VW Polo
Service and Repair Manual

A K Legg LAE MIMI and S J Drayton

Models covered

(3245-192-11AF2)

VW Polo Saloon, Hatchback & Coupe models,
including G40 (supercharged) Coupe & special/limited editions;
1043 cc & 1272 cc petrol engines

Does not cover diesel models or revised Polo range introduced September 1994

© Haynes Group Limited 2004

A book in the **Haynes Service and Repair Manual Series**

ISBN **978 1 78521 446 2**

British Library Cataloguing in Publication Data
A catalogue record for this book is available from the British Library.

**Haynes Group Limited
Haynes North America, Inc**

www.haynes.com

Contents

LIVING WITH YOUR VW POLO

Roadside repairs

Weekly checks

Lubricants, fluids and tyre pressures

MAINTENANCE

Routine maintenance and servicing

Contents

REPAIRS & OVERHAUL

REFERENCE

The updated VW Polo range was introduced in November of 1990, with a choice of 1.05 litre (1043 cc) or 1.3 litre (1272 cc) petrol engines, with either single-point or multi-point fuel injection. During Spring 1991, the G40 model was launched, equipped with a supercharged version of the 1.3 litre engine. Three body shells are available - a three-door hatchback, a two-door saloon and a three-door Coupé.

All engines are derived from the well-proven units which have appeared in previous versions of the VW Polo. The engine is of four-cylinder overhead camshaft design, mounted transversely, with the transmission mounted on the left-hand side. All models have a four or five-speed manual transmission.

All models have fully-independent front suspension and employ coil-over-damper struts, transverse lower arms and an anti-roll bar. The rear suspension is semi-independent, utilising coil-over-damper struts and incorporating trailing arms located by a torsion beam axle. A rear anti-roll bar is fitted to certain models.

A wide range of standard and optional equipment is available within the Polo range to suit most tastes, including a sliding sunroof, tinted glass, alloy wheels and remote adjustable door mirrors.

Provided that regular servicing is carried out in accordance with the manufacturer's recommendations, the VW Polo should prove reliable and very economical. The engine compartment is well-designed, and most of the items requiring frequent attention are easily accessible.

Your Polo manual

The aim of this manual is to help you get the best value from your vehicle. It can do so in several ways. It can help you decide what work must be done (even if you choose to get it done by a garage). It will also provide information on routine maintenance and servicing, and give a logical course of action and diagnosis when random faults occur. However, it is hoped that you will use the manual by tackling the work yourself. On simpler jobs it may even be quicker than booking the car into a garage and going there twice, to leave and collect it. Perhaps most important, a lot of money can be saved by avoiding the costs a garage must charge to cover its labour and overheads.

The manual has drawings and descriptions to show the function of the various components so that their layout can be understood. Tasks are described and photographed in a clear step-by-step sequence.

This manual is not a direct reproduction of the vehicle manufacturer's data, and its publication should not be taken as implying any technical approval by the vehicle manufacturers or importers.

The VW Polo Team

Haynes manuals are produced by dedicated and enthusiastic people working in close co-operation. The team responsible for the creation of this book included:

Authors	Andy Legg Spencer Drayton
Sub-editor	Carole Turk
Editor & Page Make-up	Bob Jex Pete Shoemark
Workshop manager	Paul Buckland
Photo Scans	John Martin Paul Tanswell Steve Tanswell
Cover illustration & Line Art	Roger Healing
Wiring diagrams	Matthew Marke

We hope the book will help you to get the maximum enjoyment from your car. By carrying out routine maintenance as described you will ensure your car's reliability and preserve its resale value.

Acknowledgements

Special thanks to Loders of Yeovil who provided several of the project vehicles used in the origination of this manual. Thanks are also due to Draper Tools Limited, who provided some of the workshop tools, and to all those people at Sparkford and Newbury Park who helped in the production of this manual.

We take great pride in the accuracy of information given in this manual, but vehicle manufacturers make alterations and design changes during the production run of a particular vehicle of which they do not inform us. No liability can be accepted by the authors or publishers for loss, damage or injury caused by any errors in, or omissions from, the information given.

VW Polo Boulevard

VW Polo GT Coupe

Working on your car can be dangerous. This page shows just some of the potential risks and hazards, with the aim of creating a safety-conscious attitude.

General hazards

Scalding

• Don't remove the radiator or expansion tank cap while the engine is hot.
• Engine oil, automatic transmission fluid or power steering fluid may also be dangerously hot if the engine has recently been running.

Burning

• Beware of burns from the exhaust system and from any part of the engine. Brake discs and drums can also be extremely hot immediately after use.

Crushing

• When working under or near a raised vehicle, always supplement the jack with axle stands, or use drive-on ramps. *Never venture under a car which is only supported by a jack.*
• Take care if loosening or tightening high-torque nuts when the vehicle is on stands. Initial loosening and final tightening should be done with the wheels on the ground.

Fire

• Fuel is highly flammable; fuel vapour is explosive.
• Don't let fuel spill onto a hot engine.
• Do not smoke or allow naked lights (including pilot lights) anywhere near a vehicle being worked on. Also beware of creating sparks (electrically or by use of tools).
• Fuel vapour is heavier than air, so don't work on the fuel system with the vehicle over an inspection pit.
• Another cause of fire is an electrical overload or short-circuit. Take care when repairing or modifying the vehicle wiring.
• Keep a fire extinguisher handy, of a type suitable for use on fuel and electrical fires.

Electric shock

• Ignition HT voltage can be dangerous, especially to people with heart problems or a pacemaker. Don't work on or near the ignition system with the engine running or the ignition switched on.

• Mains voltage is also dangerous. Make sure that any mains-operated equipment is correctly earthed. Mains power points should be protected by a residual current device (RCD) circuit breaker.

Fume or gas intoxication

• Exhaust fumes are poisonous; they often contain carbon monoxide, which is rapidly fatal if inhaled. Never run the engine in a confined space such as a garage with the doors shut.
• Fuel vapour is also poisonous, as are the vapours from some cleaning solvents and paint thinners.

Poisonous or irritant substances

• Avoid skin contact with battery acid and with any fuel, fluid or lubricant, especially antifreeze, brake hydraulic fluid and Diesel fuel. Don't syphon them by mouth. If such a substance is swallowed or gets into the eyes, seek medical advice.
• Prolonged contact with used engine oil can cause skin cancer. Wear gloves or use a barrier cream if necessary. Change out of oil-soaked clothes and do not keep oily rags in your pocket.
• Air conditioning refrigerant forms a poisonous gas if exposed to a naked flame (including a cigarette). It can also cause skin burns on contact.

Asbestos

• Asbestos dust can cause cancer if inhaled or swallowed. Asbestos may be found in gaskets and in brake and clutch linings. When dealing with such components it is safest to assume that they contain asbestos.

Special hazards

Hydrofluoric acid

• This extremely corrosive acid is formed when certain types of synthetic rubber, found in some O-rings, oil seals, fuel hoses etc, are exposed to temperatures above 400°C. The rubber changes into a charred or sticky substance containing the acid. *Once formed, the acid remains dangerous for years. If it gets onto the skin, it may be necessary to amputate the limb concerned.*
• When dealing with a vehicle which has suffered a fire, or with components salvaged from such a vehicle, wear protective gloves and discard them after use.

The battery

• Batteries contain sulphuric acid, which attacks clothing, eyes and skin. Take care when topping-up or carrying the battery.
• The hydrogen gas given off by the battery is highly explosive. Never cause a spark or allow a naked light nearby. Be careful when connecting and disconnecting battery chargers or jump leads.

Air bags

• Air bags can cause injury if they go off accidentally. Take care when removing the steering wheel and/or facia. Special storage instructions may apply.

Diesel injection equipment

• Diesel injection pumps supply fuel at very high pressure. Take care when working on the fuel injectors and fuel pipes.

⚠ *Warning: Never expose the hands, face or any other part of the body to injector spray; the fuel can penetrate the skin with potentially fatal results.*

Remember...

DO

• Do use eye protection when using power tools, and when working under the vehicle.

• Do wear gloves or use barrier cream to protect your hands when necessary.

• Do get someone to check periodically that all is well when working alone on the vehicle.

• Do keep loose clothing and long hair well out of the way of moving mechanical parts.

• Do remove rings, wristwatch etc, before working on the vehicle – especially the electrical system.

• Do ensure that any lifting or jacking equipment has a safe working load rating adequate for the job.

DON'T

• Don't attempt to lift a heavy component which may be beyond your capability – get assistance.

• Don't rush to finish a job, or take unverified short cuts.

• Don't use ill-fitting tools which may slip and cause injury.

• Don't leave tools or parts lying around where someone can trip over them. Mop up oil and fuel spills at once.

• Don't allow children or pets to play in or near a vehicle being worked on.

The following pages are intended to help in dealing with common roadside emergencies and breakdowns. You will find more detailed fault finding information at the back of the manual, and repair information in the main chapters.

If your car won't start and the starter motor doesn't turn

☐ Open the bonnet and make sure that the battery terminals are clean and tight.
☐ Switch on the headlights and try to start the engine. If the headlights go very dim when you're trying to start, the battery is probably flat. Get out of trouble by jump starting (see next page) using a friend's car.

If your car won't start even though the starter motor turns as normal

☐ Is there fuel in the tank?
☐ Is there moisture on electrical components under the bonnet? Switch off the ignition, then wipe off any obvious dampness with a dry cloth. Spray a water-repellent aerosol product (WD-40 or equivalent) on ignition and fuel system electrical connectors like those shown in the photos. Pay special attention to the ignition coil wiring connector and HT leads.

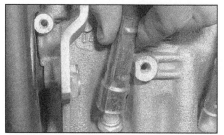

A Check that the spark plug HT leads are securely connected by pushing them down onto the plug tops

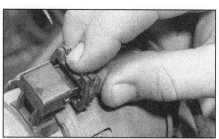

B Check that the distributor hall sender connector is firmly pushed home and free of moisture

C At the ignition coil, check that the LT and HT cable connections are secure and free of moisture

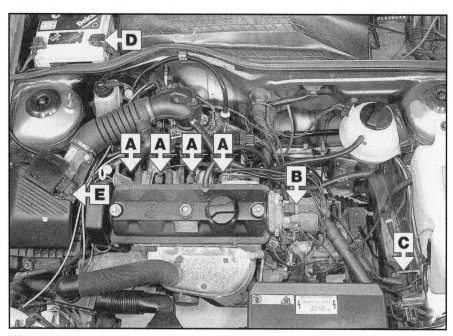

With the ignition switched **off**, check that electrical connections are secure and spray them with a water dispersant spray, such as WD40, if you suspect that moisture may be causing a problem.

D Ensure that the battery cable connections are secure

E Check that the airflow meter harness connector is secure and free of moisture

HAYNES HiNT

Jump starting will get you out of trouble, but you must correct whatever made the battery go flat in the first place. There are three possibilities:

1 *The battery has been drained by repeated attempts to start, or by leaving the lights on.*

2 *The charging system is not working properly (alternator drivebelt slack or broken, alternator wiring fault or alternator itself faulty).*

3 *The battery itself is at fault (electrolyte low, or battery worn out).*

When jump-starting a car using a booster battery, observe the following precautions:

✔ Before connecting the booster battery, make sure that the ignition is switched off.

✔ Ensure that all electrical equipment (lights, heater, wipers, etc) is switched off.

✔ Take note of any special precautions printed on the battery case.

Jump starting

✔ Make sure that the booster battery is the same voltage as the discharged one in the vehicle.

✔ If the battery is being jump-started from the battery in another vehicle, the two vehicles MUST NOT TOUCH each other.

✔ Make sure that the transmission is in neutral (or PARK, in the case of automatic transmission).

1 Connect one end of the red jump lead to the positive (+) terminal of the flat battery

2 Connect the other end of the red lead to the positive (+) terminal of the booster battery.

3 Connect one end of the black jump lead to the negative (-) terminal of the booster battery

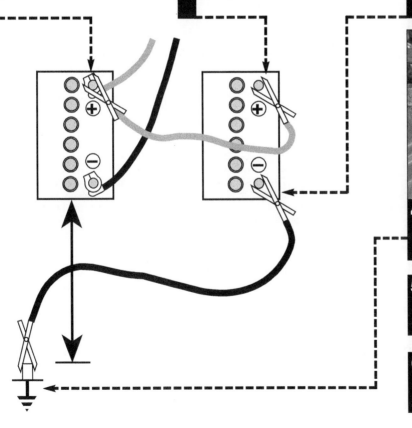

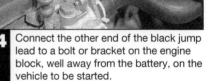

4 Connect the other end of the black jump lead to a bolt or bracket on the engine block, well away from the battery, on the vehicle to be started.

5 Make sure that the jump leads will not come into contact with the fan, drive-belts or other moving parts of the engine.

6 Start the engine using the booster battery and run it at idle speed. Switch on the lights, rear window demister and heater blower motor, then disconnect the jump leads in the reverse order of connection. Turn off the lights etc.

Wheel changing

Some of the details shown here will vary according to model. For instance, the location of the spare wheel and jack is not the same on all cars. However, the basic principles apply to all vehicles.

 Warning: Do not change a wheel in a situation where you risk being hit by other traffic. On busy roads, try to stop in a lay-by or a gateway. Be wary of passing traffic while changing the wheel – it is easy to become distracted by the job in hand.

Preparation

- ☐ When a puncture occurs, stop as soon as it is safe to do so.
- ☐ Park on firm level ground, if possible, and well out of the way of other traffic.
- ☐ Use hazard warning lights if necessary.

- ☐ If you have one, use a warning triangle to alert other drivers of your presence.
- ☐ Apply the handbrake and engage first or reverse gear (or Park on models with automatic transmission.

- ☐ Chock the wheel diagonally opposite the one being removed – a couple of large stones will do for this.
- ☐ If the ground is soft, use a flat piece of wood to spread the load under the jack.

Changing the wheel

1 The spare wheel and tools are stored in the luggage compartment. Unscrew the wing nut and lift out the spare wheel

2 The jack is located beneath the spare wheel. The wheel brace is on the right-hand side of the luggage compartment

3 Remove the wheel trim . . .

4 . . . then slacken each wheel bolt by a half turn

5 Locate the jack below the reinforced point on the sill (don't jack the vehicle at any other point of the sill) and on firm ground then turn the jack handle clockwise until the wheel is raised clear of the ground

6 Unscrew the wheel bolts and remove the wheel. Fit the spare wheel, and screw in the bolts. Lightly tighten the bolts with the brace, and lower the vehicle to the ground.

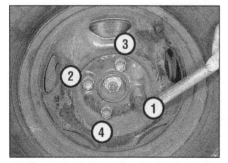

7 Securely tighten the wheel bolts in the sequence shown. Refit the wheel trim, and stow the punctured wheel and tools.

8 The wheel bolts should be slackened and retightened to the specified torque at the earliest possible opportunity

Finally...

- ☐ Remove the wheel chocks.

- ☐ Stow the jack and tools in the correct locations in the car.

- ☐ Check the tyre pressure on the wheel just fitted. If it is low, or if you don't have a pressure gauge with you, drive slowly to the nearest garage and inflate the tyre to the right pressure.

- ☐ Have the damaged tyre or wheel repaired as soon as possible.

Identifying leaks

Puddles on the garage floor or drive, or obvious wetness under the bonnet or underneath the car, suggest a leak that needs investigating. It can sometimes be difficult to decide where the leak is coming from, especially if the engine bay is very dirty already. Leaking oil or fluid can also be blown rearwards by the passage of air under the car, giving a false impression of where the problem lies.

 Warning: Most automotive oils and fluids are poisonous. Wash them off skin, and change out of contaminated clothing, without delay.

HAYNES HiNT *The smell of a fluid leaking from the car may provide a clue to what's leaking. Some fluids are distinctively coloured. It may help to clean the car and to park it over some clean paper as an aid to locating the source of the leak. Remember that some leaks may only occur while the engine is running.*

Sump oil

Engine oil may leak from the drain plug...

Oil from filter

...or from the base of the oil filter.

Gearbox oil

Gearbox oil can leak from the seals at the inboard ends of the driveshafts.

Antifreeze

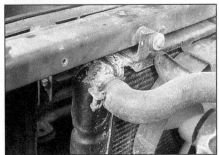

Leaking antifreeze often leaves a crystalline deposit like this.

Brake fluid

A leak occurring at a wheel is almost certainly brake fluid.

Power steering fluid

Power steering fluid may leak from the pipe connectors on the steering rack.

Towing

When all else fails, you may find yourself having to get a tow home – or of course you may be helping somebody else. Long-distance recovery should only be done by a garage or breakdown service. For shorter distances, DIY towing using another car is easy enough, but observe the following points:

☐ Use a proper tow-rope – they are not expensive. The vehicle being towed must display an 'ON TOW' sign in its rear window.
☐ Always turn the ignition key to the 'on' position when the vehicle is being towed, so that the steering lock is released, and that the direction indicator and brake lights will work.
☐ Only attach the tow-rope to the towing eyes provided.
☐ Before being towed, release the handbrake and select neutral on the transmission.
☐ Note that greater-than-usual pedal pressure will be required to operate the brakes, since the vacuum servo unit is only operational with the engine running.
☐ On models with power steering, greater-than-usual steering effort will also be required.
☐ The driver of the car being towed must keep the tow-rope taut at all times to avoid snatching.
☐ Make sure that both drivers know the route before setting off.
☐ Only drive at moderate speeds and keep the distance towed to a minimum. Drive smoothly and allow plenty of time for slowing down at junctions.
☐ The front towing eye is supplied as part of the tool kit stored in the luggage compartment. To fit the eye, carefully prise out the removable panel from the front bumper. Securely screw the eye into position, (noting that on some models it may have a **left-handed thread)** and tighten using the wheelbrace handle **(see illustration)**.

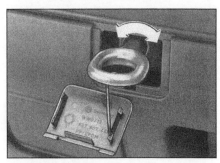

The front towing eye is supplied as part of the vehicle tool kit and must be screwed into position

Introduction

There are some very simple checks which need only take a few minutes to carry out, but which could save you a lot of inconvenience and expense.

These "Weekly checks" require no great skill or special tools, and the small amount of time they take to perform could prove to be very well spent, for example;

☐ Keeping an eye on tyre condition and pressures, will not only help to stop them wearing out prematurely, but could also save your life.

☐ Many breakdowns are caused by electrical problems. Battery-related faults are particularly common, and a quick check on a regular basis will often prevent the majority of these.

☐ If your car develops a brake fluid leak, the first time you might know about it is when your brakes don't work properly. Checking the level regularly will give advance warning of this kind of problem.

☐ If the oil or coolant levels run low, the cost of repairing any engine damage will be far greater than fixing the leak, for example.

Underbonnet check points

◀ 1.3 litre model

A *Engine oil level dipstick*
B *Engine oil filler cap*
C *Coolant expansion tank*
D *Brake fluid reservoir*
E *Screen washer fluid reservoir*
F *Battery*

Engine oil level

Before you start
✔ Make sure that your car is on level ground.
✔ Check the oil level before the car is driven, or at least 5 minutes after the engine has been switched off.

 HAYNES HiNT *If the oil is checked immediately after driving the vehicle, some of the oil will remain in the upper engine components, resulting in an inaccurate reading on the dipstick!*

The correct oil
Modern engines place great demands on their oil. It is very important that the correct oil for your car is used (See "Lubricants, fluids and tyre pressures").

Car Care
● If you have to add oil frequently, you should check whether you have any oil leaks. Place some clean paper under the car overnight, and check for stains in the morning. If there are no leaks, the engine may be burning oil. Overfilling the engine with oil may lead to catalytic converter failure.

● Always maintain the level between the upper and lower dipstick marks (see photo 3). If the level is too low severe engine damage may occur. Oil seal failure may result if the engine is overfilled by adding too much oil.

1 The dipstick top is often brightly coloured for easy identification (see *"Underbonnet check points"* on page 0•10 for exact location). Withdraw the dipstick from its tube.

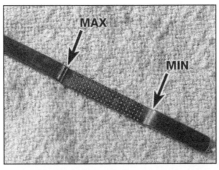
3 Note the oil level on the end of the dipstick, which should be between the upper ('MAX') mark and the lower ('MIN') mark. Adding approximately 1.0 litre of oil will raise the level from the lower to the upper mark.

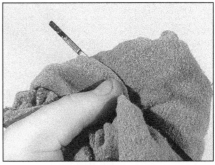
2 Using a clean rag, remove all oil from the dipstick. Insert the clean dipstick into the tube as far as it will go, then withdraw it again. Keep the handle up so the oil doesn't run along the dipstick to give a false reading.

4 Oil is added through the oil filler cap - unscrew the cap and top up the level; a funnel may help to reduce spillage. Add the oil 0.5 litre at a time, checking the level on the dipstick frequently. *DO NOT* overfill the engine (see *Car Care*).

Coolant level

 Warning: DO NOT attempt to remove the expansion tank pressure cap when the engine is hot, as there is a very great risk of scalding. Do not leave open containers of coolant about, as it is poisonous.

Car Care
● With a sealed-type cooling system, adding coolant should not be necessary on a regular basis. If frequent topping-up is required, it is likely there is a leak. Check the radiator, all hoses and joint faces for signs of staining or wetness, and rectify as necessary.

● It is important that antifreeze is used in the cooling system all year round, not just during the winter months. Don't top-up with water alone, as the antifreeze will become too diluted.

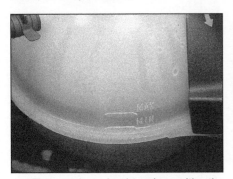
1 The coolant level varies with the temperature of the engine. When the engine is cold, the coolant level should be between the "MAX" and "MIN" marks. When hot, the level may rise above the "MAX" mark.

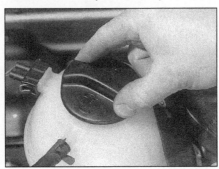
2 If topping up is necessary, wait until the engine is cold. Slowly unscrew the expansion tank cap, to release any pressure present in the cooling system, and remove it.

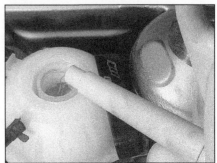
3 Add a mixture of water and antifreeze to the expansion tank until the coolant level is halfway between the level marks. Refit the cap and tighten it securely.

Brake fluid level

Warning:
● **Brake fluid can harm your eyes and damage painted surfaces, so use extreme caution when handling and pouring it.**
● **Do not use fluid that has been standing open for some time, as it absorbs moisture from the air, which can cause a dangerous loss of braking effectiveness.**

• **Make sure that your car is on level ground.**
• **The fluid level in the reservoir will drop slightly as the brake pads wear down, but the fluid level must never be allowed to drop below the "MIN" mark.**

Safety First!

● If the reservoir requires repeated topping-up this is an indication of a fluid leak somewhere in the system, which should be investigated immediately.

● If a leak is suspected, the car should not be driven until the braking system has been checked. Never take any risks where brakes are concerned.

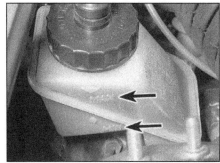

1 The "MAX" and "MIN" marks are shown on the front of the reservoir. The fluid level must be kept between the marks at all times. If topping-up is necessary, first clean around the reservoir cap.

3 Carefully add fluid, taking care not to spill it onto the surrounding components. Use only the specified fluid; mixing different types can cause damage to the system. After topping-up to the correct level, securely refit the cap and wipe off any spilt fluid

2 Unscrew the cap and carefully lift it out, taking care not to damage the level switch float. Inspect the reservoir; if the fluid is dirty the hydraulic system should be drained and refilled (see Chapter 1)

4 After topping-up the fluid level have an assistant depress the warning light test plunger on the top of the reservoir. With the ignition switched on, the warning light on the instrument panel should light up

Screen washer fluid level

Screenwash additives not only keep the winscreen clean during foul weather, they also prevent the washer system freezing in cold weather - which is when you are likely to need it most. Don't top up using plain water as the screenwash will become too diluted, and will freeze during cold weather.
On no account use coolant antifreeze in the washer system - this could discolour or damage paintwork.

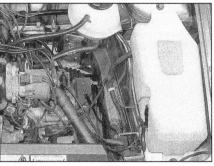

1 The screen washer fluid reservoir (arrowed) is located in the front left-hand corner of the engine compartment.

2 The screen washer level can be seen through the reservoir body. If topping-up is necessary, open the cap. When topping-up the reservoir, add a screenwash additive in the quantities recommended on the bottle.

Wiper blades

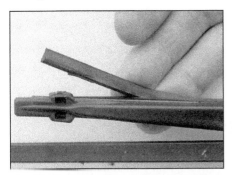

1 Check the condition of the wiper blades; if they are cracked or show any signs of deterioration, or if the glass swept area is smeared, renew them. Wiper blades should be renewed annually.

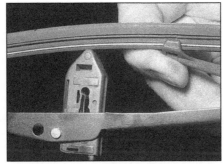

2 To remove a windscreen wiper blade, pull the arm fully away from the screen until it locks. Swivel the blade through 90° and slide it downwards . . .

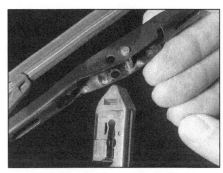

3 . . . then remove the blade from the arm.

Battery

Caution: Before carrying out any work on the vehicle battery, read the precautions given in "Safety first" at the start of this manual.

✔ Make sure that the battery tray is in good condition, and that the clamp is tight. Corrosion on the tray, retaining clamp and the battery itself can be removed with a solution of water and baking soda. Thoroughly rinse all cleaned areas with water. Any metal parts damaged by corrosion should be covered with a zinc-based primer, then painted.

✔ Periodically (approximately every three months), check the charge condition of the battery as described in Chapter 5A.

✔ If the battery is flat, and you need to jump start your vehicle, see *Roadside Repairs*.

1 The battery is located in the plenum chamber at the rear right-hand side of the engine compartment. The exterior of the battery should be inspected periodically for damage such as a cracked case or cover.

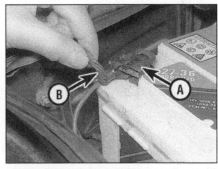

2 Check the tightness of battery clamps (A) to ensure good electrical connections. You should not be able to move them. Also check each cable (B) for cracks and frayed conductors.

HAYNES HINT

Battery corrosion can be kept to a minimum by applying a layer of petroleum jelly to the clamps and terminals after they are reconnected.

3 If corrosion (white, fluffy deposits) is evident, remove the cables from the battery terminals, clean them with a small wire brush, then refit them. Automotive stores sell a tool for cleaning the battery post . . .

4 . . . as well as the battery cable clamps

Tyre condition and pressure

It is very important that tyres are in good condition, and at the correct pressure - having a tyre failure at any speed is highly dangerous. Tyre wear is influenced by driving style - harsh braking and acceleration, or fast cornering, will all produce more rapid tyre wear. As a general rule, the front tyres wear out faster than the rears. Interchanging the tyres from front to rear ("rotating" the tyres) may result in more even wear. However, if this is completely effective, you may have the expense of replacing all four tyres at once!

Remove any nails or stones embedded in the tread before they penetrate the tyre to cause deflation. If removal of a nail does reveal that the tyre has been punctured, refit the nail so that its point of penetration is marked. Then immediately change the wheel, and have the tyre repaired by a tyre dealer.

Regularly check the tyres for damage in the form of cuts or bulges, especially in the sidewalls. Periodically remove the wheels, and clean any dirt or mud from the inside and outside surfaces. Examine the wheel rims for signs of rusting, corrosion or other damage. Light alloy wheels are easily damaged by "kerbing" whilst parking; steel wheels may also become dented or buckled. A new wheel is very often the only way to overcome severe damage.

New tyres should be balanced when they are fitted, but it may become necessary to re-balance them as they wear, or if the balance weights fitted to the wheel rim should fall off. Unbalanced tyres will wear more quickly, as will the steering and suspension components. Wheel imbalance is normally signified by vibration, particularly at a certain speed (typically around 50 mph). If this vibration is felt only through the steering, then it is likely that just the front wheels need balancing. If, however, the vibration is felt through the whole car, the rear wheels could be out of balance. Wheel balancing should be carried out by a tyre dealer or garage.

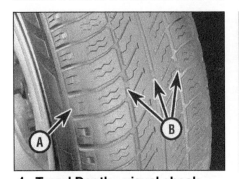

1 Tread Depth - visual check
The original tyres have tread wear safety bands (B), which will appear when the tread depth reaches approximately 1.6 mm. The band positions are indicated by a triangular mark on the tyre sidewall (A).

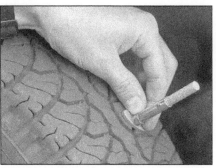

2 Tread Depth - manual check
Alternatively, tread wear can be monitored with a simple, inexpensive device known as a tread depth indicator gauge.

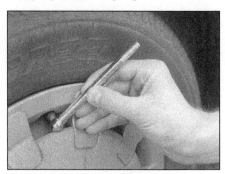

3 Tyre Pressure Check
Check the tyre pressures regularly with the tyres cold. Do not adjust the tyre pressures immediately after the vehicle has been used, or an inaccurate setting will result.

Tyre tread wear patterns

Shoulder Wear

Underinflation (wear on both sides)
Under-inflation will cause overheating of the tyre, because the tyre will flex too much, and the tread will not sit correctly on the road surface. This will cause a loss of grip and excessive wear, not to mention the danger of sudden tyre failure due to heat build-up.
Check and adjust pressures
Incorrect wheel camber (wear on one side)
Repair or renew suspension parts
Hard cornering
Reduce speed!

Centre Wear

Overinflation
Over-inflation will cause rapid wear of the centre part of the tyre tread, coupled with reduced grip, harsher ride, and the danger of shock damage occurring in the tyre casing.
Check and adjust pressures

If you sometimes have to inflate your car's tyres to the higher pressures specified for maximum load or sustained high speed, don't forget to reduce the pressures to normal afterwards.

Uneven Wear

Front tyres may wear unevenly as a result of wheel misalignment. Most tyre dealers and garages can check and adjust the wheel alignment (or "tracking") for a modest charge.
Incorrect camber or castor
Repair or renew suspension parts
Malfunctioning suspension
Repair or renew suspension parts
Unbalanced wheel
Balance tyres
Incorrect toe setting
Adjust front wheel alignment
Note: *The feathered edge of the tread which typifies toe wear is best checked by feel.*

Bulbs and fuses

✔ Check all external lights and the horn. Refer to the appropriate Sections of Chapter 12 for details if any of the circuits are found to be inoperative.

✔ Visually check all accessible wiring connectors, harnesses and retaining clips for security, and for signs of chafing or damage.

HAYNES HiNT	*If you need to check your brake lights and indicators unaided, back up to a wall or garage door and operate the lights. The reflected light should show if they are working properly.*

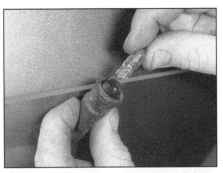

1 If a single indicator light, stop-light or headlight has failed, it is likely that a bulb has blown and will need to be replaced. Refer to Chapter 12 for details. If both stop-lights have failed, it is possible that the switch has failed (see Chapter 9).

2 If more than one indicator light or tail light has failed it is likely that either a fuse has blown or that there is a fault in the circuit. The fuses are located in the plenum chamber at the left-hand rear of the engine compartment. To replace a blown fuse, squeeze the cover and remove it from the fusebox, then simply pull out the blown fuse and fit a new one of the correct rating. If the fuse blows again, it is important that you find out why - a complete checking procedure is given in Chapter 12.

Advanced driving

Many people see the words 'advanced driving' and believe that it won't interest them or that it is a style of driving beyond their own abilities. Nothing could be further from the truth. Advanced driving is straightforward safe, sensible driving - the sort of driving we should all do every time we get behind the wheel.

An average of 10 people are killed every day on UK roads and 870 more are injured, some seriously. Lives are ruined daily, usually because somebody did something stupid. Something like 95% of all accidents are due to human error, mostly driver failure. Sometimes we make genuine mistakes - everyone does. Sometimes we have lapses of concentration. Sometimes we deliberately take risks.

For many people, the process of 'learning to drive' doesn't go much further than learning how to pass the driving test because of a common belief that good drivers are made by 'experience'.

Learning to drive by 'experience' teaches three driving skills:

☐ Quick reactions. (Whoops, that was close!)
☐ Good handling skills. (Horn, swerve, brake, horn).
☐ Reliance on vehicle technology. (Great stuff this ABS, stop in no distance even in the wet...)

Drivers whose skills are 'experience based' generally have a lot of near misses and the odd accident. The results can be seen every day in our courts and our hospital casualty departments.

Advanced drivers have learnt to control the risks by controlling the position and speed of their vehicle. They avoid accidents and near misses, even if the drivers around them make mistakes.

The key skills of advanced driving are **concentration,** effective all-round **observation, anticipation** and **planning.** When **good vehicle handling** is added to

these skills, all driving situations can be approached and negotiated in a safe, methodical way, leaving nothing to chance.

Concentration means applying your mind to safe driving, completely excluding anything that's not relevant. Driving is usually the most dangerous activity that most of us undertake in our daily routines. It deserves our full attention.

Observation means not just looking, but seeing and seeking out the information found in the driving environment.

Anticipation means asking yourself what is happening, what you can reasonably expect to happen and what could happen unexpectedly. (One of the commonest words used in compiling accident reports is 'suddenly'.)

Planning is the link between seeing something and taking the appropriate action. For many drivers, planning is the missing link.

If you want to become a safer and more skilful driver and you want to enjoy your driving more, contact the Institute of Advanced Motorists at www.iam.org.uk, phone 0208 996 9600, or write to IAM House, 510 Chiswick High Road, London W4 5RG for an information pack.

Lubricants and fluids

Engine . . . . Multigrade engine oil, viscosity SAE 10W/40 to 20W/50, to VW specification 501 01

Cooling system . . . . Ethylene glycol based antifreeze

Manual transmission . . . . Gear oil, viscosity SAE 80 or 75W-90

Braking system . . . . Hydraulic fluid to SAE J1703F or DOT4

Tyre pressures

Up to half load - bar (psi):	Front	Rear
135R13	1.9 (28)	1.9 (28)
145R13	1.7 (25)	1.7 (25)
155/70R13	1.8 (26)	1.8 (26)
165/65R13 or 175/60R13	1.8 (26)	1.8 (26)

Full load - bar (psi):	Front	Rear
135R13	2.2 (32)	2.5 (36)
145R13	1.9 (28)	2.2 (32)
155/70R13	2.1 (31)	2.4 (35)
165/65R13 or 175/60R13	2.2 (32)	2.6 (38)

Note: *Pressures apply only to original-equipment tyres, and may vary slightly if any other make of tyre is fitted; check with the tyre manufacturer or supplier for the correct pressures if necessary. The correct pressures for each individual vehicle are usually given on a sticker inside the glovebox lid or inside the fuel filler flap. This information may conflict with that shown above - in this case, consult your VW dealer for the latest recommendations.*

The spare wheel should be kept at the highest full-load pressure.

Chapter 1
Routine maintenance and servicing

Contents

Degrees of difficulty

Easy, suitable for novice with little experience	**Fairly easy,** suitable for beginner with some experience	**Fairly difficult,** suitable for competent DIY mechanic	**Difficult,** suitable for experienced DIY mechanic 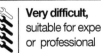	**Very difficult,** suitable for expert DIY or professional 

Lubricants and fluids - Refer to end of *"Weekly checks"*

Capacities

Engine oil

All except G40 models	3.5 litres
G40 models	3.25 litres

Cooling system	5.6 litres (approx)

Transmission

4 speed models	2.2 litres
5 speed models	3.1 litres

Fuel tank	42 litres

Washer reservoirs

Models with headlight washers	4.5 litres
Models without headlight washers	7.5 litres

Cooling system

Antifreeze mixture:

28% antifreeze	Protection down to -15°C (5°F)
50% antifreeze	Protection down to -30°C (-22°F)

Note: *Refer to antifreeze manufacturer for latest recommendations.*

Ignition system

Ignition timing, all models (basic setting)	5 ± 1° BTDC	
Spark plugs:	**Type**	**Electrode gap**
Engine codes AAU and AAV	Bosch WR 8 LT+	1.0 mm
Engine codes 3F and PY	Bosch WR 56	Not adjustable

Auxiliary drivebelt (v-belt) deflection

New belt	2 mm max.
Used belt	5 mm max.

Brakes

Brake pad friction material minimum thickness (including backplate)	7.0 mm
Brake shoe friction material minimum thickness	2.5 mm

Torque wrench settings

	Nm	lbf ft
Alternator tensioning nut:		
Initial tightening:		
New belt	8	6
Used belt	4	3
Final tightening	8	6
Alternator tensioning nut lockscrew	35	26
Alternator upper mounting screws	35	26
Alternator tensioning strut screws	20	15
G-charger bracket tensioning torque:		
New belt	135	100
Used belt	80	59
G-charger mounting bracket screws:		
M12 screws	80	59
M8 screws	30	22
Sump drain plug	30	22
Spark plugs:		
All models except G40	20	15
G40 models	25	18
Wheel bolts	110	81

The maintenance intervals in this manual are provided with the assumption that you, not the dealer, will be carrying out the work. These are the minimum maintenance intervals recommended by us for vehicles driven daily. If you wish to keep your vehicle in peak condition at all times, you may wish to perform some of these procedures more often. We encourage frequent maintenance, because it enhances the efficiency, performance and resale value of your vehicle.

When the vehicle is new, it should be serviced by a factory-authorised dealer service department, in order to preserve the factory warranty.

Weekly, or every 250 miles (400 km)

☐ See "Weekly checks"

Every 10 000 miles (15 000 km) or 12 months, whichever comes first

☐ Renew engine oil and filter (Section 1)
☐ Check the front brake pad lining thickness (Section 2)

Every 12 months - regardless of mileage

Note: *In addition to the items listed previously, carry out the following:*

☐ Check the rear brake shoes and drums (Section 3)
☐ Check clutch play (Section 4)
☐ Check all underbonnet components and hoses for fluid leaks (Section 5)
☐ Lubricate all hinges and locks (Section 6)
☐ Check all brake system components for damage or fluid leakage (Section 7)
☐ Check the condition of the exhaust system and its mountings (Section 8)
☐ Check the steering and suspension components for condition and security (Section 9)
☐ Check the condition of the driveshaft gaiters (Section 10)
☐ Check the headlight beam adjustment (Section 11)
☐ Carry out a road test (Section 12)
☐ Engine management system check (Section 13)
☐ Exhaust emission and idle speed check (Section 14)

Every 20 000 miles (30 000 km)

Note: *In addition to the items listed in the previous sub-Section, carry out the following:*

☐ Check the condition of the auxiliary drivebelt(s), and renew if necessary (Section 15)
☐ Renew the spark plugs (Section 16)
☐ Renew the air filter element and clean out the air cleaner housing (Section 17)
☐ Lubricate the sliding roof runners (Section 18)
☐ Check the underbody sealant for damage (Section 19)

Every 60 000 miles

☐ Renew the camshaft timing belt (Section 20).
☐ Renew the fuel filter (Section 21)

Every 2 years - regardless of mileage

☐ Renew the brake fluid (Section 22)
☐ Renew the coolant (Section 23)

Underbonnet view of a 1.3 litre model

1 Battery
2 Brake fluid reservoir
3 Brake servo
4 Throttle body
5 Fuel injectors
6 Spark plugs
7 Oil filler cap
8 Air cleaner/air flow meter assembly
9 Timing belt cover
10 Ignition distributor
11 Coolant expansion tank
12 Front suspension strut top mounting
13 Ignition coil
14 Exhaust CO sampling pipe

Front underbody view

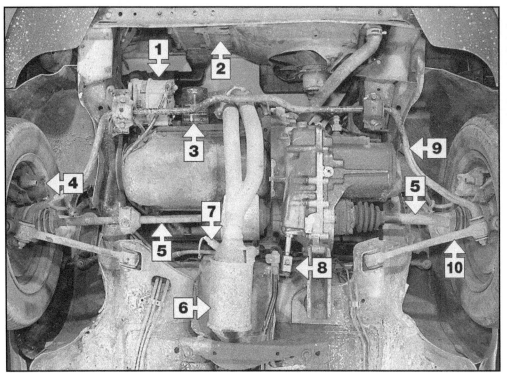

1 Alternator
2 Radiator
3 Oil filter
4 Front brake caliper
5 Driveshaft
6 Catalytic converter
7 Lambda sensor
8 Gearchange linkage
9 Anti-roll bar
10 Lower suspension arm

Rear underbody view

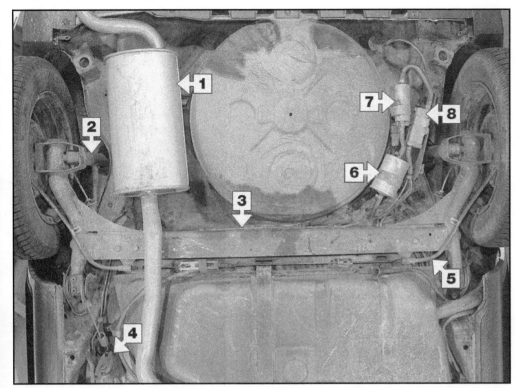

1 Exhaust tailbox
2 Rear shock absorber
3 Rear axle beam
4 Rear brake pressure
   regulating valve
5 Handbrake cable
6 Fuel filter
7 Line fuel pump
8 Accumulator

Maintenance procedures

General information

This Chapter is designed to help the home mechanic maintain his/her vehicle for safety, economy, long life and peak performance.

The Chapter contains a master maintenance schedule, followed by Sections dealing specifically with each task in the schedule. Visual checks, adjustments, component renewal and other helpful items are included. Refer to the accompanying illustrations of the engine compartment and the underside of the vehicle for the locations of the various components.

Servicing your vehicle in accordance with the mileage/time maintenance schedule and the following Sections will provide a planned maintenance programme, which should result in a long and reliable service life. This is a comprehensive plan, so maintaining some items but not others at the specified service intervals, will not produce the same results.

As you service your vehicle, you will discover that many of the procedures can -

and should - be grouped together, because of the particular procedure being performed, or because of the proximity of two otherwise-unrelated components to one another. For example, if the vehicle is raised for any reason, the exhaust can be inspected at the same time as the suspension and steering components.

The first step in this maintenance programme is to prepare yourself before the actual work begins. Read through all the Sections relevant to the work to be carried out, then make a list and gather all the parts and tools required. If a problem is encountered, seek advice from a parts specialist, or a dealer service department.

Intensive maintenance

If, from the time the vehicle is new, the routine maintenance schedule is followed closely, and frequent checks are made of fluid levels and high-wear items, as suggested throughout this manual, the engine will be

kept in relatively good running condition, and the need for additional work will be minimised.

It is possible that there will be times when the engine is running poorly due to the lack of regular maintenance. This is even more likely if a used vehicle, which has not received regular and frequent maintenance checks, is purchased. In such cases, additional work may need to be carried out, outside of the regular maintenance intervals.

If engine wear is suspected, a compression test (refer to the relevant Part of Chapter 2) will provide valuable information regarding the overall performance of the main internal components. Such a test can be used as a basis to decide on the extent of the work to be carried out. If, for example, a compression test indicates serious internal engine wear, conventional maintenance as described in this Chapter will not greatly improve the performance of the engine, and may prove a waste of time and money, unless extensive overhaul work is carried out first.

The following series of operations are those which are most often required to improve the performance of a generally poor-running engine:

Primary operations

a) Clean, inspect and test the battery (refer to "Weekly checks").
b) Check all the engine-related fluids (refer to "Weekly checks").
c) Check the condition and tension of the auxiliary drivebelt (Section 15).
d) Renew the spark plugs (Section 16).

e) Inspect the distributor cap and rotor arm (refer to the relevant Section of Chapter 5B).
f) Check the condition of the air filter, and renew if necessary (Section 17).
g) Renew the fuel filter (Section 21).
h) Check the condition of all hoses, and check for fluid leaks (Section 5).
i) Check the exhaust gas emissions (refer to Section 14).

If the above operations do not prove fully effective, carry out the following secondary operations:

Secondary operations

All items listed under "Primary operations", plus the following:

a) Check the charging system (refer to the relevant Section of Chapter 5A).
b) Check the ignition system (refer to the relevant Section of Chapter 5B).
c) Check the fuel system (see relevant Section of Chapter 4A or B as applicable).
d) Renew the distributor cap and rotor arm (refer to the relevant Section of Chapter 5B).
e) Renew the ignition HT leads (refer to the relevant Section of Chapter 5B).

10 000 mile/12 month service

1 Engine oil and filter renewal

1 Frequent oil and filter changes are the most important preventative maintenance procedures which can be undertaken by the DIY owner. As engine oil ages, it becomes diluted and contaminated, which leads to premature engine wear.
2 Before starting this procedure, gather all the necessary tools and materials. Also make sure that you have plenty of clean rags and newspapers handy, to mop up any accidental spills.
3 The oil draining procedure should ideally be carried out when the engine is warm, as warm oil runs more freely than cold oil. In addition, more built-up engine 'sludge' will be removed with the oil, as it is drained . Take care, however, not to touch the exhaust or any other hot parts of the engine when working under the vehicle. To avoid any possibility of scalding, and to protect yourself from possible skin irritants and other harmful contaminants in used engine oils, it is advisable to wear gloves when carrying out this work.
4 Access to the underside of the vehicle will be greatly improved if it can be raised on a lift,

driven onto ramps, or jacked up and supported on axle stands (see "Jacking and vehicle support"). Whichever method is chosen, make sure that the vehicle remains level, or (if it has been jacked-up at an angle), that the drain plug is at the lowest point.
5 Using a socket and wrench or a ring spanner, slacken the sump drain plug about half a turn until it can be rotated by hand (see illustration). Position the draining container under the drain plug, (noting that the stream of oil may initially run out at an angle, rather than straight down) then unscrew the plug completely (see Haynes Hint). Recover the sealing ring from the drain plug.
6 Allow some time for the old oil to drain, noting that it may be necessary to reposition the container as the oil flow slows to a trickle. If you are working outside, shield the container from draughts that may splash the stream of oil onto the ground.
7 After all the oil has drained, wipe off the drain plug with a clean rag, and fit a new sealing washer. Clean the area around the drain plug opening, and refit the plug. Tighten the plug securely.
8 If the filter is also to be renewed, move the container into position under the oil filter,

which is located on the front side of the cylinder block, below the inlet manifold.
9 Using an oil filter removal tool if necessary, slacken the filter initially (by turning it in an anticlockwise direction), then unscrew it by hand the rest of the way (see illustration). Note that the filter will still contain some oil - be prepared for an amount of leakage as the filter is unscrewed. Hold it with the sealing face uppermost until it can be emptied into the draining container.
10 Use a clean rag to remove all oil, dirt and sludge from the filter sealing area on the engine. Check the old filter to make sure that the rubber sealing ring has not stuck to the engine. If it has, carefully remove it.
11 Apply a light coating of clean engine oil to the sealing ring on the new filter, then screw it into position on the engine. Tighten the filter firmly by hand only - do not use any tools, as these may damage the outer surface filter.
12 Remove the old oil and all tools from under the car then lower the car to the ground (if applicable).
13 Remove the dipstick, then unscrew the oil filler cap from the cylinder head cover or oil filler/breather neck (as applicable). Fill the engine, using the correct grade and type of oil (refer to "Lubricants fluids and capacities"). An oil can spout or funnel may help to reduce spillage. Pour in half the specified quantity of oil first, then wait a few minutes for the oil to

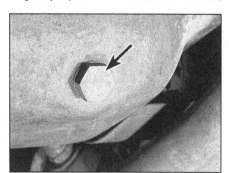

1.5 Using a socket and wrench or a ring spanner, slacken the sump drain plug (arrowed)

Keep the drain plug pressed into the sump while unscrewing it by hand the last couple of turns. As the plug releases, move it away sharply so the stream of oil from the sump runs into the container, not up your sleeve!

1.9 Turn the oil filter anticlockwise to slacken it - use a chain wrench if necessary

collect in the sump. Continue adding oil a small quantity at a time until the level is just above the lower mark on the dipstick. Adding approximately 1.0 litres will raise the level from the lower mark to the upper mark on the dipstick. Refit the filler cap.

14 Start the engine and run it for a few minutes; check for leaks around the oil filter seal and the sump drain plug. Note that there may be a delay of a few seconds before the oil pressure warning light goes out when the engine is first started, as the oil circulates through the engine oil galleries and (where applicable) the new oil filter before the pressure builds up. If the oil pressure warning light does not extinguish after the engine has started and run for several seconds, stop the engine immediately and check for leaks around the components that have been disturbed.

15 Switch off the engine, and wait a few minutes for the new oil to settle into the sump. With the new oil circulated and the filter now completely full, recheck the level on the dipstick, and add more oil as necessary.

16 Dispose of the used engine oil safely, with reference to *"General repair procedures"* in the *Reference* Sections of this manual.

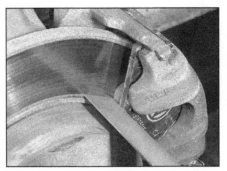

2.2a Checking the front brake outer pad linings for wear with a steel rule

2 Front brake pad check

1 Firmly apply the handbrake, then jack up the front of the car and support it securely on axle stands (see *"Jacking and vehicle support"*). Remove the front roadwheels.
2 Using a steel rule, measure the combined thickness of the lining and backing of the brake pads on both front brakes. This must not be less than 7.0 mm. Check the inner pad

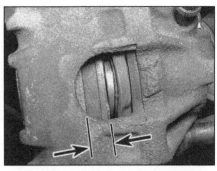

2.2b Check the front brake inner pad linings through the hole in the caliper

through the hole on the front of the caliper (see illustrations).
3 For a comprehensive check, the brake pads should be removed and cleaned. The operation of the caliper can then also be checked, and the condition of the brake disc itself can be fully examined on both sides. Refer to Chapter 9 for further information.
4 If any pad's friction material is worn to the specified thickness or less, *all four pads must be renewed as a set*. Refer to Chapter 9.
5 On completion refit the roadwheels and lower the car to the ground.

Every 12 months - regardless of mileage

3 Rear brake shoe check

1 Jack up the rear of the car and support on axle stands (see *"Jacking and vehicle support"*). Do not remove the wheels.
2 Working beneath the car remove the rubber plugs from the front of the backplates and check that the linings are not worn below the minimum thickness given in the *Specifications* **(see illustration)**. If necessary use a torch.
3 If the friction material on any shoe is worn down to the specified minimum thickness or less, all four shoes must be renewed as a set.

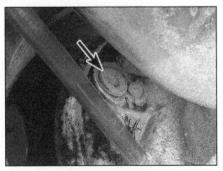

3.2 Rear brake shoe lining inspection plug location

4 At the same time check for signs of brake fluid leakage.
5 For a comprehensive check, the brake drum should be removed and cleaned. This will allow the wheel cylinders to be checked, and the condition of the brake drum itself to be fully examined (see Chapter 9).
6 Refit the rubber plugs then lower the car to the ground.

4 Clutch play

Note: *This procedure does not apply to vehicles fitted with an automatic clutch cable adjustment mechanism.*

Measurement

1 Park the vehicle and switch off the engine. Select neutral, then depress the clutch pedal several times, to settle the release mechanism components. With no pressure applied to the pedal, measure the distance between the pedal rubber and a fixed reference point, such as the bottom edge of the steering wheel - a length of batten can be used to serve as a measuring rule.
2 Gradually apply pressure to the clutch pedal, until firm resistance is felt, indicating that the release mechanism is beginning to

disengage the clutch. At this point, repeat the measurement described in paragraph 1.
3 Compare the measurement with the value listed in the *Specifications* - if the free play exceeds the maximum permitted, adjust the cable as described in the following sub-Section.

Adjustment

4 Open the bonnet and locate the clutch cable adjusting nut, on the upper surface of the transmission casing.
5 Rotate the nut through half a turn, using a spanner, to take up the slack in the cable. Measure the clutch pedal freeplay again, as described in the previous sub-Section.
6 Repeat the operations described in paragraphs 4 and 5 until the correct pedal freeplay is achieved.

5 Hose and fluid leak check

1 Visually inspect the engine joint faces, gaskets and seals for any signs of water or oil leaks. Pay particular attention to the areas around the camshaft cover, cylinder head, oil filter and sump joint faces. Bear in mind that, over a period of time, some very slight seepage from these areas is to be expected -

A leak in the cooling system will usually show up as white or rust coloured deposits on the area adjoining the leak

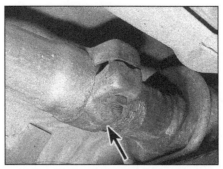

8.3a Check the exhaust pipe connections (arrowed) for evidence of leaks, severe corrosion and damage

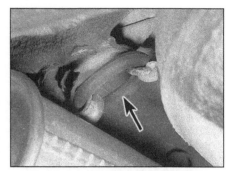

8.3b Make sure that all brackets and mountings (arrowed) are in good condition

what you are really looking for is any indication of a serious leak **(see Haynes Hint)**. Should a leak be found, renew the offending gasket or oil seal by referring to the appropriate Chapters in this manual.

2 Also check the security and condition of all the engine-related pipes and hoses. Ensure that all cable-ties or securing clips are in place and in good condition. Clips which are broken or missing can lead to chafing of the hoses, pipes or wiring, which could cause more serious problems in the future.

3 Carefully check the radiator hoses and heater hoses along their entire length. Renew any hose which is cracked, swollen or deteriorated. Cracks will show up better if the hose is squeezed. Pay close attention to the hose clips that secure the hoses to the cooling system components. Hose clips can pinch and puncture hoses, resulting in cooling system leaks.

4 Inspect all the cooling system components (hoses, joint faces etc.) for leaks. A leak in the cooling system will usually show up as white- or rust-coloured deposits on the area adjoining the leak. Where any problems of this nature are found on system components, renew the component or gasket with reference to Chapter 3.

5 On G40 models, check the oil supply and return line unions at the supercharger for leakage. Any reduction in the oil supply to the supercharger will accelerate wear and may ultimately result in failure.

6 With the vehicle raised, inspect the petrol tank and filler neck for punctures, cracks and other damage. The connection between the filler neck and tank is especially critical. Sometimes a rubber filler neck or connecting hose will leak due to loose retaining clamps or deteriorated rubber.

7 Carefully check all rubber hoses and metal fuel lines leading away from the petrol tank. Check for loose connections, deteriorated hoses, crimped lines, and other damage. Pay particular attention to the vent pipes and hoses, which often loop up around the filler neck and can become blocked or crimped. Follow the lines to the front of the vehicle,

carefully inspecting them all the way. Renew damaged sections as necessary.

8 From within the engine compartment, check the security of all fuel hose attachments and pipe unions, and inspect the fuel hoses and vacuum hoses for kinks, chafing and deterioration.

6 Hinge and lock lubrication

Lubricate the hinges of the bonnet, doors and tailgate with a light general-purpose oil. Similarly, lubricate all latches, locks and lock strikers. At the same time, check the security and operation of all the locks, adjusting them if necessary (see Chapter 11).

Lightly lubricate the bonnet release mechanism and cable with a suitable grease.

7 Brake system and fluid leakage check

Jack up the front and rear of the car and support on axle stands (see "*Jacking and vehicle support*"). Remove all wheels.

Working from the front to rear of the car, inspect the brake master cylinder, servo unit, brake lines, brake hoses, brake pressure regulator, brake calipers and rear wheel cylinders for damage and fluid leakage. Refer to Chapter 9 where repairs are necessary.

8 Exhaust system check

1 Park the vehicle on a level surface and switch off the engine. Chock the front wheels and select first gear, then raise the rear of the vehicle and rest it securely on axle stands (see "*Jacking and vehicle support*").

2 With the engine cold (wait at least an hour after switching off the engine), check the

complete exhaust system from the engine to the end of the tailpipe.

3 Check the exhaust pipes and connections for evidence of leaks, severe corrosion and damage. Make sure that all brackets and mountings are in good condition, and that all relevant nuts and bolts are tight. Leakage at any of the joints or in other parts of the system will usually show up as a black sooty stain in the vicinity of the leak **(see illustrations)**.

4 Rattles and other noises can often be traced to the exhaust system, especially the brackets and mountings. Try to move the pipes and silencers. If the components are able to come into contact with the body or suspension parts, secure the system with new mountings. Otherwise, with reference to Chapter 4C, loosen the joints between adjacent sections of the exhaust pipe by slackening the clamps (where possible) and twist the pipes as necessary to provide additional clearance. Re-tighten the exhaust pipe clamps on completion.

9 Steering and suspension check

Front suspension and steering check

1 Raise the front of the vehicle, and securely support it on axle stands (see "*Jacking and vehicle support*").

2 Visually inspect the balljoint dust covers and the steering rack-and-pinion gaiters for splits, chafing or deterioration. Any wear of these components will cause loss of lubricant, together with dirt and water entry, resulting in rapid deterioration of the balljoints or steering gear.

3 On vehicles with power steering, check the fluid hoses for chafing or deterioration, and the pipe and hose unions for fluid leaks. Also check for signs of fluid leakage under pressure from the steering gear rubber gaiters, which would indicate failed fluid seals within the steering gear.

9.4 Check for wear in the hub bearings by grasping the wheel and trying to rock it

10.1 Check the condition of the driveshaft gaiters

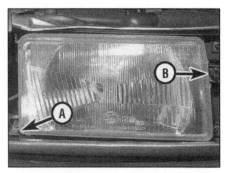

11.4 Headlight beam adjustment screws
A Vertical adjustment
B Horizontal adjustment

4 Grasp the roadwheel at the 12 o'clock and 6 o'clock positions, and try to rock it **(see illustration)**. Very slight free play may be felt, but if the movement is appreciable, further investigation is necessary to determine the source. Continue rocking the wheel while an assistant depresses the footbrake. If the movement is now eliminated or significantly reduced, it is likely that the hub bearings are at fault. If the free play is still evident with the footbrake depressed, then there is wear in the suspension joints or mountings.

5 Now grasp the wheel at the 9 o'clock and 3 o'clock positions, and try to rock it as before. Any movement felt now may again be caused by wear in the hub bearings or the steering track-rod balljoints. If the inner or outer balljoint is worn, the visual movement will be obvious.

6 Using a large screwdriver or flat bar, check for wear in the suspension mounting bushes by levering between the relevant suspension component and its attachment point. Some movement is to be expected as the mountings are made of rubber, but excessive wear should be obvious. Also check the condition of any visible rubber bushes, looking for splits, cracks or contamination of the rubber.

7 With the car standing on its wheels, have an assistant turn the steering wheel back and forth about an eighth of a turn each way. There should be very little, if any, lost movement between the steering wheel and roadwheels. If this is not the case, closely observe the joints and mountings previously described, but in addition, check the steering column universal joints for wear, and the rack-and-pinion steering gear itself.

Suspension strut/shock absorber check

8 Check for any signs of fluid leakage around the suspension strut/shock absorber body, or from the rubber gaiter around the piston rod. Should any fluid be noticed, the suspension strut/shock absorber is defective internally, and should be renewed. **Note:** *Suspension struts/shock absorbers should always be renewed in pairs on the same axle.*

9 The efficiency of the suspension strut/shock absorber may be checked by bouncing the vehicle at each corner. Generally speaking, the body will return to its normal position and stop after being depressed. If it rises and returns on a rebound, the suspension strut/shock absorber is probably suspect. Examine also the suspension strut/shock absorber upper and lower mountings for any signs of wear.

10 Driveshaft gaiter check

With the vehicle raised and securely supported on stands, turn the steering onto full lock, then slowly rotate the roadwheel. Inspect the condition of the outer constant velocity (CV) joint rubber gaiters, squeezing the gaiters to open out the folds. Check for signs of cracking, splits or deterioration of the rubber, which may allow the grease to escape, and lead to water and grit entry into the joint. Also check the security and condition of the retaining clips. Repeat these checks on the inner CV joints **(see illustration)**. If any damage or deterioration is found, the gaiters should be renewed (see Chapter 8).

At the same time, check the general condition of the CV joints themselves by first holding the driveshaft and attempting to rotate the wheel. Repeat this check by holding the inner joint and attempting to rotate the driveshaft. Any appreciable movement indicates wear in the joints, wear in the driveshaft splines, or a loose driveshaft retaining nut.

11 Headlight beam alignment check

1 Accurate adjustment of the headlight beam is only possible using optical beam-setting equipment, and this work should therefore be carried out by a VW dealer or service station with the necessary facilities. In an emergency, however, the following procedure will provide an acceptable light pattern.

2 Position the car on a level surface with tyres correctly inflated, approximately 10 metres in front of, and at right-angles to, a wall or garage door.

3 Draw a horizontal line on the wall or door at headlamp centre height. Draw a vertical line corresponding to the centre line of the car, then measure off a point either side of this, on the horizontal line, corresponding with the headlamp centres.

4 Switch on the main beam and check that the areas of maximum illumination coincide with the headlamp centre marks on the wall. If not, turn the crosshead adjustment screw located on the inner vertical edge of the headlight to adjust the beam laterally, and the crosshead adjustment screw located on the outer lower corner of the headlight to adjust the beam vertically **(see illustration)**. On models with a headlight adjustment on the instrument panel, make sure that it is set at its basic setting before making the adjustment.

12 Road test

Instruments and electrical equipment

1 Check the operation of all instruments and electrical equipment.

2 Make sure that all instruments read correctly, and switch on all electrical equipment in turn, to check that it functions properly.

Steering and suspension

3 Check for any abnormalities in the steering, suspension, handling or road "feel".

4 Drive the vehicle, and check that there are no unusual vibrations or noises.

5 Check that the steering feels positive, with no excessive "sloppiness", or roughness, and check for any suspension noises when cornering and driving over bumps.

Drivetrain

6 Check the performance of the engine, clutch, gearbox/ transmission and driveshafts.

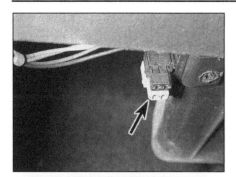

13.1 Dashboard mounted diagnostic connector (arrowed)

7 Listen for any unusual noises from the engine, clutch and gearbox/transmission.

8 Make sure that the engine runs smoothly when idling, and that there is no hesitation when accelerating.

9 Check that, where applicable, the clutch action is smooth and progressive, that the drive is taken up smoothly, and that the pedal travel is not excessive. Also listen for any noises when the clutch pedal is depressed.

10 On manual gearbox models, check that all gears can be engaged smoothly without noise, and that the gear lever action is not abnormally vague or "notchy".

11 Listen for a metallic clicking sound from the front of the vehicle, as the vehicle is driven slowly in a circle with the steering on full-lock. Carry out this check in both directions. If a clicking noise is heard, this indicates wear in a driveshaft joint, in which case renew the joint if necessary.

Braking system

12 Make sure that the vehicle does not pull to one side when braking, and that the wheels do not lock prematurely when braking hard.

13 Check that there is no vibration through the steering when braking.

14 Check that the handbrake operates correctly without excessive movement of the lever, and that it holds the car on a slope.

15 Test the operation of the brake servo unit as follows. With the engine off, depress the footbrake four or five times to exhaust the vacuum. Hold the brake pedal depressed, then start the engine. As the engine starts, there should be a noticeable "give" in the brake pedal as vacuum builds up. Allow the engine to run for at least two minutes, and then switch it off. If the brake pedal is depressed now, it should be possible to detect a hiss from the servo as the pedal is depressed. After about four or five depressions, no further hissing should be heard, and the pedal should feel considerably harder.

13 Engine management system check

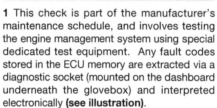

1 This check is part of the manufacturer's maintenance schedule, and involves testing the engine management system using special dedicated test equipment. Any fault codes stored in the ECU memory are extracted via a diagnostic socket (mounted on the dashboard underneath the glovebox) and interpreted electronically **(see illustration)**.

2 Unless a fault is suspected, this test is not essential, although it should be noted that it is recommended by the manufacturer.

3 The engine management system has the ability to 'override' some component failures by reverting to a 'limp-home' or 'backup' mode. Because of this, component failure may not always be immediately obvious, although some side-effects may be noticed; such as poor fuel economy, poor staring or hesitant acceleration. Having the fault log read electronically by a VW dealer will establish whether any such failures have occurred.

Caution: Although the VW Polo has a diagnostic socket, there is no safe method of extracting the fault code information

without using dedicated test equipment. The use of improvised tools for this purpose may result in internal damage to the engine management system electronic control unit.

4 If access to suitable test equipment is not possible, make a thorough check of all ignition, fuel and emission control system components, hoses, and wiring, for security and obvious signs of damage. Further details of the fuel system, emission control system and ignition system can be found in Chapter 4A, B and C and Chapter 5B.

14 Exhaust emission and idle speed check

1 Experienced home mechanics equipped with an accurate tachometer and a carefully-calibrated exhaust gas analyser may be able to check the exhaust gas CO content and the engine idle speed; if these are found to be out of specification, then the vehicle must be taken to a suitably-equipped VW dealer for assessment. Idle speed and exhaust CO adjustment screws are provided (multi-point fuel-injected models only - refer to Chapter 4B for details), but adjustment will not be possible if the engine management system has detected a fault in one of the fuelling or ignition system components. Under these circumstances, the engine management system will enter a 'back-up' mode and will not respond to adjustment. For this reason, all fault codes must be erased from the engine management system memory before the idle speed and exhaust CO settings can be checked and adjusted - this operation must be carried out by a VW dealer equipped with the required test equipment (see Section 13).

Caution: Inaccurate CO adjustment may cause overfuelling and the risk of serious catalytic converter damage.

20 000 mile service

15 Auxiliary drivebelt check and renewal

Checking

1 Disconnect the battery negative cable and position it away from the terminal.

2 Park the vehicle on a level surface, apply the handbrake and chock the rear wheels.

3 Raise the front of the vehicle, rest it securely on axle stands (see "*Jacking and vehicle support*") and remove the right-hand front roadwheel.

4 Turn the steering to full right hand lock, then remove the plug from the access hole in the inner wheel arch **(see illustration)** to expose the crankshaft pulley bolt.

5 Using a socket and wrench on the crankshaft sprocket bolt, rotate the crankshaft so that the full length of the auxiliary drivebelt can be examined. Look for cracks, splitting and fraying on the surface of the belt; check also for signs of glazing (shiny patches) and separation of the belt plies. If damage or wear is visible, the belt should be renewed.

6 Check the belt tension as follows: apply thumb pressure to the belt at a point on its longest run, midway between two pulleys and

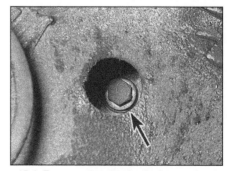

15.4 Remove the plug in the inner wheel arch to gain access to the crankshaft pulley bolt (arrowed)

15.6 Checking the auxiliary drive belt tension

assess the amount of deflection that can be caused **(see illustration)**. Compare this measurement with that listed in the *Specifications*. If necessary, refer to the relevant sub-Section and correctly tension the belt.

Tensioning

All models except G40

7 Slacken the alternator mounting screws, until the alternator can be moved by hand.
8 Working underneath the alternator, slacken the tensioning strut pivot mountings. Slacken the tensioner nut lockscrew by one turn **(see illustration)**.
9 Tighten the tensioning *nut* to the specified 'initial' torque - this sets the belt tension - then hold the nut in this position and tighten the tensioning nut lockscrew to the specified torque. **Note:** *The tensioning nut 'initial' torque figure differs for new and old belts - see Specifications for details*
10 Re-tighten the alternator and tensioning strut mounting screws to the specified torque, then start the engine and run it for about 5 minutes, to allow the belt to settle.
11 Stop the engine, then re-tension the Vee-belt, as described in paragraphs 8 to 10, but this time tighten the tensioning nut to the 'final' torque figure specified.

G40 models with single or twin auxiliary Vee-belts

12 The belt tension is set by rotating the G-charger on its mountings, as follows:

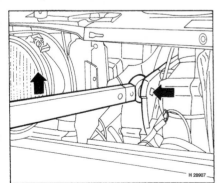

15.14a Auxiliary drivebelt tensioning - pre-December 1990 G40 models

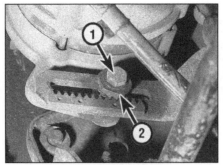

15.8 Auxiliary drivebelt tensioning strut, at the base of the alternator (all models except G40)
1 *Tensioner nut lockscrew*
2 *Tensioner nut*

13 With reference to Chapter 4B, slacken the G-charger mounting bracket screws.
14 Insert a square drive torque wrench into the adjusting hole at the edge of the G-charger mounting bracket **(see illustrations)**. **Note:** *On models built before December 1990 it will be necessary to first remove the front radiator grille - refer to Chapter 11 for details.*
15 Rotate the wrench anti-clockwise and apply the specified tensioning torque to the G-charger mounting bracket - this sets the belt tension. Hold the G-charger in this position, then tighten the mounting bracket screws to the specified torque. **Note:** *The tensioning torque figure differs for new and old belts - see Specifications for details.*
16 Refit the radiator front grille, where applicable.

Renewal

All models except G40

17 With reference to the information given in paragraph 7, slacken the alternator and adjusting strut screws, then pivot the alternator towards the engine to relieve the tension on the belt.
18 Remove the belt, then clean off any deposits that may have built up in the 'vee' of the crankshaft and alternator pulleys.

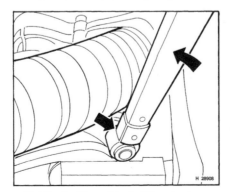

15.14b Auxiliary drivebelt tensioning - post-December 1990 G40 models

19 Fit the new belt to the crankshaft and alternator pulleys, then refer to the relevant sub-Section and adjust the belt tension.

G40 models with single or twin auxiliary V-belts

20 With reference to the information given in paragraph 13, slacken the mounting bracket screws, then allow the G-charger to pivot down towards the engine to relieve the tension on the belt(s).
21 Lift the off the belt(s), then clean off any deposits that may have built up in the 'vee' of the crankshaft, alternator and G-charger pulleys.
22 Fit the new belt over the pulleys, then refer to the relevant sub-Section and adjust the belt tension.

16 Spark plug renewal

1 The correct functioning of the spark plugs is vital for the correct running and efficiency of the engine. It is essential that the plugs fitted are appropriate for the engine (a suitable type is specified at the beginning of this Chapter). If this type is used and the engine is in good condition, the spark plugs should not need attention between scheduled replacement intervals. Spark plug cleaning is rarely necessary, and should not be attempted unless specialised equipment is available, as damage can easily be caused to the electrodes.
2 If the marks on the original-equipment spark plug (HT) leads cannot be seen, mark the leads "1" to "4", to correspond to the cylinder the lead serves (No 1 cylinder is at the timing belt end of the engine). Pull the leads from the plugs by gripping the end fitting, not the lead, otherwise the internal lead connection may be fractured **(see illustration)**.
3 It is advisable to remove any dirt from the spark plug recesses using a clean brush or compressed air before removing the plugs, to prevent dirt dropping into the cylinders **(see illustration)**. **Note:** *On engine codes AAU, AAV it will be necessary to remove the air cleaner housing to gain access to the plugs.*

16.2 Pull the leads from the plugs by gripping the end fitting

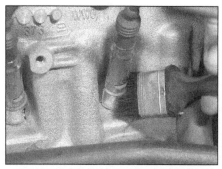

16.3 It is advisable to remove any debris from the spark plug recesses using a clean brush before removing the plugs, to prevent it from dropping into the cylinders

16.4a Unscrew the plugs using a spark plug spanner, or a spark plug socket and extension bar

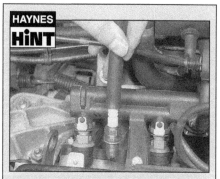

HAYNES HINT

It is very often difficult to insert spark plugs into their holes without cross-threading them. To avoid this possibility, fit a short length of 5/16 inch internal diameter rubber hose over the end of the spark plug. The flexible hose acts as a universal joint to help align the plug with the plug hole. Should the plug begin to cross-thread, the hose will slip on the spark plug, preventing thread damage to the aluminium cylinder head

16.4b Removing a spark plug

16.9 Adjusting the spark plug electrode gap

4 Unscrew the plugs using a spark plug spanner, suitable box spanner or a deep socket and extension bar. Keep the socket aligned with the spark plug - if it is forcibly moved to one side, the ceramic insulator may be broken off **(see illustrations)**. As each plug is removed, examine it as follows.

5 Examination of the spark plugs will give a good indication of the condition of the engine. If the insulator nose of the spark plug is clean and white, with no deposits, this is indicative of a weak mixture or too hot a plug (a hot plug transfers heat away from the electrode slowly, a cold plug transfers heat away quickly).

6 If the tip and insulator nose are covered with hard black-looking deposits, then this is indicative that the mixture is too rich. Should the plug be black and oily, then it is likely that the engine is fairly worn, as well as the mixture being too rich.

7 If the insulator nose is covered with light tan to greyish-brown deposits, then the mixture is correct and it is likely that the engine is in good condition.

8 The spark plug electrode gap is of considerable importance as, if it is too large or too small, the size of the spark and its efficiency will be seriously impaired. The gap should be set to the value recommended by the spark plug manufacturer.

9 To set the gap, measure it with a feeler blade and then bend open, or closed, the outer plug electrode until the correct gap is achieved. The centre electrode should never be bent, as this may crack the insulator and cause plug failure,

if nothing worse. If using feeler blades, the gap is correct when the appropriate-size blade is a firm sliding fit **(see illustration)**.

Caution: Check the spark plug packaging for the manufacturers recommendations - some types have multiple or specially-shaped electrodes, which are pre-gapped and hence not adjustable.

10 Electrode gap adjusting tools are available from most motor accessory shops, or from some spark plug manufacturers.

11 Before fitting the spark plugs, check that the threaded connector sleeves are tight, and that the plug exterior surfaces and threads are clean **(see Haynes Hint)**.

12 Remove the rubber hose (if used), and tighten the plug to the specified torque setting using the spark plug socket and a torque

wrench. Refit the remaining spark plugs in the same manner.

13 Connect the HT leads in their correct order, and refit any components removed for access.

17 Air filter renewal

1 Prise open the spring clips and lift off the air cleaner top cover **(see illustrations)**
Caution: On multi-point fuel-injected models, the air flow meter is integral with the air cleaner top cover - handle this component very carefully as it can easily be damaged.

17.1a Unclipping the air cleaner top cover - single-point fuel-injected models

17.1b Removing the air cleaner top cover/air flow meter - multi-point fuel-injected models

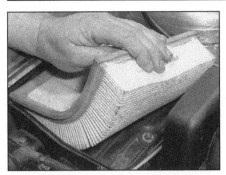

17.2a Lifting out the air cleaner element - multi-point fuel-injected models

17.2b Lifting out the air cleaner element - single-point fuel-injected models

17.5 Air cleaner top cover alignment - single-point fuel-injection models

2 Lift out the air filter element **(see illustrations)**.
3 Brush out any debris that may have collected inside the air cleaner.
4 Lay the new air filter element in position in the lower half of the air cleaner housing, ensuring that the rubberised edges are securely seated in the recess at the outer edge.
5 Refit the air cleaner top cover and snap the retaining clips into position. Where applicable on single-point fuel-injection models, the alignment arrows on the top cover must line up **(see illustration)**.

18 Sliding roof runner lubrication

1 Open the sliding roof, then clean the runners with a cloth rag.
2 Spray the runners with a suitable silicone lubricant (available from most car accessory shops).
3 Close the sliding roof.

19 Underbody sealant condition check

Jack up the front and rear of the car and support on axle stands (see "*Jacking and vehicle support*"). Alternatively position the car over an inspection pit.
Check the complete underbody, wheel housings and side sills for damage to the underbody sealant. If evident, repair as necessary.

60 000 mile service

20 Timing belt renewal

Refer to the relevant Section of Chapter 2A

21 Fuel filter renewal

Refer to the information in Chapter 4A.

Every 2 years - regardless of mileage

22 Brake fluid renewal

 Warning: Brake hydraulic fluid can harm your eyes and damage painted surfaces, so use extreme caution when handling and pouring it. Do not use fluid that has been standing open for some time, as it absorbs moisture from the air. Excess moisture can cause a dangerous loss of braking effectiveness.

1 The procedure is similar to that for the bleeding of the hydraulic system as described in Chapter 9, except that the brake fluid reservoir should be emptied by siphoning, using a clean poultry baster or similar before starting, and allowance should be made for the old fluid to be expelled when bleeding a section of the circuit.

2 Working as described in Chapter 9, open the first bleed screw in the sequence, and pump the brake pedal gently until nearly all the old fluid has been emptied from the master cylinder reservoir.

 Old hydraulic fluid is invariably darker in colour than the new, making it easy to distinguish the two.

3 Top-up to the "MAX" level with new fluid, and continue pumping until only the new fluid remains in the reservoir, and new fluid can be seen emerging from the bleed screw. Tighten the screw, and top the reservoir level up to the "MAX" level line.
4 Work through all the remaining bleed screws in the sequence until new fluid can be seen at all of them. Be careful to keep the master cylinder reservoir topped-up to above the "MIN" level at all times, or air may enter

the system and greatly increase the length of the task.
5 When the operation is complete, check that all bleed screws are securely tightened, and that their dust caps are refitted. Wash off all traces of spilt fluid, and recheck the master cylinder reservoir fluid level.
6 Check the operation of the brakes before taking the car on the road.

23 Coolant renewal

Cooling system draining

 Warning: Wait until the engine is cold before starting this procedure. Do not allow antifreeze to come in contact with your skin, or with the painted

surfaces of the vehicle. Rinse off spills immediately with plenty of water. Never leave antifreeze lying around in an open container, or in a puddle in the driveway or on the garage floor. Children and pets are attracted by its sweet smell, but antifreeze can be fatal if ingested.

1 With the engine completely cold, cover the expansion tank cap with a wad of rag, and slowly turn the cap anti-clockwise to relieve any pressure in the cooling system (a hissing sound will normally be heard). Wait until any pressure remaining in the system is released, then continue to turn the cap until it can be removed.

2 Move the heater control to the 'HOT' position. This is necessary in order to help drain the heater circuit, as a mechanical temperature valve is used in the system.

3 Position a suitable container beneath the left-hand side of the radiator, then release the retaining clip and ease the bottom hose from the radiator stub. If the hose joint has not been disturbed for some time, it will be necessary to gently twist the hose to break the joint. Do not use excessive force, or the radiator stub could be damaged. Allow the coolant to drain into the container.

4 If the coolant has been drained for a reason other than renewal, then provided it is clean and less than two years old, it can be re-used, though this is not recommended.

5 Once all the coolant has drained, reconnect the hose to the radiator and secure it in position with the retaining clip.

Cooling system flushing

6 If coolant renewal has been neglected, or if the antifreeze mixture has become diluted, then in time, the cooling system may gradually lose efficiency, as the coolant passages become restricted due to rust, scale deposits, and other sediment. The cooling system efficiency can be restored by flushing the system clean.

7 The radiator should be flushed independently of the engine, to avoid unnecessary contamination.

Radiator flushing

8 To flush the radiator disconnect the top and bottom hoses from the radiator, with reference to Chapter 3.

9 Insert a garden hose into the radiator top inlet. Direct a flow of clean water through the radiator, and continue flushing until clean water emerges from the radiator bottom outlet.

10 If after a reasonable period, the water still does not run clear, the radiator can be flushed with a good proprietary cooling system cleaning agent. It is important that the manufacturer's instructions are followed carefully. If the contamination is particularly bad, remove the radiator and invert it then insert the hose in the radiator bottom outlet and reverse-flush the radiator.

Engine flushing

11 To flush the engine, remove the thermostat as described in Chapter 3 and leave the cover disconnected.

12 With the top hose disconnected from the radiator, insert a garden hose into the radiator top hose. Direct a clean flow of water through the engine, and continue flushing until clean water emerges from the thermostat housing in the cylinder head outlet.

13 On completion of flushing, refit the thermostat and reconnect the hoses with reference to Chapter 3.

Cooling system filling

14 Before attempting to fill the cooling system, make sure that all hoses and clips are in good condition, and that the clips are tight. Note that an antifreeze mixture must be used all year round, to prevent corrosion of the engine components (see following sub-Section).

15 Check that the heater controls are set to "HOT", then remove the rubber strip and plastic cover from the plenum chamber behind the engine compartment, and loosen the bleeder screw on the heater temperature control valve.

16 Slowly pour the coolant into the expansion tank. While doing this watch the heater bleeder, and tighten the screw when bubble-free water comes out. If the coolant is being renewed, begin by pouring in a couple of litres of water, followed by the correct quantity of antifreeze, then top-up with more water.

17 Once the level in the expansion tank starts to rise, squeeze the radiator top and bottom hoses to help expel any trapped air in the system. Once all the air is expelled, top-up the coolant level to the "MAX" mark and refit the expansion tank cap.

18 Start the engine and run it until it reaches normal operating temperature and the electric cooling fan switches on, then stop the engine and allow it to cool.

19 Check for leaks, particularly around disturbed components. Check the coolant level in the expansion tank, and top-up if

necessary. Note that the system must be cold before an accurate level is indicated in the expansion tank. If the expansion tank cap is removed while the engine is still warm, cover the cap with a thick cloth, and unscrew the cap slowly to gradually relieve the system pressure (a hissing sound will normally be heard). Wait until any pressure remaining in the system is released, then continue to turn the cap until it can be removed.

20 Finally refit the plastic cover and rubber strip to the plenum chamber, and reset the heater controls as necessary.

Antifreeze mixture

21 The antifreeze should always be renewed at the specified intervals. This is necessary not only to maintain the antifreeze properties, but also to prevent corrosion which would otherwise occur as the corrosion inhibitors become progressively less effective.

22 Always use an ethylene-glycol based antifreeze which is suitable for use in mixed-metal cooling systems. The quantity of antifreeze and levels of protection are indicated in the *Specifications*.

23 Before adding antifreeze, the cooling system should be completely drained, preferably flushed, and all hoses checked for condition and security.

24 After filling with antifreeze, a label should be attached to the expansion tank, stating the type and concentration of antifreeze used, and the date installed. Any subsequent topping-up should be made with the same type and concentration of antifreeze **(see illustration)**.

25 Do not use engine antifreeze in the windscreen/tailgate washer system, as it will cause damage to the vehicle paintwork. A screenwash additive should be added to the washer system in the quantities stated on the bottle.

23.24 Topping up the cooling system with antifreeze

Chapter 2 Part A:
Engine in-car repair procedures

Contents

Degrees of difficulty

Easy, suitable for novice with little experience	**Fairly easy,** suitable for beginner with some experience	**Fairly difficult,** suitable for competent DIY mechanic	**Difficult,** suitable for experienced DIY mechanic	**Very difficult,** suitable for expert DIY or professional

Specifications

Engine type . . . .   Four cylinder in-line, overhead camshaft, transverse mounting

Engine code letters

AAU	1043 cc, single-point fuel injection, catalyst.
AAV	1272 cc, single-point fuel injection, catalyst.
3F	1272 cc, multi-point fuel injection, catalyst.
PY	1272 cc, multi-point fuel injection, supercharged, catalyst.

General

Bore x stroke:
AAU	75 x 59 mm
AAV	75 x 72 mm
3F	75 x 72 mm
PY	75 x 72 mm

Maximum power output:
AAU	33 kW @ 5200 rpm
AAV	40 kW @ 5000 rpm
3F	55 kW @ 5900 rpm
PY	83 kW @ 6000 rpm

Maximum torque:
AAU	76 Nm @ 2800 rpm
AAV	95 Nm @ 3200-3400 rpm
3F	99 Nm @ 3200-4000 rpm
PY	150 Nm @ 3600-4400 rpm

Compression ratio:
AAU	9.8:1
AAV	9.5:1
3F	10.0:1
PY	8.0:1

Compression pressures at cranking speed:
AAU, AAV, 3F:
New	10 - 15 bar
Wear limit	7 bar

PY:
New	8 - 12 bar
Wear limit	6 bar

Maximum pressure difference between adjacent cylinders	3 bar
Firing order	1-3-4-2 (No 1 at timing belt end)

Torque wrench settings

	Nm	lbf ft
Cylinder head bolts (engine cold):		
Stage 1	40	30
Stage 2	60	44
Stage 3 (angle tighten)	+ one half-turn (180°), OR + two quarter-turns (2x90°)	
Main bearing cap bolts	65	48
Camshaft cover screws	10	7
Camshaft sprocket bolt	80	59
Inlet manifold nuts/bolts	25	18
Exhaust manifold nuts/bolts	25	18
Flywheel bolts:		
Stage 1	60	44
Stage 2 (angle tighten)	+ 90°	
Sump	20	15
Oil drain plug	30	22
Oil pressure switch	25	18
Crankshaft sprocket bolt	80	59
Crankshaft oil seal housing bolts	10	7
Auxiliary drivebelt pulley bolts	20	15
Oil pump mounting bolts	20	15
Oil pump cover bolts	10	7
Oil pickup tube screws	10	7

1 General information

1 The engine is of four cylinders, in-line, overhead camshaft type mounted transversely at the front of the car, with the gearbox on the left-hand side. The top of the engine is inclined slightly forwards.

2 The crankshaft is of five bearing type, and the centre main bearing incorporates thrustwashers to control crankshaft endfloat.

3 The camshaft is driven by a toothed timing belt from a sprocket on the front of the crankshaft, and the timing belt also drives the water pump. The valves are operated by hydraulic tappets. The cylinder block is of cast iron and the cylinder head of light alloy.

4 The geared oil pump is located on the front of the cylinder block and driven by the crankshaft via a chain. A positive crankcase ventilation system is incorporated.

Major operations possible with the engine in the car

5 The following operations can be carried out without having to remove the engine from the car:

a) Removal and servicing of the cylinder head, camshaft, and timing belt*.

b) Removal of the flywheel and clutch (after removing the gearbox).

c) Renewal of the crankshaft front and rear oil seals.

d) Removal of the sump.

e) Removal of the oil pump.

f) Renewal of the engine mountings.

Major operations only possible after removal of the engine from the car

6 The following operations can only be carried out after removal of the engine from the car:

a) Renewal of the crankshaft main bearings.

b) Removal of the crankshaft.

c) Removal of the pistons/connecting rods.

*Cylinder head dismantling procedures are detailed in Chapter 2B and contain details of camshaft and hydraulic tappet removal.

Note: It is possible to remove the pistons and connecting rods (after removing the cylinder head and sump) without removing the engine from the vehicle. However, this procedure is not recommended. Work of this nature is more easily and thoroughly completed with the engine on the bench, as described in Chapter 2B.

2 Engine assembly and valve timing marks - general information and usage

General information

Note: This sub-section has been written with the assumption that the distributor, HT leads and timing belt are correctly fitted.

1 The camshaft sprocket is crankshaft-driven, by means of a timing belt. Both sprockets rotate in phase with each other and this provides the correct valve timing as the engine rotates. When the timing belt is removed during servicing or repair, it is possible for the cam and crankshafts to rotate independently of each other and the correct valve timing is then lost.

2 The design of the engines covered in this Chapter is such that potentially damaging piston-to-valve contact may occur if the camshaft is rotated when a piston is stationary at, or near, the top of its stroke.

3 For this reason, it is important that the correct phasing between the camshaft and crankshaft is preserved whilst the timing belt is off the engine. This is achieved by setting the engine in a reference condition (known as Top Dead Centre or TDC) before the timing belt is removed and then preventing the shafts from rotating until the belt is refitted. Similarly, if the engine has been dismantled for overhaul, the engine can be set to TDC during reassembly to ensure that the correct shaft phasing is restored.

4 TDC is the highest position a piston reaches within its respective cylinder - in a four stroke engine, each piston reaches TDC twice per cycle; once on the compression stroke and once on the exhaust stroke. In general, TDC normally refers to cylinder No 1 on the compression stroke. (Note that the cylinders are numbered one to four from the timing belt end of the engine).

5 The crankshaft sprocket is equipped with a marking which, when aligned with a reference marking on the timing belt cover, indicates that cylinder No 1 (and hence also No 4) is at TDC.

6 The camshaft sprocket is also equipped with a timing mark - when this is similarly aligned, the engine is correctly positioned and the timing belt can then be refitted and tensioned.

7 The following sub-Sections describe setting the engine to TDC on cylinder No 1.

Setting engine to TDC on cylinder No1 - timing belt fitted

8 Before starting work, disconnect the battery negative cable to disable the fuel ignition and ignition system and to remove the risk of electrical short circuits. Prevent any vehicle movement by putting the transmission in neutral, applying the parking brake and chocking the rear wheels.

9 On the distributor cap, note the position of the No 1 cylinder HT terminal. On some models, the manufacturer provides a marking

in the form of a small cut-out , however if the terminal is not marked, follow the HT lead from the No 1 cylinder spark plug back to the distributor cap (No 1 cylinder is at the timing belt end of the engine) and using chalk or a pen (not a pencil, as the graphite will conduct electricity), place a mark on the distributor body directly under the terminal.

10 Remove the distributor cap, as described in Chapter 5B

11 Disconnect the HT leads from the spark plugs, noting their order of connection.

12 To bring any piston up to TDC, it will be necessary to rotate the crankshaft manually. This can be done by using a wrench and socket on the bolt that retains the crankshaft pulley (refer to the following sub-Section for more detail).

13 Rotate the crankshaft in its normal direction of rotation until the distributor rotor arm electrode begins to approach the No 1 terminal marking made on the distributor body.

 HAYNES HiNT *Remove all four spark plugs; the lack of cylinder compression will make the engine easier to turn; refer to Chapter 1 for details.*

14 Carry out the following operations:

a) *Refer to Chapter 4A or B (as applicable) and remove the air cleaner assembly, to improve access.*

b) *Refer to Chapter 1 and remove the auxiliary drivebelt.*

15 Prise open the clips and lift off the upper section of the outer timing belt cover to expose the timing belt sprockets beneath. Where applicable, remove the dipstick tube and engine earth lead, if they are secured to the timing belt cover.

16 Identify the timing marks on both the camshaft sprocket and the inner section of the timing belt cover. Continue turning the crankshaft clockwise until the these marks are exactly aligned with each other. At this point, identify the timing mark on the crankshaft pulley and check that it is aligned with the 'O' marking on the lower section of the timing belt cover **(see illustration)**. **Note:** *On engine*

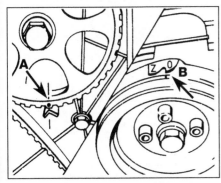

2.16 Camshaft sprocket (A) and crankshaft pulley (B) timing marks

code PY, the 'O' marking stamped on the edge of the crankshaft pulley must be aligned with the pointer on the inner timing belt cover.

17 Check that the distributor rotor arm electrode is now aligned with the No 1 terminal mark on the distributor body. If it proves impossible to align the rotor arm with the No 1 terminal whilst maintaining the alignment of the camshaft timing marks, refer to Chapter 5B and check that the distributor has been fitted correctly. **Note:** *The basic ignition advance setting may mean that the centre of the rotor arm electrode does not line up exactly with the No1 terminal marking*

18 When all the above steps have been completed successfully, the engine will be set to TDC on cylinder No 1.

Caution: If the timing belt is to be removed, ensure that the crankshaft, camshaft and intermediate shaft alignment is preserved by preventing the sprockets from rotating with respect to each other.

Setting engine to TDC on No 1 cylinder - timing belt removed

19 This procedure has been written with the assumption that the timing belt has been removed and that the alignment between the camshaft and crankshaft has been lost, for example following engine removal and overhaul.

20 On all the engines covered in this manual, it is possible for damage to be caused by the piston crowns striking the valve heads, if the camshaft is rotated with the timing belt removed and the crankshaft set to TDC. For this reason, the TDC setting procedure must be carried out in a particular order, as described in the following paragraphs.

21 Before the cylinder head is refitted, use a wrench and socket on the crankshaft pulley centre bolt to turn the crankshaft in its normal direction of rotation, until all four pistons are positioned halfway down their bores, with piston No 1 on its upstroke -i.e. 90° before TDC.

22 With the cylinder head and camshaft sprocket now fitted, identify the timing marks on both the camshaft sprocket and the inner section of the timing belt cover **(refer to illustration 2.16)**.

23 Turn the camshaft sprocket in its normal direction of rotation until the timing marks on the sprocket and timing belt inner cover are exactly aligned. Keep the camshaft in this position and prevent it from moving.

24 Temporarily refit the crankshaft auxiliary belt pulley, then identify the timing marks on the edge of pulley and the timing belt cover. Using a socket and wrench on the crankshaft sprocket retaining bolt, turn the crankshaft through 90° (quarter of a turn) in its normal direction of rotation, to bring the timing marks into alignment **(refer to illustration 2.16)**

25 Check that the distributor rotor arm electrode is now pointing roughly at the No1 cylinder terminal marking on the distributor

body. If this is not the case, refer to Chapter 5B and check that the distributor has been fitted correctly. **Note:** *The basic ignition advance setting may mean that the centre of the rotor arm electrode does not line up exactly with the No1 terminal marking.*

26 When all the above steps have been completed successfully, the engine will be set at TDC on cylinder No 1. The timing belt can now be fitted as described in Section 4. *Caution: Until the timing belt is fitted, ensure that the crankshaft and camshaft alignment is preserved by preventing the sprockets from rotating with respect to each other.*

3 Cylinder compression test

1 When engine performance is down, or if misfiring occurs which cannot be attributed to the ignition or fuel systems, a compression test can provide diagnostic clues as to the engine's condition. If the test is performed regularly, it can give warning of trouble before any other symptoms become apparent.

2 The engine must be fully warmed-up to normal operating temperature, the battery must be fully charged, and all the spark plugs must be removed (refer to Chapter 1). The aid of an assistant will also be required.

3 Disable the ignition system by disconnecting the ignition HT coil lead from the distributor cap and earthing it on the cylinder block. Use a jumper lead or similar wire to make a good connection.

4 Fit a compression tester to the No 1 cylinder spark plug hole - the type of tester which screws into the plug thread is preferable.

5 Have an assistant hold the throttle wide open, then crank the engine on the starter motor; after one or two revolutions, the compression pressure should build up to a maximum figure, and then stabilise. Record the highest reading obtained.

6 Repeat the test on the remaining cylinders, recording the pressure in each. Keep the throttle wide open.

7 All cylinders should produce very similar pressures; a difference of more than 2 bars between any two cylinders indicates a fault. Note that the compression should build up quickly in a healthy engine; low compression on the first stroke, followed by gradually-increasing pressure on successive strokes, indicates worn piston rings. A low compression reading on the first stroke, which does not build up during successive strokes, indicates leaking valves or a blown head gasket (a cracked head could also be the cause). Deposits on the undersides of the valve heads can also cause low compression.

8 Refer to the *Specifications* section of this Chapter and compare the recorded compression figures with those stated by the manufacturer. Note the lower compression ratio of the supercharged G40 model (engine code PY).

9 If the pressure in any cylinder is low, carry out the following test to isolate the cause. Introduce a teaspoonful of clean oil into that cylinder through its spark plug hole, and repeat the test.

10 If the addition of oil temporarily improves the compression pressure, this indicates that bore or piston wear is responsible for the pressure loss. No improvement suggests that leaking or burnt valves, or a blown head gasket, may be to blame.

11 A low reading from two adjacent cylinders is almost certainly due to the head gasket having blown between them; the presence of coolant in the engine oil will confirm this.

12 If one cylinder is about 20 percent lower than the others and the engine has a slightly rough idle, a worn camshaft lobe could be the cause.

13 If the compression reading is unusually high, the combustion chambers are probably coated with carbon deposits. If this is the case, the cylinder head should be removed and decarbonised.

14 On completion of the test, refit the spark plugs and restore the ignition system.

---

4   Camshaft timing belt -
removal, inspection and
refitting

General information

1 The primary function of the toothed timing belt is to drive the camshaft(s), but it is also used to drive the coolant pump. Should the belt slip or break in service, the valve timing will be disturbed and piston to valve contact may occur, resulting in serious engine damage.

2 For this reason, it is important that the timing belt is tensioned correctly and inspected regularly for signs of wear or deterioration.

Removal

3 Disconnect the battery negative cable and position it away from the terminal.

4 With reference to Section 2, remove the timing belt outer cover and set the engine to TDC on cylinder No1.

5 If the timing belt is relatively new and is to be refitted later, check to see if it has manufacturers markings to indicate the correct direction of rotation. If none are present, make your own using a dab of paint or typists correction fluid.

Caution: If the belt is refitted differently, accelerated wear leading to premature failure may occur.

6 With reference to Chapter 3, loosen the water pump retaining bolts, then turn the pump body to relieve the tension from the timing belt. Slide the timing belt from the camshaft sprocket **(see illustration)**.

4.6 Releasing the timing belt from the camshaft sprocket

7 Using an Allen bit, unbolt the auxiliary belt pulley from the crankshaft sprocket. Remove the screws, lift off the timing belt lower cover, then remove the timing belt.

Inspection

8 Examine the belt for evidence of contamination by coolant or lubricant. If this is the case, identify the source of the contamination before progressing any further. Check the belt for signs of wear or damage, particularly around the leading edges of the belt teeth. Renew the belt if its condition is in doubt; the cost of belt renewal is negligible compared with potential cost of the engine repairs, should the belt fail in service. Similarly, if the belt is known to have covered more than 60,000 miles, it is prudent to renew it regardless of condition, as a precautionary measure.

9 If the timing belt is not going to be refitted for some time, it is a wise precaution to hang a warning label on the vehicles' steering wheel, to prevent others from attempting to start the vehicle.

Refitting

10 Loop the timing belt under the crankshaft sprocket loosely, observing the direction of rotation markings.

11 Bolt the lower timing belt cover in position, then refit the auxiliary belt pulley to the crankshaft sprocket and tighten the retaining bolts to the specified torque.

12 Engage the timing belt teeth with the crankshaft sprocket, then manoeuvre it into position over the coolant pump and camshaft sprockets - avoid bending the belt back on itself or twisting it excessively as you do this. Ensure that the 'front run' of the belt is taught - ie all the slack should be in the section of the belt that passes over the coolant pump pulley.

13 With the belt fitted, ensure that the timing marks on the crankshaft pulley and camshaft sprocket are exactly aligned with their corresponding reference marks on the timing belt inner cover; refer to the illustrations in *General Information* for details.

14 Insert a stout screwdriver between the lugs on the coolant pump casting, then using the screwdriver as a lever, turn the coolant pump so that the slack in the belt is taken up **(see illustration)**.

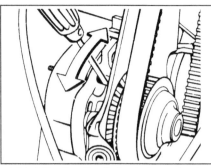

4.14 Adjusting the timing belt tension by rotating the coolant pump

15 Test the belt tension by grasping it between the fingers at a point mid-way between the coolant pump and camshaft sprockets and twisting it; the belt tension is correct when it can just be twisted through 90° (quarter of a turn) and no further **(see illustration)**.

16 When the correct belt tension has been achieved, tighten the coolant pump mounting bolts to the specified torque.

17 Using a spanner or wrench and socket on the crankshaft sprocket centre bolt, rotate the crankshaft through two complete revolutions and reset the engine to TDC on cylinder No1, with reference to Section 2. Re-check the belt tension, adjusting it if necessary.

18 Refit the timing belt cover and fasten the retaining clips securely.

---

5   Timing belt sprockets -
removal and refitting

Camshaft sprocket

Removal

1 With reference to Section 2 remove the timing belt cover, set the engine to TDC on cylinder No1 and remove the timing belt.

2 The camshaft sprocket must be held stationary whilst its retaining bolt is

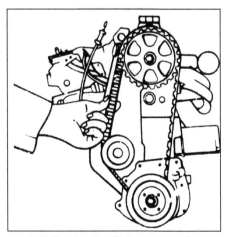

4.15 Testing the timing belt tension

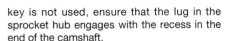

TOOL TiP

To make a camshaft sprocket holding tool, obtain two lengths of steel strip about 6 mm thick by 30 mm wide or similar, one 600 mm long, the other 200 mm long (all dimensions approximate). Bolt the two strips together to form a forked end, leaving the bolt slack so that the shorter strip can pivot freely. At the end of each 'prong' of the fork, secure a bolt with a nut and a locknut, to act as the fulcrums; these will engage with the cut-outs in the sprocket, and should protrude by about 30 mm

slackened; if access to the correct VW special tool is not possible, a simple home-made tool using basic materials may be fabricated **(see Tool Tip)**.

3 Using the home made tool, brace the camshaft sprocket and slacken and remove the retaining bolt; recover the washer where fitted.

4 Slide the camshaft sprocket from the end of the camshaft. Where applicable, recover the Woodruff key from the keyway.

5 With the sprocket removed, examine the camshaft oil seal for signs of leaking. If necessary, refer to Section 8 and renew it.

6 Wipe the sprocket and camshaft mating surfaces clean.

Refitting

7 Where applicable, fit the Woodruff key into the keyway with the plain surface facing upwards. Offer up the sprocket to the camshaft, engaging the slot in the sprocket with the Woodruff key. On engines where a

key is not used, ensure that the lug in the sprocket hub engages with the recess in the end of the camshaft.

8 Insert the camshaft sprocket bolt and tighten it to the specified torque - hold the sprocket still using the method described in the *Removal* Section.

9 Working from Section 2, check that the engine is still set to TDC on cylinder No 1, then refit and tension the timing belt, as described in Section 4. Refit the timing belt cover and fasten the retaining clips securely.

Crankshaft sprocket

Removal

10 With reference to Section 2, remove the timing belt cover, set the engine to TDC on cylinder No1 and remove the timing belt.

11 Refer to Chapter 5A and remove the starter motor. Hold the crankshaft stationary using a lever inserted between the teeth of the starter ring gear.

12 Slacken the bolt and remove the sprocket, recovering the Woodruff key, where applicable. If the sprocket is tight, carefully lever it from the end of the crankshaft using a prybar. **Note:** *Discard the sprocket retaining bolt - a new one must be used on reassembly.*

Refitting

13 Fit the Woodruff key in the crankshaft and tap the sprocket into position. On engines where a Woodruff key is not used, offer up the sprocket to the crankshaft, engaging the lug on the inside of the sprocket with the recess in the end of the crankshaft.

14 Insert a new sprocket retaining bolt and tighten it to the specified torque - hold the crankshaft stationary using a lever in the starter ring gear, as described in the *Removal* sub-Section.

15 Working from Section 2, check that the engine is still set to TDC on cylinder No 1, then refit and tension the timing belt, as described in Section 4. Refit the timing belt cover and fasten the retaining clips securely.

Coolant pump timing belt sprocket

16 The coolant pump sprocket is an integral part of the coolant pump assembly and cannot be renewed as a separate item.

6 Camshaft cover gasket - renewal

1 Disable the ignition system by unplugging the multiway wiring connector from the distributor; refer to Chapter 5B for details.

2 On models with single-point fuel injection, refer to Chapter 4A and remove the air cleaner assembly from the throttle body, to improve access.

3 Slacken the clips and disconnect the breather hoses from the camshaft cover (two hoses on G40 models). If crimp type clips are fitted, these must be removed using cutters and hence cannot be re-used.

4 Remove the protective caps, then slacken and withdraw the screws and recover the rubber seal and washers **(see illustration)**. Lift off the camshaft cover.

5 Remove the oil baffle plate **(see illustration)**, noting its orientation, then lift the camshaft cover gasket from the top of the cylinder head and inspect it for signs of deterioration or damage. If its condition is in doubt, discard it.

6 If the gasket has been leaking, inspect the mating surface of the camshaft cover carefully, as warpage due to overtighten may cause it to leak.

7 Ensure the mating surfaces of the cylinder head and the camshaft cover are completely clean, then lay a new gasket in position on the cylinder head, ensuring the lugs at the edge of the gasket fit securely over the dowels protruding from the cylinder head **(see illustration)**. Press the ends of the gasket into the recesses in the camshaft bearing caps.

8 Fit the oil baffle plate into position, then lower the camshaft cover onto the gasket.

9 Insert the cover retaining screws with the rubber seals and washers and tighten them to the specified torque. Fit the protective caps over the heads of the screws.

10 Reconnect the breather hoses to the ports on the camshaft cover. Where crimp type clips were originally fitted, fit new worm drive clips in their place.

11 On single point injected models, refer to Chapter 4A and refit the air cleaner assembly.

6.4 Camshaft cover screws (arrowed)

6.5 Showing oil baffle plate over camshaft

6.7 Camshaft cover gasket dowels (arrowed)

12 Restore the ignition system by reconnecting the distributor multiway wiring plug.

7 Camshaft oil seal - renewal

1 Disconnect the battery negative cable and position from the terminal.
2 Refer to Chapter 1 and remove the auxiliary drivebelt(s).
3 With reference to Sections 2 and 4 of this Chapter, remove the auxiliary belt pulley and timing belt cover, then set the engine to TDC on cylinder No 1 and remove the timing belt and camshaft sprocket.
4 Note that the inner timing belt cover shares mounting bolts with the coolant pump - refer to Chapter 3 and remove the coolant pump. After removing the retaining screws, lift the inner timing belt cover away from the engine block - this will expose the camshaft oil seal.
5 Drill two small holes into the existing oil seal, diagonally opposite each other. Thread two self tapping screws into the holes and using two pairs of pliers, pull on the heads of the screws to extract oil seal. Take great care to avoid drilling through into the seal housing or camshaft sealing surface.
6 Clean out the seal housing and sealing surface of the camshaft by wiping it with a lint-free cloth - avoid using solvents that may enter the cylinder head and affect component lubrication. Remove any swarf or burrs that may cause the seal to leak.

8.13a Withdraw the rear oil seal housing from the dowels on the cylinder block . . .

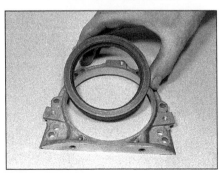

8.14 Removing the seal from its housing

7 Lubricate the lip of the new oil seal with clean engine oil and push it over the camshaft until it is positioned above its housing.
8 Using a hammer and a socket of suitable diameter, drive the seal squarely into its housing. **Note:** *Select a socket that bears only on the hard outer surface of the seal, not the inner lip which can easily be damaged.*
9 With reference to Sections 2 and 4 of this Chapter, refit the inner timing belt cover, timing sprockets, then refit and tension the timing belt. On completion, refit the timing belt outer cover.
10 With reference to Chapter 1, refit and tension the auxiliary drivebelt(s).

8 Crankshaft oil seals - renewal

Crankshaft front oil seal

1 Remove the crankshaft timing belt sprocket, with reference to Section 5.
2 If available use VW tool 2085 to remove the oil seal from the oil pump. Alternatively, drill two small holes into the existing oil seal, diagonally opposite each other. Thread two self tapping screws into the holes and using two pairs of pliers, pull on the heads of the screws to extract oil seal. Take great care to avoid drilling through into the seal housing or crankshaft sealing surface.
3 Clean out the seal housing and sealing surface of the crankshaft by wiping it with a lint-free cloth - avoid using solvents that may

8.13b . . . and recover the gasket

8.16 Driving the new oil seal into its housing

enter the oil pump and affect component lubrication. Remove any swarf or burrs that may cause the seal to leak.
4 Lubricate the lip of the new oil seal with clean engine oil and push it over the crankshaft until it is positioned above its housing.
5 Using a hammer and a socket of suitable diameter, drive the seal squarely into its housing. **Note:** *Select a socket that bears only on the hard outer surface of the seal, not the inner lip which can easily be damaged.*
6 Refit the crankshaft sprocket with reference to Section 5.

Crankshaft rear oil seal

7 Remove the flywheel (see Section 11).

Method 1

8 Drill two diagonally opposite holes in the oil seal, insert two self-tapping screws, and pull out the seal with grips.
9 Clean out the seal housing and sealing surface of the crankshaft by wiping it with a lint-free cloth - avoid using solvents that may enter the crankcase and affect component lubrication. Remove any swarf or burrs that may cause the seal to leak.
10 Using the plastic fitting tool supplied with the new oil seal, tap the seal into the housing using a suitable metal tube. **Note:** *Do not lubricate the seal to ease fitting - it is supplied with a friction-reducing coating.*
11 Refit the flywheel (see Section 11).

Method 2

12 Remove the sump (see Section 13).
13 Unscrew the bolts and withdraw the seal housing from the dowels on the cylinder block. Remove the gasket **(see illustrations)**.
14 Support the housing on blocks of wood and drive out the oil seal **(see illustration)**
15 Clean out the seal housing by wiping it with a lint-free cloth - avoid using solvents that may enter the crankcase and affect component lubrication. Remove any swarf or burrs that may cause the seal to leak.
16 Using the plastic fitting tool supplied with the new oil seal, tap the seal squarely into the housing using a block of wood **(see illustration)**. **Note:** *Do not lubricate the seal to ease fitting - it is supplied with a friction-reducing coating.*
17 Clean the mating faces then refit the housing, together with a new gasket, and tighten the bolts evenly in diagonal sequence to the specified torque.
18 Refit the sump and flywheel as described in Sections 13 and 11 respectively.

9 Cylinder head, inlet and exhaust manifolds - removal, separation and refitting

Removal

1 Select a solid, level surface to park the vehicle upon. Give yourself enough space to move around it easily.

2 Refer to Chapter 11 and remove the bonnet from its hinges - this will give extra working space and clearance when lifting off the head.

3 Disconnect the battery negative cable and position it away from the terminal. **Note:** *If the vehicle has a security coded radio, check that you have a copy of the code number before disconnecting the battery cable; refer to Chapter 12 for details.*

4 With reference to Chapter 1, carry out the following :

a) *Drain the engine oil.*
b) *Drain the cooling system.*

5 Refer to Chapter 1 and remove the auxiliary drivebelt(s).

6 With reference to Section 2 set the engine to TDC on cylinder No 1.

7 With reference to Chapter 3, slacken/remove the clips and disconnect all coolant hoses from the ports on the cylinder head and thermostat housing.

8 Where applicable, refer to Chapter 4C and unplug the Lambda sensor cabling from the main harness at the multiway connector.

9 With reference to Chapter 5B and Chapter 1, carry out the following:

a) *Remove the HT leads from the spark plugs and the distributor.*
b) *Remove the distributor from the cylinder head.*

10 On multi-point fuel-injected models, refer to Chapter 4B and remove the throttle body, the fuel rail and the fuel injectors.

11 On single point fuel-injected models, with reference to Chapter 4A, remove the air cleaner and throttle body. Disconnect the manifold pre-heater cabling at the connector.

12 With reference to Sections 6, 4 and 5 , carry out the following:

a) *Remove the camshaft cover.*
b) *Remove the timing belt outer covers, then relieve the tension from the timing belt and disengage it from the camshaft sprocket.*
c) *Remove the camshaft sprocket.*

13 Slacken and withdraw the retaining screws and lift off the inner timing belt cover. Note that the coolant pump securing bolts double up as fixings for inner timing belt cover - refer to Chapter 3 and remove the coolant pump from the cylinder block.

14 With reference to Chapter 4A or B as applicable, unplug the wiring harness from the coolant temperature sensor at the connector.

15 Refer to Chapter 4C and remove the bolts separate the exhaust down pipe from the exhaust manifold flange.

16 Where applicable, detach the warm air inlet hose from the exhaust manifold heat shield.

17 Slacken and remove the bolt securing the engine oil dipstick tube to the cylinder head.

18 Following the sequence shown in the accompanying illustration *IN REVERSE,*

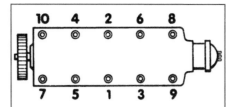

9.18 Cylinder head bolt TIGHTENING sequence

progressively slacken the cylinder head bolts, by half a turn at a time, until all bolts can be unscrewed by hand **(see illustration)**.

19 Check that nothing remains connected to the cylinder head, then lift the head away from the cylinder block; seek assistance if possible, as it is a heavy assembly, especially if it is being removed complete with the manifolds. If the head sticks, grasp either manifold and rock the head back and forth lightly, until it becomes free. Do not lever between the cylinder head and block, as the mating surfaces may be damaged.

20 Remove the gasket from the top of the block, noting the position of the locating dowels. If the dowels are a loose fit, remove them and store them with the head for safe-keeping. The gasket cannot be re-used, but do not discard it at this point - it may be needed for identification purposes, when purchasing a new gasket

21 If the cylinder head is to be dismantled for overhaul refer to Chapter 2B.

Manifold separation

22 Progressively slacken and remove the inlet and exhaust manifold retaining nuts/bolts.

23 Lift the manifolds away from the cylinder head and recover the gaskets.

24 Ensure that the mating surfaces are completely clean, then refit the manifolds, using new gaskets. Tighten the retaining nuts to the specified torque **(see illustrations)**.

Preparation for refitting

25 The mating faces of the cylinder head and cylinder block/crankcase must be perfectly clean before refitting the head. Use a hard plastic or wood scraper to remove all traces of old gasket and carbon; also clean the piston

crowns. Take particular care during the cleaning operations, as aluminium alloy is easily damaged. Also, make sure that the carbon is not allowed to enter the oil and water passages - this is particularly important for the lubrication system, as carbon could block the oil supply to the engine's components. Using adhesive tape and paper, seal the water, oil and bolt holes in the cylinder block/crankcase.

26 Check the mating surfaces of the cylinder block/crankcase and the cylinder head for nicks, deep scratches and other damage. If slight, they may be removed carefully with abrasive paper, but if excessive, machining may be the only alternative to renewal.

27 If warpage of the cylinder head gasket surface is suspected, use a straight-edge to check it for distortion. Refer to Part B of this Chapter if necessary.

28 Check the condition of the cylinder head bolts, and particularly their threads, whenever they are removed. Wash the bolts in suitable solvent, and wipe them dry. Check each for any sign of visible wear or damage, renewing any bolt if necessary. Measure the length of each bolt, to check for stretching (although this is not a conclusive test, if all bolts have stretched by the same amount). Volkswagen do not actually specify that the bolts must be renewed, however, it is strongly recommended that the bolts should be renewed as a complete set whenever they are disturbed.

29 On all the engines covered in this Chapter, it is possible for damage to be caused by the piston crowns striking the valve heads, if the camshaft is rotated with the timing belt removed and the crankshaft set to TDC. For this reason, the crankshaft must be set to a position other than TDC on cylinder No 1, before the cylinder head is refitted: use a wrench and socket on the crankshaft pulley centre bolt to turn the crankshaft in its normal direction of rotation, until all four pistons are positioned halfway down their bores, with piston No 1 on its upstroke -i.e. 90° before TDC.

Refitting

30 Lay a new head gasket on the cylinder block, engaging it with the locating dowels. Ensure that the manufacturers "TOP" and part number markings are face up **(see illustrations)**.

9.24a Fitting new exhaust . . .

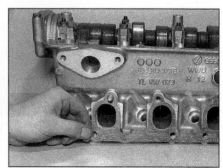

9.24b . . . and inlet manifold gaskets

9.30a Lay a new head gasket on the cylinder block, engaging it with the locating dowels

9.30b The gasket part number should face upwards

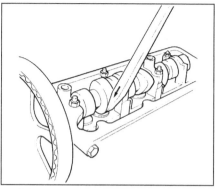

10.6 Hydraulic tappet operation check

31 With the help of an assistant, place the cylinder head and manifolds centrally on the cylinder block, ensuring that the locating dowels engage with the recesses in the cylinder head. Check that the head gasket is correctly seated before allowing the full weight of the cylinder head to rest upon it.

32 Apply a smear of grease to the threads, and to the underside of the heads, of the cylinder head bolts; use a good-quality high-melting point grease.

33 Carefully enter each bolt into its relevant hole (*do not drop them in*) and screw in, by hand only, until finger-tight.

34 Working progressively and in the sequence shown, tighten the cylinder head bolts to their Stage 1 torque setting, using a torque wrench and suitable socket **(refer to illustration 9.18)**. Repeat the exercise in the same sequence for the Stage 2 torque setting.

35 Once all the bolts have been tightened to their Stage 2 settings, working again in the given sequence, angle-tighten the bolts through the specified Stage 3 angle, using a socket and extension bar. It is recommended that an angle-measuring gauge is used during this stage of the tightening, to ensure accuracy. If a gauge is not available, use white paint to make alignment marks between the bolt head and cylinder head prior to tightening; the marks can then be used to check that the bolt has been rotated through the correct angle during tightening. Repeat the exercise for the Stage 4 setting.

36 Refit the coolant pump with reference to Chapter 3.

37 Refit the timing belt inner cover, tightening the retaining screws securely. Refer to Section 5 and refit the camshaft sprocket.

38 Refer to Section 2 and follow the procedure for setting the engine to TDC on No 1 cylinder with the timing belt removed. On completion, refer to Section 4 and refit the camshaft timing belt.

39 The remainder of refitting is a reversal of the removal procedure, as follows:

a) *Bolt the engine dipstick tube bracket to the timing belt cover, where applicable.*

b) *Refer to Chapter 4C and reconnect the exhaust downpipe to the exhaust manifold.*

c) *On multipoint fuel-injected systems, refer to Chapter 4B and refit the fuel injectors, fuel rail and the throttle body.*

d) *On single point fuel-injected models, refer to Chapter 4A and refit the throttle body and air box. Reconnect the inlet manifold pre-heater wiring.*

e) *Refer to Chapter 5B and refit the distributor and the ignition HT leads.*

f) *Refer to Section 6 and refit the camshaft cover.*

g) *Reconnect the radiator, expansion tank and heater coolant hoses, referring to Chapter 3 for guidance. Reconnect the coolant temperature sensor wiring.*

h) *Refer to Chapter 1 and refit the auxiliary drivebelt(s).*

i) *Restore the battery connection.*

j) *Refer to Chapter 11 and refit the bonnet.*

40 On completion, refer to Chapter 1 and carry out the following:

a) *Refill the engine cooling system with the correct quantity of new coolant.*

b) *Refill the engine lubrication system with the correct grade and quantity of oil.*

10 Hydraulic tappets - operation check

1 The hydraulic tappets are self-adjusting and require no attention whilst in service.

2 If the hydraulic tappets become excessively noisy, their operation can be checked as described below.

3 Run the engine until it reaches its normal operating temperature. Switch off the engine, then refer to Section 6 and remove the camshaft cover.

4 Rotate the camshaft by turning the crankshaft with a socket and wrench, until the first cam lobe over cylinder No 1 is pointing upwards.

5 Using a feeler blade, measure the clearance between the base of the cam lobe and the top of the tappet. If the clearance is greater than 0.1mm, then the tappet is defective and must be renewed.

6 If the clearance is less than 0.1 mm, press down on the top of the tappet, until it is felt to contact the top of the valve stem **(see illustration)**. Use a wooden or plastic implement that will not damage the surface of the tappet.

7 If the tappet travels more than 0.1 mm before making contact, then it is defective and must be renewed.

8 Hydraulic tappet removal and refitting is described as part of the cylinder head overhaul sequence - see Chapter 2B for details.

> ⚠️ *Warning: After fitting hydraulic tappets, wait a minimum of 30 minutes before starting the engine to allow the tappets time to settle, otherwise the increased stroke may cause the pistons to strike the valve heads.*

11 Flywheel - removal and refitting

Removal

1 Disconnect the battery negative cable and position it away from the terminal.

2 Carry out the following operations:

a) *Support the engine and remove the transmission as described in Chapter 7.*

b) *Remove the clutch assembly as described in Chapter 6.*

3 Mark the relationship between the flywheel and the end of the crankshaft with a dab of paint, to aid refitting later.

4 Hold the flywheel stationary, by means of a lever or angle iron engaged with the starter ring gear (refer to Chapter 5A for details of starter motor removal).

5 Unscrew the bolts progressively and lift the flywheel from the crankshaft.

Caution: The flywheel is a heavy, bulky component - enlist the help of an assistant if possible. Wear gloves to protect your hands from the ring gear teeth. Discard the flywheel bolts - new items must be used on refitting.

11.6a Coat the threads of the flywheel bolts with locking fluid . . .

11.6b . . . and tighten them to the specified torque

12.23 Removing the rear engine mounting block

Refitting

6 Follow the removal procedure in reverse, noting the following points **(see illustrations)**:

a) *Use the marks made during removal to align the flywheel with the crankshaft.*

b) *Use new shouldered bolts when refitting the flywheel. Tighten them diagonally and progressively to specified torque.*

12 Engine mountings - inspection and renewal

Inspection

1 If improved access is required, raise the front of the car and support it securely on axle stands (see *"Jacking and vehicle support"*).

2 Check the mounting rubbers to see if they are cracked, hardened or separated from the metal at any point; renew the mounting if any such damage or deterioration is evident.

3 Check that all the mounting's fasteners are securely tightened; use a torque wrench to check if possible.

4 Using a large screwdriver or a crowbar, check for wear in the mounting by carefully levering against it to check for free play. Where this is not possible, enlist the aid of an assistant to move the engine/transmission back and forth, or from side to side, while you watch the mounting. While some free play is to be expected even from new components, excessive wear should be obvious. If excessive free play is found, check first that the fasteners are correctly secured, then renew any worn components as described below.

Renewal

5 Disconnect the battery negative cable and position it away from the terminal.

Front left hand engine mounting

6 Position a trolley jack underneath the engine and position it that such that the jack head is directly underneath the engine /bellhousing mating surface. Alternatively, position an engine lifting beam across the engine bay, forward of the suspension strut top mountings, and support the engine using the lifting eyes provided on the cylinder head.

7 Raise the jack/lifting beam jib until it just takes the weight of the engine off the front left hand engine mounting.

8 Slacken and withdraw the engine mounting through-bolt.

9 Slacken and withdraw the engine mounting-to-transmission bolts and remove the bracket.

10 Press the engine mounting rubber blocks and bush out of the crossmember cup.

11 Refitting is a reversal of removal. Before tightening the engine mounting through-bolts, lightly rock the engine and transmission back and forth to settle the mountings. Finally, tighten all mounting bolts to the specified torque.

Right hand engine mounting

12 Mount an engine lifting beam across the engine bay and attach the jib to the engine lifting eyes on the cylinder head. Alternatively, an engine hoist can be used. Raise the hoist/lifting beam jib to take the weight of the engine off the engine mounting.

13 Refer to Chapter 1 and remove the auxiliary drivebelt(s). Refer to Chapter 5A and remove the alternator. On G40 models, refer to Chapter 4B and remove the supercharger.

14 Slacken and withdraw the engine mounting through-bolt.

15 Unbolt the engine mounting bracket from the cylinder block.

16 Unbolt the engine mounting block from the body and remove it from the engine bay.

17 Refitting is a reversal of removal. Before tightening the engine mounting through-bolts, lightly rock the engine and transmission back and forth to settle the mountings. Finally, tighten all mounting bolts to the specified torque.

Rear engine/transmission mounting

18 Disconnect the battery negative cable and position it away from the terminal.

19 Position a trolley jack underneath the engine and position it that such that the jack head is directly underneath the engine/ bellhousing mating surface. Alternatively, position an engine lifting beam across the engine bay, forward of the suspension strut top mountings, and support the engine using the lifting eyes provided on the cylinder head.

20 Raise the jack until it takes the weight of

the engine off the rear engine/transmission mounting.

21 Working underneath the vehicle, slacken and withdraw the engine mounting through-bolt. Be sure that the jack/lifting beam is taking the weight of the engine before removing the bolt completely.

22 Unbolt the mounting bracket from the end of the transmission casing.

23 Unbolt the engine mounting block from the body and remove it from the engine bay **(see illustration)**.

24 Refitting is a reversal of removal. Before tightening the engine/transmission mounting through-bolts, lightly rock the engine and transmission back and forth to settle the mountings. Finally, tighten all mounting bolts to the specified torque.

13 Sump - removal and refitting

Removal

1 Disconnect the battery negative cable, then carry out the following operations:

a) *Apply the handbrake, chock the rear wheels, then jack up the front of the car and support it on axle stands - refer to the Reference Chapter for greater detail.*

b) *Refer to Chapter 8 and disconnect the right-hand side driveshaft (Chapter 7)*

c) *Refer to Chapter 4C and unbolt the exhaust downpipe from the manifold flange.*

d) *Unclip the alternator wire from the sump.*

e) *Refer to Chapter 1 and drain the engine oil into a suitable container. Clean the drain plug and washer and refit it, tightening it to the specified torque.*

2 Unscrew the sump bolts, then break the joint by striking the sump with the palm of your hand. Lower the sump away from the engine and withdraw it from underneath the vehicle. Recover and discard the sump gasket.

3 While the sump is removed, check the oil pump pick-up/strainer for signs of clogging or disintegration. If necessary, remove the pump as described in Section 14, and clean or renew the strainer.

Refitting

4 Remove any remains of the old gasket from the sump and cylinder block - ensure that both mating surface are spotlessly clean. If the gasket has been leaking, check the mating surface of the sump for warpage that may have been caused by overtightening of the bolts. Renew the sump if it is damaged - do not attempt to repair it.

5 Apply a coating of suitable sealant to the sump and crankcase mating surfaces.

6 Lay a new sump gasket in position on the sump mating surface, then offer up the sump and refit the retaining bolts. Tighten the nuts and bolts evenly and progressively to the specified torque.

7 Refit the drive shaft, exhaust downpipe and alternator cabling.

8 Refer to Chapter 1 and refill the engine with the specified grade and quantity of oil.

9 Restore the battery connection.

---

14 Oil pump and pickup -
removal, inspection and refitting

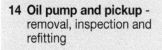

General information

1 The oil pump and pickup are both mounted at the timing belt end of the crankcase. Drive is taken from the crankshaft via a chain and sprocket **(see illustration).**

Removal

2 Refer to Section 13 and remove the sump from the crankcase.

3 With reference to Section 8, remove the front (timing belt end) crankshaft oil seal and housing.

4 Slacken and remove the bolts securing the oil pump to the end of the crankcase.

5 Remove the screws securing the oil pump pickup to the crankcase bracket.

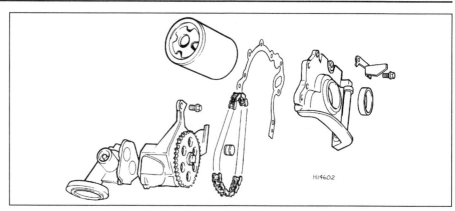

14.1 Exploded view of the oil pump assembly

6 Disengage the pump sprocket from the drive chain and remove the oil pump and pickup from the engine.

Inspection

7 Remove the screws from the mating flange and lift off the pickup tube. Recover the O-ring seal.

8 Slacken and withdraw the screws, then remove the oil pump cover.

9 Clean the pump thoroughly and inspect the gear teeth for signs of damage or wear. Where applicable, check the condition of the oil pump drive chain; if the links appear excessively worn or are particularly loose, renew the chain.

10 Check the pump backlash by inserting a feeler blade between the meshed gear teeth; rotate the gears against each other slightly, to give the maximum clearance **(see illustration)**. Compare the measurement with the limit quoted in *Specifications*.

11 Check the pump axial clearance as follows: lay an engineers straight edge across the oil pump casing, then using a feeler blade, measure the clearance between the straight edge and the pump gears **(see illustration)**. Compare the measurement with the limit quoted in *Specifications*.

12 If either of the measurements is outside of the specified limit, this indicates that the pump is worn and must be renewed.

Refitting

13 Refit the oil pump cover, then fit the screws and tighten them to the specified torque.

14 Reassemble the oil pickup to the oil pump, using a new O-ring seal. Tighten the retaining screws to the specified torque.

15 Offer up the oil pump to the end of the crankcase. Fit the drive chain over the oil pump sprocket, then engage it with the crankshaft sprocket.

16 Fit the pump mounting bolts and hand tighten them.

17 Tension the drive chain by applying finger pressure to it at a point midway between the two sprockets **(see illustration)**. Adjust the position of the pump on its mountings until the tension is within the limit given in *Specifications*. On completion tighten the mounting bolts to the specified torque.

18 Fit and tighten the fixings for the pickup tube to crankcase bracket.

19 With reference to Section 8, refit the crankshaft oil seal housing, using a new gasket and oil seal.

20 Refer to Section 13 and refit the sump.

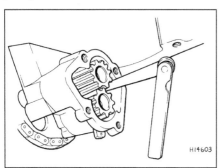

14.10 Checking the oil pump gear backlash

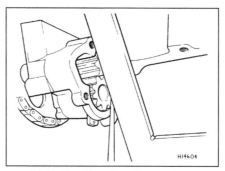

14.11 Checking the oil pump gear axial clearance

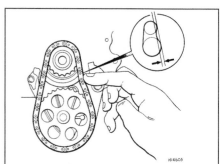

14.17 Checking the oil pump drive chain tension

Chapter 2 Part B:
Engine removal and overhaul procedures

Contents

Degrees of difficulty

Easy, suitable for novice with little experience	Fairly easy, suitable for beginner with some experience	Fairly difficult, suitable for competent DIY mechanic 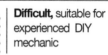	Difficult, suitable for experienced DIY mechanic	Very difficult, suitable for expert DIY or professional

Specifications

Engine designation codes

See Chapter 2A

Crankshaft

Main journal diameter (standard)	53.96 to 53.97mm
Undersizes	–0.25 mm – 0.5 mm, –0.75 mm
Crankpin journal diameter (standard)	41.96 to 41.97 mm
Undersizes	–0.25 mm, –0.5 mm, –0.75 mm
Endfloat	0.07 to 0.20 mm
Main bearing running clearance	0.03 to 0.17 mm
Crankpin running clearance	0.02 to 0.095 mm

Connecting rods

Endfloat on crankpin	0.05 to 0.40 mm

Pistons

Diameter:
Standard	74.985
Oversizes	75.235, 75.485, 75.735

Piston rings

End gap (15.0 mm from bottom of cylinder):
Compression rings	0.30 to 1.0 mm
Oil scraper ring	0.25 to 1.0 mm
Clearance in groove	0.02 to 0.15 mm

Cylinder head

Distortion (max)	0.1 mm
Minimum height for machining	135.6 mm
Minimum distance between tops of valve guides and upper surface of cylinder head:	
Exhaust	36.1 mm
Inlet	35.8 mm

Camshaft

Run-out (max)	0.01 mm
Endfloat	0.15 mm

Valves

Valve head diameter:
  Inlet
    AAU .... 32.0 mm
    All other engine codes .... 36.0 mm
  Exhaust .... 29.0 mm
Valve stem diameter:
  Inlet:
    Up to July 1992 .... 7.965 mm
    From August 1992 .... 6.970 mm
  Exhaust:
    Up to July 1992 .... 7.945 mm
    From August 1992 .... 6.050 mm
Valve deflection in guide (max):
  Inlet .... 1.0 mm (0.040 in)
  Exhaust .... 1.3 mm (0.051 in)

Lubrication system

Oil pressure at 2000 rpm and temperature of 80°C (176°F) .... 2.0 bar
Oil pressure switch:
  Off pressure (0.3 bar switch) .... 0.15 to 0.45 bar
Oil pump:
  Gear teeth backlash .... 0.05 - 0.20 mm
  Maximum axial play .... 0.15 mm
  Drive chain tension .... 2.0 - 3.0 mm

Torque wrench settings

	Nm	lbf ft
Transmission bellhousing to engine	55	41
Engine and gearbox mountings:		
M10 bolts	45	33
M8 bolts	25	18
Camshaft bearing cap nuts:		
Stage 1	6	4
Stage 2 (angle tighten)	+ one quarter-turn (90°)	
Crankshaft main bearing cap bolts	65	48
Big end bearing caps nuts:		
Stage 1	30	22
Stage 2 (angle tighten)	+ one quarter-turn (90°)	

1 Engine and transmission removal - preparation and precautions

1 If you have decided that the engine must be removed for overhaul or major repair work, several preliminary steps should be taken.

2 Locating a suitable place to work is extremely important. Adequate work space, along with storage space for the vehicle, will be needed. If a workshop or garage is not available, at the very least a solid, level, clean work surface is required.

3 If possible, clear some shelving close to the work area and use it to store the engine components and ancillaries as they are removed and dismantled. In this manner, the components stand a better chance of staying clean and undamaged during the overhaul. Laying out components in groups together with their fixings bolts, screws etc will save time and avoid confusion when the engine is refitted.

4 Clean the engine compartment and engine/transmission before beginning the removal procedure; this will help visibility and help to keep tools clean.

5 The help of an assistant should be available; there are certain instances when one person cannot safely perform all of the operations required to remove the engine from the vehicle. Safety is of primary importance, considering the potential hazards involved in this kind of operation. A second person should always be in attendance to offer help in an emergency. If this is the first time you have removed an engine, advice and aid from someone more experienced would also be beneficial.

6 Plan the operation ahead of time. Before starting work, obtain (or arrange for the hire of) all of the tools and equipment you will need. Access to the following items will allow the task of removing and refitting the engine/transmission to be completed safely and with relative ease: a heavy-duty trolley jack - rated in excess of the combined weight of the engine and transmission, complete sets of spanners and sockets as described in the front of this manual, wooden blocks, and plenty of rags and cleaning solvent for mopping up spilled oil, coolant and fuel. A selection of different sized plastic storage bins will also prove useful for keeping dismantled components grouped together. If any of the equipment must be hired, make sure that you arrange for it in advance, and perform all of the operations possible without it beforehand; this may save you time and money.

7 Plan on the vehicle being out of use for quite a while, especially if you intend to carry out an engine overhaul. Read through the whole of this Section and work out a strategy based on your own experience and the tools, time and workspace available to you. Some of the overhaul processes may have to carried out by a VW dealer or an engineering works - these establishments often have busy schedules, so it would be prudent to consult them before removing or dismantling the engine, to get an idea of the amount of time required to carry out the work.

8 When removing the engine from the vehicle, be methodical about the disconnection of external components. Labelling cables and hoses as they are removed will greatly assist the refitting process.

9 Always be extremely careful when lifting the engine/transmission assembly from the engine bay. Serious injury can result from careless actions. If help is required, it is better to wait until it is available rather than risk

personal injury and/or damage to components by continuing alone. By planning ahead and taking your time, a job of this nature, although major, can be completed successfully and without incident.

10 On all models described in this manual, the engine and transmission are removed through the top of the engine bay - access and clearance are improved by removing the bonnet from the vehicle.

11 Note that the engine and transmission should ideally be removed with the vehicle standing on all four roadwheels, however access to the driveshafts and exhaust system downpipe will be improved if the vehicle can be temporarily raised onto axle stands (see "*Jacking and vehicle support*").

2 Engine and transmission - removal, separation and refitting

Removal

1 Select a solid, level surface to park the vehicle upon. Give yourself enough space to move around it easily.

2 Refer to Chapter 11 and remove the bonnet from its hinges.

3 Disconnect the battery negative cable and position it away from the terminal. **Note:** *If the vehicle has a security coded radio, check that you have a copy of the code number before disconnecting the battery cable; refer to Chapter 12 for details.*

4 Refer to Chapter 1 and carry out the following:
a) *Drain the cooling system.*
b) *If the engine is to be dismantled, drain the engine oil.*

5 Refer to Chapter 3 and carry out the following:
a) *Remove the auxiliary cooling fan and its cowling.*
b) *Remove the radiator.*
c) *Loosen the clips and disconnect the radiator top and bottom hoses, expansion tank hose and cabin heater hoses from the thermostat housing.*

6 With reference to Chapter 4C, unplug the Lambda sensor cabling from the main harness at the multiway connector (where applicable).

7 Disconnect the ignition HT king lead from the centre terminal of the distributor cap and tie it back away from the engine.

8 Refer to Chapter 9 and disconnect the brake servo vacuum hose from the port on the inlet manifold.

9 On vehicles fitted with an activated charcoal canister emission control system, refer to Chapter 4C and disconnect the vacuum hose from the port on the throttle body. Make a careful note of the point of connection to ensure correct refitting.

Single point injection models

10 With reference to Chapter 4A, carry out the following operations:
a) *Depressurise fuel system*
b) *Remove the exhaust manifold-to-air cleaner and throttle body air box-to-air cleaner ducting from the engine bay.*
c) *Remove the air cleaner assembly from the top of the throttle body; make a note of the vacuum hose connections to ensure correct refitting later.*
d) *Disconnect the accelerator cable from the throttle spindle lever.*
e) *Disconnect the fuel supply and return hoses from the throttle body - observe the safety precautions detailed at the beginning of Chapter 4A.*

Multi point injection models

11 With reference to Chapter 4B, carry out the following operations:
a) *Depressurise fuel system.*
b) *Slacken the clips and remove the exhaust manifold-to-air cleaner and throttle body-to-air flow meter ducting from the engine bay.*
c) *Disconnect the accelerator cable from the throttle spindle lever.*
d) *Disconnect the fuel supply and return hoses from the throttle body - observe the safety precautions detailed at the beginning of Chapter 4B.*
e) *G40 models: slacken the clips and disconnect the supercharger-to-intercooler and intercooler-to-throttle body ducting.*

Caution: On G40 models, when dismantling any part of the air inlet system, take care to ensure that no foreign material can get into the G-charger air inlet port; cover the opening with a sheet of plastic, secured with an elastic band. When the engine is running, the G-charger compressor vanes rotate at very high speeds could be severely damaged if debris has been allowed to enter.

12 Refer to Chapter 5A and disconnect the wiring from the alternator, starter motor and solenoid.

13 With reference to Chapter 5B and Chapter 4A or B as applicable, identify any

sections of the ignition and fuelling system electrical harness that remain connected to sensors and actuators on the engine and disconnect them. Label each connector carefully to ensure correct refitting.

14 Refer to Chapter 7 and carry out the following:
a) *At the top of the transmission casing, disconnect the wiring from the speedometer drive transducer and reversing light switch.*
b) *Disconnect the gear selection mechanism from the transmission.*

15 Refer to Chapter 6 and disconnect the clutch cable from the release mechanism at the front of the transmission casing.

16 Refer to Chapter 8 and separate the driveshafts from the transmission differential output shafts.

17 With reference to Chapter 4C, unbolt the exhaust down pipe from the exhaust manifold. Recover and discard the gasket. Unbolt the front exhaust mounting and lower the exhaust to the floor.

18 Unbolt the engine and transmission earthing straps from the bodywork **(see illustration)**.

19 Attach the jib of an engine lifting hoist to the lifting eyelets at the cylinder head. Raise the jib until it just takes the weight of the engine and transmission.

20 With reference to Chapter 2A, slacken and withdraw the through-bolts from all three engine mountings **(see illustration)**.

21 Carry out a final check to ensure that nothing else remains connected to the engine, then slowly raise the hoist and manoeuvre the engine and transmission out through the top of the engine bay. Guide the auxiliary belt drive pulleys past the inner wing to avoid damaging the paintwork.

Separation

22 Rest the engine and transmission assembly on a firm, flat surface and use wooden blocks as wedges to keep the unit steady.

23 The transmission is secured to the engine by a combination of machine screws and studs, threaded into the cylinder block and bellhousing - the total number of fixings depends on the type of transmission and

2.18 Unbolting the engine earthing strap

2.20 Front engine mounting through-bolt

2.24 Separating the engine and transmission

vehicle specification. Note that some of these fixings also serve as mountings for the rear engine mounting.

24 Starting at the bottom, remove all the screws and nuts then carefully draw the transmission away from the engine, resting it securely on wooden blocks **(see illustration)**. Collect the locating dowels if they are loose enough to be extracted.

Caution: Take care to prevent the transmission from tilting, until the input shaft is fully disengaged from the clutch friction plate.

25 With reference to Chapter 6, remove the clutch release mechanism, pressure plate and friction plate.

Refitting

26 If the engine and transmission have not been separated, proceed from paragraph 29 onwards.

27 Smear a quantity of high-melting-point grease on the splines of the transmission input shaft. Do not use an excessive amount as there is the risk of contaminating the clutch friction plate. Carefully offer up the transmission to the cylinder block, guiding the dowels into the mounting holes in cylinder block.

28 Refit the bellhousing bolts and nuts, hand tightening them to secure the transmission in position. **Note:** *Do not tighten them to force the engine and transmission together.* Ensure that the bellhousing and cylinder block mating faces will butt together evenly without obstruction, before tightening the bolts and nuts to their specified torque.

All models

29 With reference to Chapter 2A, refit the rear engine mounting bracket and tighten the retaining bolts to the specified torque.

30 Attach the jib of an engine hoist to the lifting eyelets on the cylinder head and raise the engine and transmission from the ground.

31 Wheel the hoist up to the front of the vehicle and with the help of an assistant, guide the engine and transmission in through the top of the engine bay. Tilt the assembly slightly so that the transmission casing enters first, then guide the auxiliary belt drive pulleys past the bodywork.

32 Align the engine mounting brackets with the mounting points on the body - refer to Chapter 2A for details. Insert the engine mounting through-bolts, tightening them by hand initially.

33 Detach the engine hoist jib from the lifting eyelets.

34 Settle the engine and transmission assembly on its mountings by rocking it backwards and forwards, then tighten the mounting through-bolts to the specified torque.

35 Refer to Chapter 8 and reconnect the driveshafts to the transmission.

36 The remainder of the refitting sequence is the direct reverse of the removal procedure, noting the following points:

a) *Ensure that all sections of the wiring harness follow their original routing; use new cable-ties to secure the harness in position, keeping it away from sources of heat and abrasion.*

b) *Refer to Chapter 7 and reconnect the gear shift mechanism to the transmission, then check the overall operation of the gear shift mechanism, adjusting it if necessary.*

c) *Refer to Chapter 6 and reconnect the clutch cable to the transmission, then check the operation of the automatic adjustment mechanism (where applicable).*

d) *Ensure that all hoses are correctly routed and are secured with the correct hose clips, where applicable. If the hose clips originally fitted were of the crimp variety, they cannot be used again; proprietary worm drive clips must be fitted in their place, unless otherwise specified.*

e) *Refill the cooling system as described in Chapter 1.*

f) *Refill the engine with appropriate grades and quantities of oil, as detailed in Chapter 1.*

g) *With reference to Chapter 4A or B as applicable, reconnect the throttle cable and adjust it as necessary.*

h) *With reference to Chapter 5B, check and adjust the engine idle speed and where applicable, the ignition timing.*

37 When the engine is started for the first time , check for air, coolant, lubricant and fuel leaks from manifolds, hoses etc. If the engine has been overhauled, read the cautionary notes in Section 13 before attempting to start it.

3 Engine overhaul - preliminary information

1 It is much easier to dismantle and work on the engine if it is mounted on a portable engine stand. These stands can often be hired from a tool hire shop. Before the engine is mounted on a stand, the flywheel should be removed, so that the stand bolts can be tightened into the end of the cylinder block/crankcase.

2 If a stand is not available, it is possible to dismantle the engine with it blocked up on a sturdy workbench, or on the floor. Be very careful not to tip or drop the engine when working without a stand.

3 If you intend to obtain a reconditioned engine, all ancillaries must be removed first, to be transferred to the replacement engine (just as they will if you are doing a complete engine overhaul yourself). These components include the following:

a) *Alternator (including mounting brackets) and starter motor (Chapter 5A).*

b) *The ignition system and HT components including all sensors, distributor, HT leads and spark plugs (Chapters 1 and 5).*

c) *The fuel injection system components (Chapter 4 Parts A and B)*

d) *All electrical switches, actuators and sensors, and the engine wiring harness (Chapter 4 Parts A and B, Chapter 5B).*

e) *Inlet and exhaust manifolds (Chapter 2A).*

f) *The engine oil level dipstick (Chapter 1)*

g) *Engine mountings (Chapter 2A and B).*

h) *Flywheel (Chapter 2B)*

i) *Clutch components (Chapter 6)*

Note: *When removing the external components from the engine, pay close attention to details that may be helpful or important during refitting. Note the fitted position of gaskets, seals, spacers, pins, washers, bolts, and other small components.*

4 If you are obtaining a "short" engine (which consists of the engine cylinder block/crankcase, crankshaft, pistons and connecting rods, all fully assembled), then the cylinder head, sump and baffle plate, oil pump, timing belt (together with its tensioner and covers), auxiliary belt (together with its tensioner), coolant pump, thermostat housing, coolant outlet elbows, oil filter housing and where applicable oil cooler will also have to be removed.

5 If you are planning a complete overhaul, the engine can be dismantled in the order given below:

a) *Inlet and exhaust manifolds.*

b) *Timing belt, sprockets and tensioner.*

c) *Cylinder head.*

d) *Flywheel driveplate.*

e) *Sump.*

f) *Oil pump.*

g) *Piston/connecting rod assemblies.*

h) *Crankshaft.*

6 Before beginning the dismantling and overhaul procedures, make sure that you have all of the tools necessary. Refer to *"Tools and working facilities"* in the *Reference* Section of this manual for further information.

4.2 Remove the thermostat housing together with its O-ring (arrowed)

4.6 Keep groups of components together in labelled boxes or bags

4 Cylinder head - dismantling, cleaning, inspection and assembly

Note: *New and reconditioned cylinder heads will be available from the original manufacturer, and from engine overhaul specialists. It should be noted that some specialist tools are required for the dismantling and inspection procedures, and new components may not be readily available. It may, therefore, be more practical and economical for the home mechanic to purchase a reconditioned head, rather than to dismantle, inspect and recondition the original head.*

Dismantling

1 Remove the cylinder head from the engine block and separate the inlet and exhaust manifolds from it, as described in Part A of this Chapter.
2 Refer to Chapter 3 and remove the thermostat housing together with its O-ring **(see illustration)**. Where applicable, unscrew the coolant temperature sensor and oil pressure switch from the cylinder head.
3 Refer to Chapter 2A and remove the timing belt sprocket from camshaft.
4 Remove the spark plugs (Chapter 1).
5 Remove the distributor (Chapter 5B).
6 It is important that groups of components are kept together when they are removed and, if they are still serviceable, refitted in the same groups. If they are refitted randomly, accelerated wear leading to early failure will occur. Stowing groups of components in plastic bags or storage bins will help to keep everything in the right order - label them according to their fitted location, e.g. 'No 1 exhaust', 'No 2 inlet' , etc **(see illustration)**. (Note that No 1 cylinder is nearest the timing belt end of the engine.)
7 Check that the manufacturers identification and orientation markings are visible on camshaft bearing caps; if none can be found, make your own using a scriber or centre punch.
8 The camshaft bearing cap retaining nuts must be removed progressively and in sequence to avoid stressing the camshaft, as follows.

9 Slacken the nuts from bearing caps Nos 5, 1 and 3 first, then at bearing caps 2 and 4, slacken the nuts alternately and diagonally half a turn at a time until they can be removed by hand. **Note:** *Camshaft bearing caps are numbered 1 to 5 from the timing belt end.*
10 Slide the oil seal from the timing sprocket end of the camshaft and discard it as a new item must be used on reassembly.
11 Carefully lift the camshaft from the cylinder head - do not allow it to tilt. Support both ends as it is removed so that the journals and lobes are not damaged.
12 Lift the hydraulic tappets from their bores and store them with the valve contact surface facing downwards, to prevent the oil from draining out. Make a note of the position of each tappet, as they must be fitted to the same valves on reassembly - accelerated wear leading to early failure will result if they are interchanged.
13 Turn the cylinder head over and rest it on one side. Using a valve spring compressor, compress each valve spring in turn, extracting the split collets when the upper valve spring seat has been pushed far enough down the valve stem to free them. If the spring seat sticks, **lightly** tap the upper jaw of the spring compressor with a hammer to free it.
14 Release the valve spring compressor and remove the upper spring seat, valve spring(s) and lower spring seat. **Note:** *Depending on age and specification, engines may have concentric double valve springs, or single valve springs with no lower spring seat.*
15 Use a pair of long-nosed pliers to extract the valve stem oil seal and withdraw the valve itself from the head gasket side of the cylinder head. If the valve sticks in the guide, carefully deburr the end face with fine abrasive paper. Repeat this process for the remaining valves.

Cleaning

16 Using a suitable degreasing agent, remove all traces of oil deposits from the cylinder head, paying particular attention to the journal bearings, hydraulic tappet bores, valve guides and oilways. Scrape off any traces of old gasket from the mating surfaces, taking care not to score or gouge them. If using emery paper, do not use a grade of less than 100. Turn the head over and using a

blunt blade, scrape any carbon deposits from the combustion chambers and ports. *Caution: Do not erode the sealing surface of the valve seat. Finally, wash the entire head casting with a suitable solvent to remove the remaining debris.*
17 Clean the valve heads and stems using a fine wire brush. If the valve is heavily coked, scrape off the majority of the deposits with a blunt blade first, then use the wire brush. *Caution: Do not erode the sealing surface of the valve face.*
18 Thoroughly clean the remainder of the components using solvent and allow them to dry completely. Discard the oil seals, as new items must be fitted when the cylinder head is reassembled.

Inspection

Cylinder head casting

19 Examine the head casting closely to identify any damage sustained or cracks that may have developed. Pay particular attention to the areas around the mounting holes, valve seats and spark plug holes. If cracking is discovered between the valve seats, or between the valve seats and spark plug threads Volkswagen state that the cylinder head may be reused, provided the cracks are no larger than 0.5 mm wide or that no more than the first spark plug thread is cracked. More serious damage will mean the renewal of the cylinder head casting.
20 Moderately pitted and scorched valve seats can be repaired by lapping the valves in during reassembly, as described later in this Chapter. Badly worn or damaged valve seats may be restored by recutting ; this is a highly specialised operation involving precision machining and accurate angle measurement and as such should be entrusted to a professional cylinder head re-builder.
21 Measure any distortion of the gasketed surfaces using a straight edge and a set of feeler blades. Take one measurement longitudinally on both the inlet and exhaust manifold mating surfaces. Take several measurements across the head gasket surface, to assess the level of distortion in all planes **(see illustration)**. Compare the measurements with the figures in the *Specifications*. If the head is

4.21 Checking for cylinder head distortion using a straight edge and a set of feeler blades

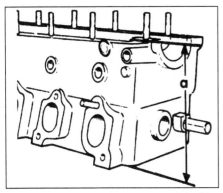

4.22a Minimum cylinder head height (a)

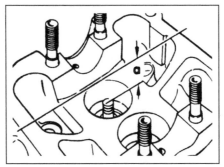

4.22b Minimum distance (a) between top of valve guides and upper surface of cylinder head

distorted out of specification, it may be possible to repair it by smoothing down any high-spots on the surface with fine abrasive paper.

22 Minimum cylinder head heights (measured between the cylinder head gasket surface and the cylinder head cover gasket surface), where quoted by the manufacturer, are listed in *Specifications*. If the cylinder head is to be professionally machined, bear in mind the following **(see illustrations)**:

a) *The minimum cylinder head height dimension (where specified) must be adhered to.*

b) *The valve seats will need to be recut to suit the new height of the cylinder head, otherwise valve to piston crown contact may occur.*

c) *Before the valve seats can be recut, check that there is enough material left on the cylinder head to allow repair; if too much material is removed, the valve stem may protrude too far above the top of the valve guide and this would prevent the hydraulic tappets from operating correctly. Refer to a professional head rebuilder or machine shop for advice.*
Note: *Depending on engine type, it may be possible to obtain new valves with shorter valve stems - refer to your VW dealer for advice.*

Camshaft

23 The camshaft is identified by means of markings stamped onto the side of the shaft, between No 1 cylinder inlet and exhaust lobes.

24 Visually inspect the camshaft for evidence of wear on the surfaces of the lobes and journals. Normally their surfaces should be smooth and have a dull shine; look for scoring, erosion or pitting and areas that appear highly polished - these are signs that wear has begun to occur. Accelerated wear will occur once the hardened exterior of the camshaft has been damaged, so always renew worn items. **Note:** *If these symptoms are visible on the tips of the camshaft lobes, check the corresponding hydraulic tappet, as it will probably be worn as well.*

25 Examine the distributor drive gear for

signs of wear or damage. Slack in the drive caused by worn gear teeth will affect ignition timing.

26 If the machined surfaces of the camshaft appear discoloured or 'blued', it is likely that it has been overheated at some point, probably due to inadequate lubrication. This may have distorted the shaft, so check the runout as follows: rotate the camshaft between two V - blocks and using a DTI gauge, measure the runout at the centre journal Compare this with the *Specifications*. If it exceeds this figure, camshaft renewal should be considered.

27 To measure the camshaft endfloat, temporarily refit the camshaft to the cylinder head, then fit the third bearing cap and tighten the fixings to the specified first stage torque setting - refer to *Reassembly* for details. Anchor a DTI gauge to the timing pulley end of the cylinder head and align the gauge probe with the camshaft axis. Push the camshaft to one end of the cylinder head as far as it will travel, then rest the DTI gauge probe on the end of the camshaft and zero the gauge display. Push the camshaft as far as it will go to the other end of the cylinder head and record the gauge reading. Verify the reading by pushing the camshaft back to its original position and checking that the gauge indicates zero again. **Note:** *The hydraulic tappets must **not** be fitted to the cylinder whilst this measurement is being taken.*

28 Check that the camshaft endfloat measurement is within the limit listed in *Specifications*. Wear outside of this limit is unlikely to be confined to any one component, so renewal of the camshaft, cylinder head and bearing caps must be considered; seek the advice of a cylinder head rebuilding specialist.

29 The difference between the outside diameters of the camshaft bearing surfaces and the internal diameters formed by the bearing caps and the cylinder head must now be measured, this dimension is known as the camshaft "running clearance".

30 The dimensions of the camshaft bearing journals are not quoted by the manufacturer, so running clearance measurement by means of a micrometer and a bore gauge or internal vernier calipers cannot be recommended in this case.

31 Another (more accurate) method of measuring the running clearance involves the use of Plastigage. This is a soft, plastic material supplied in thin "sticks" of about the same diameter as a sewing needle. Lengths of Plastigage are cut as required, laid on the camshaft bearing journals and crushed as the bearing caps are temporarily fitted and tightened. The Plastigage spreads widthways as it is crushed; the running clearance can then be determined by measuring the increase in width using the card gauge supplied with the Plastigage kit.

32 The following paragraphs describe this measurement procedure step by step, but note that a similar method is used to measure the crankshaft running clearances; refer to the illustrations in Section 10 for further guidance.

33 Ensure that the cylinder head, bearing cap and camshaft bearing surfaces are completely clean and dry. Lay the camshaft in position in the cylinder head.

34 Lay a length of Plastigage on top of each of the camshaft bearing journals.

35 Lubricate each bearing cap with a little silicone release agent, then place them in position over the camshaft and tighten the retaining nuts down to the specified *first stage* torque setting only - refer to *Reassembly* later in this Section for guidance. **Note:** *Do not rotate the camshaft whilst the bearing caps are in place, as the measurements will be affected.*

36 Carefully remove the bearing caps again, lifting them vertically away from the camshaft to avoid disturbing the Plastigage. The Plastigage should remain on the camshaft bearing surface, squashed into a uniform sausage shape. If it disintegrates as the bearing caps are removed, re-clean the components and repeat the exercise, using a little more release agent on the bearing cap.

37 Hold the scale card supplied with the kit against each bearing journal and match the width of the crushed Plastigage with the graduated markings on the card, use this to determine the running clearances.

38 Compare the camshaft running clearance measurements with those listed in the *Specifications*; if any are outside the specified tolerance, the camshaft and cylinder head should be renewed.

39 On completion, remove the bearing caps and camshaft and clean of all remaining traces of Plastigage and silicone release agent.

Valves and associated components

Note: *On all engines, the valve heads cannot be re-cut (although they may be lapped in); new or exchange units must be obtained.*

40 Examine each valve closely for signs of wear. Inspect the valve stems for wear ridges, scoring or variations in diameter; measure their diameters at several points along their lengths with a micrometer **(see illustration)**.

4.40 Measure the diameters of the valve stems at several points along their lengths using a micrometer

41 Check the overall length of each valve and compare the measurements with the figure in the *Specifications*.

42 The valve heads should not be cracked, badly pitted or charred. Note that light pitting of the valve head can be rectified by lapping-in the valves during reassembly, as described later in this Section.

43 Check that the valve stem end face is free from excessive pitting or indentation; this would be caused by defective hydraulic tappets.

44 Place the valves in a V - block and using a DTI gauge, measure the runout at the valve head. A maximum figure is not quoted by the manufacturer, but the valve should be renewed if the runout appears excessive.

45 Insert each valve into its respective guide in the cylinder head and set up a DTI gauge against the edge of the valve head. With the valve end face flush with the top of the valve guide , measure the maximum side to side deflection of the valve in its guide **(see illustration)**. If the measurement is out of tolerance, the valve and valve guide should be renewed as a pair. **Note:** *Valve guides are an interference fit in the cylinder head and their removal requires access to a hydraulic press. For this reason, it would be wise to entrust the job to an engineering workshop or head rebuilding specialist.*

46 Using vernier callipers, measure the free length of each of the valve springs. As a manufacturer's figure is not quoted, the only way to check the length of the springs is by comparison with a new component. Note that valve springs are usually renewed during a major engine overhaul.

47 Stand each spring on its end on a flat surface, against an engineers square. Check the squareness of the spring visually; if it appears distorted, renew the spring.

48 Measuring valve spring pre-load involves compressing the valve by applying a specified weight and measuring the reduction in length. This may be a difficult operation to conduct in the home workshop, so it would be wise to approach your local garage or engineering workshop for assistance. Weakened valve springs will at best, increase engine running noise and at worst, cause poor compression, so defective items should be renewed.

Reassembly

Caution: Unless all new components are to be used, maintain groups when refitting valve train components - do not mix components between cylinders and ensure that components are refitted in their original positions.

49 To achieve a gas tight seal between the valves and their seats, it will be necessary to grind, or 'lap', the valves in. To complete this process you will need a quantity of fine/coarse grinding paste and a grinding tool - this can either be of the dowel and rubber sucker type, or the automatic type which are driven by a rotary power tool.

50 Smear a small quantity of *fine* grinding paste on the sealing face of the valve head. Turn the cylinder head over so that the combustion chambers are facing upwards and insert the valve into the correct guide. Attach the grinding tool to the valve head and using a backward/forward rotary action, grind the valve head into its seat. Periodically lift the valve and rotate it to redistribute the grinding paste **(see illustration)**.

51 Continue this process until the contact between valve and seat produces an unbroken, matt grey ring of uniform width, on both faces. Repeat the operation for the remaining valves.

52 If the valves and seats are so badly pitted that coarse grinding paste must be used, check first that there is enough material left on both components to make this operation worthwhile - if too little material is left remaining, the valve stems may protrude too far above their guides, impeding the correct operation of the hydraulic tappets. Refer to a machine shop or cylinder head rebuilding specialist for advice.

53 Assuming the repair is feasible, work as described in the previous paragraph but use the coarse grinding paste initially, to achieve a dull finish on the valve face and seat. Then, wash off coarse paste with solvent and repeat the process using fine grinding paste to obtain the correct finish.

54 When all the valves have been ground in, remove all traces of grinding paste from the cylinder head and valves with solvent and allow them to dry completely.

55 Turn the head over and place it on a stand, or wooden blocks. Leave enough room underneath to allow the valves to be inserted.

56 Working on one valve at a time, lubricate the valve stem with clean engine oil and insert it into the guide. Fit one of the protective plastic sleeves supplied with the new valve stem oil seals over the valve end face - this will protect the oil seal whilst it is being fitted **(see illustrations)**.

57 Dip a new valve stem seal in clean engine oil and carefully push it over the valve and onto the top of the valve guide - take care not to damage the stem seal as it passes over the valve end face. Use a suitable long reach socket to press it firmly into position **(see illustration)**.

58 Locate the valve spring(s) over the valve stem. Where a lower spring seat is fitted, ensure that the springs locate squarely on the

4.45 Measuring the deflection of a valve in its guide

4.50 Grinding in a valve

4.56a Fitting a valve into its guide

4.56b Fitting a protective plastic sleeve over the valve end face

4.57 Pressing a new valve stem oil seal into position using a long reach socket

4.58a Fitting the inner valve spring

4.58b Fitting the outer valve spring

4.59 Spring seat being fitted over the tops of the valve springs

4.61 Refitting the hydraulic tappets

stepped surface of the seat (see illustrations). Note: Depending on age and specification, engines may have either concentric double valve springs, or single valve springs with no lower spring seat.

59 Fit the upper seat over the top of the springs, then using a valve spring compressor, compress the springs until the upper seat is pushed beyond the collet grooves in the valve stem. Refit the split collet, using a dab of grease to hold the two halves in the grooves (see illustration). Gradually release the spring compressor, checking that the collet remains correctly seated as the spring extends. When correctly seated, the upper seat should force the two halves of the collet together and hold them securely in the grooves in the end of the valve.

60 Repeat this process for the remaining sets of valve components. To settle the components after installation, strike the end of each valve stem lightly with a mallet, using an interposed block of wood to protect the stem from damage. Check before progressing any further that the split collets remain firmly held in the end of the valve stem by the upper spring seat.

61 Smear some clean engine oil onto the sides of the hydraulic tappets and fit them into position in their bores in the cylinder head. Push them down until they contact the valves, then lubricate the camshaft lobe contact surfaces (see illustration).

62 Lubricate the camshaft and cylinder head bearing journals with clean engine oil, then carefully lower the camshaft into position on the cylinder head. Support the ends of the shaft as it is inserted, to avoid damaging the lobes and journals (see illustration).

63 Oil the upper surfaces of the camshaft bearing journals, then fit the bearing caps in place. Ensure that they are fitted the right way around and in the correct locations, then fit and tighten the retaining nuts, as follows:

64 The bearing caps have their respective cylinder numbers stamped onto them and have an elongated lug on one side. When correctly fitted, the numbers should be readable from the exhaust side of the cylinder head and the lugs should face the inlet side of the cylinder head (see illustration).

65 Fit caps Nos 2 and 4 over the camshaft and tighten the retaining nuts alternately and diagonally to the specified first stage torque (see illustration).

66 Smear the cylinder head mating surfaces of caps Nos 1 and 5 with suitable sealant then fit them, together with cap No 3, over the camshaft and tighten the nuts to the specified first stage torque.

4.62 Lowering the camshaft into position

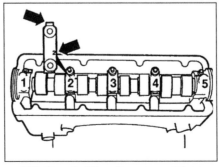

4.64 Camshaft bearing cap markings and orientation

4.65 Tightening the camshaft bearing cap nuts

4.70 Refitting the oil pressure switch

4.71 Refitting the camshaft sprocket and bolt

67 Tighten all bearing caps to the second stage torque, then fit the bolts to bearing cap No 5 and tighten them to the specified torque.
68 With reference to Chapter 2A lubricate the lip of a new camshaft oil seal with clean engine oil and locate it over the end of the camshaft. Using a mallet and a long reach socket of an appropriate diameter, drive the seal squarely into its housing until it bears against the inner stop - do not attempt to force it in any further.
69 Refit the coolant outlet elbow, using a new gasket/O-ring as necessary. Tighten the retaining bolts securely.
70 Refit the coolant sensor and oil pressure switch, using new sealing washers as appropriate **(see illustration)**.
71 With reference to Chapter 2A, carry out the following **(see illustration)**:

a) Refit the timing belt sprocket to the camshaft.
b) Refit the inlet and exhaust manifolds, complete with new gaskets.

72 Refer to Chapter 2A or B as applicable refit the cylinder head to the cylinder block.

5 Pistons and connecting rods - removal and inspection

Removal

1 Refer to Part A of this Chapter and remove the cylinder head, flywheel, sump and baffle plate, oil pump and pickup.
2 Inspect the tops of the cylinder bores; any wear ridges at the point where the pistons reach top dead centre must be removed; otherwise the pistons may be damaged when they are pushed out of their bores. This can be achieved with a scraper or ridge reamer.
3 Scribe the number of each piston on its crown, to allow identification later; note that No 1 is at the timing belt end of the engine.
4 Using a set of feeler blades, measure the big-end to crankpin web thrust clearance at each connecting rod and record the measurements for later reference **(see illustration)**.
5 Rotate the crankshaft until pistons No 1 and 4 are at bottom dead centre. Unless they are already identified, mark the big end bearing

caps and connecting rods with their respective piston numbers, using a centre punch or a scribe **(see illustration)**. Note the orientation of the bearing caps in relation to the connecting rod; it may be difficult to see the manufacturers markings at this stage, so scribe alignment arrows on them both to ensure correct reassembly. Unbolt the bearing cap bolts/nuts, half a turn at a time, until they can be removed by hand. Recover the bottom shell bearing and tape it to the cap for safe keeping. Note that if the shell bearings are to be re-used, they must be refitted to the same connecting rod.
6 On certain engines, the bearing cap bolts will remain in the connecting rod; in this case the threads of the bolts should be padded with insulating tape, to prevent them from scratching the crankpins when the pistons are removed from their bores **(see illustration)**.

5.4 Measure the big-end to crankpin web thrust clearance at each connecting rod

5.6 Pad the threads of the big end bolts with tape

7 Drive the pistons out of the top of their bores by pushing on the underside of the piston crown with a piece of dowel or a hammer handle. As the piston and connecting rod emerge, recover the top shell bearing and tape it to the connecting rod for safekeeping.
8 Turn the crankshaft through half a turn and working as described above, remove No 2 and 3 pistons and connecting rods **(see illustration)** Remember to maintain the components in their cylinder groups, whilst they are in a dismantled state.
9 Insert a small flat bladed screwdriver into the removal slot and prise the gudgeon pin circlips from each piston. Push out the gudgeon pin and separate the piston and connecting rod. Discard the circlips as new items must be fitted on reassembly. If the pin proves difficult to remove, heat the piston to 60°C with hot water - the resulting expansion will then allow the two components to be separated.

Inspection

10 Before an inspection of the pistons can be carried out, the existing piston rings must be removed, using a removal/installation tool, or an old feeler blade if such a tool is not available. Always remove the upper piston rings first, expanding them to clear the piston crown. The rings are very brittle and will snap if they are stretched too much - sharp edges are produced when this happens, so protect your eyes and hands. Discard the rings on removal, as new items must be fitted when the engine is reassembled.

5.5 Mark the big end bearing caps and connecting rods with their respective piston numbers

5.8 Removing a piston from the cylinder block

5.18 Checking the piston ring side clearance

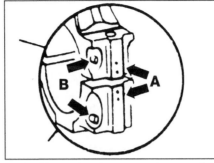

5.20a Big end bearing cap and connecting rod markings

A Identification (cylinder number) markings
B Orientation recesses

5.20b Orientation arrow on piston crown (highlighted)

11 Use a section of old piston ring to scrape the carbon deposits out of the ring grooves, taking care not to score or gouge the edges of the groove.

12 Carefully scrape away all traces of carbon from the top of the piston. A hand-held wire brush (or a piece of fine emery cloth) can be used, once the majority of the deposits have been scraped away. Be careful not to remove any metal from the piston, as it is relatively soft. **Note:** *Take care to preserve the piston number markings that were made during removal.*

13 Once the deposits have been removed, clean the pistons and connecting rods with paraffin or a suitable solvent, and dry thoroughly. Make sure that the oil return holes in the ring grooves are clear.

14 Examine the piston for signs of terminal wear or damage. Some normal wear will be apparent, in the form of a vertical 'grain' on the piston thrust surfaces and a slight looseness of the top compression ring in its groove. Abnormal wear should be carefully examined, to assess whether the component is still serviceable and what the cause of the wear might be.

15 Scuffing or scoring of the piston skirt may indicate that the engine has been overheating, through inadequate cooling, lubrication or abnormal combustion temperatures. Scorch marks on the skirt indicate that blow-by has occurred, perhaps caused by worn bores or piston rings. Burnt areas on the piston crown are usually an indication of pre-ignition, pinking or detonation. In extreme cases, the piston crown may be melted by operating under these conditions. Corrosion pit marks in the piston crown indicate that coolant has seeped into the combustion chamber and/or the crankcase. The faults causing these symptoms must be corrected before the engine is brought back into service, or the same damage will recur.

16 Check the pistons, connecting rods, gudgeon pins and bearing caps for cracks. Lay the connecting rods on a flat surface and look along the length to see if it appears bent or twisted. If you have doubts about their

condition, get them measured at an engineering workshop. Inspect the small end bush bearing for signs of wear or cracking.

17 Using a micrometer, measure the diameter of all four pistons at a point 10 mm from the bottom of the skirt, at right angles to the gudgeon pin axis. Compare the measurements with those listed in the *Specifications*. If the piston diameter is out of the tolerance band listed for its particular size, then it must be renewed. **Note:** *If the cylinder block was re-bored during a previous overhaul, oversize pistons may have been fitted. Record the measurements and use them to check the piston clearances when the cylinder bores are measured, later in this Chapter.*

18 Hold a new piston ring in the appropriate groove and measure the side clearance using a feeler blade **(see illustration)**. Note that the rings are of different widths, so use the correct ring for the groove. Compare the measurements with those listed; if the clearances are outside of the tolerance band, then the piston must be renewed. Confirm this by checking the width of the piston ring with a micrometer.

19 Using internal/external vernier callipers, measure the connecting rod small end internal diameter and the gudgeon pin external diameter. Subtract the gudgeon pin diameter from the small end diameter to obtain the clearance. If this measurement is outside its specification, then the piston and connecting rod bush will have to be resized and a new gudgeon pin installed. An engineering workshop will have the equipment needed to undertake a job of this nature.

20 The orientation of the piston with respect to the connecting rod must be correct when the two components are reassembled. The piston crown is marked with an arrow (which can easily be obscured by carbon deposits); this must point towards the timing belt end of the engine when the piston is installed in the bore. The connecting rod and its corresponding bearing cap both have recesses machined into them close to their mating surfaces - these recesses must both face in the same direction

as the arrow on the piston crown (ie towards the timing belt end of the engine) when correctly installed **(see illustrations)**. Reassemble the two components to satisfy this requirement.

21 Lubricate the gudgeon pin and small end bush with clean engine oil. Slide the pin into the piston, engaging the connecting rod small end. Fit two new circlips to the piston at either end of the gudgeon pin, so that their open ends are facing 180° away from the removal slot in the piston. Repeat this operation for the remaining pistons.

6 Crankshaft - removal and inspection

Removal

1 **Note:** *If no work is to be done on the pistons and connecting rods, then removal the cylinder head and pistons will not be necessary. Instead, the pistons need only be pushed far enough up the bores so that they are positioned clear of the crankpins. The use of an engine stand is strongly recommended.*

2 With reference to Chapter 2A, carry out the following:

a) *Remove the crankshaft timing belt sprocket.*

b) *Remove the clutch components and flywheel.*

c) *Remove the sump, baffle plate, oil pump and pickup.*

d) *Remove the front and rear crankshaft oil seals and their housings.*

3 Unbolt the pistons and connecting rods from the crankpins, as described in Section 5 (refer to the Note above).

4 Carry out a check of the crankshaft endfloat, as follows. **Note:** *This can only be accomplished when the crankshaft is still installed in the cylinder block/crankcase, but is free to move.* Set up a DTI gauge so that the probe is in line with the crankshaft axis and is in contact with a fixed point on end of the crankshaft. Push the crankshaft along its axis to the end of its travel, and then zero the

6.4 Checking the crankshaft endfloat using a DTI gauge

6.5 Checking the crankshaft endfloat using a feeler blade

6.6 Main bearing cap identification markings

6.13 Measuring the diameter main bearing journals

gauge. Push the crankshaft fully the other way, and record the endfloat indicated on the dial **(see illustration)**. Compare the result with the figure given in *Specifications* and establish whether new thrustwashers are required.

5 If a dial gauge is not available, feeler blades can be used. First push the crankshaft fully towards the flywheel end of the engine, then use a feeler blade to measure the gap between cylinder No 2 crankpin web and the main bearing thrustwasher **(see illustration)**. Compare the results with the *Specifications*.

6 Observe the manufacturers identification marks on the main bearing caps. The number relates to the position in the crankcase, as counted from the timing belt end of the engine **(see illustration)**.

7 Loosen the main bearing cap bolts one quarter of a turn at a time, until they can be removed by hand. Using a soft faced mallet, strike the caps lightly to free them from the crankcase. Recover the lower main bearing shells, taping them to the cap for safe keeping. Mark them with indelible ink to aid identification, but do not score or scratch them in any way.

8 Carefully lift the crankshaft out, taking care not to dislodge the upper main bearing shells. It would be wise to get an assistants help, as the crankshaft is quite heavy. Set it down on a clean, level surface and chock it with wooden blocks to prevent it from rolling.

9 Extract the upper main bearing shells from the crankcase and tape them to their respective bearing caps. Remove the two thrustwasher bearings from either side of No 3 crank web.

10 With the shell bearings removed, observe the recesses machined into the bearing caps and crankcase - these provide location for the lugs which protrude from the shell bearings and so prevent them from being fitted incorrectly.

Inspection

11 Wash the crankshaft in a suitable solvent and allow it to dry. Flush the oil holes thoroughly, to ensure that are not blocked - use a pipe cleaner or a needle brush if necessary. Remove any sharp edges from the edge of the hole which may damage the new bearings when they are installed.

12 Inspect the main bearing and crankpin journals carefully; if uneven wear, cracking, scoring or pitting are evident then the crankshaft should be reground by an engineering workshop, and refitted to the engine with undersize bearings.

13 Use a micrometer to measure the diameter of each main bearing journal **(see illustration)**. Taking a number of measurements on the surface of each journal will reveal if it is worn unevenly. Differences in diameter measured at 90° intervals indicate that the journal is out of round. Differences in diameter measured along the length of the journal, indicate that the journal is tapered. Again, if wear is detected, the crankshaft must be reground by an engineering workshop and refitted with undersize bearings (refer to *Reassembly*)

14 Check the oil seal journals at either end of the crankshaft. If they appear excessively scored or damaged, they may cause the new seals to leak when the engine is reassembled. It may be possible to repair the journal; seek

the advice of an engineering workshop or your VW dealer.

15 Measure the crankshaft runout by setting up a DTI gauge on the centre main bearing and rotating the shaft in V - blocks. The maximum deflection of the gauge will indicate the runout. Take precautions to protect the bearing journals and oil seal mating surfaces from damage during this procedure. A maximum runout figure is not quoted by the manufacturer, but use the figure of 0.05 mm as a rough guide. If the runout exceeds this figure, crankshaft renewal should be considered - consult your VW dealer or an engine rebuilding specialist for advice.

16 Refer to Section 8 for details of main and big-end bearing inspection.

7 Cylinder block/crankcase casting - cleaning and inspection

Cleaning

1 Remove all external components and electrical switches/sensors from the block. For complete cleaning, the core plugs should ideally be removed. Drill a small hole in the plugs, then insert a self-tapping screw into the hole. Extract the plugs by pulling on the screw with a pair of grips, or by using a slide hammer **(see illustration)**.

2 Scrape all traces of gasket and sealant from the cylinder block/crankcase, taking care not to damage the sealing surfaces.

3 Remove all oil gallery plugs (where fitted). The plugs are usually very tight - they may have to be drilled out, and the holes re-tapped. Use new plugs when the engine is reassembled.

4 If the casting is very dirty, it should be steam-cleaned. After this, clean all oil holes and galleries one more time. Flush all internal passages with water until the water runs clear. Dry thoroughly, and apply a light film of oil to all mating surfaces and cylinder bores, to prevent rusting. If you have access to compressed air, use it to speed up the drying process, and to blow out all oil holes and galleries.

⚠ *Warning: Be sure to wear eye protection when using compressed air!*

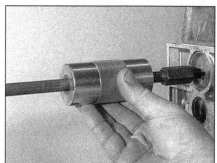

7.1 Using a slide hammer to remove a core plug

7.6 Clear out threaded holes using the correct size of tap

5 If the castings are not very dirty, you can do an adequate cleaning job with hot, soapy water and a stiff brush. Take plenty of time, and do a thorough job. Regardless of the cleaning method used, be sure to clean all oil holes and galleries very thoroughly, and to dry all components well. Protect the cylinder bores as described above, to prevent rusting.

6 All threaded holes must be clean, to ensure that fixings are tightened to the correct torque during reassembly. To clean the threads, run the correct-size tap into each of the holes to remove rust, corrosion, thread sealant or sludge, and to restore damaged threads **(see illustration)**. If possible, use compressed air to clear the holes of debris produced by this operation. **Note:** *Take extra care to exclude all cleaning liquid from blind tapped holes, as the casting may be cracked by hydraulic action if a bolt is tightened in a hole containing liquid.*

7 Apply suitable sealant to the new oil gallery plugs, and insert them into the holes in the block. Tighten them securely.

8 If the engine is not going to be reassembled immediately, cover it with a large plastic bag to keep it clean; protect all mating surfaces and the cylinder bores as described above, to prevent rusting.

Inspection

9 Visually check the casting for cracks and corrosion. Look for stripped threads in the threaded holes. If there has been any history of internal water leakage, it may be worthwhile having an engine overhaul specialist check the cylinder block/crankcase with professional equipment. If defects are found, have them repaired if possible, failing this the cylinder block should be renewed.

10 Check the cylinder bores for scuffing or scoring. Any evidence of this kind of damage should be cross-checked with an inspection of the pistons: see Section 5 of this Chapter. If the damage is in its early stages, it may be possible to repair the block by reboring it. Seek the advice of an engineering workshop before you progress.

11 To allow an accurate assessment of the wear in the cylinder bores to be made, their diameter must be measured at a number of points, as follows. Insert a bore gauge into cylinder bore No 1 and take three measurements in line with the crankshaft axis; one at the top of the bore, roughly 10 mm below the bottom of the wear ridge, one halfway down the bore and one at a point roughly 10 mm the bottom of the bore. **Note:** *Stand the cylinder block squarely on a workbench during this procedure, inaccurate results may be obtained if the measurements are taken when the engine mounted on a stand.*

12 Rotate the bore gauge through 90°, so that it is at right angles to the crankshaft axis and repeat the measurements detailed in paragraph 11 **(see illustration)**. Record all six measurements and compare them with the data listed in the *Specifications* Section. If the difference in diameter between any two cylinders exceeds the wear limit, or if any one cylinder exceeds its maximum bore diameter, then *all four* cylinders will have to be rebored and oversize pistons will have to be fitted. Note that the imbalances produced by not reboring all the cylinders together would render the engine unusable.

13 Use the piston diameter measurements recorded earlier (see Section 5) to calculate the piston to cylinder clearances. Compare these with the specified maximum and determine whether reboring and oversize pistons are required.

14 Place the cylinder block on a level work surface, crankcase downwards. Use a straight edge and a set of feeler blades to measure the distortion of the cylinder head mating surface in both planes. A maximum figure is not quoted by the manufacturer, but use the figure of 0.05 mm as a rough guide. If the measurement exceeds this figure, repair may be possible by machining - consult your dealer for advice.

15 Before the engine can be reassembled, the cylinder bores must be honed. This process involves using an abrasive tool to produce a fine, cross-hatch pattern on the inner surface of the bore. This has the effect of seating the piston rings, resulting in a good seal between the piston and cylinder. There are two types of honing tool available to the home mechanic, both are driven by a rotary power tool, such as a drill. The 'Bottle Brush' hone is a stiff, cylindrical brush with abrasive stones bonded to its bristles. The more conventional surfacing hone has abrasive stones mounted on spring loaded legs. For the inexperienced home mechanic, satisfactory results will be achieved more easily using the Bottle Brush hone. **Note:** *If you are unwilling to tackle cylinder bore honing, an engineering workshop will be able to carry out the job for you at a reasonable cost.*

16 Carry out the honing as follows; you will need one of the honing tools described above, a power drill/air wrench, a supply of clean rags, some honing oil and a pair of safety glasses.

17 Fit the honing tool in the drill chuck. Lubricate the cylinder bores with honing oil and insert the honing tool into the first bore, compressing the stones to allow it to fit. Turn on the drill at its slowest speed and as the tool rotates, move it up and down in the bore at a rate that produces a fine cross-hatch pattern on the surface. The lines of the pattern should ideally cross at about 50-60° **(see illustration)**., although some piston ring manufacturers may quote a different angle; check the literature supplied with the new rings.

⚠ *Warning: Wear safety glasses to protect your eyes from debris flying off the honing tool.*

18 Use plenty of oil during the honing process. Do not remove any more material than is necessary to produce the required finish. When removing the hone tool from the bore, do not pull it out whilst it is still rotating; maintain the up/down movement until the chuck has stopped, then withdraw the tool whilst rotating the chuck by hand, in the normal direction of rotation.

19 Wipe out the oil and swarf with a rag and proceed to the next bore. When all the bores have been honed, thoroughly clean the whole cylinder block in hot soapy water to remove all traces of honing oil and debris. The block can be considered clean when a clean rag, moistened with new engine oil does not pick up any grey residue when wiped along the bore.

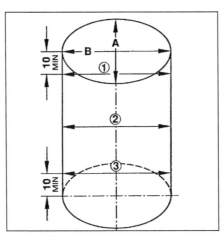

7.12 Bore measurement points

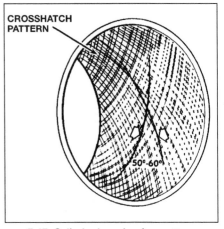

7.17 Cylinder bore honing pattern

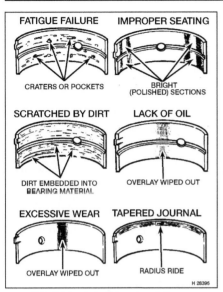

FATIGUE FAILURE

IMPROPER SEATING

CRATERS OR POCKETS

BRIGHT
(POLISHED) SECTIONS

SCRATCHED BY DIRT

LACK OF OIL

DIRT EMBEDDED INTO
BEARING MATERIAL

OVERLAY WIPED OUT

EXCESSIVE WEAR

TAPERED JOURNAL

OVERLAY WIPED OUT

RADIUS RIDE

H 28395

8.8 Typical shell bearing failures

20 Apply a light coating of engine oil to the mating surfaces and cylinder bores to prevent rust forming. Store the block in a plastic bag until reassembly.

8 Main and big-end bearings - inspection and selection

Inspection

1 Even though the main and big-end bearings should be renewed during the engine overhaul, the old bearings should be retained for close examination, as they may reveal valuable information about the condition of the engine.
2 Bearing failure can occur due to lack of lubrication, the presence of dirt or other foreign particles, overloading the engine, or corrosion. Regardless of the cause of bearing failure, the cause must be corrected before the engine is reassembled, to prevent it from happening again.
3 When examining the bearing shells, remove them from the cylinder block/crankcase, the main bearing caps, the connecting rods and the connecting rod big-end bearing caps. Lay them out on a clean surface in the same general position as their location in the engine. This will enable you to match any bearing problems with the corresponding crankshaft journal. *Do not* touch any of the shell's internal bearing surface with your fingers while checking it, or the delicate surface may be scratched.
4 Dirt and other foreign matter gets into the engine in a variety of ways. It may be left in the engine during assembly, or it may pass through filters or the crankcase ventilation system. It may get into the oil, and from there into the bearings. Metal chips from machining operations and normal engine wear are often

present. Abrasives are sometimes left in engine components after reconditioning, especially when parts are not thoroughly cleaned using the proper cleaning methods. Whatever the source, these foreign objects often end up embedded in the soft bearing material, and are easily recognised. Large particles will not embed in the bearing, but will score or gouge the bearing and journal. The best prevention for this cause of bearing failure is to clean all parts thoroughly, and keep everything spotlessly-clean during engine assembly. Frequent and regular engine oil and filter changes are also recommended.
5 Lack of lubrication (or lubrication breakdown) has a number of interrelated causes. Excessive heat (which thins the oil), overloading (which squeezes the oil from the bearing face) and oil leakage (from excessive bearing clearances, worn oil pump or high engine speeds) all contribute to lubrication breakdown. Blocked oil passages, which usually are the result of misaligned oil holes in a bearing shell, will also oil-starve a bearing, and destroy it. When lack of lubrication is the cause of bearing failure, the bearing material is wiped or extruded from the steel backing of the bearing. Temperatures may increase to the point where the steel backing turns blue from overheating.
6 Driving habits can have a definite effect on bearing life. Full-throttle, low-speed operation (labouring the engine) puts very high loads on bearings, tending to squeeze out the oil film. These loads cause the bearings to flex, which produces fine cracks in the bearing face (fatigue failure). Eventually, the bearing material will loosen in pieces, and tear away from the steel backing.
7 Short-distance driving leads to corrosion of bearings, because insufficient engine heat is produced to drive off the condensed water and corrosive gases. These products collect in the engine oil, forming acid and sludge. As the oil is carried to the engine bearings, the acid attacks and corrodes the bearing material.
8 Incorrect bearing installation during engine assembly will lead to bearing failure as well. Tight-fitting bearings leave insufficient bearing running clearance, and will result in oil starvation. Dirt or foreign particles trapped behind a bearing shell result in high spots on the bearing, which lead to failure **(see illustration)**.
9 *Do not* touch any shell's internal bearing surface with your fingers during reassembly; there is a risk of scratching the delicate surface, or of depositing particles of dirt on it.
10 As mentioned at the beginning of this Section, the bearing shells should be renewed as a matter of course during engine overhaul; to do otherwise is false economy.

Selection - main and big-end bearings

11 Main and big-end bearings for the engines described in this Chapter are available in

standard sizes and a range of undersizes to suit reground crankshafts - refer to *Specifications* for details.
12 The running clearances will need to be checked when the crankshaft is refitted with its new bearings. This procedure is described in the Section 10.

9 Engine overhaul - reassembly sequence

1 Before reassembly begins, ensure that all new parts have been obtained, and that all necessary tools are available. Read through the entire procedure to familiarise yourself with the work involved, and to ensure that all items necessary for reassembly of the engine are at hand. In addition to all normal tools and materials, thread-locking compound will be needed. A suitable tube of liquid sealant will also be required for the joint faces that are fitted without gaskets. It is recommended that the manufacturers own products are used, which are specially formulated for this purpose; the relevant product names are quoted in the text of each Section where they are required.
2 In order to save time and avoid problems, engine reassembly should ideally be carried out in the following order:

a) *Crankshaft .*
b) *Piston/connecting rod assemblies.*
c) *Oil pump (see Chapter 2A)*
d) *Sump (see Chapter 2A)*
e) *Flywheel (see Chapter 2A)*
f) *Cylinder head and gasket (see Chapter 2A)*
g) *Timing belt sprockets and timing belt (see Chapter 2A)*
h) *Engine external components and ancillaries.*
i) *Auxiliary drive pulleys and belts.*

3 At this stage, all engine components should be absolutely clean and dry, with all faults repaired. The components should be laid out (or in individual containers) on a completely clean work surface.

10 Crankshaft - refitting and running clearance check

1 Crankshaft refitting is the first stage of engine reassembly following overhaul. At this point, it is assumed that the crankshaft, cylinder block/crankcase and bearings have been cleaned, inspected and reconditioned or renewed.
2 Place the cylinder block on a clean, level work surface, with the crankcase facing upwards. Unbolt the bearing caps and carefully release them from the crankcase; lay them out in order to ensure correct reassembly. If they are still in place, remove the bearing shells from the caps and the crankcase and wipe out the

10.3 Fitting the centre main bearing upper shell

10.7 Lay a piece of Plastigage on each journal, in line with its axis

10.11 Measure the width of the crushed Plastigage using the gauge provided

inner surfaces with a clean rag - they must be kept spotlessly clean.

3 Clean the rear surface of the new bearing shells with a rag and lay them on the bearing saddles. Ensure that the orientation lugs on the shells engage with the recesses in the saddles and that the oil holes are correctly aligned **(see illustration)**. Do not hammer or otherwise force the bearing shells into place. It is critically important that the surfaces of the bearings are kept free from damage and contamination.

4 Give the newly fitted bearing shells and the crankshaft journals a final clean with a rag. Check that the oil holes in the crankshaft are free from dirt, as any left here will become embedded in the new bearings when the engine is first started.

5 Carefully lay the crankshaft in the crankcase, taking care not to dislodge the bearing shells.

Running clearance check

6 When the crankshaft and bearings are refitted, a clearance must exist between them to allow lubricant to circulate. This clearance is impossible to check using feeler blades, so Plastigage is used. This is a thin strip of soft plastic that is crushed between the bearing shells and journals when the bearing caps are tightened up. The change in its width then indicates the size of the clearance gap.

7 Cut off five pieces of Plastigage, just shorter than the length of the crankshaft journal. Lay a piece on each journal, in line with its axis **(see illustration)**.

8 Wipe off the rear surfaces of the new lower half main bearing shells and fit them to the main bearing caps, again ensuring that the locating lugs engage correctly.

9 Wipe the front surfaces of the bearing shells and give them a light coating of silicone release agent - this will prevent the Plastigage from sticking to the shell. Fit the caps in their correct locations on the bearing saddles, using the manufacturers markings as a guide. Ensure that they are correctly orientated - the caps should be fitted such that the recesses for the bearing shell locating lugs are on the same side as those in the bearing saddle.

10 Working from the centre bearing cap, tighten the bolts one half turn at a time until they are all correctly torqued *to their first stage only*. Do not allow the crankshaft to rotate at all whilst the Plastigage is in place. Progressively unbolt the bearing caps and remove them, taking care not to dislodge the Plastigage.

11 The width of the crushed Plastigage can now be measured, using the scale provided **(see illustration)**. Use the correct scale, as both imperial and metric are printed. This measurement indicates the running clearance - compare it with that listed in *Specifications*. If the clearance is outside the tolerance, it may be due to dirt or debris trapped under the bearing surface; try cleaning them again and repeat the clearance check. If the results are still unacceptable, re-check the journal diameters and the bearing sizes. Note that if the Plastigage is thicker at one end, the journals may be tapered and as such, will require regrinding.

12 When you are satisfied that the clearances are correct, carefully remove the remains of the Plastigage from the journals and bearings faces. Use a soft, plastic or wooden scraper as anything metallic is likely to damage the surfaces.

Crankshaft - final refitting

13 Lift the crankshaft out of the crankcase. Wipe off the surfaces of the bearings in the crankcase and the bearing caps. Fit the thrust bearings either side of the No 3 bearing saddle, between cylinders No 2 and 3 **(see illustration)**. Use a small quantity of grease to hold them in place; ensure that they are seated correctly in the machined recesses, with the oil grooves facing outwards.

14 Liberally coat the bearing shells in the crankcase with clean engine oil **(see illustration)**.

15 Lower the crankshaft into position so that No 2 and 3 cylinder crankpins are at TDC; No 1 and 4 cylinder crankpins will then be at BDC, ready for fitting No 1 piston.

16 Lubricate the lower bearing shells in the main bearing caps with clean engine oil, then fit the thrustwashers to either side of bearing cap No 3, noting that the lugs protruding from the washers engage the recesses in the side of the bearing cap **(see illustration)**. Make sure that the locating lugs on the shells are still engaged with the corresponding recesses in the caps.

17 Fit the main bearing caps in the correct order and orientation - No 1 bearing cap must be at the timing belt end of the engine and the bearing shell locating recesses in the bearing

10.13 Thrustwashers fitted to the No 3 bearing saddle

10.14 Liberally coat the bearing shells in the crankcase with clean engine oil

10.16 Fitting the centre main bearing cap

10.18 Tightening the main bearing bolts

11.5 Measuring the piston ring end gap using a feeler blade

saddles and caps must be adjacent to each other. Insert the bearing cap bolts and hand tighten them only.

18 Working from the centre bearing cap outwards, tighten the retaining bolts to their specified torques. Where the torque is expressed in several stages, tighten all the bolts to the first stage, then repeat the exercise in the same sequence for the subsequent stage(s) **(see illustration)**.

19 Refit the crankshaft rear oil seal housing, together with a new oil seal; refer to Part A of this Chapter for details.

20 Check that the crankshaft rotates freely by turning it by manually. If excessive resistance is felt, re-check the running clearances, as described above.

21 Carry out a check of the crankshaft endfloat as described at the beginning of Section 6. If the thrust surfaces of the crankshaft have been checked and new thrust bearings have been fitted, then the endfloat should be within specification.

11 Pistons and piston rings - assembly

1 At this point it is assumed that the pistons have been correctly assembled to their respective connecting rods and that the piston ring side clearances have been checked. If not, refer to the end of Section 5.

2 Before the rings can be fitted to the pistons, the end gaps must be checked with the rings fitted into the cylinder bores.

3 Lay out the piston assemblies and new ring sets on a clean work surface so the components are kept together in their groups during and after end gap checking. Place the crank-case on the work surface on its side, giving access to the top and bottom of the bores.

4 Take the No 1 piston top ring and insert it into the top of the bore. Using the No1 piston as a ram, push the ring close to the bottom of the bore, at the lowest point of the piston travel. Ensure that it is perfectly square in the bore by pushing firmly against the piston crown.

5 Use a set of feeler blades to measure the gap between the ends of the piston ring; the correct blade will just pass through the gap

with a minimal amount of resistance **(see illustration)**. Compare this measurement with that listed in *Specifications*. Check that you have the correct ring before deciding that a gap is incorrect. Repeat the operation for all twelve rings.

6 If new rings are being fitted, it is unlikely that the end gaps will be too small. If a measurement is found to be undersize, it must be corrected or there is the risk that the ends of the ring may contact each other during operation, possibly resulting in engine damage. This is achieved by gradually filing down the ends of the ring, using a file clamped in a vice. Fit the ring over the file such that both its ends contact opposite faces of the file. Move the ring along the file, removing small amounts of material at a time. Take great care as the rings are brittle and form sharp edges if they fracture. Remember to keep the rings and piston assemblies in the correct order.

7 When all the piston ring end gaps have been verified, they can be fitted to the pistons. Work from the lowest ring groove (oil control ring) upwards. Note that the oil control ring comprises two side rails separated by a expander ring. Note also that the two compression rings are different in cross section and so must be fitted in the correct groove and the right way up, using a piston ring fitting tool. Both of the compression rings have marks stamped on one side to indicate the top facing surface. Ensure that these marks face up when the rings are fitted.

8 Distribute the end gaps around the piston, spaced at 120° intervals to the each other. **Note:** *If the piston ring manufacturer supplies specific fitting instructions with the rings, follow these exclusively.*

12 Piston and connecting rod assemblies - refitting and big-end bearing clearance check

Big-end running clearance check

Note: *At this point, it is assumed that the crankshaft has been fitted to the engine, as described in Section 10.*

1 As with the main bearings (Section 10), a running clearance must exist between the big-end crankpin and its bearing shells to allow oil to circulate. There are two methods of checking the size of the running clearance, as described in the following paragraphs.

2 Place the cylinder block on a clean, level work surface, with the crankcase facing upwards. Position the crankshaft so that crankpins No 1 and 4 are at BDC.

3 The first method is less accurate and involves bolting bearing caps to the big-ends, away from the crankshaft, with the bearing shells in place. **Note:** *Correct orientation of the bearing caps is critical; refer to the notes in Section 5.* The internal diameter formed by the assembled big-end is then measured using internal vernier callipers. The diameter of the respective crankpin is then subtracted from this measurement and the result is the running clearance.

4 The second method of carrying out this check involves the use of Plastigage, in the same manner as the main bearing running clearance check (see Section 10) and is much more accurate than the previous method. Clean all four crankpins with a clean rag. With crankpins No 1 and 4 at BDC initially, place a strand of Plastigage on each crankpin journal.

5 Fit the upper big-end bearing shells to the connecting rods, ensuring that the locating lugs and recesses engage correctly. Temporarily refit the piston/connecting rod assemblies to the crankshaft; refit the big-end bearing caps, using the manufacturers markings to ensure that they are fitted the correct way around - refer to *Final Refitting* in the following sub-Section for details.

6 Tighten the bearing cap nuts/bolts as described below. Take care not to disturb the Plastigage or rotate the connecting rod during the tightening process.

7 Dismantle the assemblies without rotating the connecting rods. Use the scale printed on the Plastigage envelope to determine the big-end bearing running clearance and compare it with the figures listed in *Specifications*.

8 If the clearance is significantly different from that expected, the bearing shells may be the wrong size (or excessively worn, if the original shells are being re-used). Make sure that no dirt or oil was trapped between the bearing shells and the caps or connecting rods when the clearance was measured. Re-check the diameters of the crankpins. Note that if the Plastigage was wider at one end than at the other, the crankpins may be tapered. When the problem is identified, fit new bearing shells or have the crankpins reground to a listed undersize, as appropriate.

9 Upon completion, carefully scrape away all traces of the Plastigage material from the crankshaft and bearing shells. Use a plastic or wooden scraper, which will be soft enough to prevent scoring of the bearing surfaces.

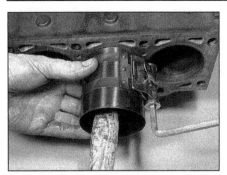

12.16 Using a piston ring compressor to install the piston assemblies

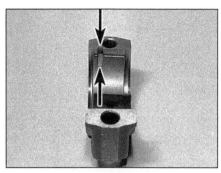

12.17 Big end bearing shell lug and locating recess (arrowed)

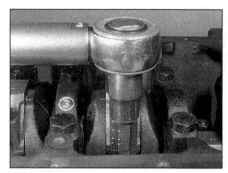

12.19 Tightening the big-end bearing caps

Piston and connecting rod assemblies - final refitting

10 Note that the following procedure assumes that the crankshaft main bearing caps are in place (see Section 10).

11 Ensure that the bearing shells are correctly fitted, as described at the beginning of this Section. If new shells are being fitted, ensure that all traces of the protective grease are cleaned off using paraffin. Wipe dry the shells and connecting rods with a lint-free cloth.

12 Lubricate the cylinder bores, the pistons, and piston rings with clean engine oil. Lay out each piston/connecting rod assembly in order on a worksurface. On engines where the big end bolts are captive in the connecting rods, fit short sections of rubber hose or tape over the bolt threads, to protect the cylinder bores during reassembly.

13 Start with piston/connecting rod assembly No 1. Make sure that the piston rings are still spaced as described in Section 12, then clamp them in position with a piston ring compressor.

14 Insert the piston/connecting rod assembly into the top of cylinder No 1. Lower the big-end in first, guiding it to protect the big-end bolts and the cylinder bores.

15 Ensure that the orientation of the piston in its cylinder is correct - the piston crown, connecting rods and big-end bearing caps are equipped with markings, which must point towards the timing belt end of the engine when the piston is installed in the bore - refer to Section 5 for details.

16 Using a block of wood or hammer handle against the piston crown, tap the assembly into the cylinder until the piston crown is flush with the top of the cylinder **(see illustration)**.

17 Ensure that the bearing shell is still correctly installed **(see illustration)**. Liberally lubricate the crankpin and both bearing shells with clean engine oil. Taking care not to mark the cylinder bores, tap the piston/connecting rod assembly down the bore and onto the crankpin. Refit the big-end bearing cap, tightening its retaining nuts/bolts finger-tight

at first. Note that the orientation of the bearing cap with respect to the connecting rod must be correct when the two components are reassembled. The connecting rod and its corresponding bearing cap both have recesses machined into them, close to their mating surfaces - these recesses must both face in the same direction as the arrow on the piston crown (ie towards the timing belt end of the engine) when correctly installed - refer to the illustrations in Section 5 for details.

19 Working progressively around each bearing cap, tighten the retaining nuts half a turn at a time to the specified torque **(see illustration)**.

20 Refit the remaining three piston/connecting rod assemblies in the same way.

21 Rotate the crankshaft by hand. Check that it turns freely; some stiffness is to be expected if new components have been fitted, but there should be no indication of binding or tight spots.

13 Engine - initial start-up after overhaul and reassembly

1 Refit the remainder of the engine components in the order listed in Section 9 of this Chapter, referring to Part A where necessary. Refit the engine (and transmission) to the vehicle as described in Section 2 of this Chapter. Double-check the engine oil and coolant levels and make a final check that everything has been reconnected. Make sure that there are no tools or rags left in the engine compartment.

2 Remove the spark plugs, referring to Chapter 1 for details.

3 The engine must be immobilised so that it can be turned over using the starter motor, without starting - disable the fuel pump by unplugging the fuel pump power relay from the relay board; refer to the relevant Part of Chapter 4 for further information.

Caution: If the vehicle is fitted with catalyst, it is potentially damaging to immobilise the engine by disabling the ignition system without first disabling the fuel system, as unburnt fuel could be supplied to the catalyst.

4 Turn the engine using the starter motor until the oil pressure warning lamp goes out. If the lamp fails to extinguish after several seconds of cranking, check the engine oil level and oil filter security. Assuming these are correct, check the security of the oil pressure switch cabling - do not progress any further until you are satisfied that oil is being pumped around the engine at sufficient pressure.

5 Refit the spark plugs, and reconnect the fuel pump relay.

6 Start the engine, but be aware that as fuel system components have been disturbed, the cranking time may be a little longer than usual.

7 While the engine is idling, check for fuel, water and oil leaks. Don't be alarmed if there are some odd smells and the occasional plume of smoke as components heat up and burn off oil deposits.

8 Assuming all is well, keep the engine idling until hot water is felt circulating through the top hose.

9 Check the ignition timing idle speed and idle mixture setting as described in Chapter 1, then switch the engine off.

10 After a few minutes, recheck the oil and coolant levels as described in Chapter 1 and top-up as necessary.

11 On all the engines described in this Chapter, there is no need to re-tighten the cylinder head bolts once the engine has been run following reassembly.

12 If new pistons, piston rings or crankshaft bearings have been fitted, the engine must be treated as new, and run-in for the first 600 miles (1000 km). *Do not* operate the engine at more than three-quarter throttle, or allow it to labour at low engine speeds in any gear. It is also recommended that the engine oil and filter are changed at the end of this period.

Chapter 3
Cooling, heating and ventilation systems

Contents

Degrees of difficulty

Easy, suitable for novice with little experience		**Fairly easy,** suitable for beginner with some experience		**Fairly difficult,** suitable for competent DIY mechanic		**Difficult,** suitable for experienced DIY mechanic		**Very difficult,** suitable for expert DIY or professional	

Specifications

General
Expansion tank cap opening pressure . . . . 1.2 to 1.5 bars

Thermostat
Opening temperatures:
   Starts to open . . . . 87°C
   Fully open . . . . 102°C
Fully open stroke (minimum) . . . . 7.0 mm

Electric cooling fan thermoswitch
Operating temperatures:
   Single-stage switch
      Switches on . . . . 93° to 98°C
      Switches off . . . . 88° to 93°C
   Two-stage switch
      Stage 1 speed:
         Switches on . . . . 92° to 97°C
         Switches off . . . . 84° to 91°C
      Stage 2 speed:
         Switches on . . . . 99° to 105°C
         Switches off . . . . 91° to 98°C

Torque wrench settings

Torque wrench settings	Nm	lbf ft
Radiator mounting bolts	10	7
Thermostat cover bolts	10	7
Thermostat housing bolts	20	15
Cooling fan retaining nuts	10	7
Cooling fan cowling bolts	10	7
Cooling fan thermostatic switch	25	18
Coolant pump	10	7

1 General information and precautions

General information

1 The cooling system is of pressurised type, including a pump, an aluminium crossflow radiator, electric cooling fan, and a thermostat. The system functions as follows. Cold coolant is pumped around the cylinder block, head passages, expansion tank, inlet manifold and heater matrix by the coolant pump. After cooling the cylinder bores, combustion surfaces and valve seats, the coolant is returned to the water pump via the metal tube at the rear of the engine. With the engine cold, the thermostat is initially closed and there is no circulation through the radiator.

2 When the coolant reaches a predetermined temperature, the thermostat opens and the coolant passes through to the radiator. As the coolant circulates through the radiator it is cooled by the inrush of air when the car is in forward motion. Airflow is supplemented by the action of the electric cooling fan when necessary. From the bottom of the radiator the coolant passes through the thermostat to the coolant pump and the cycle is repeated. In this system the thermostat is located in the return line to the coolant pump.

3 The electric cooling fan mounted on the rear of the radiator is controlled by a thermostatic switch. At a predetermined coolant temperature the switch actuates the fan.

Precautions

 Warning: Do not attempt to remove the expansion tank filler cap or disturb any part of the cooling system while the engine is hot, as there is a high risk of scalding. If the expansion tank filler cap must be removed before the engine and radiator have fully cooled (even though this is not recommended) the pressure in the cooling system must first be relieved. Cover the cap with a thick layer of cloth, to avoid scalding, and slowly unscrew the filler cap until a hissing sound can be heard. When

the hissing has stopped, indicating that the pressure has reduced, slowly unscrew the filler cap until it can be removed; if more hissing sounds are heard, wait until they have stopped before unscrewing the cap completely. At all times keep well away from the filler cap opening.

 Warning: Do not allow antifreeze to come into contact with skin or painted surfaces of the vehicle. Rinse off spills immediately with plenty of water. Never leave antifreeze in an open container or in a puddle in the driveway or on the garage floor. Children and pets are attracted by its sweet smell. Antifreeze can be fatal if ingested.

 Warning: If the engine is hot, the electric cooling fan may start rotating even if the engine is not running, so be careful to keep hands, hair and loose clothing well clear when working in the engine compartment.

2 Cooling system hoses - disconnection and renewal

Note: *Refer to the warnings given in Section 1 of this Chapter before proceeding.*

1 If the checks described in Chapter 1 reveal a faulty hose, it must be renewed as follows.

2 First drain the cooling system (see Chapter 1). If the coolant is not due for renewal, it may be re-used if it is collected in a clean container.

3 To disconnect a hose, release its retaining clips, then move them along the hose, clear of the relevant inlet/outlet union. Carefully work the hose free. **Do not** attempt to disconnect any part of the system while it is still hot.

4 Note that the radiator inlet and outlet unions are fragile; do not use excessive force when attempting to remove the hoses. If a hose proves to be difficult to remove, try to release it by rotating the hose ends before attempting to free it.

5 When fitting a hose, first slide the clips onto the centre of the hose, then work the hose into position. If clamp type clips were

originally fitted, it is a good idea to replace them with screw type clips when refitting the hose. If the hose is stiff, use a little soapy water as a lubricant.

> **HAYNES HiNT** *If all else fails, cut the hose with a sharp knife, then slit it so that it can be peeled off in two pieces. Although this may prove expensive if the hose is otherwise undamaged, it is preferable to buying a new radiator.*

6 Work the hose into position, checking that it is correctly routed, then slide each clip along the hose until it passes over the flared end of the relevant inlet/outlet union, before securing it in position with the retaining clip.

7 Refill the cooling system with reference to Chapter 1.

8 Check thoroughly for leaks as soon as possible after disturbing any part of the cooling system.

3 Radiator - removal, inspection and refitting

Removal

1 Disconnect the battery negative lead. **Note:** *Make sure you know the anti-theft code for the radio so that it can be reactivated later.*

2 Drain the cooling system as described in Chapter 1 by disconnecting the radiator bottom hose.

3 Disconnect the wiring from the thermo-switch and cooling fan motor **(see illustrations)**.

4 Disconnect the top hose from the radiator **(see illustration)**.

5 Remove the upper mounting screws and washers, move the top of the radiator rearwards, and withdraw the mounting rubbers **(see illustrations)**.

6 Lift the radiator out of the lower mounting rubbers and withdraw it from the engine compartment taking care not to damage the matrix.

7 Remove the screws and withdraw the cowling and fan from the radiator.

3.3a Disconnect the wiring from the thermoswitch . . .

3.3b . . . and cooling fan motor

3.4 Disconnecting the top hose

3.5a Removing the radiator upper mounting screws

3.5b Removing the radiator upper mounting rubbers

4.2a Unscrew the socket head bolts . . .

Inspection

8 If the radiator has been removed due to suspected blockage, reverse flush it as described in Chapter 1. Clean dirt and debris from the radiator fins, using an air line (in which case, wear eye protection) or a soft brush. Be careful, as the fins are easily damaged, and are sharp.

9 If necessary, a radiator specialist can perform a "flow test" on the radiator, to establish whether an internal blockage exists.

10 A leaking radiator must be referred to a specialist for permanent repair. Do not attempt to weld or solder a leaking radiator, as damage may result.

11 In an emergency, minor leaks from the radiator can be cured by using a suitable radiator sealant in accordance with the manufacturers instructions with the radiator *in situ*.

12 If the radiator is to be sent for repair or renewed, remove the thermostatic switch.

Refitting

13 Refitting is a reversal of removal, but if necessary renew the radiator mounting rubbers. Fill the cooling system as described in Chapter 1.

4 Thermostat - removal, testing and refitting

Removal

1 The thermostat is located in the outlet housing on the left-hand end of the cylinder head. To remove it, first drain the cooling system as described in Chapter 1.

2 Unscrew the bolts and remove the thermostat cover **(see illustrations)**. Place the cover with top hose still attached to one side.

3 Remove the sealing ring **(see illustration)**.

4 Extract the thermostat from the outlet housing.

Testing

5 To test whether the unit is serviceable, suspend it with a piece of string in a container

of water. Gradually heat the water and note the temperature at which the thermostat starts to open. Continue heating the water to the specified fully open temperature then check that the thermostat has opened by at least the minimum amount given in the *Specifications*. Remove the thermostat from the water and check that it is fully closed when cold.

6 Renew the thermostat if it fails to operate correctly.

7 Clean the thermostat seating and the mating faces of the outlet housing and cover.

Refitting

8 Refitting is a reversal of removal, but fit a new sealing ring and tighten the cover bolts to the specified torque. Fill the cooling system as described in Chapter 1.

5 Electric cooling fan - testing, removal and refitting

Testing

1 The cooling fan is supplied with current through the ignition switch, fuse and radiator thermoswitch which is mounted in the left-hand end of the radiator. Either a single- or two-stage fan is fitted. The two-stage fan has two speed settings; the thermostatic switch actually contains two switches one for the stage 1 fan speed setting and another for the stage 2 fan speed setting. Testing of the

cooling fan circuit is as follows noting that where applicable the following check should be carried out on both the stage 1 speed circuit and the stage 2 speed circuit (see wiring diagrams at the end of Chapter 12).

2 If the fan does not work, first check the fuses. If they are good, run the engine until normal operating temperature is reached, then allow it to idle. If the fan does not cut in within a few minutes, switch off the ignition and disconnect the wiring plug from the cooling fan thermoswitch. Bridge the relevant two contacts in the wiring plug using a length of spare wire, and switch on the ignition. If the fan now operates, the switch is probably faulty and should be renewed.

3 If the switch appears to work, the motor can be checked by disconnecting the motor wiring connector and connecting a 12 volt supply directly to the motor terminals.

4 If the fan still fails to operate, check the cooling fan circuit wiring with reference to Chapter 12. Check each wire for continuity and make sure all connections are clean and free from corrosion. If the motor is faulty, it must be renewed, as no spares are available.

Removal

5 Disconnect the battery negative lead. **Note:** *Make sure you know the anti-theft code for the radio so that it can be re-activated when the battery is reconnected.*

6 Disconnect the wiring from the cooling fan motor.

7 Remove the four screws and lift the cowling together with the cooling fan and motor from the radiator.

4.2b . . . and remove the thermostat cover

4.3 Removing the thermostat cover sealing ring

8 Remove the nuts and lift the cooling fan and motor from the cowling **(see illustration)**.
9 If necessary the fan can be separated from the motor by prising off the clamp washer. Assemble the components in reverse order using a new clamp washer.

Refitting

10 Refitting is a reversal of removal.

---

6 Cooling system electrical switches - testing, removal and refitting

---

Electric cooling fan thermostatic switch

Testing

1 Testing the switch is described in Section 5, as part of the cooling fan test procedure.

Removal

2 The switch is located in the left-hand side of the radiator. The engine and radiator should be cold before removing the switch.
3 Disconnect the battery negative lead. **Note:** *Make sure you know the anti-theft code for the radio so that it can be reactivated later.*
4 Either drain the cooling system to below the level of the switch (as described in Chapter 1), or have ready a suitable plug which can be used to plug the switch aperture in the radiator whilst the switch is removed. If a plug is used, take great care not to damage the radiator, and do not use anything which will allow foreign matter to enter the radiator.
5 Disconnect the wiring plug from the switch **(see illustration)**.
6 Carefully unscrew the switch from the radiator. Recover the washer.

Refitting

7 Refitting is a reversal of removal, but fit a new washer and tighten the switch to the specified torque setting. On completion, refill the cooling system as described in Chapter 1 or top-up as described in *"Weekly checks"*.
8 Start the engine and run it until it reaches normal operating temperature, then continue to run the engine and check that the cooling fan cuts in and functions correctly.

Coolant temperature gauge sensor

Testing

9 The coolant temperature gauge, mounted in the instrument panel, is fed with a stabilised voltage supply from the instrument panel feed (through the ignition switch and a fuse), and its earth is controlled by the sensor.
10 The sensor unit is clipped into the coolant outlet housing on the left-hand end of the cylinder head **(see illustration)**. The sensor contains a thermistor, which consists of an electronic component whose electrical resistance decreases at a predetermined rate as its temperature rises. When the coolant is cold, the sensor resistance is high, therefore current flow through the gauge is reduced, and the gauge needle points towards the "cold" end of the scale. If the sensor is faulty, it must be renewed.
11 If the gauge develops a fault, first check the other instruments; if they do not work at all, check the instrument panel electrical feed. If the readings are erratic, there may be a fault in the instrument panel assembly. If the fault lies in the temperature gauge alone, check it as follows.
12 If the gauge needle remains at the "cold" end of the scale, disconnect the wiring connector from the sensor unit, and earth the temperature gauge wire (see *"Wiring diagrams"* for details) to the cylinder head. If the needle then deflects when the ignition is switched on, the sensor unit is proved faulty, and should be renewed. If the needle still does not move, remove the instrument panel (Chapter 12) and check the continuity of the wiring between the sensor unit and the gauge, and the feed to the gauge unit. If continuity is shown, and the fault still exists, then the gauge is faulty and should be renewed.
13 If the gauge needle remains at the "hot" end of the scale, disconnect the sensor wire. If the needle then returns to the "cold" end of the scale when the ignition is switched on, the sensor unit is proved faulty and should be renewed. If the needle still does not move, check the remainder of the circuit as described previously.

Removal

14 Either partially drain the cooling system to just below the level of the sensor (as described in Chapter 1), or have ready a suitable plug which can be used to plug the sensor aperture whilst it is removed. If a plug is used, take great care not to damage the sensor unit aperture, and do not use anything which will allow foreign matter to enter the cooling system.
15 Disconnect the wiring from the sensor.
16 Depress the sensor unit and slide out its retaining clip. Withdraw the sensor from the coolant elbow and recover its sealing ring.

Refitting

17 Fit a new sealing ring to the sensor unit. Push the sensor fully into the coolant elbow and secure it in position with the retaining clip.
18 Reconnect the wiring connector then refill the cooling system as described in Chapter 1 or top-up as described in *"Weekly checks"*.

---

7 Coolant pump - removal, inspection and refitting

Removal

1 Drain the cooling system (see Chapter 1).
2 Where necessary, remove the air cleaner and air ducting as described in Chapter 4, and disconnect the battery negative lead.
3 Unbolt and remove the timing belt cover.
4 Turn the engine with a spanner on the crankshaft pulley bolt until the timing belt inner cover retaining bolt is visible through the camshaft sprocket hole. Unscrew and remove the bolt.
5 Align the timing marks and release the timing belt from the water pump and camshaft sprocket with reference to Chapter 2. Also unbolt and remove the camshaft sprocket.
6 Remove the bolts and withdraw the timing belt inner cover followed by the water pump. Remove the sealing ring **(see illustrations)**.

Inspection

7 It is not possible to repair the water pump; if faulty it must be renewed. Clean the mating faces of the water pump and cylinder block.

5.8 Cooling fan and mounting nuts

6.5 Cooling fan motor thermoswitch

6.10 Coolant temperature gauge sensor clipped into the coolant outlet housing on the left-hand end of the cylinder head

7.6a Removing the water pump

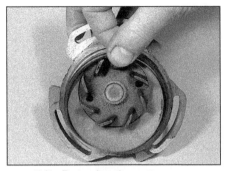

7.6b Removing the water pump sealing ring

Refitting

8 Refitting is a reversal of removal, but fit a new sealing ring and refer to Chapter 2 when fitting the camshaft sprocket and tensioning the timing belt. If a reconditioned coolant pump is being fitted, check if the number "5" is stamped on the mounting flange - if so, use an oversize sealing ring of 5 mm diameter. Fill the cooling system as described in Chapter 1.

8 Heating and ventilation system - general information

1 The heating/ventilation system consists of a four-speed blower motor (housed in the engine compartment plenum chamber), face-level vents in the centre and at each end of the facia, and air ducts to the front footwells.
2 The control unit is located in the facia, and the controls operate flap valves to deflect and mix the air flowing through the various parts of the heating/ventilation system. The flap valves are contained in the air distribution housing, which acts as a central distribution unit, passing air to the various ducts and vents.
3 Cold air enters the system through the grille at the rear of the engine compartment.
4 The airflow, which can be boosted by the blower, then flows through the various ducts, according to the settings of the controls. Stale air is expelled through ducts at the rear of the passenger compartment. If warm air is required, the cold air is passed through the heater matrix, which is heated by the engine coolant.
5 If necessary, the outside air supply can be closed off, allowing the air inside the vehicle to be recirculated. This can be useful to prevent unpleasant odours entering from outside the vehicle, but should only be used briefly, as the recirculated air inside the vehicle will soon deteriorate.
6 Certain models may be fitted with heated front seats. The heat is produced by electrically-heated mats in the seat and backrest cushions. The temperature is regulated automatically by a thermostat, and cannot be adjusted.

9 Heater/ventilation components - removal and refitting

Heater unit (including blower motor and matrix)

1 Drain the cooling system with reference to Chapter 1.
2 Remove the sealing strip and cover from the plenum chamber at the rear of the engine compartment.
3 Pull the wiring block from the terminals on the heater **(see illustration)**.
4 Note the locations of the hoses then loosen the clips and disconnect them **(see illustration)**.
5 Release the clip and disconnect the temperature control cable **(see illustration)**.
6 Prise out the clips, ease the heater from the fresh air box, and withdraw it from the bulkhead. Remove all traces of gasket and sealing compound **(see illustrations)**.
7 Refitting is a reversal of removal, but fit a new gasket and fill and bleed the cooling system with reference to Chapter 1. Make sure the hoses are fitted the correct way

9.3 Disconnecting the heater wiring block

9.4 Disconnecting the heater hoses

9.5 Showing heater temperature control and cable

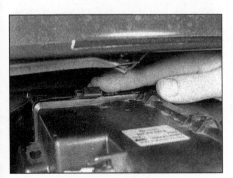

9.6a Prise off the clips . . .

9.6b . . . and withdraw the heater

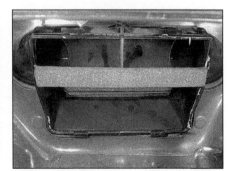

9.6c The heater air box on the bulkhead (heater removed)

9.7 The flow direction arrow on the upper heater outlet - beneath the outlet with temperature valve fitted

9.10 Series resistor and motor connections

9.13a Matrix retaining screw locations in the heater body

round - the direction of flow is indicated on the outlet elbow **(see illustration)**.

Heater blower motor

Note: *The blower motor is fixed in the heater unit housing and cannot be obtained as a separate item.*

8 Remove the heater unit as described previously.

9 Remove the matrix as described later in this sub-Section.

10 Remove the series resistor from the housing **(see illustration)**. If necessary, separate the housing halves and remove the motor.

11 Refitting is a reversal of removal, but fit a new gasket and fill and bleed the cooling system with reference to Chapter 1.

Heater matrix

12 Remove the heater unit as described previously.

13 Remove the cross-head screws and slide the matrix from the housing **(see illustrations)**.

14 Check the condition of the gasket between the matrix and the housing and renew if necessary.

15 Refitting is a reversal of removal but fit a new housing gasket and fill and bleed the cooling system with reference to Chapter 1.

Air distribution housing (passenger compartment)

16 Remove the heater unit as previously described.

17 Remove the facia (see Chapter 11).

18 Disconnect the air ducts from the housing.

19 Note the positions of the control cables then disconnect them.

20 Unscrew the mounting bolts and remove the air distribution housing from inside the car.

21 Refitting is a reversal of removal, but fit a new housing gasket and fill and bleed the cooling system with reference to Chapter 1. If

9.13b Removing the heater matrix

necessary adjust the control cables as described in the following paragraphs.

Heater/ventilation control panel and cables

22 Remove the radio and ashtray insert as described in Chapter 12.

23 Where necessary, remove the switches for the seat heating, rear window heating and foglights as described in Chapter 12.

24 Unscrew the screws securing the heater control panel to the facia and withdraw it **(see illustration)**.

25 Note the positions of the control cables on the air distribution housing then disconnect them. Withdraw the cables from

9.24 Removing the heater control panel securing screws

9.13c Heater matrix and temperature control valve

the facia and if necessary disconnect them from the controls **(see illustration)**.

26 Refitting is a reversal of removal, but adjust them as follows.

27 To adjust the regulator valve cable turn the temperature knob fully anticlockwise to the "cold" position, then remove the clip which secures the inner cable to the lever on the housing. With the outer cable securely clipped to the housing, move the lever to the "cold" position then refit the inner cable clip.

28 To adjust the distribution cable turn the knob fully anticlockwise and remove the outer cable clip from the housing. Move the housing lever to the "dash panel outlet" position and refit the outer cable clip.

9.25 Heater control panel and cable connections

Chapter 4 Part A:
Fuel system: single-point injection models

Contents

Degrees of difficulty

Easy, suitable for novice with little experience	Fairly easy, suitable for beginner with some experience	Fairly difficult, suitable for competent DIY mechanic	Difficult, suitable for experienced DIY mechanic	Very difficult, suitable for expert DIY or professional

Specifications

System type . . . . Bosch Mono-Motronic

Fuel system data

Fuel pump type . . . . Electric lift pump immersed in fuel tank and electric in-line pump mounted adjacent fuel tank.

Fuel pump delivery rate (minimum):
   Lift pump . . . . 1800 cm^3 /min approx. (battery voltage of 12.0 V)
   In-line pump . . . . 1250 cm^3 / min approx.(battery voltage of 12.0 V)
Regulated fuel pressure . . . . 0.8 to 1.2 bar
Engine idle speed . . . . 750 - 850 rpm (non-adjustable, electronically controlled)
Maximum engine speed . . . . 6500 rpm (governed electronically)
Injector electrical resistance . . . . 1.2 to 1.6 Ω at 15 to 30 °C

Recommended fuel

Minimum octane rating:
   Engine code:
     PY . . . . 95 RON unleaded
     3F . . . . 95 RON unleaded
     AAU . . . . 91 RON unleaded
     AAV . . . . 91 RON unleaded

Torque wrench settings

	Nm	lbft
Throttle body air cleaner retaining nuts	10	7
Throttle body through-bolts	15	11
Fuel pipe to throttle body banjo bolts	25	18
Inlet manifold retaining bolts	25	18
Inlet manifold heater retaining screws	10	7
Injector cap/inlet air temperature sensor housing screw	5	4
Throttle valve positioning module screws	6	4
Fuel tank retaining strap nuts	25	18
Lambda sensor	50	37

1 General information and precautions

General information

1 The Bosch Mono-Motronic system is a self-contained engine management system, which controls both the fuel injection and ignition. This Chapter deals with the fuel injection system components only - refer to Chapter 5A for details of the ignition system components.
2 The fuel injection system comprises a fuel tank, an electric fuel lift pump an electric fuel line pump, a fuel filter, fuel supply and return lines, a throttle body with an integral electronic fuel injector, and an Electronic Control Unit (ECU) together with its associated sensors, actuators and wiring.
3 The fuel lift and line pumps deliver a constant supply of fuel through an accumulator/coarse mesh filter and a fine mesh cartridge filter to the throttle body, at a slightly higher pressure than required. The fuel pressure regulator (integral with the throttle body) maintains a constant fuel pressure at the fuel injector and returns excess fuel to the tank via the return line. This constant flow system also helps to reduce fuel temperature and prevents vaporisation, aiding hot starting.
4 The fuel injector is an electromagnetically operated pintle valve, which is opened and closed many times per second by an Electronic Control Unit (ECU). When the valve is open, fuel is sprayed in conical pattern onto the back of the throttle disc. The ECU calculates the injection timing and duration according to engine speed, throttle position and rate of opening, inlet air temperature, coolant temperature, road speed and exhaust gas oxygen content information, received from sensors mounted on the engine.
5 Inlet air is drawn into the engine through the air cleaner, which contains a renewable paper filter element. The inlet air temperature is regulated by a vacuum operated valve mounted in the air cleaner, which blends air at ambient temperature with hot air, heated by the exhaust manifold.
6 Idle speed control is achieved as follows. An electronic throttle positioning module, mounted on the side of the throttle body alters the amount of air entering the engine and hence the idle speed. The ignition system provides idle speed stability by increasing and decreasing the engines torque through making small alterations to the ignition timing. As a result, manual adjustment of the engine idle speed is not necessary.
7 To improve cold starting and idling, an electric heating element is mounted on the underside of the inlet manifold; this prevents fuel vapour condensation on the manifold walls when the engine is cold. Power is supplied to the heater by a relay, which is in turn controlled by the ECU.
8 The exhaust gas oxygen content is

constantly monitored by the ECU via the Lambda sensor, which is mounted in the exhaust pipe. The ECU then uses this information to modify the injection timing and duration to maintain the optimum air:fuel ratio - a result of this is that manual adjustment of the idle exhaust CO content is not necessary. In addition, certain models are fitted with an exhaust catalyst - see Chapter 4C for details.
9 The ECU also controls the operation of the activated charcoal filter evaporative loss system - refer to Chapter 4C for further details.
10 It should be noted that fault diagnosis of the Bosch Mono-Motronic engine management system is only possible with dedicated electronic test equipment. Problems with the systems operation should therefore be referred to a VW dealer for assessment. Once the fault has been identified, the removal/refitting sequences detailed in the following Sections will then allow the appropriate component(s) to renewed as required.
Note: *Throughout this Chapter, engines are frequently referred to by their code number, rather than by capacity - refer to Chapter 2A for engine code number listings.*

Precautions

⚠️ *Warning: Petrol is extremely flammable - great care must be taken when working on any part of the fuel system. Do not smoke, or allow any naked flames or uncovered light bulbs near the work area. Note that gas powered domestic appliances with pilot flames, such as heaters boilers and tumble-dryers, also present a fire hazard - bear this in mind if you are working in an area where such appliances are present. Always keep a suitable fire extinguisher close to the work area and familiarise yourself with its operation before starting work. Wear eye protection when working on fuel systems and wash off any fuel spilt on bare skin immediately with soap and water. Note that fuel vapour is just as dangerous as liquid fuel; a vessel that has been emptied of liquid fuel will still contain vapour and can be potentially explosive.*
11 Many of the operations described in this Chapter involve the disconnection of fuel lines, which may cause an amount of fuel spillage. Before commencing work, refer to the above *Warning* and the information in *Safety First !* at the beginning of this manual.
12 Residual fuel pressure always remain in the fuel system, long after the engine has been switched off. This pressure must be relieved in a controlled manner before work can commence on any component in the fuel system - refer to Section 9 for details.
13 When working with fuel system components, pay particular attention to cleanliness - dirt entering the fuel system may cause blockages which will lead to poor running.
14 In the interests of personal safety and

equipment protection, many of the procedures in this Chapter suggest that the negative cable be removed from the battery terminal. This firstly eliminates the possibility of accidental short circuits being caused as the vehicle is being worked upon, and secondly prevents damage to electronic components (eg sensors, actuators, ECU's) which are particularly sensitive to the power surges caused by disconnection or reconnection of the wiring harness whilst they are still "live".
15 It should be noted, however, that certain engine management systems described in this Chapter (and Chapter 5B) have a "learning" capability, that allows the system to adapt to the engine's running characteristics as it wears with use. This "learnt" information is lost when the battery is disconnected and the system will then take a short period of time to "re-learn" the engines' characteristics - this may be manifested (temporarily) as rough idling, reduced throttle response and possibly a slight increase in fuel consumption, until the system re-adapts. The re-adaptation time will depend on how often the vehicle is used and the driving conditions encountered.

2 Air cleaner and inlet system - removal and refitting

Removal

1 Slacken the worm drive clips and disconnect the air ducting from the air cleaner assembly, including the warm air ducting from the exhaust manifold.
2 Prise open the retaining clips, lift the cover from the top of the air cleaner and recover the filter element, as described in Chapter 1.
3 Unscrew the retaining nuts, lift off the retaining ring and remove the air cleaner from the top of the throttle body **(see illustration)**.
4 Disconnect the air temperature regulator vacuum hoses from the ports on the underside of the air cleaner - make a careful note of their order of connection to aid refitting.

Refitting

5 Refit the air cleaner by following the removal procedure in reverse.

3 Inlet air temperature regulator - removal and refitting

Removal

1 Disconnect the vacuum hoses from the temperature regulator, noting their order of connection.
2 Remove the throttle body air cleaner, as described in Section 2.
3 Prise off the metal spring clip **(refer to**

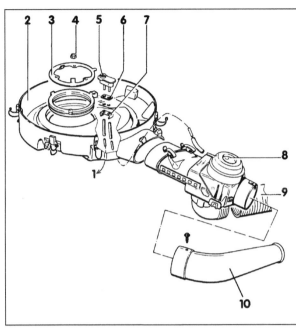

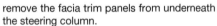

**2.3 Air cleaner assembly -
models with single-point
fuel injection**

1 To throttle body
  vacuum tapping
2 Air cleaner housing
3 Retaining ring
4 Retaining nut
5 Inlet air temperature
  regulator valve
6 Gasket
7 Spring clip
8 Intake air temperature
  regulating flap
9 Warm air ducting
10 Cold air ducting

illustration 2.3) and remove the temperature regulator from the air cleaner housing. Recover the gasket.

Refitting

4 Refit the regulator by following the removal procedure in reverse. Use a new gasket.

4 Accelerator cable - removal, refitting and adjustment

Removal

1 Remove the throttle body air box/air cleaner as described in Section 2.
2 At the throttle body, disconnect the accelerator cable inner from the throttle valve spindle plate (see illustration).
3 Remove the adjustment clip and extract the cable outer from the mounting bracket (refer to illustration 4.2).
4 To improve access, refer to Chapter 11 and remove the facia trim panels from underneath the steering column.
5 Working under the facia, depress the accelerator pedal slightly, then unclip the accelerator cable end from the pedal extension lever (see illustration).
6 At the point where the cable passes through into the engine bay, prise the grommet out from the bulkhead.
7 Release the cable from its clips (where applicable) and guide it out through the aperture in the bulkhead, into the engine bay.

Refitting

8 Refit the accelerator cable by following the removal procedure in reverse.

Adjustment

9 At the throttle body, fix the position of the cable outer in its mounting bracket by inserting the metal clip in one the locating slots, such that when the accelerator is depressed fully, the throttle valve is held wide open to its end stop.

5 Fuel injection system components - removal and refitting

⚠ **Warning: Observe the precautions in Section 1 before working on any component in the fuel system.**

Throttle body

Removal

1 Refer to Section 2 and remove the air cleaner/throttle body air box.
2 Refer to Section 9 and depressurise the fuel system, then disconnect the battery negative cable and position it away from the terminal.
3 Disconnect the fuel supply and return hoses from the ports on the side of the throttle body. Note the arrows that denote the direction of fuel flow, and mark the hoses accordingly (see illustration).
4 Unplug the wiring harness from the throttle body at the connectors, labelling them to aid correct refitting later. Similarly, disconnect all vacuum hoses from the throttle body and label them carefully; it is essential that the hoses are reconnected to the correct vacuum ports on reassembly.
5 Refer to Section 4 and disconnect the accelerator cable from the throttle body.
6 Remove the through-bolts and lift the upper and lower sections of the throttle body away from the inlet manifold.
7 The lower section of the throttle body may be separated from the upper section by releasing the clips. If required, the inter-mediate flange may be detached from the inlet manifold by removing the nuts from the four through-bolts.

Refitting

8 Refitting is a reversal of removal; renew all gaskets where appropriate. Finally, check and if necessary adjust the accelerator cable.

Fuel injector

Removal

9 Refer to Section 2 and remove the air cleaner housing.

4.2 Accelerator cable mounting arrangement at the throttle body

A Throttle valve spindle plate
B Adjustment clip

4.5 Unclip the accelerator cable inner (arrowed) from the pedal extension lever

5.3 Throttle body fuel supply and return hoses and ports

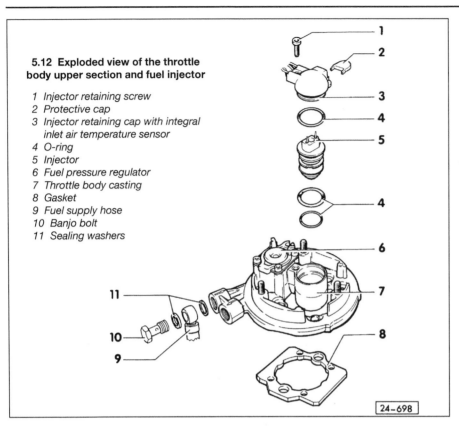

5.12 Exploded view of the throttle body upper section and fuel injector

1 Injector retaining screw
2 Protective cap
3 Injector retaining cap with integral inlet air temperature sensor
4 O-ring
5 Injector
6 Fuel pressure regulator
7 Throttle body casting
8 Gasket
9 Fuel supply hose
10 Banjo bolt
11 Sealing washers

24-698

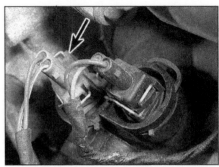

5.30 Two coolant temperature sensors are fitted; the one colour-coded blue (arrowed) serves the engine management system

10 Refer to Section 9 and depressurise the fuel system, then disconnect the battery negative cable and position it away from the terminal.

11 Unplug the wiring harness from the injector at the connector(s), labelling them to aid correct refitting later.

12 Remove the screw and lift off the injector retaining cap/inlet air temperature sensor housing **(see illustration)**

13 Lift the injector out of the throttle body, recovering the O-ring seals. Check the injector electrical resistance using a multimeter and compare the result with the *Specifications*.

Refitting

14 Refit the injector by following the removal procedure in reverse, renewing all O-ring seals. Tighten the retaining screw to the specified torque.

Inlet air temperature sensor

15 The inlet air temperature sensor is an integral part of the fuel injector retaining cap. Removal is as described in the previous sub-Section. Its electrical resistance may be checked using a multimeter **(refer to illustration 5.12)**.

Fuel pressure regulator

16 The fuel pressure regulator components are matched to the upper section of the throttle body and can only be renewed as part of a complete assembly.

Throttle valve positioning module

Removal

17 Disconnect the battery negative cable and position it away from the terminal. Remove the air cleaner/throttle body air box, with reference to Section 2.

18 Refer to Section 4 and disconnect the accelerator cable from the throttle body.

19 Unplug the connector from the side of the throttle valve positioning module.

20 Remove the retaining screws and lift the module together with the accelerator cable outer mounting bracket away from the throttle body.

Refitting

21 Refitting is a reversal of removal. Check that the idle switch plunger lines up with the plastic stop on the lower section of the throttle body. If necessary, adjust the position of the throttle valve positioning module bracket after loosening the mounting screws.

Throttle valve potentiometer

22 Refer to the relevant sub-Section and remove the throttle body. The throttle valve potentiometer is an integral part of the lower section of the throttle body and cannot be renewed separately.

Idle switch

23 Refer to the relevant sub-Section and remove the throttle valve positioning module. The idle switch is an integral part of the module and cannot be renewed separately.

Lambda sensor

Removal

24 The lambda sensor is threaded into the exhaust pipe, at the front of the catalyst.

25 Disconnect the battery negative cable and position it away from the terminal, then unplug the wiring harness from the lambda sensor at the connector, located at the rear of the engine, beneath the throttle body.

26 **Note:** *As a flying lead remains connected to the sensor after is has been disconnected, if the correct size spanner is not available, a slotted socket will be required to remove the sensor.* Working under the vehicle, slacken and withdraw the sensor, taking care to avoid damaging the sensor probe as it is removed.

Refitting

27 Apply a little anti-seize grease to the sensor threads - take care to avoid contaminating the probe tip.

28 Refit the sensor to its housing, tightening it to the correct torque. Restore the harness connection.

Coolant temperature sensor

Removal

29 Disconnect the battery negative cable and position it away from the terminal, then refer to Chapter 3 and drain approximately one quarter of the coolant from the engine.

30 The temperature sensor is located on the left hand side of the cylinder head, under the heater coolant outlet elbow **(see illustration)**. There are two sensors fitted; the one colour coded blue serves the engine management system, the black one produces a signal for the instrument panel temperature gauge.

31 Unplug the wiring harness from the sensor at the connector, then extract the clip and lift the sensor from its housing, recovering the O-ring - be prepared for an amount of coolant loss.

Refitting

32 Refit the sensor by reversing the removal procedure, using a new O-ring. Refer to Chapter 1 and top-up the cooling system.

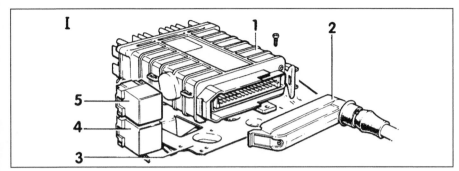

5.40 Location of engine management system ECU and relays

1 Bosch Mono-Motronic ECU
2 Multiway harness connector
3 Mounting bracket

4 Fuel injection pump relay
5 Inlet manifold pre-heater relay

Electronic Control Unit (ECU)

Removal

Caution: Electronic Control Units (ECUs) contain components that are sensitive to the levels of static electricity generated during normal activity. Once the multiway harness connector has been unplugged, the exposed ECU connector pins can freely conduct stray static electricity to these components, damaging or even destroying them - the damage will be invisible and may not manifest itself immediately. Expensive repairs can be avoided by observing the following basic handling rules:

a) *Handle a disconnected ECU by its case only; do not allow fingers or tools to come into contact with the pins.*

b) *When carrying an ECU around, "ground" yourself from time to time, by touching a metal object such as an unpainted water pipe, this will discharge any potentially damaging static that may have built up.*

c) *Do not leave the ECU unplugged from its connector for any longer than is absolutely necessary.*

d) *Make no attempt to 'test' the ECU using multimeters or other non-dedicated test equipment.*

e) *Only unplug the ECU multiway connector after the battery supply has been disconnected.*

33 The ECU is located on the engine bulkhead, beneath a water shield.
34 Disconnect the battery negative cable and position it away from the terminal.
35 Remove the clips and lift off the water shield.
36 Release the spring clip and unplug the multiway connector from the ECU.
37 Remove the securing screws and lift the ECU away from the mounting bracket.

Refitting

38 Refitting is a reversal of removal.

Hall effect sensor

39 This sensor is an integral part of the ignition HT distributor assembly. It can be removed and renewed separately, but dismantling of the distributor will be necessary. It is therefore recommended that this operation is entrusted to a automotive electrical specialist.

Relays

Fuel pump relay

40 The fuel pump relay is located on the engine bulkhead, beneath a water shield. It is the lower of the two relays mounted on the same bracket as the engine management system ECU **(see illustration)**.
41 Disconnect the battery negative cable and position it away from the terminal.
42 Remove the clips and lift off the water shield.
43 Pull the relay from its socket.
44 Refitting is a reversal of removal.

Inlet manifold preheater relay

45 The manifold preheater relay is located on the engine bulkhead, beneath a water shield. It is the upper of the two relays, mounted on the same bracket as the engine management system ECU **(refer to illustration 5.40)**.
46 Disconnect the battery negative cable and position it away from the terminal.
47 Remove the clips and lift off the water shield.
48 Pull the relay from its socket.
49 Refitting is a reversal of removal.

---

6   Fuel filter - renewal

 Warning: Observe the precautions in Section 1 before working on any component in the fuel system.

Removal

1 The fuel filter is mounted behind the fuel tank, at the rear of the vehicle. Access is from the underside of the vehicle.
2 Refer to Section 9 and depressurise the fuel system.

 If proprietary hose clamps are not available, fit two sockets over the jaws of a pair of mole grips and use these to clamp off the hose. the rounded surfaces of the sockets will prevent the jaws from pinching the hose and damaging it

3 Park the vehicle on a level surface, apply the handbrake, select first gear and chock the front roadwheels. Raise the rear of the vehicle and support it securely on axle stands (see "Jacking and vehicle support").
4 Clamp off the fuel lines using proprietary hose clamps - do not use a G-clamp or any similar tool, as the flat jaws may pinch the hose and damage the walls internally **(see Tool Tip)**.
5 Slacken the hose clips and disconnect the fuel lines from either side of the filter unit **(see illustration)**. If the clips are of the crimp type, snip them off with cutters and replace them with equivalent size worm drive clips upon reconnection.
6 Release the filter retaining ring by slackening the upper clamp bolt, then lower the filter unit away from its mounting bracket.
Note: *The fuel accumulator also contains a filter element, but this has a coarse mesh and should not require renewal except in extreme circumstances, e.g. after exposure to contaminated fuel.*

Refitting

7 Refitting is a reversal of removal. Note the direction of flow arrow marked on the side of the filter unit casing - this must point towards the engine when fitted **(see illustration)**.

---

7   Fuel pumps and gauge sender unit - removal and refitting

 Warning: Observe the precautions in Section 1 before working on any component in the fuel system.

General information

1 The fuel lift pump and gauge sender unit are combined in one assembly, which is mounted inside the fuel tank. Access is via a hatch provided in the load space floor and its removal involves exposing the contents of the fuel tank to atmosphere.

 Warning: Avoid direct contact skin contact with fuel - wear protective clothing and gloves when handling fuel system components. Ensure that the work area is well ventilated to prevent the build up of fuel vapour.

2 The line fuel pump is mounted on a bracket, at the front of the fuel tank, next to the fuel filter.

6.5 Slacken the hose clips and disconnect the fuel lines from either side of the filter

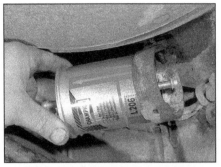

6.7 The direction of flow arrow marking must point towards the engine

Lift pump and fuel gauge sender assembly

Removal

3 It is advisable to carry out this operation when the fuel tank is almost empty.

4 Refer to Section 9 and depressurise the fuel system.

5 Ensure that the vehicle is parked on a level surface, then disconnect the battery negative cable and position it away from the terminal.

6 Refer to Chapter 11 and pivot the rear seat cushion upwards and forwards.

7 Slacken and withdraw the access hatch screws and lift the hatch away from the floorpan (see illustration).

8 Unplug the wiring harness connector from the pump/sender unit (see illustration).

9 Pad the area around the supply and return fuel hoses with rags to absorb any split fuel, then slacken the hose clips and remove them from the ports at the sender unit. Make a note of their order of connection to ensure correct refitting later; note that the fuel return hose is colour-coded blue (see illustration).

10 Grip the slotted outer ring and turn it anticlockwise to release the pump/sender unit from the fuel tank aperture.

> **TOOL TiP** *Use a large pair of water pump pliers to grip and rotate the outer slotted ring*

11 Carefully manoeuvre the pump/sender unit out of the fuel tank, taking care to avoid damaging the float arm. Hold the unit above the level of the fuel in the tank until the excess fuel has drained out (see illustration). Recover the rubber seal.

12 Remove the lift pump/sender unit from the vehicle and lay it on an absorbent card or rag, in a well ventilated area (see illustration). Inspect the float at the end of the sender unit arm for punctures and fuel ingress - renew the unit if it appears damaged.

13 Inspect the sender unit wiper and track; carefully clean off any dirt and debris that may have accumulated and look for breaks or corrosion on the track windings.

14 Inspect the rubber seal from the fuel tank aperture for signs of fatigue - renew it if necessary (see illustration).

Refitting

15 Refit the sender unit by following the removal procedure in reverse, noting the following points:

a) Smear the tank aperture rubber seal with clean fuel before fitting it in position.

b) Reconnect the fuel supply and return hoses according to the notes made during removal.

Line fuel pump

Removal

> ⚠ **Warning: Observe the precautions in Section 1 before working on any component in the fuel system.**

16 The line fuel pump is mounted alongside the fuel accumulator, behind the fuel tank, at

7.7 Remove the access hatch screws and lift the hatch away from the floorpan

7.8 Unplug the wiring harness connector from the pump/sender unit

7.9 Fuel pump connections
1 Supply hose   2 Return hose

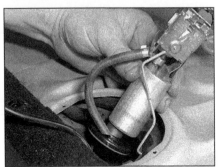

7.11 Carefully manoeuvre the pump/sender unit out of the fuel tank

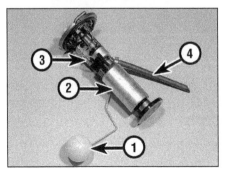

7.12 Fuel pump/gauge sender unit
1 Float and arm   2 Fuel pump
3 Sender unit track and wiper
4 Fuel return hose

7.14 Inspect the rubber seal from the fuel tank aperture for signs of fatigue - renew it if necessary

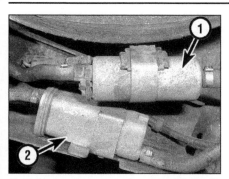

7.16 Line fuel pump and accumulator unit
1 Line fuel pump   2 Accumulator

the rear of the vehicle. Access is from the underside of the vehicle **(see illustration)**.

17 Refer to Section 9 and depressurise the fuel system.

18 Park the vehicle on a level surface, apply the handbrake, select first gear (manual transmission) and chock the front roadwheels. Raise the rear of the vehicle and support it securely on axle stands (see *"Jacking and vehicle support"*).

19 Slacken the hose clips and disconnect the fuel lines from either side of the pump. If the clips are of the crimp type, snip them off with cutters and replace them with equivalent size worm drive clips upon reconnection.

20 Prise off the metal retaining clip and lower the pump unit away from its mounting bracket. Disconnect the wiring harness at the connector.

Refitting

21 Refitting is reversal of removal.

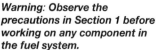

8 Fuel tank -
removal and refitting

> **Warning: Observe the precautions in Section 1 before working on any component in the fuel system.**

Removal

1 Before the tank can be removed, it must be drained of as much fuel as possible. As no drain plug is provided, it is preferable to carry out this operation with the tank almost empty.

2 Disconnect the battery negative cable and position it away from the terminal. Using a hand pump or syphon, remove any remaining fuel from the bottom of the tank.

3 Refer to Section 7 and carry out the following:

a) *Disconnect the wiring harness from the top of the pump sender unit at the multiway connector.*

b) *Disconnect the fuel supply and return hoses from the pump/sender unit*

4 Select first gear and chock the front roadwheels. Remove the centre caps and slacken the right hand rear roadwheel bolts.

5 Raise the rear of the vehicle, support it securely on axle stands (see *"Jacking and vehicle support"*) and remove the right hand rear roadwheel.

6 Refer to Chapter 4C and unhook the exhaust tailbox from its mounting bracket.

7 With reference to Chapter 9, detach the handbrake cable and its mounting bracket from the rear axle beam.

8 Refer to Chapter 10 and unbolt the right hand axle beam mounting from the vehicle underside. Support the axle on blocks to prevent straining the bushes.

9 Position a trolley jack under the centre of the tank. Insert a block of wood between the jack head and the tank to prevent damage to the tank surface. Raise the jack until it just takes the weight of the tank.

10 Working inside the rear right hand wheel arch, slacken and withdraw the screws that secure the tank filler neck to the inside of the wheel arch. Open the fuel filler flap and peel the rubber sealing flange away from the bodywork.

11 Detach the breather hoses from the filler neck, making a note of their order of fitment.

12 Remove the retaining screws from the tank securing straps, keeping one hand on the tank to steady it, as it is released from its mountings.

13 Lower the jack and tank away from the underside of the vehicle; disconnect the charcoal canister vent pipe from the port on the filler neck as it is exposed. Locate the earthing strap and disconnect it from the terminal at the filler neck.

14 If the tank is contaminated with sediment or water, remove the fuel lift pump/sender unit (see Section 7) and swill the tank out with clean fuel.

Refitting

15 Refitting is the reverse of the removal procedure noting the following points.

a) *When lifting the tank back into position make sure the mounting rubbers are correctly positioned and take great care to ensure that none of the hoses become trapped between the tank and vehicle body.*

b) *The large breather hose must be secured to the filler neck before the tank is secured in position.*

c) *Ensure that all breather pipes and hoses are correctly routed, free of kinks and securely held in position with their retaining clips.*

d) *Reconnect the earth strap to its terminal on the filler neck.*

e) *Tighten the tank retaining strap bolts to the specified torque.*

f) *If a new tank has been fitted, it must be coated with underseal before the vehicle is brought back into service.*

g) *On completion, refill the tank with fuel and check for signs of leakage prior to taking the vehicle out on the road.*

9 Fuel injection system -
depressurisation

> **Warning: Observe the precautions in Section 1 before working on any component in the fuel system.**

The following procedure will merely relieve the pressure in the fuel system - remember that fuel will still be present in the system components and take precautions accordingly before disconnecting any of them.

1 The fuel system referred to in this Section is defined as the tank-mounted fuel lift pump, the line fuel pump, the fuel filter, the fuel injector, the throttle body mounted fuel pressure regulator and the metal pipes and flexible hoses of the fuel lines between these components. All these contain fuel which will be under pressure while the engine is running and/or while the ignition is switched on. The pressure will also remain for some time *after* the ignition has been switched off and must be relieved before any of these components are disturbed for servicing work. The engine should be allowed to cool completely before work commences.

2 Refer to Section 5 and locate the fuel pump relay. Remove the relay from its socket, then crank the engine for a few seconds. The engine may fire and run for a while, but continue cranking until it stops. The fuel injector should have opened enough times during cranking to considerably reduce the line fuel pressure.

3 Switch off the ignition ,then disconnect the battery negative cable and position it away from the terminal

4 Place a suitable container beneath the connection/union that is to be disconnected, and have a rag ready to soak up any escaping fuel not being caught by the container.

5 Slowly loosen the connection or union nut (as applicable) to avoid a sudden release of pressure and position the rag around the connection to catch any fuel spray which may be expelled. Once the pressure has been released, disconnect the fuel line completely and insert plugs to minimise fuel loss and to prevent the entry of dirt into the fuel system.

10 Fuel injection system
adjustment - general
information

1 If a fault appears in the fuel injection system first ensure that all the system wiring connectors are securely connected and free of corrosion. Then ensure that the fault is not due to poor maintenance; ie, check that the air cleaner filter element is clean, the spark plugs are in good condition and correctly gapped, the cylinder compression pressures are correct, the ignition timing is correct and the engine breather hoses are clear and undamaged, referring to Chapter 1, Chapter 2 and Chapter 5B for further information.

2 If these checks fail to reveal the cause of the problem the vehicle should be taken to a suitably equipped VW dealer for testing. A diagnostic connector is incorporated in the engine management system wiring harness, into which a dedicated electronic test equipment can be plugged. This equipment is capable of "interrogating" the engine management ECU electronically and accessing its internal fault log. In this manner, faults can be pinpointed quickly and simply, even if their occurrence is intermittent. Testing all the system components individually in an attempt to locate the fault by elimination is a time consuming operation that is unlikely to be fruitful (particularly if the fault occurs dynamically) and carries high risk of damage the ECU's internal components.

3 Experienced home mechanics equipped with a tachometer and an accurately-calibrated exhaust gas analyser may be able to check the exhaust gas CO content and the engine idle speed; if these are found to be out of specification, then the vehicle must be taken to a suitably-equipped VW dealer for assessment. Neither the air/fuel mixture (exhaust gas CO content) nor the engine idle speed are manually adjustable; incorrect test results indicate a fault within the fuel injection system.

11 Unleaded petrol -
general information and usage

Note: *The information given in this Chapter is correct at the time of writing and applies only to petrols currently available in the UK. Check with a VW dealer as more up to date information may be available. If travelling abroad consult one of the motoring organisations (or a similar authority) for advice on the petrols available and their suitability for your vehicle.*

The fuel recommended by VW is given in *Specifications* of this Chapter.

RON and MON are different testing standards; RON stands for Research Octane Number (also written as RM), while MON stands for Motor Octane Number (also written as MM).

Chapter 4 Part B:
Fuel system: multi-point injection models

Contents

Degrees of difficulty

Easy, suitable for novice with little experience	Fairly easy, suitable for beginner with some experience	Fairly difficult, suitable for competent DIY mechanic	Difficult, suitable for experienced DIY mechanic	Very difficult, suitable for expert DIY or professional

Specifications

Fuel system data

Fuel pump type	Electric lift pump immersed in fuel tank and electric in-line pump mounted adjacent to fuel tank
Fuel pump delivery rate(minimum):	
Lift pump	1800 cm³ /min approx. (battery voltage of 12.0 V)
In-line pump	1250 cm³ / min approx.(battery voltage of 12.0 V)
Regulated fuel pressure:	
Engine code 3F	2.5 bar (3.0 bar with regulator vac hose disconnected)
Engine code PY	1.9 bar (2.5 bar with regulator vac hose disconnected)
G-charger boost pressure	0.5 ± 0.05 bar
Engine idle speed:	
Engine code 3F	900 - 950 rpm
Engine code PY	850 - 950 rpm
Maximum engine speed:	
Engine code 3F	6800 rpm
Engine code PY	6600 rpm
Idle exhaust gas CO content:	
Engine code 3F	1.0 - 1.4 %
Engine code PY	0.4 - 1.0 %
Injector electrical resistance	15 - 20 Ω

Recommended fuel

Minimum octane rating:	
Engine code 3F	95 RON
Engine code PY	95 RON

Torque wrench settings

	Nm	lbf ft
Throttle body screws	10	7
Lambda sensor	50	37
Fuel pressure regulator screws	10	7
Fuel line to fuel rail banjo bolts	10	7
Fuel rail bracket to inlet manifold	20	15

1 General information and precautions

General information

1 The Digifant system is a completely self-contained engine management system, which controls both the fuel injection and ignition. This Chapter deals with the fuel injection system components only - refer to Chapter 5A for details of the ignition system components.

2 The fuel injection system comprises a fuel tank, an electric fuel lift pump an electric fuel line pump, a fuel filter, fuel supply and return lines, a throttle body, a fuel rail, a fuel pressure regulator, four electronic fuel injectors, and an Electronic Control Unit (ECU) together with its associated sensors, actuators and wiring.

3 The fuel pump delivers a constant supply of fuel through a cartridge filter to the fuel rail, at a slightly higher pressure than required - the fuel pressure regulator maintains constant fuel pressure to the fuel injectors and returns excess fuel to the tank via the return line. This constant flow system also helps to reduce fuel temperature and prevents vaporisation.

4 The fuel injectors are electromagnetically operated pintle valves, which are opened and closed many times per second by an Electronic Control Unit (ECU). The ECU calculates the injection timing and duration according to engine speed, crankshaft position, throttle position and rate of opening, inlet air volume flow rate, inlet air temperature, coolant temperature, road speed and exhaust gas oxygen content information, received from sensors mounted on and around the engine.

5 Inlet air is drawn into the engine through the air cleaner assembly, which contains a renewable paper filter element. An air flow meter is also integrated into the air cleaner assembly. This sensor is part of the engine management system and monitors engine load by measuring the volume flow rate of the inlet air entering the engine. It sends this information to the ECU in the form of a varying electrical signal.

6 On engine code 3F, the inlet air temperature is regulated by a vacuum operated valve mounted in the air cleaner, which blends air at an ambient temperature with hot air, drawn over the exhaust manifold.

7 On engine code PY, inlet air is supplied to the engine at a positive pressure by a belt driven supercharger. The filtered air is drawn into the supercharger, where it is compressed to a maximum pressure of around 0.5 bar, depending on engine speed and load. An intercooler, mounted in the air flow through the engine bay, cools the inlet air, increasing its density and maximising the amount of oxygen entering the combustion chambers. This helps to keep combustion temperatures

down and increases engine power and torque. An air bypass valve directs excess air back to the supercharger inlet when the engine load is low, i.e. on part throttle or overrun.

8 Idle speed control is achieved by means of an auxiliary air valve, mounted in parallel with the throttle body, which allows a variable amount of air to bypass the throttle disc and enter the engine. The ignition system provides idle speed stability by increasing and decreasing the engines torque through small alterations to the ignition timing.

9 The exhaust gas oxygen content is constantly monitored by the ECU via the Lambda sensor, which is mounted in the exhaust pipe. The ECU then uses this information to modify the injection timing and duration to maintain the optimum air:fuel ratio. In addition, certain models are fitted with an exhaust catalyst - see Chapter 4C for details.

10 The ECU also controls the operation of the activated charcoal filter evaporative loss system - refer to Chapter 4C for further details.

11 It should be noted that comprehensive fault diagnosis of the engine management system is only possible with dedicated electronic test equipment. Problems with the systems operation should therefore be referred to a VW dealer for assessment. Once the fault has been identified, the removal/refitting sequences detailed in the following Sections will then allow the appropriate component(s) to be renewed as required.

Note: *Throughout this Chapter, vehicles are frequently referred to by their engine code, rather than by their engine capacity - refer to Chapter 2A for engine code listings.*

Precautions

Warning: Petrol is extremely flammable - great care must be taken when working on any part of the fuel system. Do not smoke, or allow any naked flames or uncovered light bulbs near the work area. Note that gas powered domestic appliances with pilot flames, such as heaters, boilers and tumble-dryers, also present a fire hazard - bear this in mind if you are working in an area where such appliances are present. Always keep a suitable fire extinguisher to hand and familiarise yourself with its operation before starting work. Wear eye protection when working on fuel systems and wash off any fuel spilt on bare skin immediately with soap and water. Note that fuel vapour is just as dangerous as liquid fuel; a vessel that has been emptied of liquid fuel will still contain vapour and can be potentially explosive.

12 Many of the operations described in this Chapter involve the disconnection of fuel lines, which may cause an amount of fuel spillage. Before commencing work, refer to

the above **Warning** and the information in *Safety First!* at the beginning of this manual.

13 Residual fuel pressure always remains in the fuel system, long after the engine has been switched off. This pressure must be relieved in a controlled manner before work can commence on any component in the fuel system - refer to Section 8 for details.

14 When working with fuel system components, pay particular attention to cleanliness - dirt entering the fuel system may cause internal blockages which could lead to running problems later.

15 In the interests of personal safety and equipment protection, many of the procedures in this Chapter suggest that the negative cable be removed from the battery terminal. This firstly eliminates the possibility of accidental short circuits being caused as the vehicle is being worked upon, and secondly prevents damage to electronic components (eg sensors, actuators, ECU's) which are particularly sensitive to the power surges caused by disconnection or reconnection of the wiring harness whilst they are still "live".

16 It should be noted, however, that the engine management system described in this Chapter (and Chapter 5B) has a "learning" capability, that allows the system to adapt to the engines running characteristics as it wears with normal use. This "learnt" information is lost when the battery is disconnected - on reconnection the system will then take a short period of time to "re-learn" the engines' characteristics. This may be manifested (temporarily) as rough idling, reduced throttle response and possibly an increase in fuel consumption, until the system re-adapts. The re-adaptation time will depend on how often the vehicle is used and the driving conditions encountered.

2 Air cleaner and inlet system - removal and refitting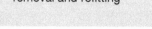

Removal

1 With reference to Chapter 1, carry out the following:

   a) *Slacken the worm drive clips and disconnect the air ducting from the air flow meter.*
   b) *Disconnect the wiring harness from the air flow meter at the multiway connector.*
   c) *Prise open the retaining clips and lift the top cover and air flow meter from the air cleaner.*
   Caution: The air flow meter is a delicate component - handle it carefully.
   d) *Remove the air cleaner filter element.*

2 Detach the cold inlet air ducting from the cowling above the radiator **(see illustration)**

3 Detach the warm inlet air ducting from the

2.2 Detach the cold inlet air ducting from the cowling above the radiator

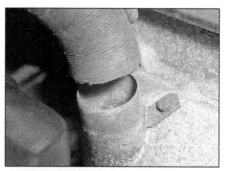

2.3 Detach the warm inlet air ducting from the shield on the exhaust manifold

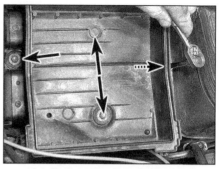

2.4 Remove the four air cleaner retaining nuts (arrowed)

shield on the exhaust manifold **(see illustration)**
4 Remove the four retaining nuts, then lift the air cleaner out of the engine bay and recover the rubber mountings **(see illustration)**. To improve access, detach the charcoal canister vacuum hoses, but make a careful note of the order of fitting to ensure correct refitting.

Refitting

5 Refit the air cleaner by following the removal procedure in reverse.

---

3 Inlet air temperature system - general information and component renewal

General information

1 The inlet air regulation system consists of a temperature controlled vacuum switch,

mounted in the air inlet ducting, a vacuum operated flap valve and several lengths of interconnecting vacuum hose. The switch senses the temperature of the inlet air and opens when a preset lower limit is reached. It then directs manifold vacuum to the flap valve which opens, allowing warm air drawn from around the exhaust manifold to blend with the inlet air.

Component renewal

Temperature switch

2 Remove the screw and detach the inlet air ducting from the top of the throttle body.
3 Disconnect the vacuum hoses from the temperature switch, noting their order of connection to ensure correct refitting **(see illustration)**.
4 Prise the metal retaining clip off the temperature switch ports, then press the

switch body inside the ducting. Recover the gaskets **(see illustration)**.
5 Refitting is a reversal of removal.

Flap valve

6 The flap valve is removed with the air cleaner inlet ducting - remove the screw and detach the ducting from the front of the air cleaner.

---

4 Accelerator cable - removal, refitting and adjustment

> ⚠ **Warning: Observe the precautions in Section 1 before working on any component in the fuel system.**

Removal

1 Remove the ducting from the top of the throttle body, as described in Section 5, to improve access.
2 Prise off the clip and disconnect the accelerator cable inner from the throttle valve spindle plate **(see illustrations)**.
3 Remove the metal clip and extract the cable outer from the mounting bracket **(see illustration)**.
4 Refer to Chapter 11 and remove the facia trim panels from underneath the steering column.
5 Depress the accelerator pedal slightly, then unclip the accelerator cable end from the pedal extension lever.
6 At the point where the cable passes

3.3 Disconnect the vacuum hoses from the temperature switch

3.4 The temperature switch (arrowed) is located inside the throttle body inlet duct

4.2a Prise off the clip . . .

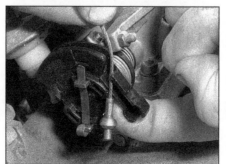

4.2b . . . and disconnect the accelerator cable inner from the throttle valve spindle plate

4.3 Remove the metal clip and extract the cable outer from the mounting bracket

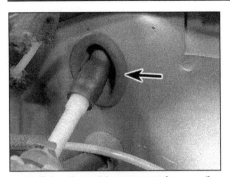

4.6 Prise the cable grommet (arrowed) from the bulkhead

5.4 Remove the air flow meter retaining screws (arrowed)

5.7 Unplug the wiring harness from the potentiometer at the connector (arrowed)

through into the engine bay, prise the grommet from the bulkhead **(see illustration)**.
7 Release the cable from its securing clips and guide it out through the bulkhead into the engine bay.

Refitting

8 Refit the accelerator cable by following the removal procedure in reverse.

Adjustment

9 At the throttle body, fix the position of the cable outer in its mounting bracket by inserting the metal clip in one of the locating slots, such that when the accelerator is depressed fully, the throttle valve is held wide open to its end stop.

---

5 Digifant fuel injection system components - removal and refitting

⚠ *Warning: Observe the precautions in Section 1 before working on any component in the fuel system.*

Air flow meter

Removal

1 Disconnect the battery negative cable and position it away from the terminal.
2 With reference to Section 2 and Chapter 1, remove the top cover from the air cleaner assembly.
3 Unplug the harness connector from the air flow meter.
4 Remove the retaining screws and detach the meter from the air cleaner top cover - recover the seal **(see illustration)**.
Caution: Handle the air flow meter carefully - its internals are easily damaged.

Refitting

5 Refitting is a reversal of removal. Renew the seal if it appears damaged.

Throttle valve potentiometer (engine code 3F only)

Removal

6 Disconnect the battery negative cable and position it away from the terminal.

5.11 The inlet air temperature sensor (arrowed) is an integral part of the air flow meter

7 Unplug the harness connector from the potentiometer **(see illustration)**.
8 Remove the retaining screws and locking plate, then lift the potentiometer away from the throttle body. Recover the O-ring seal.

Refitting

9 Refitting is a reversal of removal, noting the following:

 a) *Renew the O-ring seal if it appears damaged.*
 b) *Ensure that the potentiometer drive engages correctly with the throttle spindle extension.*

10 On completion, the potentiometer must be "matched" electronically to the Digifant Electronic Control Unit (ECU). This operation requires access to dedicated electronic test equipment, refer to a VW dealer for advice.

Inlet air temperature sensor

Removal

11 The sensor is an integral part of the air flow meter and cannot be renewed separately (see illustration).

Auxiliary air valve

Removal

12 The valve is mounted on a bracket below the inlet manifold - access is extremely limited with the inlet manifold in position.
13 Unplug the harness connector from the valve.
14 Release the clips and disconnect the

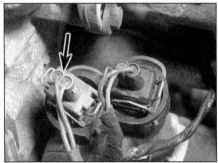

5.17 Two coolant temperature sensors are fitted; the one colour coded blue (arrowed) serves the engine management system

hoses from the auxiliary valve. Note their order of connection to aid correct refitting.
15 Remove the screw and detach the valve from its mountings.

Refitting

16 Refitting is a reversal of removal.

Coolant temperature sensor

Removal

17 The coolant temperature sensor is mounted at the left hand side of the cylinder head, directly underneath the ignition distributor. Two sensors are fitted; the one colour coded blue serves the engine management system, the black one produces a signal for the instrument panel temperature gauge **(see illustration)**.
18 Unplug the harness connector from the sensor.
19 Refer to Chapter 3 and drain approximately one quarter of the coolant from the engine.
20 Extract the retaining clip and lift the sensor from the coolant elbow - be prepared for coolant loss. Recover the O-ring.

Refitting

21 Refit the sensor by reversing the removal procedure, using a new O-ring. Refer to Chapter 1 and top-up the cooling system.

Engine speed Hall sender

22 This sensor is an integral part of the ignition HT distributor assembly. It can be removed and renewed separately, but dismantling of the distributor will be

necessary. It is therefore recommended that this operation is entrusted to a automotive electrical specialist.

Throttle body

Removal

23 Refer to Section 4 and detach the accelerator cable from the throttle valve lever.
24 Slacken the clips and detach the inlet air ducting from the top of the throttle body inlet. Remove the bolts, lift off the throttle body inlet elbow and recover the seal **(see illustrations)**.
25 On engine code 3F, remove the through-bolt and detach the inlet housing from the top of the throttle body. On engine code PY, remove the screws and detach the bypass valve housing from the top of the throttle body.
26 Disconnect the battery negative cable and position it away from the terminal, then unplug the harness connector from the throttle potentiometer.
27 Disconnect the vacuum hoses from the ports on the throttle body, noting their order of fitment. Release the wiring harness from the guide clip.
28 Slacken and withdraw the bolts **(see illustration)**, then lift the throttle body away from the inlet manifold. Recover and discard the gasket.

Refitting

29 Refitting is a reversal of removal, noting the following:
a) *Use a new throttle body-to-inlet manifold gasket.*
b) *Observe the correct tightening torque when refitting the throttle body through-bolts/screws.*
c) *Ensure that all vacuum hoses and electrical connectors are refitted securely.*
d) *With reference to Section 4, check and if necessary adjust the accelerator cable.*

Fuel injectors and fuel rail

 Warning: Observe the precautions in Section 1 before working on any component in the fuel system. Ideally this operation should be carried out when the engine is cold.

Removal

30 Disconnect the battery negative cable and position it away from the terminal.
31 Refer to the relevant sub-Section in this Chapter and remove the throttle body.
32 Unplug the injector wiring harness at the multiway connector, which is located at the end of the fuel rail **(see illustration)**.
33 Refer to Section 8 and depressurise the fuel system.
34 Disconnect the vacuum hose from the port on the top of the fuel pressure regulator **(see illustration)**.
35 Slacken the clips and disconnect the fuel supply and return hoses from the ports on the fuel rail and pressure regulator

5.24a Slacken the clips and detach the inlet air ducting from the top of the throttle body inlet

5.24c . . . and recover the seal

(see illustrations). *Carefully* note the fitted positions of the hoses - the supply hose is colour-coded black and the return hose is colour-coded with a blue band.

5.32 Unplug the injector wiring harness at the multiway connector

5.35a Slacken the clips and disconnect the fuel supply hose. . .

5.24b Remove the bolts, lift off the throttle body inlet elbow . . .

5.28 Slacken and withdraw the four throttle body retaining bolts (three arrowed, one hidden)

36 Slacken and withdraw the fuel rail retaining screws, then carefully lift the fuel rail away from the inlet manifold, together with the injectors. Recover the injector lower O-ring

5.34 Disconnect the vacuum hose from the top of the fuel pressure regulator

5.35b . . . and return hose (arrowed)

5.36a Slacken and withdraw the fuel rail retaining screws (arrowed) . . .

5.36b . . . then carefully lift the fuel rail away from the inlet manifold, together with the injectors

5.37a Unclip both halves of the plastic shielding from the injector body

5.37b Remove the insulating shroud

5.37c Unplug the wiring harness connector

5.37d Extract the retaining clip

5.37e Prise out the injector

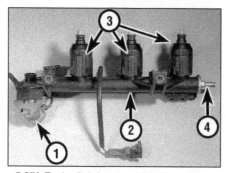

5.37f Fuel rail, injector and fuel pressure regulator assembly (No 1 injector removed)
1 Fuel pressure regulator   2 Fuel rail
3 Fuel injectors   4 Fuel pressure test point

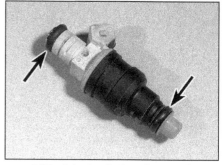

5.37g Injector O-rings (arrowed)

seals as they emerge from the manifold, if they work loose **(see illustrations)**.
37 To remove individual injectors from the fuel rail, proceed as follows **(see illustrations)**:

a) *Unclip both halves of the plastic shielding from the injector body.*
b) *Remove the insulating shroud.*
c) *Unplug the wiring harness connector.*
d) *Extract the retaining clip.*
e) *Prise out the injector.*

38 If required, remove the fuel pressure regulator, referring to the relevant sub-Section for guidance.
39 Check the electrical resistance of the injectors using a multimeter connected across the injector terminals - compare the results with the *Specifications*.

40 Moisten the injector O-rings with clean engine oil, then refit the injectors to the fuel rail, ensuring that the O-ring seals are correctly seated and that the retaining clips are firmly in place.

Refitting

41 Refit the injectors and fuel rail by following the removal procedure in reverse, noting the following points:

a) *Renew the injector O-ring seals if they appear worn or damaged.*
b) *Ensure that the injector retaining clips are securely seated.*
c) *Check that the fuel supply and return hoses are reconnected correctly - refer to the colour coding described in "Removal".*

d) *Check that all vacuum and electrical connections are remade correctly and securely.*
e) *On completion, check exhaustively for fuel leaks before bringing the vehicle back into service.*

Fuel pressure regulator

Warning: Observe the precautions in Section 1 before working on the fuel system. Ideally this operation should be carried out when the engine is cold.

Removal

42 Disconnect the battery negative cable and position it away from the terminal.
43 Refer to Section 8 and depressurise the fuel system.

5.46 Remove the retaining screws (arrowed) and lift off the regulator body

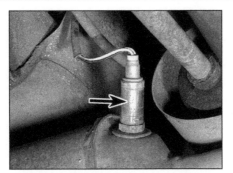

5.48 The Lambda sensor (arrowed) is threaded into the exhaust pipe, at the front of the catalyst

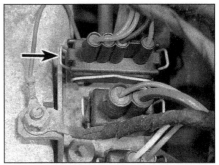

5.49 Unplug the wiring harness from the Lambda sensor at the connector (arrowed), mounted at the rear of the engine, on the side of the inlet manifold

44 Disconnect the vacuum hose from the port on the top of the fuel pressure regulator.
45 Slacken the clip and disconnect the fuel supply hose from the end of the fuel rail. This will allow the majority of fuel in the regulator to drain out. Be prepared for an amount of fuel loss - position a small container and some old rags underneath the fuel regulator housing.
46 Remove the retaining screws and lift off the regulator body, recovering the O-ring seal **(see illustration)**.

Refitting

47 Refit the fuel pressure regulator by following the removal procedure in reverse, noting the following points.

a) Renew the O-ring seals if they appear worn or damaged
b) Ensure that the regulator retaining screws are tightened to the correct torque.
c) Refit the regulator vacuum hose securely.

Lambda sensor

Removal

48 The Lambda sensor is threaded into the exhaust pipe, at the front of the catalyst **(see illustration)**.
49 Disconnect the battery negative cable and position it away from the terminal, then unplug the wiring harness from the Lambda sensor at the connector, located at the rear of the engine, beneath the throttle body **(see illustration)**.
50 Note: *As a flying lead remains connected to the sensor after is has been disconnected, if the correct size spanner is not available, a slotted socket will be required to remove the sensor.* Working under the vehicle, slacken and withdraw the sensor, taking care to avoid damaging the sensor probe as it is removed.

Refitting

51 Apply a little anti-seize grease to the sensor threads - take care to avoid contaminating the probe tip.
52 Refit the sensor to its housing, tightening it to the correct torque. Restore the harness connection.

Electronic Control Unit (ECU)

Removal

Caution: Electronic Control Units (ECUs) contain components that are sensitive to the levels of static electricity generated during normal activity. Once the multiway harness connector has been unplugged, the exposed ECU connector pins can freely conduct stray static electricity to these components, damaging or even destroying them - the damage will be invisible and may not manifest itself immediately. Expensive repairs can be avoided by observing the following basic handling rules:

a) Handle a disconnected ECU by its case only; do not allow fingers or tools to come into contact with the pins.
b) When carrying an ECU around, "ground" yourself from time to time, by touching a metal object such as an unpainted water pipe, this will discharge any potentially damaging static that may have built up.
c) Do not leave the ECU unplugged from its connector for any longer than is absolutely necessary.
d) Do not 'test' the ECU using multimeters or other non-dedicated test equipment.
e) Only unplug the ECU connector after the battery supply has been disconnected.

53 The ECU is located on the engine bulkhead, beneath a water shield.
54 Disconnect the battery negative cable and position it away from the terminal.
55 Remove the clips and lift off the water shield.
56 Release the spring clip and unplug the multiway connector from the ECU.
57 Remove the screws and lift the ECU away from the mounting bracket **(see illustration)**.

Refitting

58 Refitting is a reversal of removal.

Fuel pump relay

59 The fuel pump relay is located on the engine bulkhead, beneath a water shield. It is the lower of the two relays mounted on the same bracket as the engine management system ECU.

60 Disconnect the battery negative cable and position it away from the terminal.
61 Remove the clips and lift off the water shield.
62 Pull the relay from its socket.
63 Refitting is a reversal of removal.

6 Fuel filter - renewal

Refer to the information in Chapter 4A.

7 Fuel pumps and gauge sender unit - removal and refitting

Refer to the information in Chapter 4A.

8 Fuel injection system - depressurisation

Refer to the information in Chapter 4A.

9 Fuel tank - removal and refitting

Refer to the information in Chapter 4A.

5.57 Remove the securing screws and lift the ECU away from the mounting bracket

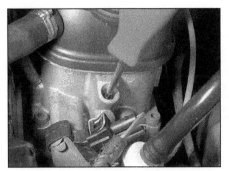

10.3a Idle speed adjustment screw location

10.3b Exhaust CO adjustment screw location

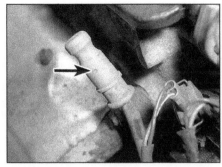

10.3c Protective cap (arrowed) fitted to exhaust CO pre-catalyst sampling pipe (not fitted to later vehicles)

10 Fuel injection system adjustment - general information

1 If a fault appears in the fuel injection system first ensure that all the system wiring connectors are securely connected and free of corrosion. Then ensure that the fault is not due to poor maintenance; ie, check that the air cleaner filter element is clean, the spark plugs are in good condition and correctly gapped, the cylinder compression pressures are correct, the ignition timing is correct and the engine breather hoses are clear and undamaged, referring to Chapter 1, Chapter 2A and Chapter 5B for further information.

2 If these checks fail to reveal the cause of the problem the vehicle should be taken to a suitably equipped VW dealer for testing. A diagnostic connector is incorporated in the engine management system wiring harness, into which a dedicated electronic test equipment can be plugged. The test equipment is capable of "interrogating" the engine management system ECU electronically and accessing its internal fault log. In this manner, faults can be pinpointed quickly and simply, even if their occurrence is intermittent. Testing all the system components individually in an attempt to locate the fault by elimination is a time consuming operation that is unlikely to be fruitful (particularly if the fault occurs dynamically) and carries a high risk of damage to the ECU's internal components.

3 Experienced home mechanics equipped with an accurate tachometer and a carefully-calibrated exhaust gas analyser may be able to check the exhaust gas CO content and the engine idle speed; if these are found to be out of specification, then the vehicle must be taken to a suitably-equipped VW dealer for assessment. Idle speed and exhaust CO adjustment screws are provided **(see illustrations)**, but adjustment will not be possible if the engine management system has detected and stored a fault in one of the fuelling or ignition system components. For this reason, all fault codes must be erased from the engine management system memory before the idle speed and exhaust CO settings can be

checked and adjusted - this operation must be carried out by a VW dealer with the required test equipment.
Caution: Inaccurate CO adjustment may cause overfuelling and the risk of serious catalytic converter damage.

11 G-charger - removal and refitting

General information

1 The G-charger develops its maximum pressure at full load and so cannot be tested with the vehicle stationary. It is recommended that the boost pressure is measured by a VW dealer, using a rolling road. However, if this is not possible, the measurement may be made as follows.

2 Connect a vacuum hose T-piece in line with the vacuum supply to the fuel pressure regulator. Route a length of vacuum hose from the T-piece to a pressure test gauge in the cabin. Close the bonnet, ensuring that the vacuum hose is not trapped. Enlist the help of an assistant to hold the gauge and read off measurements from the passenger seat.

3 Drive the vehicle on a strip of private road (not the public highway) at full throttle in second gear whilst simultaneously depressing the footbrake to maintain an engine speed of 4000 rpm. Have your assistant record the maximum boost pressure indicated.
Caution: Do not maintain these driving conditions for more than 10 seconds.

4 Compare the measurement with that listed in the *Specifications*. If the boost pressure is low, check the tension of the drivebelts (as described in Chapter 1) and make sure that there are no leaks or blockages in the inlet system, before condemning the G-charger.

Removal

Warning: Do not run the engine with the G-charger air inlet hose disconnected; the depression at the inlet can build up very suddenly if the engine speed raised and there is the risk of foreign objects being sucked in.

Caution: Thoroughly clean around all oil pipe unions before disconnecting them, to prevent the ingress of dirt. Store components in a sealed container to prevent contamination. Cover the G-charger air inlet ducts to prevent debris entering and clean using lint-free cloths only.

5 Remove the screws and lift off the G-charger cover plates.
6 Remove the auxiliary drivebelts (Chapter 1).
7 Slacken the clips and detach the air inlet and delivery ducting from the G-charger ports. Cover the open ports with plastic sheeting secured with elastic bands, to prevent the ingress of foreign material.
8 Slacken and withdraw the banjo bolts at the oil supply and return unions. Recover the sealing washers and discard them - new ones must be used on refitting. Plug the open oilways to minimise oil loss and prevent contamination.
9 Slacken and withdraw the G-charger mounting bracket bolts, supporting the unit as the last bolt is withdrawn.
10 Remove the G-charger from the engine bay together with its mounting bracket and the drivebelt pulleys.

Refitting

11 Refit the G-charger by following the removal procedure in reverse, noting the following points:

a) Ensure that the air inlet ducting is completely free of debris, before refitting it and securing the clips.
b) Use new sealing washers when reconnecting the oil supply and return unions; tighten the banjo bolts to the specified torque.
c) With reference to Chapter 1, refit and tension the auxiliary drivebelts.

12 Unleaded petrol - general information and usage

Refer to the information in the Specifications at the start of this Chapter, and in Chapter 4A.

Chapter 4 Part C:
Emission control and exhaust systems

Contents

Degrees of difficulty

Easy, suitable for novice with little experience	Fairly easy, suitable for beginner with some experience	Fairly difficult, suitable for competent DIY mechanic	Difficult, suitable for experienced DIY mechanic	Very difficult, suitable for expert DIY or professional

Specifications

Torque wrench settings	Nm	lbf ft
Exhaust system clamp bolts	25	18
Exhaust downpipe-to-exhaust manifold nuts	25	18

1 General information

Emission control systems

1 All petrol engine models have the ability to use unleaded petrol and are controlled by engine management systems that are "tuned " to give the best compromise between driveability, fuel consumption and exhaust emission production. In addition, a number of systems are fitted that help to minimise other harmful emissions: a crankcase emission-control system that reduces the release of pollutants from the engines lubrication system is fitted to all models, catalytic converters that reduce exhaust gas pollutants are fitted to most models and an evaporative loss emission control system that reduces the release of gaseous hydrocarbons from the fuel tank is fitted to all models.

Crankcase emission control

2 To reduce the emission of unburned hydrocarbons from the crankcase into the atmosphere, the engine is sealed and the blow-by gases and oil vapour are drawn from inside the crankcase, through a wire mesh oil separator, into the inlet tract to be burned by the engine during normal combustion.

3 Under conditions of high manifold depression (idling, deceleration) the gases will be sucked out of the crankcase. Under conditions of low manifold depression (acceleration, full-throttle running) the gases are forced out of the crankcase by the (relatively) higher crankcase pressure. If the

engine is worn, the raised crankcase pressure (due to increased blow-by) will cause some of the flow to return under all manifold conditions. On certain engines, a pressure regulating valve (mounted on the side of the cylinder head) controls the flow of gases from the crankcase.

4 On engine code PY, the excess inlet air generated by the G-charger, when the engine is on part throttle or overrun, is directed through the camshaft cover by the bypass valve.

Exhaust emission control

5 To minimise the amount of pollutants which escape into the atmosphere, most models are fitted with a catalytic converter in the exhaust system. On all models where a catalytic converter is fitted, the fuelling system is of the closed-loop type, in which a Lambda sensor in the exhaust system provides the engine management system ECU with constant feedback, enabling the ECU to adjust the air/fuel mixture to optimise combustion.

6 The Lambda sensor has a heating element built-in that is controlled by the ECU through the Lambda sensor relay to quickly bring the sensor's tip to its optimum operating temperature. The sensor's tip is sensitive to oxygen and relays a voltage signal to the ECU that varies according on the amount of oxygen in the exhaust gas. If the inlet air/fuel mixture is too rich, the exhaust gases are low in oxygen so the sensor sends a low-voltage signal, the voltage rising as the mixture weakens and the amount of oxygen rises in the exhaust gases. Peak conversion efficiency of all major pollutants occurs if the inlet air/fuel mixture is maintained at the

chemically-correct ratio for complete combustion. This equates to 14.7 parts (by weight) of air to 1 part of fuel (the `stoichiometric' ratio). The sensor output voltage alters in a large step at this point, the ECU using the signal change as a reference point and correcting the inlet air/fuel mixture accordingly by altering the fuel injector pulse width. Details of the Lambda sensor removal and refitting are given in Chapter 4A or B as applicable .

Evaporative emission control

7 To minimise the escape of unburned hydrocarbons into the atmosphere, an evaporative loss emission control system is fitted to all petrol models. The fuel tank filler cap is sealed and a charcoal canister is mounted underneath the front right-hand wing to absorb the vapour released from the fuel contained in the fuel tank. It stores them until they can be drawn from the canister via the purge valve into the inlet tract, where they are then burned by the engine during normal combustion. On single-point injection models, the purge valve is controlled electronically by the engine management system ECU. On models with multi-point injection, the purge valve is controlled by vacuum supplied from the inlet manifold.

8 To ensure that the engine runs correctly when it is cold and/or idling and to protect the catalytic converter from the effects of overfuelling, the purge control valve(s) are not opened by the ECU until the engine has warmed up, and the engine is under load; the valve solenoid is then modulated on and off to allow the stored vapour to pass into the inlet tract.

Exhaust systems

9 The exhaust system comprises the exhaust manifold, a number of silencer units (depending on model and specification), a catalytic converter (where fitted), a number of mounting brackets and a series of connecting pipes.

2   Evaporative loss control system - general information and component renewal

General information

1 The evaporative loss emission control system consists of the purge valve, the activated charcoal filter canister and a series of connecting vacuum hoses.
2 The purge valve is mounted on a bracket behind the air cleaner housing, and the charcoal canister is mounted on a bracket above the right hand front wheel housing.

Purge valve

3 On single-point injection models, ensure that the ignition is switched off, then unplug the wiring harness from the purge valve at the connector.
4 Slacken the clips and pull the vacuum (where applicable) and vapour hoses off the purge valve ports. Make a note of their orientation to aid refitting later. Remove the valve from the engine bay **(see illustration)**.
5 Refitting is a reversal of removal.

Charcoal canister

6 Open the bonnet and locate the canister in the right hand wing **(see illustration)**. Disconnect the vapour hoses from it and make a note of their order of connection to aid correct refitting later.
7 Remove the screws from the securing bracket and lift the canister out of its aperture.
8 Refitting is a reversal of removal.

3   Crankcase emission system - general information

The crankcase emission control system consists of a series of hoses that connect the crankcase vent to the camshaft cover vent

and the air inlet, a pressure regulating valve (where applicable) and an oil separator unit.
The components of this system require no attention other than to check at regular intervals that the hose(s) are free of blockages and undamaged.

4   Exhaust manifold - removal and refitting

The exhaust manifold removal is described as part of the cylinder head dismantling sequence; refer to Chapter 2A.

5   Exhaust system - general information and component removal

General information

1 The exhaust system is made up of the downpipe, (with integral catalytic converter, where fitted), the intermediate pipe and the tail section which contains the rear silencer.
2 On all models, the system is suspended throughout its entire length by rubber mountings, which are secured to the underside of the vehicle by metal brackets.

Removal

3 Each exhaust section can be removed individually or, alternatively, the complete system can be removed as a unit.
4 To remove the system or part of the system, first jack up the front or rear of the car and support it on axle stands (see "*Jacking and vehicle support*"). Alternatively position the car over an inspection pit or on car ramps.

Downpipe

5 Place blocks of wood under the catalytic converter/front silencer to act as a support. Where applicable, refer to Chapter 4A or B and remove the Lambda sensor from the exhaust pipe.
6 Slacken the clamp and separate the down pipe from the intermediate pipe.
7 Undo the nuts and separate the downpipe from the exhaust manifold. Recover the gasket.

Catalytic converter

8 Where fitted, the catalytic converter is integral with the down pipe.

Intermediate pipe

9 Slacken the clamping ring bolts and disengage the clamp from the intermediate pipe-to-tailpipe joint and the intermediate pipe-to-catalytic converter/front silencer joint.
10 Disengage the intermediate pipe from the tailpipe and the catalytic converter/front silencer and remove it from underneath the vehicle.

Tailpipe

11 Slacken the clamping ring bolts and disengage the tailpipe at the joint.
12 Unhook the tailpipe from its mounting rubbers and remove it from the vehicle.

Complete system

13 Disconnect the down pipe from the manifold as described earlier in this Section.
14 With the aid of an assistant, free the system from all its mounting rubbers and manoeuvre it out from underneath the vehicle.

Heatshields

15 The heatshields, where fitted, are secured to the underside of the body by a combination of nuts, bolts and clips. Each shield can be removed once the relevant exhaust section has been removed. Note that if the shield is being removed to gain access to a component located behind it, in some cases it may prove sufficient to remove the retaining nuts and/or bolts and simply lower the shield, removing the need to disturb the exhaust system.

Refitting

16 Each section is refitted by a reverse of the removal sequence, noting the following points.

a) *Ensure that all traces of corrosion have been removed from the flanges and renew all necessary gaskets.*

b) *Inspect the rubber mountings for signs of damage or deterioration and renew as necessary.*

c) *On joints which are secured by clamping rings, apply a smear of exhaust system jointing paste to the joint mating surfaces to ensure an air-tight seal. Tighten the clamping ring nuts evenly and progressively to the specified torque so that the clearance between the clamp halves is equal on either side.*

d) *Prior to tightening the exhaust system fasteners, ensure that all rubber mountings are correctly located and that there is adequate clearance between the exhaust system and vehicle underbody.*

2.4 Purge valve location - engine code 3F shown

2.6 Charcoal canister location - engine code 3F shown

6 Catalytic converter - general information and precautions

The catalytic converter is a reliable and simple device which needs no maintenance in itself, but there are some facts of which an owner should be aware if the converter is to function properly for its full service life.

a) DO NOT use leaded petrol in a car with a catalytic converter - the lead will coat the precious metals reagents, reducing their converting efficiency and will eventually destroy the converter.

b) Always keep the ignition and fuel systems well-maintained in accordance with the manufacturer's schedule.

c) If the engine develops a misfire, do not drive the car at all (or at least as little as possible) until the fault is cured.

d) DO NOT push- or tow-start the car - this will soak the catalytic converter in unburned fuel, causing it to overheat when the engine eventually starts.

e) DO NOT switch off the ignition at high engine speeds.

f) In some cases a sulphurous smell (like that of rotten eggs) may be noticed from the exhaust. This is common to many catalytic converter-equipped cars and once the car has covered a few thousand miles the problem should disappear. Low quality fuel with a high sulphur content will exacerbate this effect.

g) The catalytic converter, used on a well-maintained and well-driven car, should last for between 50 000 and 100 000 miles - if the converter is no longer effective it must be renewed.

h) DO NOT use fuel or engine oil additives - these may contain substances harmful to the catalytic converter.

i) DO NOT continue to use the car if the engine burns oil to the extent of leaving a visible trail of blue smoke as this will contaminate the catalyst.

j) The catalytic converter operates at very high temperatures. DO NOT park the car in dry undergrowth, over long grass or piles of dead leaves after a long run.

k) Remember that the catalytic converter is FRAGILE - do not strike it with tools during servicing work.

Notes

Chapter 5 Part A:
Starting and charging systems

Contents

Degrees of difficulty

Easy, suitable for novice with little experience	**Fairly easy,** suitable for beginner with some experience	**Fairly difficult,** suitable for competent DIY mechanic 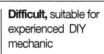	**Difficult,** suitable for experienced DIY mechanic	**Very difficult,** suitable for expert DIY or professional

Specifications

System type . . . . 12 V, negative earth

Battery
Capacity . . . . 36 Ah or 45 Ah
Minimum voltage (under load) . . . . 9.6 V at 110 A

Alternator
Type . . . . Bosch or Motorola
Output at 3000 rpm (engine speed) . . . . 30 A (45 A model) 45 A (65 A model)
Regulator voltage . . . . 12.5 to 14.5 V
Minimum brush length . . . . 5.0 mm
Rotor winding resistance:
    45 amp . . . . 3.4 to 3.7 ohms
    65 amp . . . . 2.8 to 3.0 ohms

Starter motor
Minimum brush length . . . . 13.0 mm

Torque wrench settings	**Nm**	**lbf ft**
Starter	25	18
Alternator bracket:		
Engine	45	33
Alternator	30	22

1 General information and precautions

General information

The engine electrical system consists mainly of the charging and starting systems. Because of their engine-related functions, these components are covered separately from the body electrical devices such as the lights, instruments, etc (which are covered in Chapter 12). Refer to Part B of Chapter 5 for information on the ignition system.

The electrical system is of the 12-volt negative earth type.

The battery may be of the low maintenance or 'maintenance-free' (sealed for life) type and is charged by the alternator, which is belt-driven from the crankshaft pulley.

The starter motor is of the pre-engaged type incorporating an integral solenoid. On starting, the solenoid moves the drive pinion into engagement with the flywheel ring gear before the starter motor is energised. Once the engine has started, a one-way clutch prevents the motor armature being driven by the engine until the pinion disengages from the flywheel.

Precautions

Further details of the various systems are given in the relevant Sections of this Chapter.

While some repair procedures are given, the usual course of action is to renew the component concerned. The owner whose interest extends beyond mere component renewal should obtain a copy of the 'Automobile Electrical & Electronic Systems Manual', available from the publishers of this manual.

It is necessary to take extra care when working on the electrical system to avoid damage to semi-conductor devices (diodes, transistors and integrated circuits), and to avoid the risk of personal injury. In addition to the precautions given in 'Safety first!' at the beginning of this manual, observe the following when working on the system:

Always remove rings, watches, etc before working on the electrical system. Even with

the battery disconnected, capacitive discharge could occur if a component's live terminal is earthed through a metal object. This could cause a shock or nasty burn.

Do not reverse the battery connections. Components such as the alternator, electronic control units, or any other components having semiconductor circuitry could be irreparably damaged.

If the engine is being started using jump leads and a slave battery, connect the batteries positive-to-positive and negative-to-negative (see `Booster battery (jump) starting'). This also applies when connecting a battery charger.

Never disconnect the battery terminals, the alternator, any electrical wiring or any test instruments when the engine is running.

Do not run the alternator with its output open circuit disconnected.

Never 'test' for alternator output by 'flashing' the output lead to earth.

Never use an ohmmeter or continuity tester of the type incorporating a hand-cranked generator for circuit or continuity testing.

Always ensure that the battery negative lead is disconnected when working on the electrical system.

Before using electric-arc welding equipment on the car, disconnect the battery, alternator and components such as the engine management system electronic control unit to protect them from the risk of damage.

Certain radio/cassette units fitted as standard equipment by VW are equipped with a built-in security code to deter thieves. Refer to 'Radio/cassette unit anti-theft system precaution' in the Reference section of this manual for further information.

2 Battery - removal and refitting

Removal

1 The battery is located under the bonnet on the right-hand side of the bulkhead **(see illustration)**.
2 Loosen the battery terminal clamp nuts and disconnect the negative lead followed by the positive lead.
3 Unscrew the bolt and remove the battery retaining clamp.
4 Lift the battery from its platform and remove it from the engine bay.

Refitting

5 Refitting is a reversal of removal, but make sure that the leads are fitted to their correct terminals, and do not overtighten the lead clamp nuts or the battery retaining clamp bolt. Finally, smear a little petroleum jelly on the terminals and clamps to prevent corrosion.

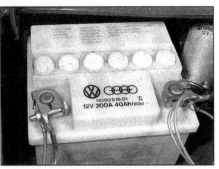

2.1 The battery is located under the bonnet, on the right-hand side of the bulkhead

3 Battery - testing and charging

Standard and low maintenance battery - testing

1 If the vehicle covers a small annual mileage it is worthwhile checking the specific gravity of the electrolyte every three months to determine the state of charge of the battery. Use a hydrometer to make the check and compare the results with the following table. The temperatures quoted are ambient (air) temperatures.

	Above 25°C	Below 25°C
Fully charged	1.210 to 1.230	1.270 to 1.290
70% charged	1.170 to 1.190	1.230 to 1.250
Discharged	1.050 to 1.070	1.110 to 1.130

Note that the specific gravity readings assume an electrolyte temperature of 15°C (59°F); for every 10°C (50°F) below 15°C (59°F) subtract 0.007. For every 10°C (50°F) above 15°C (59°F) add 0.007.
2 If the battery condition is suspect, first check the specific gravity of electrolyte in each cell. A variation of 0.040 or more between any cells indicates loss of electrolyte or deterioration of the internal plates.
3 If the specific gravity variation is 0.040 or more, the battery should be renewed. If the cell variation is satisfactory but the battery is discharged, it should be charged as described later in this Section.

Maintenance-free battery - testing

4 In cases where a `sealed for life' maintenance-free battery is fitted, topping-up and testing of the electrolyte in each cell is not possible. The condition of the battery can therefore only be tested using a battery condition indicator or a voltmeter.
5 Certain models may be fitted with a maintenance-free battery, with a built-in charge condition indicator. The indicator is located in the top of the battery casing, and indicates the condition of the battery from its colour. If the indicator shows green, then the

battery is in a good state of charge. If the indicator turns darker, eventually to black, then the battery requires charging, as described later in this Section. If the indicator shows clear/yellow, then the electrolyte level in the battery is too low to allow further use, and the battery should be renewed. **Do not** attempt to charge, load or jump start a battery when the indicator shows clear/yellow.
6 If testing the battery using a voltmeter, connect the voltmeter across the battery and compare the result with those given in the *Specifications* under `charge condition'. The test is only accurate if the battery has not been subjected to any kind of charge for the previous six hours. If this is not the case, switch on the headlights for 30 seconds, then wait four to five minutes before testing the battery after switching off the headlights. All other electrical circuits must be switched off, so check that the doors and tailgate are fully shut when making the test.
7 If the voltage reading is less than 12.2 volts, then the battery is discharged, whilst a reading of 12.2 to 12.4 volts indicates a partially discharged condition.
8 If the battery is to be charged, remove it from the vehicle and charge it as described later in this Section.

Standard and low maintenance battery - charging

Note: *The following is intended as a guide only. Always refer to the manufacturer's recommendations (often printed on a label attached to the battery) before charging a battery.*
9 Charge the battery at a rate equivalent to 10% of the battery capacity (eg for a 45 Ah battery charge at 4.5 A) and continue to charge the battery at this rate until no further rise in specific gravity is noted over a four hour period.
10 Alternatively, a trickle charger charging at the rate of 1.5 amps can be used overnight.
11 Specially rapid `boost' charges which are claimed to restore the power of the battery in 1 to 2 hours are not recommended, as they can cause serious damage to the battery plates through overheating.
12 While charging the battery, note that the temperature of the electrolyte should never exceed 37.8°C (100°F).

Maintenance-free battery - charging

Note: *The following is intended as a guide only. Always refer to the manufacturer's recommendations (often printed on a label attached to the battery) before charging a battery.*
13 This battery type takes considerably longer to fully recharge than the standard type, the time taken being dependent on the extent of discharge, but it can take anything up to three days.
14 A constant voltage type charger is required, to be set to 13.9 to 14.9 volts with a

5.4a Location of the brush holder/voltage regulator module

5.4b Lifting the brush holder/voltage regulator module away from the alternator

5.5 Measure the free length of the brush contacts

5.6 Inspect the surfaces of the slip rings (arrowed), at the end of the alternator shaft

screws, then prise open the clips and lift the plastic cover from the rear of the alternator.

4 Slacken and withdraw the brush holder/voltage regulator module screws, then lift the module away from the alternator **(see illustrations)**.

5 Measure the free length of the brush contacts - take the measurement from the manufacturers emblem etched on the side of the brush contact, to the shallowest part of the curved end face of the brush. Check the measurement with the *Specifications*; renew the module if the brushes are worn below the minimum limit **(see illustration)**.

6 Inspect the surfaces of the slip rings, at the end of the alternator shaft **(see illustration)**. If they appear excessively worn, burnt or pitted, then renewal must be considered; refer to an automobile electrical system specialist for further guidance.

7 Reassemble the alternator by following the dismantling procedure in reverse. Refit the alternator as described in Section 6.

6 Alternator – removal and refitting

Removal

1 Disconnect the battery negative lead.

2 Release the clip and pull the multi-plug from the rear of the alternator **(see illustration)**.

3 Loosen the auxiliary belt tensioner nut and lockscrew, then slacken the tensioner strut pivot bolt **(see illustrations)**. Push the alternator in towards the engine and slip the drivebelt from the alternator and crankshaft pulleys, (and G-charger pulley on G40 models) - refer to auxiliary belt tensioning procedure in Chapter 1 for greater detail.

4 Remove the adjustment link nut and washer.

5 Support the alternator then remove the pivot bolt and withdraw the unit from the engine **(see illustration)**.

Refitting

6 Refitting is a reversal of removal, but before fully tightening the pivot and tensioner nuts/bolts, tension the auxiliary drivebelt as described in Chapter 1.

6.2 Release the clip and pull the multi-plug from the rear of the alternator

charger current below 25 amps. Using this method, the battery should be usable within three hours, giving a voltage reading of 12.5 volts, but this is for a partially discharged battery and, as mentioned, full charging can take considerably longer.

15 If the battery is to be charged from a fully discharged state (condition reading less than 12.2 volts), have it recharged by your VW dealer or local automotive electrician, as the charge rate is higher and constant supervision during charging is necessary.

4 Alternator/charging system - testing in vehicle

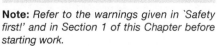

Note: *Refer to the warnings given in 'Safety first!' and in Section 1 of this Chapter before starting work.*

1 If the ignition warning light fails to illuminate when the ignition is switched on, first check the alternator wiring connections for security. If satisfactory, check that the warning light bulb has not blown, and that the bulbholder is secure in its location in the instrument panel. If the light still fails to illuminate, check the continuity of the warning light feed wire from the alternator to the bulbholder. If all is satisfactory, the alternator is at fault and should be renewed or taken to an auto-electrician for testing and repair.

2 If the ignition warning light illuminates when the engine is running, stop the engine and check that the drivebelt is correctly tensioned (see Chapter 2A or B) and that the alternator

connections are secure. If all is so far satisfactory, check the alternator brushes as described in Section 5 . If the fault persists, the alternator should be renewed, or taken to an auto-electrician for testing and repair.

3 If the alternator output is suspect even though the warning light functions correctly, the regulated voltage may be checked as follows.

4 Connect a voltmeter across the battery terminals and start the engine.

5 Increase the engine speed until the voltmeter reading remains steady; the reading should be approximately 12 to 13 volts, and no more than 14 volts.

6 Switch on as many electrical accessories (eg, the headlights, heated rear window and heater blower) as possible, and check that the alternator maintains the regulated voltage at around 13 to 14 volts.

7 If the regulated voltage is not as stated, the fault may be due to worn brushes, weak brush springs, a faulty voltage regulator, a faulty diode, a severed phase winding or worn or damaged slip rings. The brushes may be checked (see Section 5), but if the fault persists, the alternator should be renewed or taken to an auto-electrician for testing and repair.

5 Alternator - brush holder/regulator module renewal

1 Remove the alternator (see Section 6).

2 Place the alternator on a clean work surface, with the pulley facing down.

3 Where applicable, remove the retaining

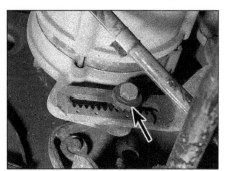

6.3a Auxiliary belt tensioner nut and lockscrew (arrowed)

6.3b Loosening the tensioner strut pivot bolt

6.5 Removing the alternator upper pivot bolt

7 Starting system - testing

Note: *Refer to the precautions given in 'Safety first!' and in Section 1 of this Chapter before starting work. Take great care to avoid causing short circuits by accidentally touching the bodywork or other components with 'live' wiring.*

1 If the starter motor fails to operate when the key is turned to the correct position, the following possible causes may be to blame.

a) *The battery is faulty.*
b) *The electrical connections between the switch, solenoid, battery and starter motor are somewhere failing to pass the necessary current from the battery through the starter to earth.*
c) *The solenoid is faulty.*
d) *The starter motor is mechanically or electrically defective.*

2 To check the battery, switch on the headlights. If they dim after a few seconds, this indicates that the battery is discharged - recharge (see Section 3) or renew the battery. If the headlights glow brightly, operate the ignition switch and observe the lights. If they dim, then this indicates that current is reaching the starter motor, therefore the fault must lie in the starter motor. If the lights continue to glow brightly (and no clicking sound can be heard from the starter motor solenoid), this indicates that there is a fault in the circuit or solenoid - see following paragraphs. If the starter motor turns slowly when operated, but the battery is in good condition, then this indicates that either the starter motor is faulty, or there is considerable resistance somewhere in the circuit.

3 If a fault in the circuit is suspected, disconnect the battery leads (including the earth connection to the body), the starter/solenoid wiring and the engine/transmission earth strap. Thoroughly clean the connections, and reconnect the leads and wiring, then use a voltmeter or test lamp to check that full battery voltage is available at the battery positive lead connection to the solenoid, and that the earth is sound. Smear petroleum jelly around the battery terminals to prevent corrosion -

corroded connections are amongst the most frequent causes of electrical system faults.

4 If the battery and all connections are in good condition, check the circuit by disconnecting the wire from the solenoid blade terminal. Connect a voltmeter or test lamp between the wire end and a good earth (such as the battery negative terminal), and check that the wire is live when the ignition switch is turned to the 'start' position. If it is, then the circuit is sound - if not the circuit wiring can be checked as described in Chapter 12.

5 The solenoid contacts can be checked by connecting a voltmeter or test lamp between the battery positive feed connection on the starter side of the solenoid, and earth. With the ignition switch turned to the 'start' position, there should be a reading or lighted bulb, as applicable. If not, the solenoid is faulty and should be renewed.

6 If the circuit and solenoid are proved sound, the fault must lie in the starter motor - remove it (see Section 9), and have the brushes and motor windings checked by an automotive electrical specialist. Check on the availability and cost of spares before considering having the starter motor overhauled, as it may prove more economical to obtain a new or exchange motor.

8 Starter motor testing - general information

If the starter motor is suspect, it should be removed and taken to an auto-electrician for assessment. In the majority of cases, new starter motor brushes can be fitted at a reasonable cost. However, check the cost of repairs first as it may prove more economical to purchase a new or exchange motor.

9 Starter motor – removal and refitting

Removal

1 To improve access, remove the air cleaner with reference to Chapter 4A or B as applicable.

2 Disconnect the battery negative lead.
3 Identify the wiring for position then disconnect it from the solenoid.
4 Jack up the front of the car and support it on axle stands (see "*Jacking and vehicle support*"). Apply the handbrake.
5 Unscrew the bolt securing the exhaust pipe to the support strap beneath the starter.
6 Where applicable unscrew the nuts and bolts and remove the support bracket from the cylinder block.
7 Unscrew and remove the retaining bolts, then unbolt the exhaust bracket and withdraw the starter motor **(see illustrations)**.

Refitting

8 Refitting is a reversal of removal, but tighten the bolts to the specified torque. Where a support bracket is fitted, do not fully tighten the nuts and bolts until the bracket is correctly located and free of any tension.

9.7a Starter motor retaining bolts, showing exhaust bracket location

9.7b Removing the starter motor

Chapter 5 Part B:
Ignition systems

Contents

Degrees of difficulty

Easy, suitable for novice with little experience	**Fairly easy,** suitable for beginner with some experience	**Fairly difficult,** suitable for competent DIY mechanic 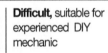	**Difficult,** suitable for experienced DIY mechanic	**Very difficult,** suitable for expert DIY or professional

Specifications

General
Type:
Engine codes AAU, AAV	Bosch Mono-Motronic
Engine codes 3F, PY	Digifant

Ignition coil
Primary winding resistance	0.5 - 1.2 Ω
Secondary resistance	3000 - 4000 Ω

Distributor
Type	Breakerless, incorporating Hall sender.
Rotor arm resistance	600 - 1400 Ω
Dwell angle	Controlled by engine management system
Ignition timing:	
Basic setting	5 ± 1° BTDC
Advance	Controlled by engine management system

Sensors
Coolant sensor resistance:
At 90° C	220 - 280 Ω
At 50° C	700 - 900 Ω

Spark plugs
Refer to Chapter 1

Torque wrench settings	Nm	lbf ft
Spark plugs:		
Engine code AAU, AAV, 3F	20	15
Engine code PY	25	18
Knock sensor bolt	20	15
Distributor clamp bolt	10	7

1 General description

1 The Bosch Mono-Motronic and Digifant systems are self-contained engine management systems, which control both the fuel injection and ignition. This Chapter deals with the ignition system components only - refer to Chapter 4A or B for details of the fuel injection system components.

2 The ignition system comprises four spark plugs, five HT leads, the distributor, an electronic ignition coil, and an Electronic Control Unit (ECU) together with its associated sensors, actuators and wiring. The component layout varies from system to system but the basic operation is the same for all models.

3 The operation is as follows: the ECU supplies a voltage to the input stage of the ignition coil which causes the primary windings in the coil to be energised. As the engine rotates, the ECU is triggered to interrupt the coil primary supply voltage by the distributor-mounted Hall sender. This results in the collapse of a primary magnetic field, which then induces a much larger voltage in the secondary coil, called the HT voltage. This voltage is directed by the distributor, rotor arm and HT leads, to the spark plug in the cylinder on its ignition stroke. The spark plug electrodes form a gap small enough for the HT voltage to arc across, and the resulting spark ignites the fuel/air mixture in the cylinder. The timing of this sequence of events is critical and is regulated solely by the ECU. The basic ignition setting can be adjusted by turning the distributor body on its mountings - refer to Section 5 for greater detail.

4 The ECU calculates and controls the ignition timing and dwell angle primarily according to engine speed, crankshaft position and inlet air volume flow rate information, received from sensors mounted on and around the engine. Other parameters that affect ignition timing are throttle position and rate of opening, inlet air temperature, coolant temperature and on certain systems, engine knock. Again, these are monitored via sensors mounted on the engine.

5 On systems where knock control is employed, the knock sensor is mounted on the cylinder block - this has the ability to detect engine pre-ignition (or 'pinking') before performance is affected or engine damage is caused. If pre-ignition occurs, the ECU retards the ignition timing of the cylinder that is pre-igniting in steps until the pre-ignition ceases. The ECU then advances the ignition timing of that cylinder in steps until it is restored to normal, or until pre-ignition occurs again.

6 Idle speed control is achieved partly by an electronic throttle valve positioning module (or auxiliary air valve, depending on system type -

see Chapter 4A or B for details) and partly by the ignition system, which gives fine control of the idle speed by altering the ignition timing.

7 On certain systems, the ECU has the ability to perform multiple ignition cycles during cold starting. During cranking, each spark plug fires several times per ignition stroke, until the engine starts. This greatly improves the engines cold starting performance.

8 It should be noted that comprehensive fault diagnosis of all the engine management systems described in this Chapter is only possible with dedicated electronic test equipment. Problems with the systems operation that cannot be pinpointed by following the basic guidelines in Section 2 should therefore be referred to a VW dealer for assessment. Once the fault has been identified, the removal/refitting sequences detailed in the following Sections will then allow the appropriate component(s) to renewed as required.

Note: *Throughout this Chapter, vehicles are frequently referred to by their engine code, rather than by engine capacity - refer to Chapter 2A for engine code listings.*

2 Ignition system - testing

Warning: Extreme care must be taken when working on the system with the ignition switched on; it is possible to get a substantial electric shock from a vehicle's ignition system. Persons with cardiac pacemaker devices should keep well clear of the ignition circuits, components and test equipment. Always switch off the ignition before disconnecting or connecting any component and when using a multi-meter to check resistances.

General information

1 Comprehensive fault diagnosis of all the engine management systems described in this Chapter is only possible with dedicated electronic test equipment. Problems with the systems operation that cannot be pinpointed by following the basic guidelines described in this Section should therefore be referred to a VW dealer for assessment. Once the fault has been identified, the removal/refitting sequences detailed in the following Sections will then allow the appropriate component(s) to renewed as required.

2 Most ignition system faults are likely to be due to loose or dirty connections or to 'tracking' (unintentional earthing) of HT voltage due to dirt, dampness or damaged insulation, rather than by the failure of any of the system's components. Always check all wiring thoroughly before condemning an electrical component and work methodically to eliminate all other possibilities before deciding that a particular component is faulty.

3 The old practice of checking for a spark by

holding the live end of an HT lead a short distance away from the engine is not recommended. Similarly, no attempt should be made to 'diagnose' misfires by pulling off one HT lead at a time. Not only is there a high risk of an electric shock, but the HT coil and/or exhaust catalyst could easily be damaged.

4 Problems with the systems operation that cannot be pinpointed by using the guidelines in the following paragraphs should be referred to a VW dealer for assessment.

Engine will not start

5 If the engine either will not turn over at all, or only turns very slowly, check the battery and starter motor . Connect a voltmeter across the battery terminals (meter positive probe to battery positive terminal), disconnect Hall sender multiway connector from the distributor, then note the voltage reading obtained while turning over the engine on the starter for (no more than) ten seconds. If the reading obtained is less than approximately 9.5 volts, first check the battery, starter motor and charging systems (see Chapter 5A).

6 If the engine turns over at normal speed but will not start, check the HT circuit by connecting a timing light (following the manufacturer's instructions) and turning the engine over on the starter motor; if the light flashes, voltage is reaching the spark plugs, so these should be checked first. If the light does not flash, check the HT leads themselves followed by the distributor cap, carbon brush and rotor arm using the information given in Chapter 1.

7 If there is a spark, check the fuel system for faults referring to the relevant part of Chapter 4 for further information.

8 If there is still no spark, then the problem must lie within the engine management system. In these cases, the vehicle should be referred to a VW dealer for assessment.

Engine misfires

9 An irregular misfire suggests either a loose connection or intermittent fault on the primary circuit, or an HT fault on the coil side of the rotor arm.

10 With the ignition switched off, check carefully through the system ensuring that all connections are clean and securely fastened.

11 Check that the HT coil, the distributor cap and the HT leads are clean and dry. Check the leads themselves and the spark plugs (by substitution, if necessary), then check the distributor cap, carbon brush and rotor arm as described in Chapter 1.

12 Regular misfiring is almost certainly due to a fault in the distributor cap, HT leads or spark plugs. Use a timing light (paragraph 4 above) to check whether HT voltage is present at all leads.

13 If HT voltage is not present on one particular lead, the fault will be in that lead or in the distributor cap. If HT is present on all leads, the fault will be in the spark plugs;

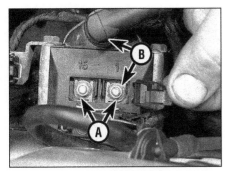

3.3 Ignition coil primary and secondary winding terminals
A Primary winding terminals
B Secondary winding terminals

check and renew them if there is any doubt about their condition.
14 If no HT voltage is present, check the ignition coil; its secondary windings may be breaking down under load.

3 Ignition coil -
testing, removal and refitting

Testing

1 The resistance of the coil windings may be tested without removing the unit from the engine bay. Note that the measurements taken will be affected by ambient temperature, so it is good idea to conduct this test after the engine has been running for a while, as the coil will then be at its normal operating temperature.
2 Disconnect the battery negative cable and position it away from the terminal.
3 Connect the probes of a multimeter set to the resistance measurement function across the primary winding terminals (1 and 15) **(see illustration)**. Record the resistance indicated. **Note:** *On G40 models with a cylindrical ignition coil, the primary resistance is measured between the '+' and '-' terminals.*
4 Repeat the measurement at the secondary winding terminals (4 and 15) **(refer to illustration 3.3)**. **Note:** *On G40 models with a cylindrical ignition coil, the secondary*

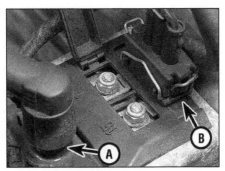

3.8 Ignition coil connectors
A HT cable connector
B LT cable multiway connector

resistance is measured between the HT lead terminal and '-' terminal.
5 Compare the measurements with the *Specifications* and renew the coil if necessary.
Note: *This test pinpoints short or open circuits within the ignition coil, but does not allow diagnosis of failures that occur whilst the coil is under load. Under these circumstances, the coil should be tested by an automotive electrical specialist.*

Removal

6 On all models, the ignition coil is mounted at the front left hand corner of the engine bay.
7 Disconnect the battery negative cable and position it away from the terminal.
8 Unplug the HT lead from the ignition coil at the connector **(see illustration)**.

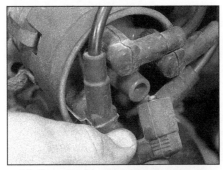

4.3 If required, unplug all five HT leads from the distributor cap

4.5 Disconnect the Hall sender cable from the distributor at the multiway connector (arrowed)

9 Disconnect the LT cable from the ignition coil at the multiway connector **(refer to illustration 3.8)**.
10 Slacken and withdraw the mounting screws, remove the brackets and detach the earthing strap (where applicable). Remove the ignition coil from the engine bay.

Refitting

11 Refitting is a reversal of removal.

4 Distributor - removal, inspection and refitting

Removal

1 Disconnect the battery negative cable and position it away from the terminal.
2 Set the engine to TDC on cylinder No 1, referring to of Chapter 2A for guidance.
3 If required, unplug all five HT leads from the distributor cap - label them to aid refitting later **(see illustration)**.
4 Unplug the screening cap earth strap from the distributor body **(see illustration)**.
5 Unplug the Hall sensor cable from the distributor body at the connector **(see illustration)**.
6 Remove the screws or prise off the retaining clips (as applicable), then lift off the distributor cap. Check at this point that the centre of the rotor arm electrode is aligned with the cylinder No 1 marking on the distributor body **(see illustrations)**.

4.4 Unplug the screening cap earth strap from the distributor body

4.6b ... then lift off the distributor cap

4.6a Prise off the retaining clips ...

4.7a Carefully prise off the rotor arm . . .

4.7b . . . then lift off the moisture shield

4.8a Slacken and remove
the clamp bolts . . .

7 Carefully prise off the rotor arm, then lift off the moisture shield **(see illustrations)**.
8 Mark the relationship between the distributor body and the drive gear case flange by scribing arrows on each. Slacken and remove the clamp bolts, then withdraw the distributor body from the cylinder head. Recover the seals, shims and washers (where applicable), noting their order of fitment to ensure correct reassembly later **(see illustrations)**.

Inspection

9 Recover the O-ring seal from the bottom of the distributor and inspect them. Renew them if they appear at all worn or damaged.
10 Inspect the teeth of the distributor drive gear for signs of wear or damage. Any slack in the distributor drive train will affect ignition timing. Renew the distributor if the teeth of the drive gear appear worn or chipped.

Refitting

11 Before progressing, check that the engine is still set to TDC on cylinder No 1 - refer to Chapter 2A for guidance.
12 Install the distributor and loosely fit the clamp bolt; it may be necessary to rotate the shaft slightly to allow it to engage with the camshaft drive gear. Rotate the distributor body such that the alignment marks made during removal line up.
13 The shaft is engaged at the correct angle when the rotor arm electrode is pointing at the No 1 cylinder mark on the distributor body (taking into account the offset for the basic ignition timing setting).
14 Refit the distributor cap, pressing the retaining clips firmly into place/ tightening the retaining screws (as applicable).
15 Reconnect the Hall sensor cabling to the distributor.
16 Where applicable, refit the screening cap, tightening the screws securely.
17 Working from the No 1 terminal, connect the HT leads between the spark plugs and the distributor cap. Note that the firing order is 1-3-4-2.
18 Fit the HT king lead between the coil and the centre terminal on the distributor cap.
19 It will now be necessary to have the ignition timing checked and if necessary adjusted - refer to the notes in Section 5.

4.8b . . . then withdraw the distributor
body from the cylinder head . . .

5 Ignition timing - adjustment

Note: *The engine should be at normal operating temperature to ensure correct results*
Note: *Accurate checking and setting of the ignition timing is only possible using a special instrument connected to the flywheel TDC sender unit through the aperture in the top of the gearbox bellhousing. This will not normally be available to the home mechanic, so a method using a stroboscopic timing light is described below. It should be noted that this only provides an approximate setting - it is recommended that the vehicle be checked by a VW dealer at the earliest opportunity.*
1 Disable the engine by unplugging the multiway Hall sender connector from the distributor.
2 Using a spanner or socket and wrench on the crankshaft pulley, turn the engine manually until the crankshaft pulley timing mark (a notch cut into the edge of the pulley) becomes visible. Clean the edge of the pulley, then highlight the timing mark with chalk or a dab of white paint. On G40 models, there are two marks: the timing mark has a 'Z' stamped next to it on the crankshaft pulley (the TDC mark is indicated by an 'O').
3 Reconnect the distributor multiway plug, then connect the stroboscopic timing light to the engine in accordance with the manufacturer's instructions, so that it is triggering from the No 1 cylinder HT lead.

4.8c Recover the seals

4 Start the engine and run it at idling speed. Direct the beam from the timing light at the pointer protruding from the timing belt cover. The stroboscopic effect should 'freeze' the motion of the crankshaft pulley and the highlighted timing mark. If the mark appears to be moving back and forth, this may be due erratic idling - check that all of the cars electrical accessories are switched off and that the auxiliary cooling fan is not running. The engine should be at normal operating temperature, but the idle speed may be become unstable if it is particularly hot day and the engine has been idling for some time.
5 The highlighted timing mark should appear to be stationary and aligned with the pointer on the timing belt cover **(see illustrations)**. If they are not aligned, the basic ignition setting requires adjustment.
6 To adjust the basic ignition timing setting, first switch off the engine, to avoid the risk of a getting a shock from the HT voltage. Refer

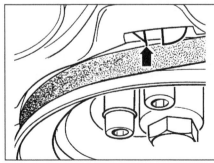

5.5a Ignition timing marks -
all models except G40

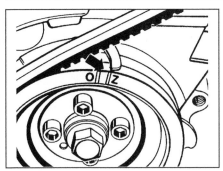

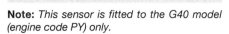

5.5b Ignition timing marks - G40 models

to Section 4 and slacken the distributor retaining bolts. **Note:** *Mark the relationship between the distributor body and the cylinder head with a dab of paint, before adjustment is attempted. This gives a reference point that can be reverted to if the timing setting is lost.*
7 Turn the distributor *by a small amount* clockwise to advance (or anti-clockwise to retard) the ignition timing. Tighten the bolts lightly and repeat the timing light test.

Continue until the timing setting is correct, then tighten the distributor bolts to the specified torque.

6 Knock sensor - removal and refitting

Note: *This sensor is fitted to the G40 model (engine code PY) only.*

Removal

1 The knock sensor is located on the rear of the cylinder block, below the inlet manifold.
2 Ensure the ignition is off, then unplug the wiring from the sensor at the connector.
3 Slacken and withdraw the mounting bolt and lift off the sensor.

Refitting

4 Refitting is a reversal of removal, but note that the sensor's operation will be affected if its mounting bolt is not tightened to the correct torque.

7 Rotor arm - renewal

Removal

1 With reference to Section 4, remove the distributor cap and its screening shield (where applicable).
2 Pull the rotor arm from the end of the distributor shaft **(refer to illustration 4.7a)**.
3 Inspect the distributor shaft contacts and clean them if necessary, using contact cleaning solution - do not use abrasive paper or a wire brush as this will accelerate contact wear.

Refitting

4 Refitting is a reversal of removal - ensure that the rotor arm alignment lug engages with the recess in the distributor shaft, before refitting the distributor cap.

Notes

Chapter 6
Clutch

Contents

Degrees of difficulty

Easy, suitable for novice with little experience	**Fairly easy,** suitable for beginner with some experience	**Fairly difficult,** suitable for competent DIY mechanic 	**Difficult,** suitable for experienced DIY mechanic	**Very difficult,** suitable for expert DIY or professional

Specifications

General

Type	Single dry plate, diaphragm spring with spring-loaded hub
Operation	Cable with automatic adjustment mechanism
Diameter:	
All models except G40	190 mm
G40 models	200 mm
Pressure plate distortion (maximum)	0.2 mm
Pressure plate spring finger wear (depth, maximum)	0.3 mm
Driven plate runout (maximum)	0.8 mm (measured 2.5 mm from outer edge)

Torque wrench settings

	Nm	lbf ft
Pressure plate to flywheel bolts:		
4 speed transmission	25	18
5 speed transmission	20	15

1 General information

All vehicles are fitted with a cable-operated, single dry plate clutch system. The layout of the clutch components is conventional; the flywheel is bolted to a flange on the crankshaft, the pressure plate bolted to the flywheel with the driven plate sandwiched between the two. The release bearing slides on a guide sleeve, over the transmission input shaft.

When the clutch pedal is depressed, effort is transmitted to the clutch release lever and shaft by means of a self-adjusting cable. The release shaft rotates against a return spring and pushes the release bearing into contact with the centre of the pressure plate diaphragm spring. This action causes the friction surface of the pressure plate to withdraw from the flywheel, releasing the driven plate and disconnecting the drive to the transmission input shaft.

Removal of the clutch driven plate, pressure plate and release bearing can be carried out after removing the transmission, leaving the engine in situ.

2 Clutch cable - renewal

Removal

1 The clutch cable self-adjusting mechanism is located within the cable and automatically adjusts the free play to cater for cable stretch and wear of the clutch friction linings.

2.3 Disconnect the clutch cable end fitting from the release lever (arrowed)

2 To remove the cable, first fully depress the clutch pedal several times.

3 Pull the release arm on the transmission away from the cable in order to compress the adjustment mechanism, then hold the end fitting and disconnect it from the release lever **(see illustration)**.

4 Prise the rubber grommet from the bracket on the transmission, then disconnect the cable from the pedal and withdraw it from the steering gear housing **(see illustration)**.

2.4 Pulling the clutch cable through the hole in the steering gear

Refitting

5 Refitting is a reversal of removal, but note the following points:

a) *Make sure the flats on the cable are located correctly on the steering gear housing.*

b) *Grease the cable attachment point on the pedal, but do not grease the cable before fitting it to the steering gear housing, as there is a danger of grease blocking the breather vent.*

c) *Check that the clutch operates correctly: depress the pedal several times, then pull the release lever approximately 10 mm away from the cable to check that it is free.*

3 Clutch pedal - removal and refitting

Removal

1 Disconnect the clutch cable from the release arm on the transmission clutch housing and from the top of the clutch pedal with reference to Section 3.

2 Prise the clip from the end of the pedal pivot shaft.

3 On left-hand drive models, withdraw the pivot shaft just enough to allow the clutch pedal to be removed from the bracket. On right-hand drive models, the pivot shaft must first be withdrawn through the brake pedal.

4 Clean the pedal and pivot shaft and examine them for wear. If the bushes are worn they can be removed using a soft metal drift, and the new bushes installed using a vice to press then into position. Check the rubber foot pad and the stop rubber on the bracket, and renew them if necessary.

Refitting

5 Refitting is a reversal of removal, but apply a little multi-purpose grease to the pivot shaft and bushes.

4 Clutch components - removal, inspection and refitting

Removal

1 Remove the transmission as described in Chapter 7.

2 Mark the position of the pressure plate cover with respect to the flywheel, to ensure correct alignment on refitting.

3 Using an Allen key or hex bit, unscrew the pressure plate bolts progressively in a diagonal sequence (see illustration). If necessary, prevent the flywheel from rotating by inserting a screwdriver between the starter ring gear teeth and the cylinder block.

4 Withdraw the pressure plate assembly and the driven plate from the flywheel. Note that one side of the pressure plate hub houses the torsional damping springs and protrudes by a greater amount - this side faces the pressure plate.

5 Check the condition of the clutch components as described in the following sub-Section.

Inspection

6 Examine the surfaces of the pressure plate and flywheel for signs of heavy scoring. Light scoring is normal, but if excessive the pressure plate must be renewed and the flywheel either machined or renewed.

7 Inspect the ends of the pressure plate diaphragm spring fingers; look for wear caused by contact with the release bearing. If the scoring appears excessive, renew the assembly.

8 Using a straight edge and feeler blade, check that the inward taper of the pressure plate does not exceed the maximum amount given in the *Specifications* (see illustration). Also check for loose riveted joints and for any cracks in the pressure plate components.

9 Check the driven plate linings for wear; renew the plate if the linings are worn to within 1.0 mm (0.04in) of the lining material securing rivets.

10 Check that the driven plate damper springs and all rivets are secure, and that the linings are not contaminated with oil. Temporarily fit the disc to the transmission input shaft and check that the run-out does not exceed that given in the *Specifications*.

11 If the clutch components are contaminated with oil, the leak should be found and rectified. The procedure for renewing the crankshaft oil seal is described in Chapter 2A; the procedure for renewing the transmission input shaft oil seal is described in Chapter 7.

12 Having checked the clutch disc and pressure plate, check the release bearing with reference to Section 7.

Refitting

13 Before commencing the refitting procedure, a tool must be obtained for aligning the driven plate, otherwise difficulty will be experienced when refitting the transmission. If the driven plate is not aligned centrally before the pressure plate is fitted, it will not be possible to engage the transmission input shaft with it. If a centralising tool is not available, a wooden mandrel may be made to the dimensions shown (see illustration).

14 Clean the friction faces of the flywheel and pressure plate, then fit the centralising tool to the crankshaft and locate the driven plate on it with the hub extension facing outwards (see illustration).

15 Fit the pressure plate assembly to the flywheel (using the alignment marks made during removal, if the original component is being refitted). Ensure that the friction surface lies flat against the driven plate, then insert the retaining bolts and tighten them progressively in diagonal sequence to the specified torque (see illustration).

16 Refit the transmission as described in Chapter 7, then reconnect the clutch cable as described in Section 2.

4.3 Removing the pressure plate bolts

4.8 Checking the clutch pressure plate for taper

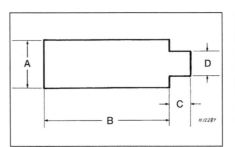

4.13 Clutch driven plate centralising tool dimensions
A 18.24 mm   B 70.0 mm
C 20.0 mm   D 14.81 mm

4.14 Driven plate fitted with centralising tool in place

4.15 Fitting the pressure plate assembly

5 Release bearing and shaft - removal, inspection and refitting

Four speed transmission

Removal

1 With the transmission removed, unhook the return spring from the release arm **(see illustration)**.

2 Turn the release arm to move the release bearing up the guide sleeve, then disengage the two spring clips from the release fork and withdraw the bearing **(see illustration)**.

3 Note how the springs and clips are fitted **(see illustration)**, then prise the clips from the release bearing.

4 Using a splined socket, unbolt and remove the guide sleeve from the clutch housing.

5 Using a narrow drift, drive the release shaft outer bush from the clutch housing. Alternatively prise out the bush.

6 Pull the release shaft from the inner bearing then withdraw the shaft and arm from the housing.

Inspection

7 Spin the release bearing by hand and check it for roughness, then attempt to move the outer race laterally against the inner race. If any excessive roughness or wear is evident, renew the bearing. Do not wash the bearing in solvent if it is to be re-used.

8 Check the bushes and bearing surfaces of the release shaft for wear and also check the guide sleeve for scoring. The inner bush may be removed using a soft metal drift and the new bush driven in until flush.

Refitting

9 Refitting is a reversal of removal, but lubricate all bearing surfaces with a little high-melting-point grease. Make sure that the release shaft outer bush is correctly sealed with the tab located in the cut-out in the clutch housing **(see illustration)**.

5.1 Clutch release arm return spring

5.2 Release bearing in place on the release shaft arms (four speed transmission)

5.3 Release bearing showing retaining clips (arrowed)

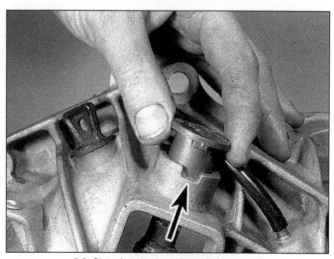

5.9 Showing the location tab (arrowed) on the release shaft outer bush

Five-speed transmission

Removal

10 Remove the transmission as described in Chapter 7. Removal and checking procedures for the release bearing are the same as for the four-speed transmission, as described in the previous sub-Section.

11 Extract the circlips securing the release lever to the release shaft, then withdraw the shaft from its bushes and the release lever **(see illustration)**. Note that there is a master spline on the shaft and lever allowing fitment in only one position.

Inspection

12 Check the bushes and bearing surfaces of the shaft for wear, and also check the release bearing guide sleeve for scoring. The bushes may be removed using a drift, and new bushes fitted in a similar fashion. Fit the bushes so that the oil seal will be flush with the housing when in position.

Refitting

13 Refitting is a reversal of removal, but lubricate all bearing surfaces with a high-melting-point grease.

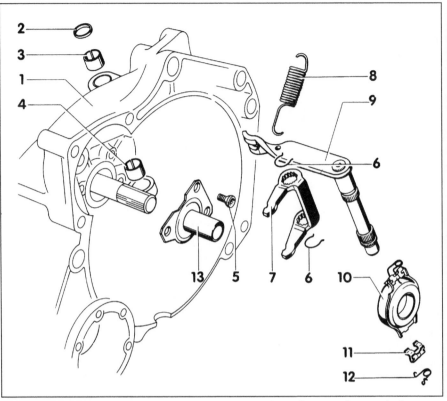

5.11 Exploded view of the clutch release mechanism - five speed transmission

1 Clutch housing	5 Guide sleeve	8 Spring	12 Spring clip
2 Seal	retaining screw	9 Release shaft	13 Guide sleeve
3 Bush	6 Circlip	10 Release bearing	
4 Bush	7 Release lever	11 Retaining clip	

Chapter 7
Manual transmission

Contents

Degrees of difficulty

Easy, suitable for novice with little experience	Fairly easy, suitable for beginner with some experience	Fairly difficult, suitable for competent DIY mechanic	Difficult, suitable for experienced DIY mechanic	Very difficult, suitable for expert DIY or professional

Specifications

General

Type	Transverse mounted, front wheel drive layout with integral transaxle differential/final drive. 4 or 5 forward speeds,1 reverse speed
Oil capacity:	
4 speed transmission	2.2 litres
5 speed transmission	3.1 litres
Oil type/specification	See end of "Weekly checks"

Transmission codes

4 speed:	
Engine code AAU (1.05 litre, 33 kW)	AKV, AKY, CEL, CEN
Engine code AAV (1.3 litre, 40 kW)	AKY, CEL
5 Speed:	
Engine code AAU (1.05 litre, 33kW)	AHZ, AYZ, CEE, CEM
Engine code AAV (1.3 litre, 40 kW)	CEG, 8P
Engine code 3F (1.3 litre, 55 kW)	AHD, CEH
Engine code PY (1.3 litre, 83 kW)	CEK, ATV

Torque wrench settings

	Nm	lbf ft
Transmission to engine:		
5 speed transmission	55	41
4 speed transmission	80	59
Gearshift lever lower housing nuts	15	11
Drive flange centre bolts	25	18
Selector rod clamp nut	20	15
Bearing cover	20	15
Filler and drain plugs	25	18

1 General information

Description

1 The manual transmission is mounted transversely in the engine bay, bolted directly to the engine. This layout has the advantage of providing the shortest possible drive path to the front wheels, as well as locating the transmission in the airflow through engine bay, optimising cooling. The unit is cased in aluminium alloy.

2 Drive from the crankshaft is transmitted via the clutch to the transmission input shaft, which is splined to accept the clutch driven plate.
3 All forward gears are fitted with syncromeshes. When a gear is selected, the movement of the cabin floor-mounted gear lever is communicated to the transmission by a selector rod. This in turn actuates a series of selector forks inside the transmission which are slotted onto the synchromesh sleeves. The sleeves, which are locked to the transmission shafts but can slide axially by means of splined hubs, press baulk rings into contact with the respective gear/pinion. The coned surfaces between the baulk rings and the pinion/gear act as a friction clutch, that progressively matches the speed of the synchromesh sleeve (and hence the transmission shaft) with that of the gear/pinion. The dog teeth on the outside of the baulk ring prevent the synchromesh sleeve ring from meshing with the gear/pinion until their speeds are exactly matched; this allows gear changes to be carried out smoothly and greatly reduces the noise and mechanical wear caused by rapid gear changes.
4 Drive is transmitted to the differential crownwheel, which rotates the differential

case and planetary gears, thus driving the sun gears and driveshafts. The rotation of the planetary gears on their shaft allows the inner roadwheel to rotate at a slower speed than the outer roadwheel during cornering.

5 Transmission fluid drain and filler plugs are provided, and a magnetic swarf collector is located in the bottom of the transmission casing.

6 When overhauling the transmission, due consideration should be given to the costs involved, since it is often more economical to obtain a service exchange or good secondhand transmission rather than fit new parts to the existing transmission.

7 This Chapter covers the 084 4-speed and 085 5-speed transmissions.

Manual transmission overhaul - general information

8 The overhaul of a manual transmission is a complex (and often expensive) engineering task for the DIY home mechanic to undertake, which requires access to specialist equipment. It involves the dismantling and reassembly of many small components, the precise measurement of clearances and if necessary, adjustment by the selection shims and spacers. Internal transmission components are also often difficult to obtain and in many instances, extremely expensive. Because of this, if the transmission develops a fault or becomes noisy, the best course of action is to have the unit overhauled by a specialist repairer or to obtain an exchange, reconditioned unit.

9 Nevertheless, it is not impossible for the more experienced mechanic to overhaul the transmission if the special tools are available and the job is carried out in a deliberate step-by-step manner, to ensure that nothing is overlooked.

10 The tools necessary for an overhaul include internal and external circlip pliers, bearing pullers, a slide hammer, a set of pin punches, a dial test indicator and possibly a hydraulic press. In addition, a large, sturdy workbench and a vice will be required.

11 During dismantling of the transmission, make careful notes of how each component is fitted to make reassembly easier and accurate.

12 Before dismantling the transmission, it will help if you have some idea of where the problem lies. Certain problems can be closely related to specific areas in the transmission which can make component examination and renewal easier. Refer to *"Fault finding"* at the end of this manual for more information.

2 Transmission – removal and refitting

Note: *The following paragraphs describe how to remove the transmission leaving the engine in situ. However, if work is necessary on the engine as well, the engine and transmission can be removed as one unit then separated on the bench as described in Chapter 2B.*

Removal

1 The engine must be supported before the transmission can be removed and it is recommended that a hoist or lifting beam is used. As the transmission is removed from underneath the engine bay, first jack up the front of the car and support it securely on axle stands (see *"Jacking and vehicle support"*), then apply the handbrake. Take the weight of the engine with the hoist or lifting beam.

2 Remove the air cleaner/throttle body ducting as described in Chapter 4A or B as applicable.

3 Disconnect the battery negative cable and position it away from the terminal.

4 Remove the windscreen washer bottle (see Chapter 12) and place it to one side.

5 Disconnect the clutch cable from the transmission with reference to Chapter 6.

6 Unscrew and remove the engine to transmission bolts that can be reached from the top of the transmission.

7 Remove the starter motor with reference to Chapter 5A.

8 Loosen the clip securing the support bracket to the coolant pipe at the rear of the engine, remove the upper starter bolt if necessary, and move the bracket away from the transmission **(see illustration)**.

9 Remove the left-hand front engine mounting bracket by unscrewing the nuts securing it to the transmission, removing the mounting bolt, and removing the bolt securing the earth strap.

10 Working beneath the car, unbolt and remove the cover plate from the clutch housing **(see illustration)**.

11 Disconnect the wiring from the reversing light switch **(see illustration)**

12 Disconnect the inner ends of the driveshafts from the transmission flanges with reference to Chapter 8 and tie them out of the way.

13 Refer to Chapter 12 and unscrew the collar and disconnect the speedometer cable from the transmission.

14 Unscrew and remove the remaining engine to transmission bolts noting the location of the rear mounting bracket **(see illustrations)**

15 Unscrew the rear mounting nut and remove the bracket, or leave the mounting on the bracket and remove the mounting bolts **(see illustration)**.

2.8 Coolant pipe support bracket location

2.10 Clutch housing cover plate

2.11 Reversing light switch (arrowed)

2.14a Engine rear mounting bracket

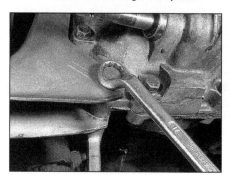

2.14b Removing the rear mounting bracket bolts

2.15 Removing the rear engine mounting and bracket

2.16a Disconnecting the shift rod coupling

4 Gearchange mechanism - removal, refitting and adjustment

Removal

1 Jack up the front of the car and support on axle stands (see "*Jacking and vehicle support*"). Apply the handbrake.
2 With neutral selected, mark the shift rod and coupling in relation to each other, then unscrew the coupling clamp and pull out the shift rod.
3 Working inside the car unscrew the gear knob and remove the gaiter.
4 Unscrew the nuts from the ball housing stop plate, and withdraw the complete gearchange mechanism upwards into the car **(see illustration)**. Recover the spacers.
5 Dismantle the mechanism as necessary and examine the components for wear and damage. Renew those showing signs of wear or deterioration. Note that the selector rod bush is in two parts, and both parts are destroyed when removing the mechanism. When fitting the new bush, ensure that the two plastic cups are not pushed apart.

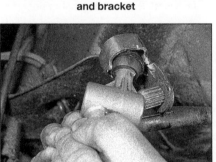

2.16b Removing the shift rod coupling

2.16c Shift rod adapter and bush

Refitting

6 Lubricate the joints and bearing surfaces with high-melting-point grease then refit using a reversal of the removal procedure. If a new coupling has been fitted it will be necessary to adjust the coupling position – this is best carried out by a VW dealer, as a specially shaped template is required, but if necessary the method described in the following sub-Section can be used in an emergency.

Adjustment

7 With the car raised and supported on axle stands (see "*Jacking and vehicle support*"), loosen the shift rod clamp bolt.
8 Have an assistant position the gear lever as shown **(see illustration)**. Use a twist drill for dimension (a), and align the lever so that the reverse gear catch is exactly opposite the recess in the housing.
9 With the transmission still in neutral, tighten the clamp bolt.
10 Check that all gears can be selected easily.

16 Remove the screw from the shift rod coupling and ease the coupling from the rod. The screw threads are coated with a liquid locking agent and if difficulty is experienced it may be necessary to heat up the coupling with a blowlamp, however take the necessary fire precautions. If required, remove the coupling ball from the adapter **(see illustrations)**.
17 Support the transmission on a trolley jack then withdraw it from the engine keeping it in a horizontal position until clear of the clutch. If necessary use a lever to free the transmission from the locating dowels.
Caution: Do not allow the transmission to tilt until it the input shaft is clear of the clutch driven plate, or damage to the plate may occur.
18 Lower the transmission and remove it from under the car.

Refitting

19 Refitting is a reversal of removal, but first smear a little molybdenum disulphide based grease on the splines of the input shaft, and make sure the engine rear plate is correctly located on the dowels. Delay fully tightening the mounting nuts and bolts until the transmission is in its normal position. Adjust the gearchange if necessary (see Section 4).

3 Drive flange oil seals - renewal

1 Jack up the front of the car, support it on axle stands (see "*Jacking and vehicle support*") and apply the handbrake.

2 Detach the inner ends of the driveshafts from the drive flanges with reference to Chapter 8 and tie the driveshafts to one side.
3 Unscrew the bolt from the centre of each drive flange using a bar and two temporarily inserted bolts to hold the flange stationary.
4 Place a container beneath the transmission then remove the drive flanges and lever out the old oil seals. Identify the flanges side for side.
5 Clean the recesses then drive in the new oil seals using a suitable length of metal tubing.
6 Smear a little grease on the lips of the oil seals, and insert the drive flanges.
7 Insert the bolts and tighten them to the specified torque using the bar and bolts to hold the flanges stationary.
8 Refit the driveshafts with reference to Chapter 8.
9 Check and if necessary top-up the transmission oil level then lower the car to the ground.

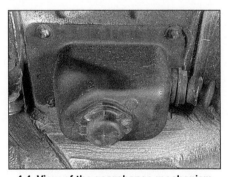

4.4 View of the gearchange mechanism housing

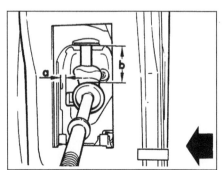

4.8 Gear lever adjustment dimensions
a 11.0 mm   b 43.0 mm

5.8a Disconnect the wiring . . .

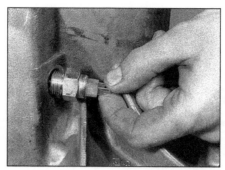

5.8b . . . and remove the reversing light switch (4 speed transmission shown)

6.2 Speedometer drive cable locknut (arrowed) at the differential casing

5 Reversing lamp switch - testing, removal and refitting

Testing

1 Ensure the ignition switch is 'OFF'.
2 Unplug the wiring harness from the reversing lamp switch at the connector. The switch is threaded into the transmission casing, at the front of the unit on 085 5 speed transmissions, and at the rear of the unit on 084 4 speed transmissions.
3 Connect the probes of a continuity tester, or multimeter set to the resistance measurement function, across the terminals of the reverse lamp switch.
4 The switch contacts are normally open, so with any gear other than reverse selected, the tester/meter should indicate an open circuit. When reverse gear is then selected, the switch contacts should close, causing the tester/meter to indicate a short circuit.

5 If the switch appears to be constantly open or short circuit, or is intermittent in its operation, it should be renewed.

Removal

6 Ensure that the ignition switch is turned to the 'OFF' position.
7 Unplug the wiring harness from the reversing lamp switch at the connector.
8 Slacken the switch body using a ring spanner and withdraw it from the transmission. Recover the sealing ring. (see illustrations).

Refitting

9 Refitting is a reversal of removal.

6 Speedometer drive - removal and refitting

Removal

1 Trace the speedometer drive cable back to the connection point on the differential

housing, at the rear of the transmission casing.
2 Unscrew the locknut and withdraw the end of the drive cable (see illustration). Where fitted, recover the washer.
3 Using a ring spanner, unscrew and withdraw the speedometer drive guide sleeve.
4 Remove the drive shaft and gear from the transmission casing.
5 Clean the gear thoroughly and examine the teeth for signs of wear or damage. Renew the component if necessary, but bear in mind that the drive pinion inside the differential casing may be worn as well and this can only be renewed as part of a complete transmission overhaul.

Refitting

6 Refitting is a reversal of removal.

Chapter 8
Driveshafts

Contents

Degrees of difficulty

Easy, suitable for novice with little experience		**Fairly easy,** suitable for beginner with some experience		**Fairly difficult,** suitable for competent DIY mechanic		**Difficult,** suitable for experienced DIY mechanic		**Very difficult,** suitable for expert DIY or professional	

Specifications

Type . . . . Solid (left) and tubular (right) driveshafts with constant velocity joints at each end

Torque wrench settings	**Nm**	**lbf ft**
Driveshaft to flange	45	33
Driveshaft nut	210	155

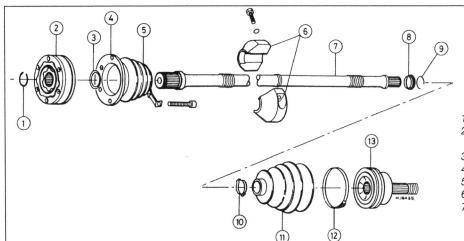

1.1 Exploded view of the right-hand driveshaft

1 Circlip
2 Inner constant velocity joint
3 Dished washer
4 Protective cap
5 Rubber gaiter
6 Balance weight
7 Shaft
8 Dished washer
9 Circlip
10 Clip
11 Rubber gaiter
12 Hose clip
13 Outer constant velocity joint

1 General information

Drive is transmitted from the differential to the front wheels by means of two driveshafts of unequal length **(see illustration)**. The right-hand driveshaft is longer than the left-hand, due to the position of the transmission. The left-hand driveshaft is of solid construction and the right-hand one is of tubular construction.

Both driveshafts are splined at their outer ends to enter the wheel hubs, and are threaded and secured with large nuts. The inner ends of the driveshafts are bolted to the transmission drive flanges.

Constant velocity (CV) ball-and-cage type joints are fitted to each end of the driveshafts to ensure that the smooth and efficient transmission of drive at all the angles possible as the roadwheels move up and down with the suspension, and as they turn from side to side under steering.

2 Driveshaft - removal and refitting

Note: *A new driveshaft retaining nut will be required on refitting.*

Removal

1 Remove the wheel trim from the relevant wheel.
2 With the handbrake applied loosen the driveshaft nut. The nut is tightened to a high torque and a socket extension may be required.
3 Jack up the front of the car and support it on axle stands (see "*Jacking and vehicle support*"). Remove the roadwheel.
4 Using a suitable splined key, unscrew and remove the bolts securing the inner CV joint to the final drive flange. Note the location of the spacer plates. Support the inner end of the driveshaft on an axle stand.
5 Remove the outer nut and washer, then turn the steering on full lock and tap the driveshaft from the splined hub using a soft head mallet. When removing the right-hand driveshaft it is advantageous to disconnect the anti-roll bar front mountings and the track control arm from the strut. Do not move the car on its wheels with either driveshaft removed otherwise damage may occur to the wheel bearings **(see illustration)**.

Refitting

6 Refitting is a reversal of removal, but first clean the hub and driveshaft splines and the mating faces of the inner CV joint and final drive flange. Smear a little molybdenum based grease on the splines. Fit a new outer nut and tighten it to the specified torque with the car lowered to the ground. Tighten the inner bolts to the specified torque. On the

2.5 The driveshaft inner joint

2.6a Fitting the driveshaft to the final drive flange

right-hand driveshaft make sure that the balance weight is located with its conical side facing the gearbox and the opposite side in the groove on the driveshaft. Where there is no groove, locate it on the point mark at the dimension shown **(see illustrations)**.

2.6b Location of the balance weight on the right-hand driveshaft

Dimension a = 151.0 mm

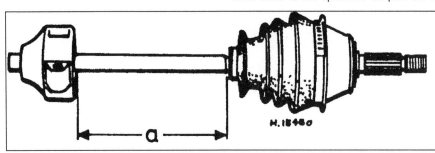

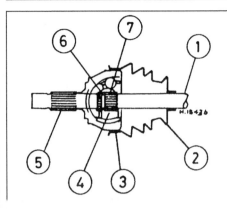

3.2 Cross-section diagram of the driveshaft outer joint

1 *Driveshaft*
2 *Rubber gaiter*
3 *Clip*
4 *Bearing race*
5 *Splined shaft*
6 *Distance washer*
7 *Dished washer*

3.4 Correct fitted position of the dished washer

3 Driveshaft rubber gaiters - renewal

Outer rubber gaiter

1 Remove the driveshaft from the car as described in Section 2 and secure it in a vice equipped with soft jaws.
2 Loosen the clips and release the large diameter end from the joint **(see illustration)**. If necessary cut the clips free.
3 Using a soft faced mallet drive the outer joint from the driveshaft.
4 Extract the circlip from the driveshaft and remove the spacer (if fitted) and dished washer noting that the concave side faces the end of the driveshaft **(see illustration)**.
5 Slide the rubber gaiter and clips from the driveshaft. Scoop out the grease from the joint.
6 Wipe clean the driveshaft then slide on the new rubber gaiter and clips.
7 Fit the dished washer and spacer (if applicable) to the driveshaft and insert the circlip in the groove.
8 Locate the outer joint on the driveshaft and using a soft faced mallet, drive it fully into position until the circlip is engaged.
9 Insert the special grease in the joint then locate the gaiter and tighten the clips.
10 Refit the driveshaft as described in Section 2.

Inner rubber gaiter

11 Remove the driveshaft from the car as described in Section 2 and secure it in a vice equipped with soft jaws.
12 Extract the retaining circlip from the inner end of the driveshaft **(see illustration)**.
13 Using a small drift drive the plastic cap from the joint housing **(see illustration)**.
14 Loosen the clips and slide the rubber gaiter away from the joint. If necessary cut the clips free.
15 Support the joint over the jaws of the vice and using a soft metal drift, drive out the driveshaft.
16 Remove the dished washer from the driveshaft noting that the concave side faces the end of the driveshaft.
17 Slide the rubber gaiter and clips from the driveshaft. Scoop out the grease from the joint.
18 Fit the new rubber gaiter and clips to the driveshaft followed by the dished washer, concave side facing the end of the driveshaft.
19 Mount the driveshaft in the vice then drive on the joint using a suitable metal tube or socket on the hub.
20 Fit the retaining circlip in its groove.
21 Insert the special grease in the joint then tap the plastic cap into position.
22 With the rubber gaiter correctly located, tighten the clips.
23 Refit the driveshaft as described in Section 2.

4 Driveshaft - checking and cleaning

Checking

1 If any of the checks described in Chapter 1 reveal wear in any driveshaft joint, first remove the roadwheel trims and check that the driveshaft retaining nuts are tight.
2 Road test the vehicle, and listen for a metallic clicking from the front as the vehicle is driven slowly in a circle on full lock. If evident, this indicates wear in the outer constant velocity joint(s). This means that the joint(s) must be renewed; reconditioning is not possible.
3 If vibration, consistent with road speed, is felt through the car when accelerating, there is a possibility of wear in the inner constant velocity joint(s).
4 The procedure for removing or renewing the joints is described in Section 3, however if necessary the joints may be dismantled as follows for examination or for cleaning where the gaiters have broken and the joints have been contaminated with dirt or water.

Cleaning

Outer joint

5 With the joint removed as described in Section 3, mark the hub in relation to the cage and joint housing.
6 Swivel the hub and cage and remove the balls one at a time.

3.12 The retaining circlip on the driveshaft inner joint

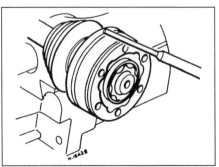

3.13 Removing the plastic cap from the inner joint housing

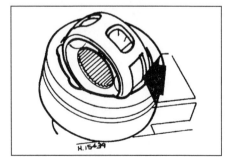

4.7 Removing the cage and hub from the outer joint housing
Arrow shows rectangular aperture

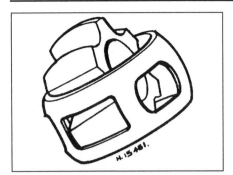

4.8 Removing the outer joint hub
from the cage

4.16 Removing the inner joint
hub and cage

4.17a Inner joint hub, cage and housing

7 Turn the cage until the rectangular apertures are aligned with the housing then withdraw the cage and hub **(see illustration)**.
8 Turn the hub and insert one of the segments into one of the rectangular apertures, then swivel the hub from the cage **(see illustration)**.
9 Note that the joint components including the balls form a matched set and must only be fitted to the correct side.
10 Clean the components in paraffin and examine them for wear and damage. Excessive wear will have been evident when driving the car especially when changing from acceleration to overrun.
11 Commence reassembly by inserting half the amount of special grease (ie 45g) into the joint housing.
12 Fit the hub to the cage by inserting one of the segments into the rectangular aperture.

13 With the rectangular apertures aligned with the housing, fit the hub and cage to the housing in its original position.
14 Swivel the hub and cage and insert the balls from alternate sides.

Inner joint

15 Mark the hub in relation to the cage and joint housing.
16 Turn the hub and cage 90° to the housing and press out the hub and cage. Keep the balls in their correct positions during this procedure **(see illustration)**.
17 Extract the balls then turn the hub so that one of the track grooves is located on the rim of the cage, and withdraw the hub **(see illustrations)**.
18 Note that the joint components including the balls form a matched set and must only be fitted to the correct side.
19 Clean the components in paraffin and

examine them for wear and damage. Excessive wear will have been evident when driving the car especially when changing from acceleration to overrun.
20 Commence reassembly by fitting the hub to the cage.
21 Insert the balls into position using the special grease to hold them in place.
22 Press the hub and cage into the housing making sure that the wide track spacing on the housing will be adjacent to the narrow spacing on the hub **(see illustration)** when fully assembled. Note also that the chamfer on the hub splines must face the large diameter side of the housing.
23 Swivel the cage ahead of the hub so that the balls enter their respective tracks then align the hub and cage with the housing.
24 Check that the hub can be moved freely through its operating arc.

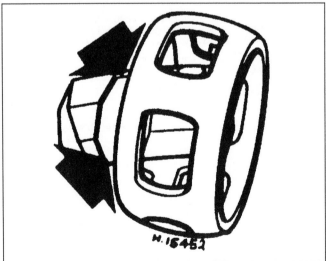

4.17b Removing the inner joint hub from the cage

Arrows indicate position of hub

4.22 Assembly of the inner joint cage and hub to the housing

"a" must be aligned with "b"

Chapter 9
Braking system

Contents

Degrees of difficulty

Easy, suitable for novice with little experience		Fairly easy, suitable for beginner with some experience		Fairly difficult, suitable for competent DIY mechanic		Difficult, suitable for experienced DIY mechanic		Very difficult, suitable for expert DIY or professional	

Specifications

Front brakes

Disc type:
VW1 (except G40 Coupe models)	Standard
VW2 (G40 Coupe models)	Ventilated
Disc diameter	239 mm

Disc thickness (new):
VW1 (except G40 Coupe models)	10 mm
VW2 (G40 Coupe models)	20 mm

Disc thickness (minimum):
VW1 (except G40 Coupe models)	8 mm
VW2 (G40 Coupe models)	18 mm
Maximum disc runout	0.06 mm

Brake pad thickness including backing (new):
VW1 (except G40 Coupe models)	12.0 mm
VW2 (G40 Coupe models)	10.0 mm

Brake pad thickness including backing (minimum):
VW1 (except G40 Coupe models)	7.0 mm
VW2 (G40 Coupe models)	5.0 mm

Rear drum brakes

Drum diameter:
New	180 mm
Maximum diameter	181 mm
Maximum drum out-of-round	0.05 mm
Brake shoe friction material thickness (minimum)	2.5 mm

Torque wrench settings

	Nm	lbf ft
Brake servo mounting bracket to servo	20	15
Master cylinder	20	15
Servo mounting bracket	15	11
Front brake caliper to fixed member	25	19
Front brake caliper fixed member to bearing housing	70	52
Front brake backplate	10	7
Handbrake lever	20	15
Rear brake backplate	60	44

1 General information

The braking system is of servo-assisted hydraulic, dual circuit type with discs at the front and self-adjusting drum brakes at the rear. The hydraulic circuit is split diagonally so that with the failure of one circuit, one front and rear brake remain operative. A load sensitive pressure regulator is incorporated in the rear hydraulic circuits on some models to prevent the rear wheels locking in advance of the front wheels during heavy application of the brakes. The regulator proportions the hydraulic pressure between the front and rear brakes according to the load being carried.

The handbrake operates on the rear wheels only and the lever incorporates a switch which illuminates a warning light on the instrument panel when the handbrake is applied. The same warning light is wired into the low hydraulic fluid switch circuit.

2 Hydraulic system - bleeding

⚠️ **Warning: Hydraulic fluid is poisonous; wash off immediately in the case of skin contact, and seek medical advice if any fluid is swallowed or gets into the eyes. Certain types of hydraulic fluid are flammable, and may ignite when allowed into contact with hot components; when servicing any hydraulic system, it is safest to assume that the fluid IS flammable, and to take precautions against the risk of fire. Hydraulic fluid is also an effective paint stripper, and will attack plastics; if any is spilt, it should be washed off immediately, using copious quantities of fresh water. Finally, it is hygroscopic (it absorbs moisture from the air) - old fluid may be contaminated and unfit for further use. Excess moisture content lowers the fluid's boiling point, making it potentially dangerous. When topping-up or renewing the fluid, always use the recommended type, and ensure that it comes from a freshly-opened sealed container.**

General

1 The correct operation of any hydraulic system is only possible after removing all air from the components and circuit; this is achieved by bleeding the system.
2 During the bleeding procedure, add only clean, unused hydraulic fluid of the recommended type; never re-use fluid that has already been bled from the system.
3 If there is any possibility of incorrect fluid being already in the system, the brake components and circuit must be flushed completely with uncontaminated, correct fluid, and new seals should be fitted to the various components.
4 If hydraulic fluid has been lost from the system, or air has entered because of a leak, ensure that the fault is cured before continuing further.
5 Park the vehicle on level ground, or alternatively (for better access to the bleed screws) jack up the car and support on axle stands (see "*Jacking and vehicle support*") and remove the wheels.
6 Check that all pipes and hoses are secure, unions tight and bleed screws closed. Clean any dirt from around the bleed screws.
7 Unscrew the master cylinder reservoir cap, and if necessary top-up to the "MAX" level line; refit the cap loosely, and remember to maintain the fluid level at least above the "MIN" level line throughout the procedure, or there is a risk of air entering the system.
8 There are a number of one-man, do-it-yourself brake bleeding kits currently available from motor accessory shops. It is recommended that one of these kits is used whenever possible, as they greatly simplify the bleeding operation, and reduce the risk of expelled air and fluid being drawn back into the system. If such a kit is not available, the basic (two-man) method must be used, which is described in detail below.
9 If a kit is to be used, prepare the vehicle as described previously and follow the kit manufacturer's instructions, since the procedure may vary slightly according to the type being used.
10 Whichever method is used, the same sequence must be followed (paragraphs 11 and 12) to ensure the removal of all air from the system.

Bleeding sequence

11 If the system has been only partially disconnected, and suitable precautions were taken to minimise fluid loss, it should only be necessary to bleed that part of the system.
12 If the complete system is to be bled, then it should be done working in the following sequence:
 a) Right-hand rear brake.
 b) Left-hand rear brake.
 c) Right-hand front brake.
 d) Left-hand front brake.

Bleeding - basic (two-man) method

13 Collect together a clean glass jar of reasonable size, a suitable length of plastic or rubber tubing which is a tight fit over the bleed screw, and a ring spanner to fit the screw. The help of an assistant will also be required.
14 Remove the dust cap from the first screw in the sequence **(see illustration)**. Fit the spanner and tube to the screw, place the other end of the tube in the jar, and pour in sufficient fluid to cover the end of the tube.
15 Ensure that the master cylinder reservoir fluid level is maintained at least above the

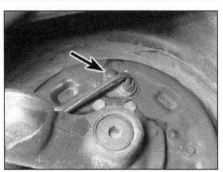

2.14 Dust cap (arrowed) over the bleed screw on a rear brake wheel cylinder

"MIN" level line throughout the procedure.
16 Have the assistant fully depress the brake pedal several times to build up pressure, then maintain it on the final downstroke.
17 While pedal pressure is maintained, unscrew the bleed screw (approximately one turn) and allow the compressed fluid and air to flow into the jar. The assistant should maintain pedal pressure, following it down to the floor if necessary, and should not release it until instructed to do so. When the flow stops, tighten the bleed screw again, have the assistant release the pedal slowly, and recheck the reservoir fluid level.
18 Repeat the steps given in paragraphs 16 and 17 until the fluid emerging from the bleed screw is free from air bubbles. If the master cylinder has been drained and refilled, and air is being bled from the first screw in the sequence, allow approximately five seconds between cycles for the master cylinder passages to refill.
19 When no more air bubbles appear, tighten the bleed screw securely, remove the tube and spanner, and refit the dust cap. Do not overtighten the bleed screw.
20 Repeat the procedure on the remaining screws in the sequence, until all air is removed from the system and the brake pedal feels firm again.

Bleeding - using a one-way valve kit

21 As their name implies, these kits consist of a length of tubing with a one-way valve fitted, to prevent expelled air and fluid being drawn back into the system; some kits include a translucent container, which can be positioned so that the air bubbles can be seen more easily flowing from the end of the tube.
22 The kit is connected to the bleed screw, which is then opened. The user returns to the driver's seat, depresses the brake pedal with a smooth, steady stroke, and slowly releases it; this is repeated until the expelled fluid is clear of air bubbles.
23 Note that these kits simplify work so much that it is easy to forget the master cylinder reservoir fluid level; ensure that this is maintained at least above the "MIN" level line at all times.

4.4a Undo the caliper mounting bolts using an Allen key

4.4b Removing the caliper mounting bolts

4.4c Lifting the caliper from the front brake pads

Bleeding - using a pressure-bleeding kit

24 These kits are usually operated by pressurised air contained in a spare tyre. However, note that it will probably be necessary to reduce the pressure to a lower level than normal; refer to the instructions supplied with the kit.

25 By connecting a pressurised, fluid-filled container to the master cylinder reservoir, bleeding can be carried out simply by opening each screw in turn (in the specified sequence), and allowing the fluid to flow out until no more air bubbles can be seen in the expelled fluid.

26 This method has the advantage that the large reservoir of fluid provides an additional safeguard against air being drawn into the system during bleeding.

27 Pressure-bleeding is particularly effective when bleeding "difficult" systems, or when bleeding the complete system at the time of routine fluid renewal.

All methods

28 When bleeding is complete, and a firm pedal feel is restored, tighten the bleed screws securely and refit their dust caps, then wash off any spilt fluid.

29 Check the hydraulic fluid level in the master cylinder reservoir, and top-up if necessary (see *"Weekly Checks"*).

30 Discard any hydraulic fluid that has been bled from the system; it will not be fit for re-use.

31 Check the feel of the brake pedal. If it feels at all spongy, air must still be present in the system, and further bleeding is required. Failure to bleed satisfactorily after a repetition of the bleeding procedure may be due to worn master cylinder seals.

3 Hydraulic pipes and hoses - renewal

Note: *Refer to the warning in Section 2 concerning the dangers of hydraulic fluid.*

1 If any pipe or hose is to be renewed, minimise fluid loss by first removing the master cylinder reservoir cap, then tightening

it down onto a piece of polythene to obtain an airtight seal. Alternatively, flexible hoses can be sealed, if required, using a proprietary brake hose clamp; metal brake pipe unions can be plugged (if care is taken not to allow dirt into the system) or capped immediately they are disconnected. Place a wad of rag under any union that is to be disconnected, to catch any spilt fluid.

2 If a flexible hose is to be disconnected, unscrew the brake pipe union nut before removing the spring clip which secures the hose to its mounting bracket.

3 To unscrew the union nuts, it is preferable to obtain a "split" brake pipe spanner of the correct size; these are available from most large motor accessory shops. Failing this, a close-fitting open-ended spanner will be required, though if the nuts are tight or corroded, their flats may be rounded-off if the spanner slips. In such a case, a self-locking wrench is often the only way to unscrew a stubborn union, but it follows that the pipe and the damaged nuts must be renewed on reassembly. Always clean a union and surrounding area before disconnecting it. If disconnecting a component with more than one union, make a careful note of the connections before disturbing any of them.

4 If a brake pipe is to be renewed, it can be obtained cut to length and with the union nuts and end flares in place, from VW dealers. All that is then necessary is to bend it to shape, following the line of the original, before fitting it to the car. Alternatively, most motor accessory shops can make up brake pipes from kits, but this requires very careful measurement of the original, to ensure that the replacement is of the correct length. The safest answer is usually to take the original to the shop as a pattern.

5 On refitting, do not overtighten the union nuts. Where given, only tighten the nuts to the specified torque setting.

6 Ensure that the pipes and hoses are correctly routed, with no kinks, and that they are secured in the clips or brackets provided. After fitting, remove the polythene from the reservoir, and bleed the hydraulic system as described in Section 2. Wash off any spilt fluid, and check carefully for fluid leaks.

4 Front brake pads - renewal

⚠ *Warning: Renew BOTH sets of brake pads at the same time - NEVER renew the pads on only one wheel, as uneven braking may result. Note that the dust created by wear of the pads may contain asbestos, which is a health hazard. Never blow it out with compressed air, and DO NOT inhale any of it. An approved filtering mask should be worn when working on the brakes. DO NOT use petrol or petroleum-based solvents to clean brake parts; use brake cleaner or methylated spirit only.*

1 Apply the handbrake, then jack up the front of the vehicle and support it on axle stands (see *"Jacking and vehicle support"*). Remove the front wheels.

2 Trace the brake pad wear sensor wiring (where fitted) back from the pads, and disconnect it from the wiring connector. Note the routing of the wiring, and free it from any relevant retaining clips.

3 Where necessary to improve access, undo the retaining bolts and remove the air deflector shield from the caliper.

4 Using an Allen key, slacken and remove the two caliper mounting bolts, then lift the caliper away from the brake pads and hub, and tie it to the suspension strut using a suitable piece of wire **(see illustrations)**. Do not allow the

4.5 Removing the front brake pads

4.10a Fit the anti-rattle springs to the carrier bracket, making sure they are correctly located . . .

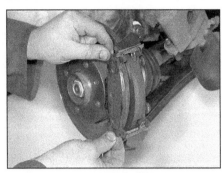

4.10b . . . and install the brake pads with their friction material facing the disc

caliper to hang unsupported on the flexible brake hose.

5 Withdraw the two brake pads from the carrier bracket and recover the anti-rattle springs, noting their correct fitted locations **(see illustration)**. Note that the springs are different and are not interchangeable.

6 First measure the thickness of each brake pad (including the backing plate). If either pad is worn at any point to the specified minimum thickness or less, all four pads must be renewed. Also, the pads should be renewed if any are fouled with oil or grease as there is no satisfactory way of degreasing friction material, once contaminated. If any of the brake pads are worn unevenly, or are fouled with oil or grease, trace and rectify the cause before reassembly. New brake pad kits are available from VW dealers.

7 If the brake pads are still serviceable, carefully clean them using a clean, fine wire brush or similar, paying particular attention to the sides and back of the metal backing. Clean out the grooves in the friction material (where applicable), and pick out any large embedded particles of dirt or debris. Carefully clean the pad locations in the caliper body/mounting bracket.

8 Prior to fitting the pads, check that the spacers/sleeves are free to slide easily in the caliper body bushes, and are a reasonable tight fit. Brush the dust and dirt from the caliper and piston, but *do not* inhale it, as it is injurious to health. Inspect the dust seal around the piston for damage, and the piston for evidence of fluid leaks, corrosion or damage. If attention to any of these components is necessary, refer to Section 8.

9 If new brake pads are to be fitted, the caliper piston must be pushed back into the cylinder to make room for them. Either use a G-clamp or similar tool, or use suitable pieces of wood as levers. Provided that the master cylinder reservoir has not been overfilled with hydraulic fluid, there should be no spillage, but keep a careful watch on the fluid level while retracting the piston. If necessary, the surplus should be syphoned off or ejected through a plastic tube connected to the bleed screw (see Section 2). **Note:** *Do not syphon the fluid by mouth, as it is poisonous; use a syringe or an old poultry baster.*

10 Fit the new anti-rattle springs to the carrier bracket, making sure they are correctly positioned and fit the pads, and ensuring that the friction material of each pad is against the brake disc. Note that, where necessary, the pad with the wear sensor wire should be installed as the inner pad **(see illustrations)**.

11 Position the caliper over the pads, and pass the pad warning sensor wiring (where fitted) through the caliper aperture.

12 Press the caliper into position sufficiently until it is possible to install the caliper mounting bolts. **Note:** *Do not exert excess pressure on the caliper in either direction, as this will deform the pad springs, resulting in noisy operation of the brakes.* Tighten the mounting bolts to the specified torque setting.

13 Reconnect the brake pad wear sensor wiring connectors, ensuring that the wiring is correctly routed. Where necessary, refit the air deflector shield to the caliper.

14 Depress the brake pedal repeatedly, until the pads are pressed into firm contact with the brake disc, and normal (non-assisted) pedal pressure is restored.

15 Repeat the above procedure on the remaining front brake caliper.

16 Refit the roadwheels, then lower the vehicle to the ground and tighten the roadwheel bolts to the specified torque.

17 New pads will not give full braking efficiency until they have bedded-in. Be prepared for this, and avoid hard braking as far as possible for the first hundred miles or so after pad renewal.

5 Rear brake shoes - renewal

> **Warning: Renew BOTH sets of brake shoes at the same time - NEVER renew the shoes on only one wheel, as uneven braking may result. Note that the dust created by wear of the shoes may contain asbestos, which is a health hazard. Never blow it out with compressed air, and DO NOT inhale any of it. An approved filtering mask should be worn when working on the brakes. DO NOT use petrol or petroleum-based solvents to clean brake parts; use brake cleaner or methylated spirit only.**

1 Remove the brake drum (see Section 7).

2 Working carefully, and taking the necessary precautions, remove all traces of brake dust from the brake drum, backplate and shoes.

3 Measure the thickness of the friction material of each brake shoe at several points; if either shoe is worn at any point to the specified minimum thickness or less, all four shoes must be renewed as a set. The shoes should also be renewed if any are fouled with oil or grease; there is no satisfactory way of degreasing friction material, once contaminated.

4 If any of the brake shoes are worn unevenly, or fouled with oil or grease, trace and rectify the cause before reassembly.

5 To renew the brake shoes, continue as follows. If the brake shoes are not worn excessively and all is well, refit the brake drum as described in Section 7.

6 Note the position of the brake shoes and springs, and mark the webs of the shoes, if necessary, to aid refitting.

7 Using a pair of pliers, remove the shoe retainer spring cups by depressing and turning them through 90°. With the cups removed, lift off the springs and withdraw the retainer pins **(see illustrations)**.

8 Ease the shoes out one at a time from the lower pivot point, to release the tension of the return spring, then disconnect the lower return spring from both shoes. Use a pair of pliers or an adjustable spanner to release the shoes **(see illustrations)**.

5.7a Using pliers, remove the spring cup and spring . . .

5.7b . . . and withdraw the retainer pin from the rear of the backplate

5.8a Unhook the shoes from the lower pivot point using an adjustable spanner . . .

5.8b . . . and remove the lower return spring

5.9a Note the elastic band (arrowed) used to retain pistons

9 Ease the upper end of both shoes out from their wheel cylinder locations, taking care not to damage the wheel cylinder seals, and disconnect the handbrake cable from the trailing shoe. The brake shoe assembly can then be manoeuvred out of position and away from the backplate. Do not depress the brake pedal until the brakes are reassembled and the drum refitted; wrap a strong elastic band around the wheel cylinder pistons to retain them **(see illustrations)**.

10 Make a note of the correct fitted positions of all components then unhook the upper return spring, and disengage the wedge key spring **(see illustrations)**.

11 Unhook the tensioning spring, and remove the pushrod from the trailing shoe, together with the wedge key **(see illustrations)**.

12 Examine all components for signs of wear or damage and renew as necessary. Although

linings are available separately (without shoes) from VW dealers, renewal of the shoes complete with linings is to be preferred, unless the necessary skills and equipment are available to fit new linings to the old shoes.

13 Peel back the rubber protective caps, and check the wheel cylinder for fluid leaks or other damage; check that both cylinder pistons are free to move easily. Refer to Section 9, if necessary, for information on wheel cylinder overhaul.

14 Apply a little brake grease to the contact areas of the pushrod and handbrake lever.

15 Hook the tensioning spring into the trailing shoe. Engage the pushrod with the opposite end of the spring and pivot the pushrod into position on the trailing shoe.

16 Fit the wedge key between the trailing shoe and pushrod making sure it is fitted the correct way around.

17 Locate the handbrake lever on the leading shoe in the pushrod, and fit the upper return spring using a pair of pliers.

18 Fit the spring to the wedge key and hook it onto the trailing shoe.

19 Prior to installation, clean the backplate, and apply a thin smear of high-temperature brake grease or anti-seize compound to all those surfaces of the backplate which bear on the shoes, particularly the wheel cylinder pistons and lower pivot point. Do not allow the lubricant to foul the friction material.

20 Remove the elastic band from the wheel cylinder and offer up the shoe assembly.

21 Connect the handbrake cable to the handbrake lever and locate the top of the shoes in the wheel cylinder piston slots.

22 Fit the lower return spring to the shoes, then lever the bottom of the shoes onto the bottom anchor.

5.9b Disconnecting the handbrake cable from the trailing shoe

5.10a Prior to dismantling, note the correct fitted location of the shoe components

5.10b Wedge key and spring

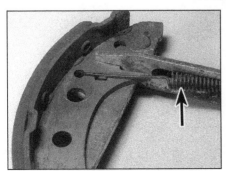

5.11a Unhook the tensioning spring (arrowed) . . .

5.11b . . . and remove the pushrod from the trailing shoe

6.3 Measuring brake disc thickness with a micrometer

23 Tap the shoes to centralise them with the backplate, then refit the shoe retainer pins and springs, and secure them in position with the spring cups.

24 Refit the brake drum as described in Section 7.

25 Repeat the above procedure on the remaining rear brake.

26 Once both sets of rear shoes have been renewed, adjust the lining-to-drum clearance by repeatedly depressing the brake pedal.

27 Check and, if necessary, adjust the handbrake as described in Section 14.

28 On completion, check the hydraulic fluid level as described in Chapter 1.

29 New shoes will not give full braking efficiency until they have bedded in. Be prepared for this, and avoid hard braking as far as possible for the first hundred miles or so after shoe renewal.

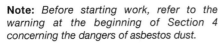

6 Brake disc - inspection, removal and refitting

Note: *Before starting work, refer to the warning at the beginning of Section 4 concerning the dangers of asbestos dust.*

Inspection

Note: *If either disc requires renewal, BOTH should be renewed at the same time, to ensure even and consistent braking. New brake pads should also be fitted.*

1 Apply the handbrake, then jack up the front of the car and support it on axle stands (see *"Jacking and vehicle support"*). Remove the appropriate front roadwheel.

2 Slowly rotate the brake disc so that the full area of both sides can be checked; remove the brake pads if better access is required to the inboard surface. Light scoring is normal in the area swept by the brake pads, but if heavy scoring or cracks are found, the disc must be renewed.

3 It is normal to find a lip of rust and brake dust around the disc's perimeter; this can be scraped off if required. If, however, a lip has formed due to excessive wear of the brake pad swept area, then the disc's thickness must be measured using a micrometer **(see illustration)**. Take measurements at several

places around the disc, at the inside and outside of the pad swept area; if the disc has worn at any point to the specified minimum thickness or less, the disc must be renewed.

4 If the disc is thought to be warped, it can be checked for run-out. Either use a dial gauge mounted on any convenient fixed point, while the disc is slowly rotated, or use feeler blades to measure (at several points all around the disc) the clearance between the disc and a fixed point, such as the caliper mounting bracket. If the measurements obtained are at the specified maximum or beyond, the disc is excessively warped, and must be renewed; however, it is worth checking first that the hub bearing is in good condition (Chapters 1 and/or 10). If the run-out is excessive, the disc must be renewed.

5 Check the disc for cracks, especially around the wheel bolt holes, and any other wear or damage, and renew if necessary.

Removal

6 Remove the brake pads as described in Section 4. If necessary unbolt the caliper carrier bracket from the swivel hub.

7 Use chalk or paint to mark the relationship of the disc to the hub, then remove the screw securing the brake disc to the hub, and remove the disc **(see illustration)**. If it is tight, lightly tap its rear face with a hide or plastic mallet.

Refitting

8 Refitting is the reverse of the removal procedure, noting the following points:
 a) *Ensure that the mating surfaces of the disc and hub are clean and flat.*

6.7 Undo the retaining screw and remove the front brake disc

7.3a Remove the split pin . . .

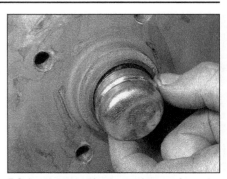

7.2 Lever out and remove the cap from the centre of the brake drum

 b) *Align (if applicable) the marks made on removal, and securely tighten the disc retaining screw.*
 c) *If a new disc has been fitted, use a suitable solvent to wipe any preservative coating from the disc, before refitting the caliper.*
 d) *Refit the pads as described in Section 4.*
 e) *Refit the roadwheel, then lower the car to the ground and tighten the roadwheel bolts to the specified torque. On completion, repeatedly depress the brake pedal until normal pedal pressure returns.*

7 Rear brake drum - removal, inspection and refitting

Note: *Before starting work, refer to the warning at the beginning of Section 5 concerning the dangers of asbestos dust.*

Removal

1 Chock the front wheels, then jack up the rear of the vehicle and support it on axle stands (see *"Jacking and vehicle support"*). Remove the appropriate rear wheel. Release the handbrake lever.

2 Using a hammer and a large flat-bladed screwdriver, carefully tap and prise the cap out of the centre of the brake drum **(see illustration)**. Discard the cap if it is disfigured during removal.

3 Extract the split pin and remove the locking cap **(see illustrations)**. Discard the split pin; a new one must be used on refitting.

7.3b . . . and locking cap . . .

7.4a ... then unscrew the retaining nut ...

7.4b ... remove the toothed washer ...

7.4c ... and withdraw the outer bearing

4 Unscrew and remove the rear hub nut, then slide off the toothed washer and remove the outer bearing from the centre of the drum **(see illustrations)**.

5 It should now be possible to withdraw the brake drum assembly from the stub axle by hand **(see illustration)**. However it may be difficult to remove the drum, due to the tightness of the hub bearing on the stub axle, or due to the brake shoes binding on the inner circumference of the drum. If the bearing is tight, tap the periphery of the drum using a hide or plastic mallet, or use a universal puller, secured to the drum with the wheel bolts, to pull it off. If the brake shoes are binding, first check that the handbrake is fully released, then continue as follows.

6 Check that the handbrake is fully released.

7 Insert a screwdriver through one of the wheel bolt holes in the brake drum, and lever up the wedge key in order to allow the brake shoes to retract fully **(see illustration)**. The brake drum can now be withdrawn.

Inspection

Note: *If either drum requires renewal, BOTH should be renewed at the same time, to ensure even and consistent braking. New brake shoes should also be fitted.*

8 Working carefully, remove all traces of brake dust from the drum, but avoid inhaling the dust as it may contain asbestos and be injurious to health.

9 Clean the outside of the drum, and check it for obvious signs of wear or damage, such as cracks around the roadwheel bolt holes; renew the drum if necessary.

10 Examine the inside of the drum. Light scoring of the friction surface is normal, but if heavy scoring is found, the drum must be renewed. It is usual to find a lip on the drum's inboard edge which consists of a mixture of rust and brake dust; this should be scraped away.

11 If the drum is thought to be excessively worn, or oval, its internal diameter must be measured at several points using an internal micrometer. Take measurements in pairs, the second at right-angles to the first, and compare the two, to check for signs of ovality. Provided that it does not enlarge the drum to beyond the specified maximum diameter, it may be possible to have the drum refinished by skimming or grinding; if this is not possible, the drums on both sides must be renewed. Note that if the drum is to be skimmed, BOTH drums must be refinished to maintain a consistent internal diameter on both sides.

Refitting

12 If new brake drums are to be installed, use a suitable solvent to remove any preservative coating that may have been applied to the friction surfaces. If necessary, install the bearing races, inner bearing and oil seal as described in Chapter 10, and thoroughly grease the outer bearing.

13 Prior to refitting, fully retract the brake shoes by lifting up the wedge key.

14 Apply a smear of grease to the drum oil seal, and carefully slide the assembly onto the stub axle.

15 Fit the outer bearing and toothed thrustwasher, ensuring its tooth is correctly engaged in the axle slot.

16 Refit the hub nut and moderately tighten it whilst rotating the brake drum to settle the hub bearings in position. Gradually slacken the hub nut until the position is found where it is just possible to move the toothed washer from side-to-side using a screwdriver **(see illustration)**. **Note:** *Only finger pressure should be needed to move the washer. Do not turn or lever the screwdriver.* When the hub nut is correctly positioned, refit the locking cap and secure the nut in position with a new split pin.

17 Fit the cap to the centre of the brake drum, tapping it fully into position with a light hammer.

18 Depress the footbrake several times to operate the self-adjusting mechanism.

19 Repeat the above procedure on the remaining rear brake assembly (where necessary), then check and if necessary adjust the handbrake cable (see Section 14).

20 On completion, refit the roadwheel(s), then lower the vehicle to the ground and tighten the wheel bolts to the specified torque.

8 Front brake caliper - removal, overhaul and refitting

Note: *Before starting work, refer to the warning at the beginning of Section 2 concerning the dangers of hydraulic fluid, and to the warning at the beginning of Section 4 concerning the dangers of asbestos dust.*

7.5 ... and remove the brake drum

7.7 Release the brake shoes by inserting a screwdriver through the drum hole

7.16 Checking the adjustment of the rear hub bearing with a screwdriver

Removal

1 Apply the handbrake, then jack up the front of the vehicle and support it on axle stands (see "*Jacking and vehicle support*"). Remove the appropriate roadwheel.

2 Minimise fluid loss by first removing the master cylinder reservoir cap, and then tightening it down onto a piece of polythene, to obtain an airtight seal. Alternatively, use a brake hose clamp, a G-clamp or a similar tool to clamp the flexible hose.

3 Clean the area around the union, then loosen the brake hose union nut.

4 Follow the procedure described in Section 4 for the removal of the brake pads, however leave the pads in the carrier bracket.

5 Unscrew the caliper from the end of the brake hose and remove it from the vehicle.

Overhaul

6 With the caliper on the bench, wipe away all traces of dust and dirt, but *avoid inhaling the dust, as it is injurious to health.*

7 Withdraw the partially ejected piston from the caliper body, and remove the dust seal.

 HAYNES HiNT *If the piston cannot be withdrawn by hand, it can be pushed out by applying compressed air to the brake* hose union hole. Only low pressure should be required, such as is generated by a foot pump. As the piston is expelled take great care not to trap your fingers between the piston and caliper.

8 Using a small screwdriver, extract the piston hydraulic seal, taking great care not to damage the caliper bore **(see illustration)**.

9 Thoroughly clean all components, using only methylated spirit, isopropyl alcohol or clean hydraulic fluid as a cleaning medium. Never use mineral-based solvents such as petrol or paraffin, as they will attack the hydraulic system's rubber components. Dry the components immediately, using compressed air or a clean, lint-free cloth. Use compressed air to blow clear the fluid passages.

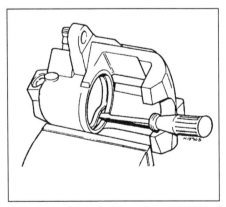

8.8 Extracting the piston seal - take care not to scratch the surface of the bore

10 Withdraw the spacers/sleeves from the caliper body bushes.

11 Check all components, and renew any that are worn or damaged. Check particularly the cylinder bore and piston; these should be renewed (note that this means the renewal of the complete body assembly) if they are scratched, worn or corroded in any way.

12 Similarly check the condition of the spacer sleeves and their bushes/bores; both spacer sleeves should be undamaged and (when cleaned) a reasonably tight sliding fit in their bores. If there is any doubt about the condition of any component, renew it.

13 If the assembly is fit for further use, obtain the appropriate repair kit.

14 Renew all rubber seals, dust covers and caps disturbed on dismantling as a matter of course.

15 On reassembly, ensure that all components are spotlessly clean.

16 Dip the piston and the new piston (fluid) seal in clean hydraulic fluid. Smear clean fluid on the cylinder bore surface.

17 Fit the new piston (fluid) seal, using only your fingers (no tools) to manipulate it into the cylinder bore groove. Fit the new dust seal to the piston, and refit the piston to the cylinder bore using a twisting motion; ensure that the piston enters squarely into the bore. Press the piston fully into the bore, then press the dust seal into the caliper body.

18 Apply the grease supplied in the repair kit, or a good quality high-temperature brake grease or anti-seize compound, to the spacer sleeves and insert them into their bushes.

Refitting

19 Screw the caliper fully onto the flexible hose union.

20 Check that the brake pads are correctly located in the carrier bracket, then refit the caliper with reference to Section 4.

21 Securely tighten the brake hose union nut.

22 Remove the brake hose clamp or polythene, as applicable, and bleed the hydraulic system as described in Section 2. Note that, providing the precautions described were taken to minimise brake fluid loss, it should only be necessary to bleed the relevant front brake.

23 Refit the roadwheel, then lower the vehicle to the ground and tighten the roadwheel bolts to the specified torque.

9 Rear wheel cylinder - removal, overhaul and refitting

Note: *Before starting work, refer to the warning at the beginning of Section 2 concerning the dangers of hydraulic fluid, and to the warning at the beginning of Section 5 concerning the dangers of asbestos dust.*

Removal

1 Remove the brake drum (see Section 7).

2 Using pliers, carefully unhook the upper brake shoe return spring, and remove it from both brake shoes. Pull the upper ends of the shoes away from the wheel cylinder to disengage them from the pistons.

3 Minimise fluid loss by first removing the master cylinder reservoir cap, and then tightening it down onto a piece of polythene, to obtain an airtight seal. Alternatively, use a brake hose clamp, G-clamp or a similar tool to clamp the flexible hose at the nearest convenient point to the wheel cylinder.

4 Wipe away all traces of dirt around the brake pipe union at the rear of the wheel cylinder, and unscrew the union nut. Carefully ease the pipe out of the wheel cylinder, and plug or tape over its end to prevent dirt entry. Wipe off any spilt fluid immediately.

5 Unscrew the two wheel cylinder retaining bolts from the rear of the backplate, and remove the cylinder, taking great care not to allow surplus hydraulic fluid to contaminate the brake shoe linings.

Overhaul

6 Brush the dirt and dust from the wheel cylinder, but take care not to inhale it.

7 Pull the rubber dust seals from the ends of the cylinder body.

8 The pistons will normally be ejected by the pressure of the coil spring, but if they are not, tap the end of the cylinder body on a piece of wood, or apply low air pressure - eg, from a foot pump - to the hydraulic fluid union hole to eject the pistons from their bores.

9 Inspect the surfaces of the pistons and their bores in the cylinder body for scoring, or evidence of metal-to-metal contact. If evident, renew the complete wheel cylinder assembly.

10 If the pistons and bores are in good condition, remove and discard the seals and obtain a repair kit, which will contain all the necessary renewable items. Note the correct fitted orientation of the seals to ensure correct fitment of the new seals.

11 Lubricate the new piston seals with clean brake fluid, and fit them onto the pistons with their larger diameters innermost.

12 Insert the spring in the cylinder.

13 Insert the pistons into the cylinder bores using a twisting motion.

14 Fit the dust seals, and check that the pistons can move freely in their bores.

Refitting

15 Ensure that the backplate and wheel cylinder mating surfaces are clean, then spread the brake shoes and manoeuvre the wheel cylinder into position.

16 Insert the brake pipe, and screw in the union nut two or three turns to ensure that the thread has started.

17 Insert the two wheel cylinder retaining bolts, and tighten them to the specified torque. Now fully tighten the brake pipe union nut.

18 Remove the clamp from the flexible brake hose, or the polythene from the master cylinder reservoir (as applicable).

19 Ensure that the brake shoes are correctly located in the cylinder pistons, then refit the brake shoe upper return spring, using a screwdriver to stretch the spring into position.
20 Refit the brake drum (see Section 7).
21 Bleed the brake hydraulic system as described in Section 2. Providing suitable precautions were taken to minimise loss of fluid, it should only be necessary to bleed the relevant rear brake.

10 Master cylinder - removal, overhaul and refitting

Note: *Before starting work, refer to the warning at the beginning of Section 2 concerning the dangers of hydraulic fluid.*

Removal

1 Disconnect the battery negative terminal. Where necessary, to improve access to the master cylinder, remove the air inlet duct as described in the relevant Part of Chapter 4.
2 Remove the master cylinder reservoir cap, and syphon the hydraulic fluid from the reservoir. **Note:** *Do not syphon the fluid by mouth, as it is poisonous; use a syringe or an old poultry baster.* Alternatively, open any convenient bleed screw in the system, and gently pump the brake pedal to expel the fluid through a plastic tube connected to the screw (see Section 2). Disconnect the wiring plug from the brake fluid level sender unit.
3 Wipe clean the area around the brake pipe unions on the side of the master cylinder, and place absorbent rags beneath the pipe unions to catch any surplus fluid. Make a note of the correct fitted position of the unions, then unscrew the union nuts and carefully withdraw the pipes **(see illustration)**. Plug or tape over the pipe ends and master cylinder orifices, to minimise the loss of brake fluid, and to prevent the entry of dirt into the system. Wash off any spilt fluid immediately with cold water.
4 Slacken and remove the two nuts and washers securing the master cylinder to the vacuum servo unit, then withdraw the unit from the engine compartment. Remove the O-ring from the rear of the master cylinder and discard it.

10.3 Brake master cylinder location on the front of the servo unit

Overhaul

5 If the master cylinder is faulty, it must be renewed. Repair kits are not available from VW dealers, so the cylinder must be treated as a sealed unit.
6 The only items which can be renewed are the mounting seals for the fluid reservoir; if these show signs of deterioration, pull off the reservoir and remove the old seals. Lubricate the new seals with clean brake fluid, and press them into the master cylinder ports. Ease the fluid reservoir into position, and push it fully home.

Refitting

7 Remove all traces of dirt from the master cylinder and servo unit mating surfaces, and fit a new O-ring to the groove on the master cylinder body.
8 Fit the master cylinder to the servo unit, ensuring that the servo unit pushrod enters the master cylinder bore centrally. Refit the master cylinder mounting nuts and washers, and tighten them to the specified torque.
9 Wipe clean the brake pipe unions, then refit them to the master cylinder ports and tighten them securely.
10 Refill the master cylinder reservoir with new fluid, and bleed the complete hydraulic system as described in Section 2.

11 Brake pedal - removal, overhaul and refitting

Removal

1 Disconnect the battery negative terminal.
2 Working inside the car extract the clip, remove the pin and disconnect the vacuum servo pushrod from the pedal.
3 Unhook the return spring from the pedal.
4 Prise the clip from the end of the pedal pivot shaft.
5 Withdraw the pivot shaft sufficient to remove the brake pedal.
6 If necessary the pedal bracket can be removed after removing the clutch pedal and mounting nuts and bolts.

Overhaul

7 Clean the pedal and pivot shaft and examine them for wear. If the bushes are worn, they can be removed using a soft metal drift, and the new bushes installed using a vice to press them into position. Check the rubber foot pad and renew if necessary.

Refitting

8 Refitting is a reversal of removal, but apply a little multi-purpose grease to the pivot shaft and bushes and check the adjustment of the brake pedal as follows. Before refitting the servo pushrod loosen the locknut, then with the pedal at its rest position, turn the pushrod while holding the clevis stationary until the holes in the pedal and clevis are aligned with each other. Insert the pin and tighten the locknut. Retain the pin with its clip.
9 If the clutch pedal was removed, refit it with reference to Chapter 6.

12 Vacuum servo unit - testing, removal and refitting

Testing

1 To test the operation of the servo unit, depress the footbrake several times to exhaust the vacuum, then start the engine whilst keeping the pedal firmly depressed. As the engine starts, there should be a noticeable "give" in the brake pedal as the vacuum builds up. Allow the engine to run for at least two minutes, then switch it off. If the brake pedal is now depressed, it should feel normal, but further applications should result in the pedal feeling firmer, with the pedal stroke decreasing with each application.
2 If the servo does not operate as described, first inspect the servo unit check valve as described in Section 13.
3 If the servo unit still fails to operate satisfactorily, the fault lies within the unit itself. Repairs to the unit are not possible - if faulty, the servo unit must be renewed.

Removal

4 The vacuum servo unit is removed together with the master cylinder, then dismantled on the bench. First disconnect the battery negative terminal. To improve access to the master cylinder, remove the air inlet duct as described in the relevant Part of Chapter 4.
5 Remove the master cylinder reservoir cap, and syphon the hydraulic fluid from the reservoir. **Note:** *Do not syphon the fluid by mouth, as it is poisonous; use a syringe or an old poultry baster.* Alternatively, open any convenient bleed screw in the system, and gently pump the brake pedal to expel the fluid through a plastic tube connected to the screw (see Section 2). Disconnect the wiring plug from the brake fluid level sender unit.
6 Wipe clean the area around the brake pipe unions on the side of the master cylinder, and place absorbent rags beneath the pipe unions to catch any surplus fluid. Make a note of the correct fitted position of the unions, then unscrew the union nuts and carefully withdraw the pipes. Plug or tape over the pipe ends and master cylinder orifices, to minimise the loss of brake fluid, and to prevent the entry of dirt into the system. Wash off any spilt fluid immediately with cold water.
7 Working inside the car extract the clip, remove the pin and disconnect the vacuum servo pushrod from the pedal.
8 Working in the engine compartment, carefully ease out the vacuum hose from the servo unit sealing grommet.

9 Unscrew the nuts and remove the washers securing the servo unit to the bulkhead. Where applicable, note the location of the retaining plate on the upper stud. Remove the assembly from the engine compartment.
10 Slacken and remove the two nuts and washers securing the master cylinder to the vacuum servo unit, then withdraw the master cylinder and recover the rubber O-ring.

Filter renewal

11 If necessary the filter may be removed as follows. Loosen the locknut then unscrew the clevis from the pushrod - to ensure correct refitting note carefully the position of the clevis. Unscrew the locknut.
12 Slide the protective sleeve from the servo unit, then use a hooked instrument to remove the filter and damping washer.
13 Clean the filter location then insert a new filter and damping washer making sure that the slots of each item are offset by 180° from each other.
14 Refit the sleeve followed by the locknut and clevis. After positioning the clevis in its previously noted position, tighten the locknut.

Refitting

15 Remove all traces of dirt from the master cylinder and servo unit mating surfaces, and fit a new O-ring to the groove on the master cylinder body.
16 Fit the master cylinder to the servo unit, ensuring that the servo unit pushrod enters the master cylinder bore centrally. Refit the master cylinder mounting nuts and washers, and tighten them to the specified torque.
17 Refit the assembly to the bulkhead and tighten the mounting nuts. Where applicable, make sure the location plate is located on the upper stud.
18 Ease the vacuum hose back into position in the servo unit, taking care not to displace the sealing grommet.
19 Inside the car connect the pushrod to the pedal with the pin and retain with the clip. **Note:** *If a new servo unit has been fitted adjust the pushrod as described in Section 11.*
20 Wipe clean the brake pipe unions, then refit them to the master cylinder ports and tighten them securely.
21 Refill the master cylinder reservoir with

new fluid, and bleed the complete hydraulic system as described in Section 2.
22 Refit the air inlet duct (where removed) and reconnect the battery negative terminal.

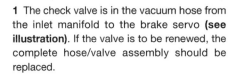

13 Vacuum servo unit non-return valve - removal, testing and refitting

1 The check valve is in the vacuum hose from the inlet manifold to the brake servo **(see illustration)**. If the valve is to be renewed, the complete hose/valve assembly should be replaced.

Removal

2 Ease the vacuum hose out of the servo unit, taking care not to displace the grommet.
3 Note the routing of the hose, then slacken the clip and disconnect the opposite end of the hose assembly from the manifold and remove it from the car.

Testing

4 Examine the check valve and vacuum hose for signs of damage, and renew if necessary.
5 The valve may be tested by blowing through it in both directions, air should flow through the valve in one direction only; when blown through from the servo unit end of the valve. Renew the valve if this is not the case.
6 Examine the servo unit rubber sealing grommet for signs of damage or deterioration, and renew as necessary.

Refitting

7 Ensure that the sealing grommet is correctly fitted to the servo unit.
8 Ease the hose union into position in the servo, taking great care not to displace or damage the grommet.
9 Ensure that the hose is correctly routed, and connect it to the inlet manifold, tightening its retaining clip securely.
10 On completion, start the engine and check the check valve to servo unit connection for signs of air leaks.

14 Handbrake - adjustment

1 To check the handbrake adjustment, first apply the footbrake firmly several times to establish correct shoe-to-drum clearance, then apply and release the handbrake several times.
2 Applying normal moderate pressure, pull the handbrake lever to the fully-applied position, counting the number of clicks on the handbrake ratchet mechanism. If adjustment is correct, there should be approximately 4 to 7 clicks before the handbrake is fully applied. If this is not the case, adjust as follows.
3 Remove the plastic cover from the handbrake lever **(see illustration)**.
4 Chock the front wheels, then jack up the rear of the vehicle and support it on axle stands (see "*Jacking and vehicle support*").
5 With the handbrake set on the 4th notch of the ratchet mechanism, rotate the adjusting nut until it is difficult to turn both rear wheels by hand **(see illustration)**. Once this is so, release the handbrake lever, and check that the wheels rotate freely. Check the adjustment by applying the handbrake fully, counting the clicks from the handbrake ratchet and, if necessary, re-adjust.
6 Where necessary refit the centre console section, then lower the car to the ground.

15 Handbrake lever - removal and refitting

Removal

1 Remove the plastic cover from the lever and fully release the lever.
2 Where necessary remove the rear section of the centre console with reference to Chapter 11.
3 Pull back the carpet, then unscrew the adjusting nut from the front end of the handbrake cable.
4 Unscrew the mounting bolts and lift the lever from the floor at the same time sliding the pin from the cable adjustment end fitting.

13.1 Vacuum servo unit non-return valve

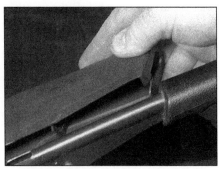

14.3 Removing the plastic cover from the handbrake lever

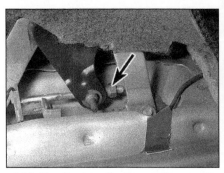

14.5 Handbrake adjusting nut (arrowed)

Refitting

5 Refitting is a reversal of the removal procedure, but finally adjust the handbrake as described in Section 14.

16 Handbrake cables - removal and refitting

Front cable

Removal

1 Chock the front wheels then jack up the rear of the car and support on axle stands (see "*Jacking and vehicle support*"). Release the handbrake.
2 If fitted, remove the plastic cover from the handbrake lever **(see illustration)**. Where necessary remove the rear section of the centre console with reference to Chapter 11.
3 Pull back the carpet, then unscrew the adjusting nut from the front end of the handbrake cable. Release the cable from the handbrake.

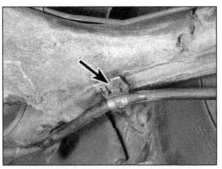

16.10 Release the retaining clips (arrowed) and detach the handbrake cable from the trailing arm

4 Working beneath the car, unhook the rear end of the inner cable from the compensator.
5 Release the cable from the underbody supports and clips and withdraw from under the car.

Refitting

6 Refitting is a reversal of removal but adjust the cable as described in Section 14.

16.11 With the shoes removed, detach the cable from the backplate

Rear cable

Removal

7 Chock the front wheels then jack up the rear of the car and support on axle stands (see "*Jacking and vehicle support*"). Release the handbrake.
8 Remove the rear brake shoes on the relevant side as described in Section 5.
9 Working beneath the car, unhook the inner cable from the compensator.
10 Release the outer cable from the support and clips **(see illustration)**.
11 Withdraw the cable from the rear brake backplate and remove from under the car **(see illustration)**.

Refitting

12 Refitting is a reversal of removal but adjust the cable as described in Section 14.

17 Rear brake pressure-regulating valve - removal, refitting and adjustment

Note: *Before starting work refer to the warning at the beginning of Section 2 concerning the dangers of hydraulic fluid.*

Removal

1 A brake pressure regulator is fitted in the rear brake circuit of most models and its purpose is to prevent the rear wheels locking in advance of the front wheels during heavy application of the brakes. The regulator is also load sensitive in order to vary the pressure according to the load being carried. The regulator is located on the underbody, in front of the left-hand rear wheel.
2 Minimise fluid loss by first removing the master cylinder reservoir cap, and then tightening it down onto a piece of polythene, to obtain an airtight seal.
3 Chock the front wheels then jack up the rear of the car and support on axle stands (see "*Jacking and vehicle support*").
4 Working beneath the car unhook the spring from the regulator.
5 Identify each hydraulic brake line for position, then unscrew the union nuts and

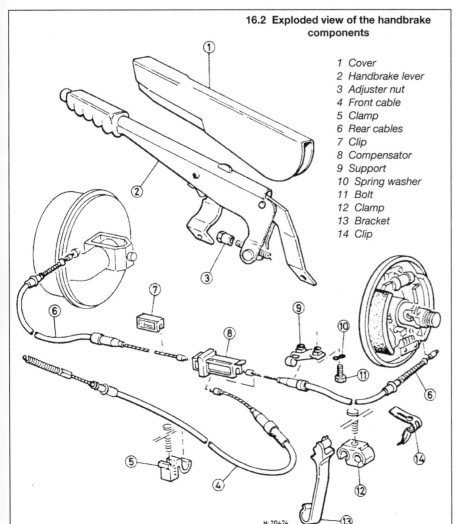

16.2 Exploded view of the handbrake components

1 Cover
2 Handbrake lever
3 Adjuster nut
4 Front cable
5 Clamp
6 Rear cables
7 Clip
8 Compensator
9 Support
10 Spring washer
11 Bolt
12 Clamp
13 Bracket
14 Clip

H.20474

withdraw the lines so that they are just clear of the regulator. Tape the ends of the brake lines to prevent entry of dust and dirt.

6 Unscrew the mounting bolts and withdraw the regulator from under the car.

Refitting

7 Before refitting the regulator check that the brake line apertures and sealing surfaces are clean.

8 Locate the regulator on the underbody, insert the bolts and tighten securely.

9 Remove the tape and wipe clean the ends of the hydraulic lines then insert them into their correct positions and tighten the union nuts. To ensure that the nuts are not cross-threaded, initially tighten them by hand only.

10 Hook the spring onto the regulator and adjustment roller.

11 Remove the polythene from the master cylinder then bleed the complete hydraulic circuit as described in Section 2.

12 Lower the car to the ground.

13 The initial operation of the regulator can be checked as follows. Have an assistant depress the brake pedal rapidly and check that the regulator lever moves at the same time.

Adjustment

14 Checking and adjustment of the regulator is best left to a VW garage as special pressure gauges and spring tensioning tools are required. Adjustment is made by varying the spring tension, but this must be carried out by the garage.

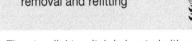

18 Stop-light switch - removal and refitting

1 The stop-light switch is located either on the pedal bracket or on the master cylinder.

18.2 Stoplight switch location on the pedal bracket

Pedal bracket-mounted type

Removal

2 Reach up behind the facia and disconnect the wiring connector from the switch on the pedal bracket **(see illustration)**.

3 Twist the switch through 90° and release it from the mounting bracket. **Note:** *The switch for RHD and LHD models is different.*

Refitting

4 Prior to installation, fully extend the stoplight switch plunger.

5 Fully depress and hold the brake pedal, then manoeuvre the switch into position. Secure the switch in position by twisting it through 90° and release the brake pedal.

6 Reconnect the wiring connector, and check the operation of the stop-lights. The stop-lights should illuminate after the brake pedal has travelled about 5 mm. If the switch is not functioning correctly, it is faulty and must be renewed; no adjustment is possible.

Master cylinder-mounted type

Removal

7 Have ready a suitable plastic or rubber bung which will be a close fit in the switch aperture in the master cylinder. Place some cloth rags beneath the switch.

19.3 Unscrewing the handbrake warning light switch mounting screw

8 Disconnect the wiring from the switch. Loosen and unscrew the switch until it is on its last threads, then quickly unscrew and remove it and the washer, and fit the bung.

Refitting

9 Fit a new washer onto the switch.

10 Remove the bung and fit the switch as quickly as possible, then tighten it securely.

11 Wipe clean the exterior of the master cylinder and reconnect the wiring.

12 Bleed the complete hydraulic circuit as described in Section 2.

19 Handbrake "on" warning light switch - removal and refitting

Removal

1 Remove the plastic cover from the handbrake lever and fully apply the lever.

2 Pull back the carpet, then disconnect the wiring from the warning light switch which is mounted on a bracket on the floor.

3 Unscrew the mounting screw and lift the switch out **(see illustration)**.

Refitting

4 Refitting is a reversal of removal.

Chapter 10
Suspension and steering

Contents

Degrees of difficulty

Easy, suitable for novice with little experience	Fairly easy, suitable for beginner with some experience	Fairly difficult, suitable for competent DIY mechanic	Difficult, suitable for experienced DIY mechanic	Very difficult, suitable for expert DIY or professional

Specifications

Front suspension

Type . . . . Independent with spring struts, lower track control arms, and anti-roll bar. Telescopic shock absorbers incorporated in struts

Rear suspension

Type . . . . Semi-independent incorporating torsion axle beam, trailing arms, and spring struts/shock absorbers. Anti-roll bar incorporated in beam on multi-point fuel injection (Mpi), GT and G40 models

Steering

Type . . . . Rack and pinion with safety column
Steering roll radius . . . . Negative 4.17 mm
Steering wheel turns lock to lock 3.66
Steering ratio . . . . 17.6 to 1

Front wheel alignment

Total toe . . . . 0° ± 10' (0 ± 1 mm)
Camber:
    Except Mpi, GT and G40 (AAU and AAV engine models) . . . . +20' ± 30'
    Mpi and GT (3F engine models) . . . . +10' ± 30'
    G40 (PY engine models) . . . . -20' ± 30'
    Maximum difference side to side . . . . 30'
Castor . . . . 2° 20' ± 30'
    Maximum difference side to side . . . . 1°

Rear wheel alignment

Total toe . . . . +20' ± 10'
Camber . . . . -1° 30' ± 10'
    Maximum difference side to side . . . . 20'

Wheels

Type	....	Pressed steel disc or alloy
Size	....	4.5J x 13 or 5.5J x 13

Tyres

Pressures - see end of *"Weekly checks"*.
Sizes:*
  Roadwheels:

4.5J x13	....	135 R 13, 145 R 13 or 155/70 R 13
5.5J x 13	....	165/65 R 13 or 175/60 R 13

Consult your handbook, a VW dealer or a tyre dealer for the correct size for your vehicle.

Torque wrench settings

	Nm	lbf ft
Front suspension		
Strut to body	60	44
Shock absorber rod to top mounting	50	37
Strut cap	150	110
Steering knuckle to track control arm	50	37
Track control arm to body	55	41
Anti-roll bar to control arm	75	55
Anti-roll bar to body	30	22
Anti-roll bar mounting	120	89
Rear suspension		
Trailing arm to trunnion	40	30
Trunnion to body	120	89
Stub axle	60	44
Shock absorber to trailing arm	45	33
Shock absorber to body	20	15
Steering		
Tie-rod (outer)	35	26
Flange tube	25	18
Column tube	20	15
Steering wheel	50	37
Steering lock housing	10	7
Steering gear	25	18
Inner column clamp to steering gear	30	22
Tie-rod inner	30	22
Tie-rod carrier	40	30
Tie-rod locknut	40	30
Wheel bolts	110	81

1 General information

The front suspension is of independent type with spring struts, lower track control arms and an anti-roll bar. Each strut incorporates a telescopic shock absorber which can be renewed separately in the event of failure. The track control arms are attached to the wheel bearing housings/struts by balljoints. The pivot points of the struts are positioned to give a negative roll in the interests of steering stability. The anti-roll bar which stabilises the car when cornering, also acts as a radius arm for each track control arm. The front wheel hubs are mounted in twin track ball bearings in the wheel bearing housings.

The rear suspension is of semi-independent type with trailing arms located at each end of the torsion axle beam. The shock absorbers are an integral part of the spring struts. The axle beam is attached to the trailing arms behind the pivot points.

The steering is of rack and pinion type mounted on the front of the bulkhead, and the column is of telescopic (safety) design. On early models the bottom end of the inner column is connected directly to the steering gear pinion by means of a clamp, however on later models a universal joint is fitted. Some models are fitted with a steering damper attached to the steering gear end fitting.

2 Front suspension strut - removal and refitting

Removal

1 Remove the wheel trim from the relevant wheel.

2 With the handbrake applied loosen the driveshaft nut **(see illustration)**. The nut is tightened to a high torque and a socket extension may be required.

3 Jack up the front of the car and support it on axle stands (see *"Jacking and vehicle support"*). Remove the roadwheel.

2.2 Driveshaft nut

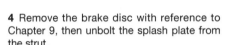

2.10a Removing the front suspension strut top cap

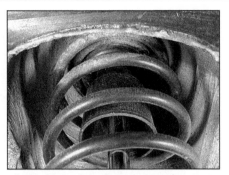

2.10b View of the front suspension strut upper mounting from below

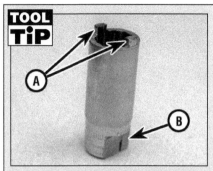

In the absence of the special VW tool, a replacement can be fabricated from a long-reach 13 mm socket. Cut the lower end of the socket to leave two teeth (A) which will engage with the slots in the strut nut, and file the upper end of the socket (B) so that it can be held with an open-ended spanner

4 Remove the brake disc with reference to Chapter 9, then unbolt the splash plate from the strut.
5 Unscrew the nut securing the steering tie-rod end to the strut, then use a balljoint separator to release the tie-rod.
6 Remove the anti-roll bar as described in Section 7. Alternatively the track control arm and anti-roll bar can be levered downwards later (paragraph 8).
7 Unscrew and remove the clamp bolt securing the track control arm to the wheel bearing housing/strut noting that the bolt head faces forward.
8 Push the control arm down to disconnect the balljoint then move the strut sideways.
9 Unscrew the driveshaft nut, then pull the strut out and at the same time tap the driveshaft through the hub with a mallet.
10 Working in the engine compartment prise the cap from the top of the strut then unscrew the self-locking nut while supporting the strut from below **(see illustrations)**. If necessary hold the shock absorber rod stationary with a spanner.
11 Lower the strut from under the car.
12 If necessary remove the cups and rubber mountings from the front suspension tower.

Refitting

13 Refitting is a reversal of removal, but renew the upper rubber mountings if necessary. Refer to Section 7 when refitting the anti-roll bar, Chapter 9 when refitting the brake disc and Chapter 8 when tightening the driveshaft nut. Finally check and if necessary adjust the front wheel alignment as described in Section 20. If difficulty is experienced fitting the upper rubber mounting first dust it with talcum powder.

3 Front coil spring -
removal and refitting

Warning: Before attempting to dismantle the suspension strut, a suitable tool to hold the coil spring in compression must be obtained. Adjustable coil spring compressors are readily available, and are recommended for this operation. Any attempt to dismantle the strut without such a tool is likely to result in damage or personal injury.
Note: *A special slotted socket is required to remove and refit the upper spring seat retaining nut; alternatives to the VW tool are available from specialist automotive tool manufacturers (eg. Sykes Pickavant)* **(see Tool Tip).**

Removal

1 Remove the front suspension strut as described in Section 2.
2 Using a spring compression tool compress the coil spring until it is clear of the upper retainer.
3 Using the special slotted socket, unscrew the slotted nut from the shock absorber rod and withdraw the spring retainer, washer, bump stop, boot, and coil spring **(see illustration)**. If a special tool to engage the slotted nut is not available, use a pair of grips.
4 Remove the compressor tool.

Refitting

5 Refitting is a reversal of removal with reference to Section 2 when refitting the strut. Tighten the slotted nut to the specified torque.

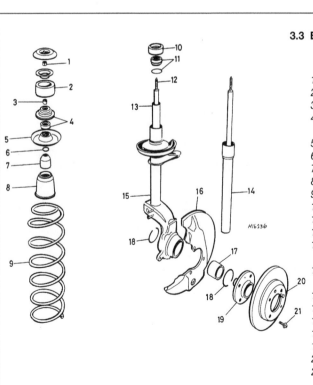

3.3 Exploded view of front suspension strut

1 Self-locking nut
2 Damping ring
3 Slotted nut
4 Suspension strut bearing
5 Spring retainer
6 Washer
7 Bump stop
8 Boot
9 Coil spring
10 Screw cap
11 Piston rod guide seal
12 Shock absorber
13 'Wet type' shock absorber
14 Shock absorber cartridge
15 Wheel bearing housing
16 Splash plate
17 Wheel bearing
18 Circlip
19 Wheel hub
20 Brake disc
21 Wheel bolt

4 Front shock absorber - renewal

Note: *VW tool 40-201 B is necessary in order to unscrew the screw cap from the top of the strut.*

1 A faulty shock absorber will normally make a knocking noise as the car is driven over rough surfaces.

2 To remove the shock absorber first remove the front coil spring as described in Section 3.

3 Using VW tool 40-201 B unscrew the screw cap from the top of the strut and remove the piston rod guide and seal. If necessary first mount the strut in a vice.

4 Pull the shock absorber out of the strut then pour the remaining fluid out and discard it. Clean the inside of the strut with paraffin and wipe dry.

5 Replacement shock absorbers are supplied as dry type cartridges, the wet type are only fitted by the factory when new.

6 With the new shock absorber upright, operate it fully several times and check that the resistance is even without any tight spots.

7 Insert the shock absorber in the strut and fit the guide together with a new seal.

8 Fit the screw cap and tighten it to the specified torque.

9 Refit the coil spring as described in Section 3.

5 Front wheel bearings - testing and renewal

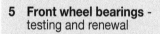

Testing

1 Jack up the front of the car and support on axle stands (see *"Jacking and vehicle support"*). With neutral selected, spin the wheel. A rumbling noise will be evident if the bearings are worn and excessive play will be apparent when the wheel is rocked, however check that the lower balljoint is not responsible for the play.

Renewal

2 To renew the wheel bearings first remove the suspension strut as described in Section 2.

3 Support the outside of the strut, then using a suitable metal tube, drive the hub from the wheel bearing. The outer bearing race will be forced from the bearing during this procedure and therefore it is not possible to re-use the bearing.

4 Mount the hub in a vice and use a suitable puller to remove the race **(see illustration)**.

5 Extract the circlips then support the strut again and use a suitable metal tube to drive out the wheel bearing.

6 Clean the inside of the bearing housing in the strut.

7 Fit the outer circlip to the strut.

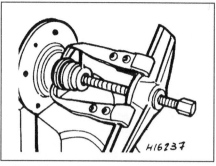

5.4 Using a puller to remove the outer wheel bearing race from the hub

8 Support the strut then smear a little grease on the bearing contact surfaces and drive in the bearing using a metal tube on the outer race only. Fit the inner circlip.

9 Place the hub upright on the bench and smear a little grease on the bearing contact area.

10 Locate the strut horizontally on the hub, then using a metal tube on the bearing inner race drive the bearing fully onto the hub.

11 Refit the suspension strut as described in Section 2.

6 Front track control arm and balljoint - removal and refitting

Removal

1 Jack up the front of the car and support on axle stands (see *"Jacking and vehicle support"*). Apply the handbrake and remove the roadwheel.

2 Unscrew the clamp bolt securing the control arm balljoint to the strut. Press the control arm down from the strut. Note that the bolt head faces forward.

3 Unscrew the nut and remove the bolt from the inner end of the control arm. Note that the bolt head faces forward, and also mark its position on the bracket.

4 Press the control arm down from the bracket, then unscrew the nut from the end of the anti-roll bar and pull off the control arm.

5 If the balljoint is worn excessively, renew the complete control arm. Check the condition of the bushes and if necessary press them out using a metal tube, nut and bolt, and washers. Fit the new bushes using the same method, but first dip them in soapy water. **Note:** *On G40 models the inner end of the track control arm is attached to the underbody by a fully enclosed ball joint which cannot be renewed separately.*

Refitting

6 Refitting is a reversal of removal, but delay fully tightening the inner pivot bolt and the anti-roll bar nut until the full weight of the car is on the roadwheels. Note that where camber angle adjustment has been made, the bolt

7.3 Top view of the anti-roll bar front mounting bracket (engine removed from car)

hole in the bracket may have been elongated and in this case it is imperative that the special bush and bolt are refitted in their original position otherwise the adjustment will have to be repeated.

7 Front anti-roll bar - removal and refitting

Removal

1 Jack up the front of the car and support with axle stands (see *"Jacking and vehicle support"*). Remove both wheels and apply the handbrake.

2 Note that with the anti-roll bar correctly fitted, the bend in the front of the bar faces upwards.

3 Unscrew the bolts and remove the mounting clamps securing the front of the bar to the underbody bracket **(see illustration)**.

4 Unscrew and remove the nuts and washers from the ends of the anti-roll bar.

5 Pull the anti-roll bar from the control arms and withdraw it from under the car. If difficulty is experienced, temporarily jack up the control arms to give a little extra width for the removal of the bar.

6 Check the bar and rubber bushes for wear and deterioration and renew as necessary. If the bush in the control arm is worn, renew it with reference to Section 6. **Note:** *The bushes fitted to the G40 model are harder than those fitted to other models.*

Refitting

7 Refitting is a reversal of removal, but delay fully tightening the nuts and bolts until the full weight of the car is on the roadwheels. The bend in the front section of the bar must face upwards. Note that the castor angle is determined by the position of the control arms on the anti-roll bar, therefore any adjustment washers should be refitted in their original locations.

8.2 Remove the cap from the top of the rear suspension strut

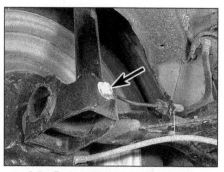

8.5a Rear suspension strut lower mounting bolt

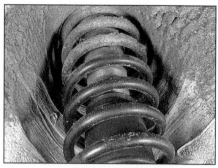

8.5b View of the rear suspension strut upper mounting from below

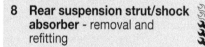

8 Rear suspension strut/shock absorber - removal and refitting

Note: *Removal of both suspension struts at the same time is not recommended, due to the excessive stresses which would be subjected to the bonded rubber bushes. If unavoidable, support the trailing arms on axle stands.*

Removal

1 Chock the front wheels then jack up the rear of the car and support on axle stands. Remove the rear wheel.

2 Working inside the rear of the car, remove the parcel tray then remove the cap from the top of the strut by twisting it anti-clockwise **(see illustration)**.
3 Support the trailing arm with a trolley jack.
4 Unscrew the nut from the top of the shock absorber rod, if necessary holding the rod stationary with a spanner. Remove the cup and upper buffer.
5 Working beneath the car remove the lower mounting bolt, then lower the trailing arm sufficient to withdraw the strut/shock absorber. Keep the coil spring, seat and bump stop components in their fitted positions **(see illustrations)**.

6 Remove the upper spring seat, coil spring, lower buffer, washer, bump stop and bellows and, if the unit is to be renewed, the lower spring retainer **(see illustration)**.
7 If the shock absorber is faulty it will normally make a knocking noise as the car is driven over rough surfaces, however with the unit removed uneven resistance tight spots will be evident as the central rod is operated. Check the condition of the buffers, bump stop and bellows and renew them if necessary. Before fitting the strut/shock absorber operate it fully several times in an upright position and check that the resistance is even and without any tight spots.

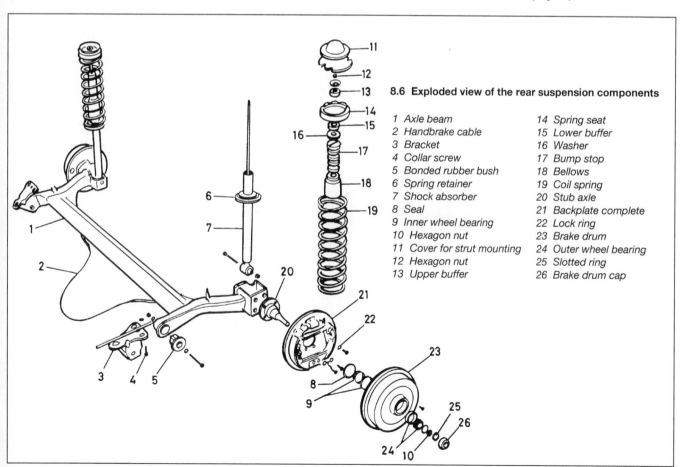

8.6 Exploded view of the rear suspension components

1 Axle beam	14 Spring seat
2 Handbrake cable	15 Lower buffer
3 Bracket	16 Washer
4 Collar screw	17 Bump stop
5 Bonded rubber bush	18 Bellows
6 Spring retainer	19 Coil spring
7 Shock absorber	20 Stub axle
8 Seal	21 Backplate complete
9 Inner wheel bearing	22 Lock ring
10 Hexagon nut	23 Brake drum
11 Cover for strut mounting	24 Outer wheel bearing
12 Hexagon nut	25 Slotted ring
13 Upper buffer	26 Brake drum cap

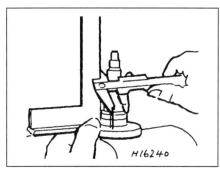

9.3 Checking the rear wheel stub axle for distortion

Refitting

8 Refitting is a reversal of removal, but make sure that the coil spring is correctly located in the seats. Delay tightening the lower mounting bolt until the full weight of the car is on the roadwheels.

9 Rear stub axle - removal and refitting

Removal

1 Remove the rear brake shoes and wheel cylinder as described in Chapter 9.
2 Unscrew the bolts and remove the brake backplate followed by the stub axle.
3 Clean the stub axle and check it for distortion using a try-square and vernier calipers as shown **(see illustration)**. Compare

the readings at a minimum of three points and if the difference between the maximum and minimum readings exceeds 0.25 mm, renew the stub axle.

Refitting

4 Refitting is a reversal of removal, but make sure that all mating faces are clean and tighten the bolts to the specified torque. Refer to Section 10 as necessary and adjust the wheel bearings.

10 Rear wheel bearings - testing and renewal

Testing

1 Chock the front wheels, then jack up the rear of the car and support on axle stands (see "*Jacking and vehicle support*"). Release the handbrake.
2 Spin the wheel. A rumbling noise will be evident if the bearings are worn in which case they must be renewed.

Renewal

3 Remove the wheel then prise off the central hub cap and extract the split pin. Remove the locking ring **(see illustrations)**.
4 Unscrew the hub nut and remove the thrustwasher and outer wheel bearing **(see illustrations)**.
5 Withdraw the brake drum. If difficulty is experienced, the brake shoes must be backed away from the drum first. To do this, insert a

screwdriver through one of the bolt holes and push the automatic adjuster wedge upwards against the spring tension. This will release the shoes from the drum.
6 Prise the seal from the inside of the drum with a screwdriver.
7 Remove the inner bearing, then using a soft metal drift, drive out the bearing outer races **(see illustration)**.
8 Clean the components in paraffin, wipe them dry, then examine them for wear and deterioration. Check the rollers and races for signs of pitting. Renew the bearings as necessary and obtain a new oil seal. Wipe clean the stub axle.
9 Using a suitable metal tube or socket, drive the outer races into the drum/hub **(see illustration)**.
10 Lubricate the bearings with lithium based grease then locate the inner bearing in its race **(see illustration)**.

10.3a Removing the rear wheel hub cap

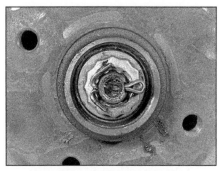

10.3b Rear wheel bearing split pin and locking ring

10.4a Rear wheel bearing thrustwasher

10.4b Removing the rear wheel outer bearing

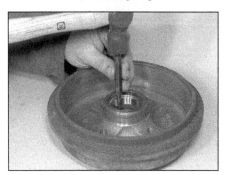

10.7 Drive the outer races out of position using a hammer and punch

10.9 Drive the outer races securely into position using a socket on the outer edge

10.10 Work grease into the taper roller bearings prior to fitting them to the hub

10.11 Grease the lips of the seal, and press it into the rear of the hub

11 Smear the lips of the new seal with a little grease. Using a block of wood drive the seal squarely into the drum/hub with the lips facing inwards **(see illustration)**.
12 Refit the drum and locate the outer bearing on the stub axle.
13 Fit the thrustwasher and hub nut, and tighten the nut hand tight.
14 Refit the wheel.
15 With the hub cap, split pin, and locking ring removed, tighten the hub nut firmly while turning the wheel in order to settle the bearings.
16 Back off the nut then tighten it until it is just possible to move the thrustwasher laterally with a screwdriver under finger pressure. Do not twist the screwdriver or lever it **(see illustration)**.
17 Fit the locking ring together with a new split pin, then tap the hub cap into the drum with a mallet.
18 Lower the car to the ground.

11 Rear axle beam -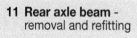
removal and refitting

Removal

Note: *If the axle beam is suspected of being distorted it should be checked in position by a VW garage using an optical alignment instrument*

1 Remove the rear stub axles as described in Section 9.

10.16 Checking the rear wheel bearing adjustment with a screwdriver (see text)

2 Support the weight of the trailing arms with axle stands then disconnect the struts/shock absorbers by removing the lower mounting bolts.
3 Remove the tail section of the exhaust system with reference to Chapter 4. Alternatively release the rear exhaust from the rubber mountings and position it to one side.
4 Disconnect the handbrake cables from the axle beam with reference to Chapter 9.
5 Remove the brake fluid reservoir filler cap and tighten it down onto a piece of polythene sheet in order to reduce the loss of hydraulic fluid. Alternatively fit brake hose clamps to the rear flexible hoses.
6 Lower the axle beam and disconnect the brake hydraulic hoses with reference to Chapter 9.
7 Support the weight of the axle beam with axle stands then unscrew and remove the pivot bolts and lower the axle beam to the ground. Note that the pivot bolt heads face outwards **(see illustration)**.
8 If the bushes are worn renew them as described in Section 12. If necessary the trunnion brackets can be removed by unscrewing the bolts. Discard the bolts.

Refitting

9 Refit the trunnion brackets if removed, but coat the new bolt threads with locking compound before tightening them to the specified torque.
10 Refitting the rear axle beam is a reversal of removal, but delay tightening the strut/shock absorber lower mounting bolts

and the axle beam pivot bolts to the specified torques until the full weight of the car is on the roadwheels. Bleed the brake hydraulic system as described in Chapter 9.

12 Rear axle beam pivot bushes
- renewal

1 Chock the front wheels then jack up the rear of the car and support on axle stands (see "*Jacking and vehicle support*"). Release the handbrake and remove the rear wheels.
2 Remove the tail section of the exhaust system with reference to Chapter 4.
3 Disconnect the handbrake cables from the underbody brackets and axle beam with reference to Chapter 9.
4 Unscrew and remove the pivot bolts and lower the axle beam onto axle stands making sure the flexible brake hoses are not strained.
5 Using a two-arm puller, force the bushes from the axle beam **(see illustration)**. Dip the new bushes in soapy water before pressing them in from the outside with the puller.
6 Refit the pivot bolts, handbrake cables, exhaust and rear wheels using a reversal of the removal procedure, but delay tightening the pivot bolt nuts to the specified torque until the full weight of the car is on the roadwheels.

13 Steering wheel -
removal and refitting

Removal

1 Set the front wheels in the straight-ahead position.
2 Prise the cover from the centre of the steering wheel, note the location of the wires and disconnect them from the terminals on the cover.
3 Mark the steering wheel, inner column and adapter sleeve in relation to each other, then unscrew the nut, remove the washer and withdraw the steering wheel. If it is tight, try rocking it slowly but firmly. Remove the washer **(see illustrations)**.

11.7 Rear axle pivot bolt

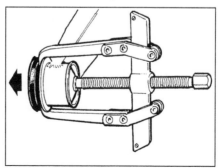

12.5 Use a puller to remove the rear axle beam pivot bushes

13.3a Unscrew the nut . . .

13.3b . . . and remove the washer

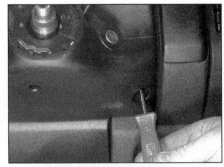

14.3a Remove the screws . . .

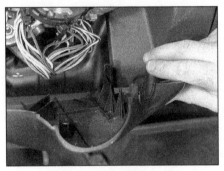

14.3b . . . and withdraw the
lower shroud . . .

14.3c . . . and upper shroud

14.6 Steering column lower clamp

Refitting

4 Refitting in a reversal of removal, but make sure that the turn signal lever is in its neutral position, otherwise damage may occur to the cancelling arm. Make sure that the 3 mm thick washer is fitted beneath the retaining nut, and also check that when fitted a clearance of 3 mm exists between the bottom edge of the steering wheel and the steering column switch. Tighten the nut to the specified torque.

14 Steering column - removal and refitting

Removal

1 Disconnect the battery negative lead.
2 Remove the steering wheel as described in Section 13.
3 Remove the screws and withdraw the steering column lower then upper shrouds (see illustrations).
4 Remove the three screws and withdraw the combination switch. Disconnect the wiring plug.
5 Remove the screws and withdraw the lower facia trim panel.
6 Mark the position of the clamp on the bottom of the inner column in relation to the steering gear pinion, then unscrew and remove the bolt (see illustration).
7 Remove the column mounting bolts (see illustration). An Allen key is required to

unscrew one bolt, but the remaining bolt is a shear bolt and therefore its head must be drilled out using an 8.5 mm diameter drill.
8 Lift the steering column and disconnect the inner column from the steering gear pinion splines, then withdraw the column from the car. Disconnect the ignition switch wiring plug, and unscrew the old shear bolt.

Refitting

9 Refitting is a reversal of removal, but make sure that the column is correctly positioned before tightening the shear bolt until its head is broken off. On models manufactured from late 1991, make sure that there is a clearance of 1.0 mm between the end of the steering gear pinion and the adjacent part of the universal joint (see illustration).

15 Steering column - overhaul

1 With the steering column removed as described in Section 14 mark the splined adapter in relation to the top of the inner column, then use a suitable puller to remove the adapter (see illustration).
2 Remove the spring from the top of the inner column.
3 Using an Allen key unscrew the clamp bolt securing the steering lock and withdraw the lock. Note that the ignition key must be inserted and the lock released.

14.7 Steering column mounting bolts

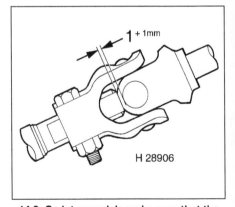

14.9 On later models make sure that the clearance shown is maintained between the end of the steering gear pinion and the universal joint

15.1 Draw the splined adapter off the steering column using a puller

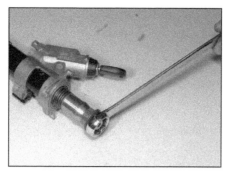

15.7 Use the steering wheel nut to press the adapter onto the inner column

16.2 Removing the splined adapter and spring from the top of the inner column

16.6 Unscrewing the steering lock clamp bolt

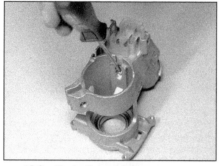

16.8a Undo the retaining screw . . .

16.8b . . . and remove the ignition switch from the steering column lock assembly

4 Withdraw the inner column from the outer column and remove the support ring.

5 Clean the components and examine them for wear and damage. The metal tab on the bottom section of the inner column must be visible in the hole of the top section - if not, the column may be damaged. On models manufactured from late 1991, examine the universal joint for wear. Renew the components as necessary.

6 Before reassembling the column, temporarily fit the components to the top of the column and check that there is a clearance of 3.0 mm ± 1.5 mm between the bottom of the steering wheel and the steering column switch.

7 Reassembly is a reversal of dismantling, but lubricate bearing surfaces with multi-purpose grease. The splined adapter is refitted using the steering wheel retaining nut to press it on the top of the inner column **(see illustration)**.

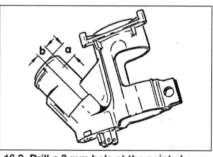

16.9 Drill a 3 mm hole at the point shown to reveal the lock cylinder detent plunger

a 12 mm   b 10 mm

3 Remove the screws and withdraw the steering column lower shroud.
4 Remove the three screws and withdraw the combination switch. Disconnect the wiring plug.
5 Remove the spring from the top of the inner column.
6 Using an Allen key unscrew the clamp bolt securing the steering lock **(see illustration)**.
7 Disconnect the wiring plug and withdraw the steering lock from the top of the column together with the upper shroud. Note that the ignition key must be inserted to ensure that the lock is in its released position.
8 Remove the screw and withdraw the switch from the lock housing **(see illustrations)**.
9 To remove the lock cylinder, drill a 3.0 mm diameter hole in the location shown **(see illustration)**, depress the spring pin, and extract the cylinder.

16 Steering lock - removal and refitting

Removal

1 Disconnect the battery negative lead.
2 Remove the steering wheel as described in Section 13, and the splined adapter as described in Section 15 paragraph 1 **(see illustration)**. However it is not necessary to remove the steering column for this work.

17.5 Clutch cable hole (arrowed) in the steering gear housing

Refitting
10 Refitting is a reversal of removal.

17 Steering gear - removal, refitting and adjustment

Removal

1 Disconnect the battery negative lead.
2 Remove the air duct and air cleaner as described in Chapter 4.
3 Lift out the windscreen washer bottle and place it to one side.
4 Inside the car, remove the screws and withdraw the lower facia panel shelf from around the steering column.
5 Disconnect the clutch cable from the transmission with reference to Chapter 6, and

17.10a Steering gear location (engine removed from car)

17.10b Right-hand side mounting clamp on the steering gear

19.2 Steering tie-rod centre bolts

disengage it from the steering gear **(see illustration)**.

6 Set the front wheels in the straight-ahead position then unscrew the clamp bolt securing the inner column to the steering gear pinion. Where applicable, remove the trim panel for access to the clamp bolt.

7 Prise the inner column up from the pinion as far as it will go. Do not bend the clamp open.

8 Unscrew and remove the tie-rod centre bolts and move the tie-rods to one side. Where applicable unscrew the bolt and disconnect the steering damper.

9 Jack up the front of the car and support on axle stands (see "*Jacking and vehicle support*"). Apply the handbrake and remove the front wheels.

10 Unscrew the nuts and remove the mounting clamps **(see illustrations)**.

11 Withdraw the steering gear upwards.

Refitting and adjustment

12 Refitting is a reversal of removal, but do not fully tighten the mounting clamp nuts until the steering gear is correctly aligned.

13 With the front of the car supported on axle stands turn the steering from lock to lock and check that there are no tight spots or excessive play. If necessary turn in the self-locking adjusting screw on the bottom of the steering gear to reduce play or turn out to reduce tight spots. Turn the screw in 20° stages and initially make the adjustment with the front wheels in the straight ahead position.

14 Finally check and if necessary adjust the clutch with reference to Chapter 6.

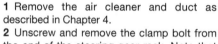

18 Steering gear rubber gaiters - renewal

1 Remove the air cleaner and duct as described in Chapter 4.

2 Unscrew and remove the clamp bolt from the end of the steering gear rack. Note that the bolt engages a groove on the side of the rack. Separate the bracket from the rack.

3 Loosen the clip and withdraw the bellows from the steering gear together with the retaining ring.

4 Smear a little steering gear grease on the rack then fit the new bellows together with the inner clip. Locate the bellows on the housing and tighten the clip.

5 Push on the retaining ring and locate the bellows in the outer groove.

6 Fit the bracket then insert the bolt so that it engages the groove and tighten the nut.

7 Refit the air cleaner with reference to Chapter 4.

19 Tie-rods and balljoints - removal and refitting

Removal

1 If the steering tie-rod and balljoints are worn, play will be evident as the roadwheel is rocked from side to side, and the balljoint must then be renewed. On RHD models the left-hand tie-rod is adjustable and the balljoint on this tie-rod can be renewed separately, however the right-hand tie-rod must be renewed complete. On LHD models the tie-rods are vice versa.

2 If the complete tie-rod is to be removed unscrew the centre bolt preferably with the weight of the car on the wheels otherwise the rubber bush may be damaged **(see illustration)**.

3 Jack up the front of the car and support on axle stands (see "*Jacking and vehicle support*"). Apply the handbrake and remove the front wheel(s).

4 Unscrew the balljoint nut then use a balljoint separator tool to release the joint from the strut **(see illustrations)**.

5 Withdraw the tie-rod or, if removing only the tie-rod end, loosen the locknut and unscrew the tie-rod end.

Refitting

6 Refitting is a reversal of removal, but tighten the nuts to the specified torque and check the front wheel alignment (refer to Section 20).

20 Wheel alignment and steering angles - general information

Definitions

1 A car's steering and suspension geometry is defined in four basic settings - all angles are expressed in degrees (toe settings are also expressed as a measurement); the steering

19.4a Unscrew the nut . . .

19.4b . . . then use a balljoint separator tool . . .

19.4c . . . to release the tie-rod

axis is defined as an imaginary line drawn through the axis of the suspension strut, extended where necessary to contact the ground.

2 Camber is the angle between each roadwheel and a vertical line drawn through its centre and tyre contact patch, when viewed from the front or rear of the car. Positive camber is when the roadwheels are tilted outwards from the vertical at the top; negative camber is when they are tilted inwards.

3 Camber angle does not normally require adjustment, but refer to Section 6. It can be checked using a camber checking gauge.

4 Castor is the angle between the steering axis and a vertical line drawn through each roadwheel's centre and tyre contact patch, when viewed from the side of the car. Positive castor is when the steering axis is tilted so that it contacts the ground ahead of the vertical; negative castor is when it contacts the ground behind the vertical.

5 Castor angle does not normally require adjustment, but refer to Section 7. It can be checked using a castor checking gauge - if the figure obtained is significantly different from that specified, the vehicle must be taken for careful checking by a professional. Where necessary a 3.0 mm washer can be inserted at the anti-roll bar bush on the front of the lower suspension arm.

6 Toe is the difference, viewed from above, between lines drawn through the roadwheel centres and the car's centre-line. "Toe-in" is when the roadwheels point inwards, towards each other at the front, while "toe-out" is when they splay outwards from each other at the front.

7 The front wheel toe setting is adjusted by screwing the left-hand track rod (RHD models) or right-hand track rod (LHD models) in or out of its balljoint, to alter the effective length of the track rod assembly.

8 Rear wheel toe setting is not adjustable, and is given for reference only. While it can be checked, if the figure obtained is significantly different from that specified, the vehicle must be taken for careful checking by a professional, as the fault can only be caused by wear or damage to the body or suspension components.

Checking and adjustment

Front wheel toe setting

9 Due to the special measuring equipment necessary to check the wheel alignment, and the skill required to use it properly, the checking and adjustment of these settings is best left to a VW dealer or similar expert. Note that most tyre-fitting shops now possess sophisticated checking equipment.

10 To check the toe setting, a tracking gauge must first be obtained. Two types of gauge are available, and can be obtained from motor accessory shops. The first type measures the distance between the front and rear inside edges of the roadwheels, as previously described, with the vehicle stationary. The second type, known as a 'scuff plate', measures the actual position of the contact surface of the tyre, in relation to the road surface, with the vehicle in motion. This is achieved by pushing or driving the front tyre over a plate, which then moves slightly according to the scuff of the tyre, and shows this movement on a scale. Both types have

their advantages and disadvantages, but either can give satisfactory results if used correctly and carefully.

11 Make sure that the steering is in the straight-ahead position when making measurements.

12 If adjustment is necessary, apply the handbrake then jack up the front of the vehicle and support it securely on axle stands (see "*Jacking and vehicle support*").

13 First clean the track rod threads; if they are corroded, apply penetrating fluid before starting adjustment.

14 Retain the track rod with a suitable spanner and slacken the locknuts. Alter the length of the track rod by turning the tie-rod as necessary.

15 When the setting is correct, hold the track rod and tighten the locknuts. If after adjustment, the steering wheel spokes are no longer horizontal when the wheels are in the straight-ahead position, remove the steering wheel and reposition it (see Section 13).

16 Check that the toe setting has been correctly adjusted by lowering the vehicle to the ground and re-checking; re-adjust if necessary.

Rear wheel toe setting

17 The procedure for checking the rear toe setting is same as described for the front in paragraph 10. The setting is not adjustable.

Front wheel camber angle

18 Checking and adjusting of the front wheel camber angle should be entrusted to a VW dealer or other suitably equipped specialist. Note that most tyre-fitting shops now possess sophisticated checking equipment.

Notes

Chapter 11
Bodywork and fittings

Contents

Degrees of difficulty

Easy, suitable for novice with little experience	Fairly easy, suitable for beginner with some experience	Fairly difficult, suitable for competent DIY mechanic	Difficult, suitable for experienced DIY mechanic	Very difficult, suitable for expert DIY or professional

Specifications

Torque wrench settings	Nm	lbf ft
Tailgate lock	23	17
Window regulator	8	6
Door	55	41
Exterior handle:		
To outside of door	2	1.5
To edge of door	8	6
Bumpers	5	4
Seat belts:		
Reel	40	30
Stalk	60	44
Anchor	40	30
Tailgate lock	23	17

1 General information

The bodyshell is made of pressed-steel sections, and is available in three-door Hatchback, three-door Coupe and two-door Saloon versions. Most components are welded together, but some use is made of structural adhesives; the front wings are bolted on.

The bonnet, door, and some other vulnerable panels are made of zinc-coated metal, and are further protected by being coated with an anti-chip primer before being sprayed.

Extensive use is made of plastic materials, mainly in the interior, but also in exterior components. The front and rear bumpers and front grille are injection-moulded from a synthetic material that is very strong and yet light. Plastic components such as wheel arch liners are fitted to the underside of the vehicle, to improve the body's resistance to corrosion.

2 Maintenance - bodywork and underframe

The general condition of a vehicle's bodywork is the one thing that significantly affects its value. Maintenance is easy, but needs to be regular. Neglect, particularly after minor damage, can lead quickly to further deterioration and costly repair bills. It is important also to keep watch on those parts of the vehicle not immediately visible, for instance the underside, inside all the wheel arches, and the lower part of the engine compartment.

The basic maintenance routine for the bodywork is washing - preferably with a lot of water, from a hose. This will remove all the loose solids which may have stuck to the vehicle. It is important to flush these off in such a way as to prevent grit from scratching the finish. The wheel arches and underframe need washing in the same way, to remove any accumulated mud which will retain moisture and tend to encourage rust. Strangely enough, the best time to clean the underframe and wheel arches is in wet weather, when the mud is thoroughly wet and soft. In very wet weather, the underframe is usually cleaned of large accumulations automatically, and this is a good time for inspection.

Periodically, except on vehicles with a wax-based underbody protective coating, it is a good idea to have the whole of the underframe of the vehicle steam-cleaned, engine compartment included, so that a thorough inspection can be carried out to see what minor repairs and renovations are necessary. Steam cleaning is available at many garages, and is necessary for the removal of the accumulation of oily grime, which sometimes is allowed to become thick in certain areas. If steam-cleaning facilities are not available, there are some excellent grease solvents available which can be brush-applied; the dirt can then be simply hosed off. Note that these methods should not be used on vehicles with wax-based underbody protective coating, or the coating will be removed. Such vehicles should be inspected annually, preferably just before Winter, when the underbody should be washed down, and repair any damage to the wax coating. Ideally, a completely fresh coat should be applied. It would also be worth considering the use of such wax-based protection for injection into door panels, sills, box sections, etc, as an additional safeguard against rust damage, where such protection is not provided by the vehicle manufacturer.

After washing paintwork, wipe off with a chamois leather to give an unspotted clear finish. A coat of clear protective wax polish will give added protection against chemical pollutants in the air. If the paintwork sheen has dulled or oxidised, use a cleaner/polisher combination to restore the brilliance of the shine. This requires a little effort, but such dulling is usually caused because regular washing has been neglected. Care needs to be taken with metallic paintwork, as special non-abrasive cleaner/polisher is required to avoid damage to the finish. Always check that the door and ventilator opening drain holes and pipes are completely clear, so that water can be drained out. Brightwork should be treated in the same way as paintwork. Windscreens and windows can be kept clear of the smeary film which often appears, by proprietary glass cleaner. Never use any form of wax or other body or chromium polish on glass.

3 Maintenance - upholstery and carpets

Mats and carpets should be brushed or vacuum-cleaned regularly, to keep them free of grit. If they are badly stained, remove them from the vehicle for scrubbing or sponging, and make quite sure they are dry before refitting. Seats and interior trim panels can be kept clean by wiping with a damp cloth. If they do become stained (which can be more apparent on light-coloured upholstery), use a little liquid detergent and a soft nail brush to scour the grime out of the grain of the material. Do not forget to keep the headlining clean in the same way as the upholstery. When using liquid cleaners inside the vehicle, do not over-wet the surfaces being cleaned. Excessive damp could get into the seams and padded interior, causing stains, offensive odours or even rot. If the inside of the vehicle gets wet accidentally, it is worthwhile taking some trouble to dry it out properly, particularly where carpets are involved. *Do not leave oil or electric heaters inside the vehicle for this purpose.*

4 Minor body damage - repair

Repairs of minor scratches in bodywork

If the scratch is very superficial, and does not penetrate to the metal of the bodywork, repair is very simple. Lightly rub the area of the scratch with a paintwork renovator or a very fine cutting paste to remove loose paint from the scratch, and to clear the surrounding bodywork of wax polish. Rinse the area with clean water.

Apply touch-up paint to the scratch using a fine paint brush; continue to apply fine layers of paint until the surface of the paint in the scratch is level with the surrounding paintwork. Allow the new paint at least two weeks to harden, then blend it into the surrounding paintwork by rubbing the scratch area with a paintwork renovator or a very fine cutting paste. Finally, apply wax polish.

Where the scratch has penetrated right through to the metal of the bodywork, causing the metal to rust, a different repair technique is required. Remove any loose rust from the bottom of the scratch with a penknife, then apply rust-inhibiting paint to prevent the formation of rust in the future. Using a rubber or nylon applicator, fill the scratch with bodystopper paste. If required, this paste can be mixed with cellulose thinners to provide a very thin paste which is ideal for filling narrow scratches. Before the stopper-paste in the scratch hardens, wrap a piece of smooth cotton rag around the top of a finger. Dip the finger in cellulose thinners, and quickly sweep it across the surface of the stopper-paste in the scratch; this will ensure that the surface of the stopper-paste is slightly hollowed. The scratch can now be painted over as described earlier in this Section.

Repairs of dents in bodywork

When deep denting of the vehicle's bodywork has taken place, the first task is to pull the dent out, until the affected bodywork almost attains its original shape. There is little point in trying to restore the original shape completely, as the metal in the damaged area will have stretched on impact, and cannot be reshaped fully to its original contour. It is better to bring the level of the dent up to a point which is about 3 mm below the level of the surrounding bodywork. In cases where the dent is very shallow anyway, it is not worth trying to pull it out at all. If the underside of the dent is accessible, it can be hammered out gently from behind, using a mallet with a wooden or plastic head. Whilst doing this, hold a suitable block of wood firmly against the outside of the panel, to absorb the impact from the hammer blows and thus prevent a large area of the bodywork from being "belled-out".

Should the dent be in a section of the bodywork which has a double skin, or some other factor making it inaccessible from behind, a different technique is called for. Drill several small holes through the metal inside the area - particularly in the deeper section. Then screw long self-tapping screws into the holes, just sufficiently for them to gain a good purchase in the metal. Now the dent can be pulled out by pulling on the protruding heads of the screws with a pair of pliers.

The next stage of the repair is the removal of the paint from the damaged area, and from an inch or so of the surrounding "sound" bodywork. This is accomplished most easily by using a wire brush or abrasive pad on a power drill, although it can be done just as effectively by hand, using sheets of abrasive paper. To complete the preparation for filling, score the surface of the bare metal with a screwdriver or the tang of a file, or alternatively, drill small holes in the affected area. This will provide a good "key" for the filler paste.

To complete the repair, see the Section on filling and respraying.

Repairs of rust holes or gashes in bodywork

Remove all paint from the affected area, and from an inch or so of the surrounding "sound" bodywork, using an abrasive pad or a wire brush on a power drill. If these are not available, a few sheets of abrasive paper will do the job most effectively. With the paint removed, you will be able to judge the severity of the corrosion, and therefore decide whether to renew the whole panel (if this is possible) or to repair the affected area. New body panels are not as expensive as most people think, and it is often quicker and more satisfactory to fit a new panel than to attempt to repair large areas of corrosion.

Remove all fittings from the affected area, except those which will act as a guide to the original shape of the damaged bodywork (eg headlamp shells etc). Then, using tin snips or a hacksaw blade, remove all loose metal and any other metal badly affected by corrosion. Hammer the edges of the hole inwards, to create a slight depression for the filler paste.

Wire-brush the affected area to remove the powdery rust from the surface of the remaining metal. Paint the affected area with rust-inhibiting paint; if the back of the rusted area is accessible, treat this also.

Before filling can take place, it will be necessary to block the hole in some way. This can be achieved with aluminium or plastic mesh, or aluminium tape.

Aluminium or plastic mesh, or glass-fibre matting, is probably the best material to use for a large hole. Cut a piece to the approximate size and shape of the hole to be filled, then position it in the hole so that its edges are below the level of the surrounding bodywork. It can be retained in position by several blobs of filler paste around its periphery.

Aluminium tape should be used for small or very narrow holes. Pull a piece off the roll, trim it to the approximate size and shape required, then pull off the backing paper (if used) and stick the tape over the hole; it can be overlapped if the thickness of one piece is insufficient. Burnish down the edges of the tape with the handle of a screwdriver or similar, to ensure that the tape is securely attached to the metal underneath.

Bodywork repairs - filling and respraying

Before using this Section, see the Sections on dent, deep scratch, rust holes and gash repairs.

Many types of bodyfiller are available, but generally speaking, those proprietary kits which contain a tin of filler paste and a tube of resin hardener are best for this type of repair which can be used directly from the tube. A wide, flexible plastic or nylon applicator will be found invaluable for imparting a smooth and well-contoured finish to the surface of the filler.

Mix up a little filler on a clean piece of card or board - measure the hardener carefully (follow the maker's instructions on the pack), otherwise the filler will set too rapidly or too slowly. Using the applicator, apply the filler paste to the prepared area; draw the applicator across the surface of the filler to achieve the correct contour and to level the surface. When a contour that approximates to the correct one is achieved, stop working the paste - if you carry on too long, the paste will become sticky and begin to "pick-up" on the applicator. Continue to add thin layers of filler paste at 20-minute intervals, until the level of the filler is just proud of the surrounding bodywork.

Once the filler has hardened, the excess can be removed using a metal plane or file. From then on, progressively-finer grades of abrasive paper should be used, starting with a 40-grade production paper, and finishing with a 400-grade wet-and-dry paper. Always wrap the abrasive paper around a flat rubber, cork, or wooden block - otherwise the surface of the filler will not be completely flat. During the smoothing of the filler surface, the wet-and-dry paper should be periodically rinsed in water. This will ensure that a very smooth finish is imparted to the filler at the final stage.

At this stage, the "dent" should be surrounded by a ring of bare metal, which in turn should be encircled by the finely "feathered" edge of the good paintwork. Rinse the repair area with clean water, until all the dust produced by the rubbing-down operation has gone.

Spray the whole area with a light coat of primer - this will show up any imperfections in the surface of the filler. Repair these imperfections with fresh filler paste or bodystopper, and again smooth the surface with abrasive paper. If bodystopper is used, it can be mixed with cellulose thinners, to form

a thin paste which is ideal for filling small holes. Repeat this spray-and-repair procedure until you are satisfied that the surface of the filler, and the feathered edge of the paintwork, are perfect. Clean the repair area with clean water, and allow to dry fully.

The repair area is now ready for final spraying. Paint spraying must be carried out in a warm, dry, windless and dust-free atmosphere. This condition can be created artificially if you have access to a large indoor working area, but if you are forced to work in the open, you will have to pick your day very carefully. If you are working indoors, dousing the floor in the work area with water will help to settle the dust which would otherwise be in the atmosphere. If the repair area is confined to one body panel, mask off the surrounding panels; this will help to minimise the effects of a slight mis-match in paint colours. Bodywork fittings (eg chrome strips, door handles etc) will also need to be masked off. Use genuine masking tape, and several thickness of newspaper, for the masking operations.

Before starting to spray, agitate the aerosol can thoroughly, then spray a test area (an old tin, or similar) until the technique is mastered. Cover the repair area with a thick coat of primer; the thickness should be built up using several thin layers of paint, rather than one thick one. Using 400 grade wet-and-dry paper, rub down the surface of the primer until it is smooth. While doing this, the work area should be thoroughly doused with water, and the wet-and-dry paper periodically rinsed in water. Allow to dry before spraying on more paint.

Spray on the top coat, again building up the thickness by using several thin layers of paint. Start spraying in the centre of the repair area, and then, using a circular motion, work outwards until the whole repair area and about 2 inches of the surrounding original paintwork is covered. Remove all masking material 10 to 15 minutes after spraying on the final coat of paint.

Allow the new paint at least two weeks to harden, then, using a paintwork renovator or a very fine cutting paste, blend the edges of the paint into the existing paintwork. Finally, apply wax polish.

Plastic components

With the use of more and more plastic body components by the vehicle manufacturers (eg bumpers, spoilers, and in some cases major body panels), rectification of more serious damage to such items has become a matter of either entrusting repair work to a specialist in this field, or renewing complete components. Repair of such damage by the DIY owner is not feasible, owing to the cost of the equipment and materials required for effecting such repairs. The basic technique involves making a groove along the line of the crack in the plastic, using a rotary burr in a power drill. The damaged part is then welded back together, using a hot air gun to heat up and fuse a plastic filler rod into the groove. Any excess plastic is then removed, and the area rubbed down to a smooth finish. It is important that a filler rod of the correct plastic is used, as body components can be made of a variety of different types (eg polycarbonate, ABS, polypropylene).

Damage of a less serious nature (abrasions, minor cracks etc) can be repaired by the DIY owner using a two-part epoxy filler repair material which can be used directly from the tube. Once mixed in equal proportions, this is used in similar fashion to the bodywork filler used on metal panels. The filler is usually cured in twenty to thirty minutes, ready for sanding and painting.

If the owner is renewing a complete component himself, or if he has repaired it with epoxy filler, he will be left with the problem of finding a suitable paint for finishing which is compatible with the type of plastic used. At one time, the use of a universal paint was not possible, owing to the complex range of plastics met with in body component applications. Standard paints, generally speaking, will not bond to plastic or rubber satisfactorily, but professional matched paints, to match any plastic or rubber finish, can be obtained from some dealers. However, it is now possible to obtain a plastic body parts finishing kit which consists of a pre-primer treatment, a primer and coloured top coat. Full instructions are normally supplied with a kit, but basically the method of use is to first apply the pre-primer to the component concerned, and allow it to dry for up to 30 minutes. Then the primer is applied, and left to dry for about an hour before finally applying the special-coloured top coat. The result is a correctly coloured component, where the paint will flex with the plastic or rubber, a property that standard paint does not normally posses.

5 Major body damage - repair

Where serious damage has occurred, or large areas need renewal due to neglect, it means that complete new panels will need

welding-in, and this is best left to professionals. If the damage is due to impact, it will also be necessary to check completely the alignment of the bodyshell, and this can only be carried out accurately by a VW dealer using special jigs. If the body is left misaligned, it is primarily dangerous, as the car will not handle properly, and secondly, uneven stresses will be imposed on the steering, suspension and possibly transmission, causing abnormal wear, or complete failure, particularly to such items as the tyres.

6 Radiator grille - removal and refitting

Removal

1 Support the bonnet in its open position.
2 Release the clips from the top of the grille by pressing them down with a screwdriver **(see illustration)**.
3 Move the top of the grille forwards then lift it from the lower mounting holes in the front valance **(see illustration)**.

Refitting

4 Refitting is a reversal of removal.

7 Front bumper - removal and refitting

Removal

1 Jack up the front of the car and support on axle stands (see "*Jacking and vehicle support*"). Apply the handbrake.
2 Remove the radiator grille (see Section 6).
3 Unscrew the three upper mounting bolts from the top edge of the front bumper.
4 Unscrew the lower mounting bolts, then pull the bumper forwards and disengage it from the side guide plates **(see illustration)**. Where headlamp washers are fitted, disconnect the tubing from the jets.

Refitting

5 Refitting is a reversal of removal.

8 Rear bumper - removal and refitting

Removal

Hatchback and Coupe models

1 Open the tailgate then prise out the covers and unscrew the upper mounting bolts from the top edge of the rear bumper **(see illustration)**.
2 Unscrew the lower mounting bolts then pull the rear bumper rearwards and disengage it from the side guide plates **(see illustration)**.

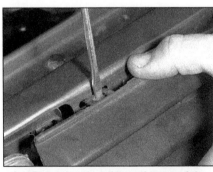

6.2 Releasing the clips at the top of the radiator grille with a screwdriver

6.3 Removing the radiator grille

7.4 Front bumper mounting bolt

8.1 Rear bumper upper mounting bolt and cover

8.2 Rear bumper lower mounting bolt

Saloon models

3 Remove the number plate lights from the rear bumper as described in Chapter 12.
4 Unscrew the mounting bolts securing the rear bumper to the underbody bracket. If necessary, access can be improved by raising the rear of the car and supporting on axle stands (see "*Jacking and vehicle support*").
5 Pull the rear bumper rearwards and disengage it from the side guide plates.

Refitting

6 Refitting is a reversal of removal.

9 Bonnet - removal, refitting and adjustment

Removal

1 Support the bonnet in its open position, and place some cardboard or rags beneath the corners by the hinges.
2 Mark the location of the hinges with a pencil then loosen the four retaining bolts.
3 With the help of an assistant, release the stay, remove the bolts, and withdraw the bonnet from the car.

Refitting and adjustment

4 Refitting is a reversal of removal, but adjust the hinges to their original positions and check that the bonnet is level with the surrounding bodywork. If necessary adjust the height of the bonnet front edge by screwing the rubber buffers in or out, and also adjust the bonnet lock if necessary with reference to Section 11.

10 Bonnet release cable - removal and refitting

Removal

1 Open the bonnet, unbolt the bonnet lock from the engine compartment front cross-member and disconnect the cable.

10.3 Bonnet release handle beneath the left-hand side of the facia

2 Inside the car, remove the lower facia panel on the left-hand side under the facia.
3 Remove the bonnet catch release handle and bracket (two screws), then disconnect the cable **(see illustration)**. Tie a piece of thin wire or cord to the inside end and pull that into the place the cable occupied to make fitting a new cable more simple. Release the cable from the retainers in the engine compartment and release the rubber grommet from the bulkhead.

Refitting

4 Refitting is a reversal of removal, but make sure that the cable is positioned without any sharp bends.

11 Bonnet lock - removal and refitting

Removal

1 To remove the lock, open the bonnet then mark the position of the bonnet lock on the engine compartment front crossmember **(see illustration)**.
2 Unscrew the mounting bolts, withdraw the lock and disconnect the cable.

Refitting

3 Refitting is a reversal of removal, but if necessary adjust the height of the bonnet front edge by loosening the retaining bolts

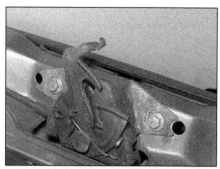
11.1 The bonnet lock located on the engine compartment front crossmember

and repositioning the lock within the elongated holes. The safety catch and anti-rattle spring should be checked for condition at the same time. Check that the bonnet is supported by the rubber buffers when shut, and if necessary adjust the height of the buffers by screwing them in or out.

12 Door - removal, refitting and adjustment

Removal

1 Open the door then prise off the special washer and remove the check strap pivot pin **(see illustration)**.
2 Mark the position of the door hinge brackets in relation to each other.
3 Support the door then unscrew and remove the lower hinge bolt followed by the upper hinge bolt, and withdraw the door from the car **(see illustration)**.

Refitting and adjustment

4 Refitting is a reversal of removal, but if necessary adjust the position of the door on the hinges so that, when closed, it is level with the surrounding bodywork and central within the body aperture. Lubricate the hinges with a little oil and the check strap with grease. If necessary adjust the position of the door striker.

12.1 Door check strap and pivot pin

12.3 Door upper hinge bolt

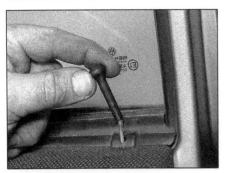

13.1 Removing the locking knob

13.2 Slide the inner handle surround to the rear to remove it

13.3a Removing the exterior mirror control knob . . .

13.3b . . . and boot

13.4a Prise out the trim cover . . .

13.4b . . . unscrew the mounting screws . . .

13.4c . . . and release the door pull from the trim

13.5a Prise off the cover . . .

13.5b . . . remove the screw . . .

13 Door inner trim panel - removal and refitting

Removal

1 If required, unscrew and remove the locking knob from the top of the inner trim panel **(see illustration)**. This is not essential as the trim panel is slotted to allow it to be removed with the knob in position.

2 Remove the inner handle surround by sliding it to the rear **(see illustration)**.

3 Remove the exterior mirror control knob and boot from the top of the door pull **(see illustrations)**.

4 Prise the trim cover from the door pull, remove the cross-head screws, then move the rear of the door pull outwards. Note the location lug **(see illustrations)**.

13.5c . . . and withdraw the window regulator handle from the splines

5 Note the position of the window regulator handle with the window shut then prise off the cover, remove the cross-head screw and withdraw the handle **(see illustrations)**.

6 Where applicable, remove the self-tapping screws and withdraw the storage compart-

13.7 Cross-head screw securing the inner trim panel to the door

ment panel. This is not required on all models.

7 Prise out the stoppers and remove the cross-head screws from the trim panel **(see illustration)**.

8 Using a wide blade screwdriver carefully prise the trim panel clips from the door inner

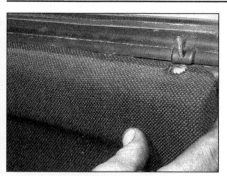

13.8 Releasing the inner trim panel from the weatherseal

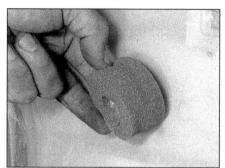

13.9 Removing the window regulator handle packing

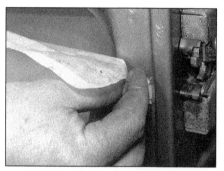

13.10 Peeling the protective sheet from the door

14.1 Screw securing the exterior handle to the rear edge of the door

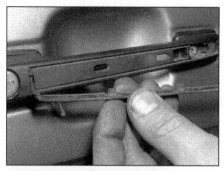

14.2 Removing the plastic strip insert from the exterior door handle

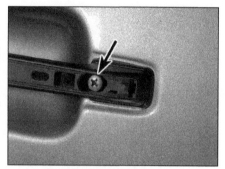

14.3a Remove the screw . . .

panel taking care not to damage the trim. Remove the panel and release it from the upper inner door weatherseal **(see illustration)**.

9 Remove the window regulator handle packing **(see illustration)**.

10 If necessary peel the protective sheet from the door **(see illustration)**. The trim clips are fitted over the sheet - it will be necessary to cut round them to prevent tearing the sheet.

Refitting

11 Refitting is a reversal of removal.

---

14 Door exterior handle and lock components - removal and refitting

Exterior handle

Removal

1 Open the door and unscrew the single screw securing the handle to the rear edge of the door **(see illustration)**.

2 Using a small screwdriver lever the plastic strip insert from the exterior door handle **(see illustration)**.

3 Remove the cross-head screw and withdraw the exterior handle from the door **(see illustrations)**. **Note:** *The handle is not connected directly with the door lock.*

Refitting

4 Refitting is a reversal of removal, but check the sealing gasket and fit a new one if necessary.

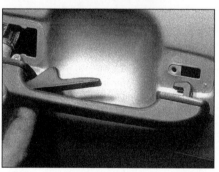

14.3b . . . then release the exterior handle from the door

Door lock

Removal

5 Remove the trim panel, locking knob and protective sheeting (refer to Section 13), then remove the packing from around the inner

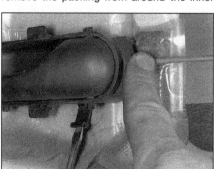

14.6a Use a screwdriver to release the inner door handle . . .

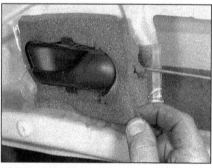

14.5 Packing around the inner door handle

door handle **(see illustration)**. The locking knob must also be unscrewed from the control rod before removing the door lock.

6 Using a screwdriver release the inner door handle from the door inner panel, then unhook it from the control rod **(see illustrations)**.

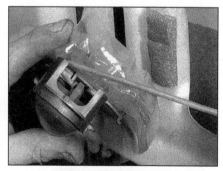

14.6b . . . then unhook it from the control rod

14.7a Unscrew the mounting screws . . .

14.7b . . . and withdraw the lock from the door

15.3a Bolts securing the window regulator to the door

15.3b Bolts securing the lifting plate to the window channel

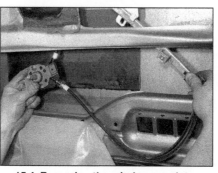

15.4 Removing the window regulator through the door aperture

15.5 Unclip the mouldings from the window aperture

7 Unscrew the two screws securing the door lock to the rear edge of the door, then withdraw the lock while guiding the locking control rod and main control rods from the door **(see illustrations)**. Keep the locking knob engaged with the lock.

Refitting

8 Refitting is a reversal of removal, but make sure that the locking knob control rod remains engaged with the lock while guiding it through the hole in the top of the door. Also make sure the main control rod is located on the inner (protective sheet) side of the window channel before connecting it to the inner door handle.

15 Door window glass and regulator - removal and refitting

Removal

1 Remove the trim panel as described in Section 13.
2 Temporarily refit the window regulator handle and lower the window until the lifting plate is visible.
3 Remove the bolts securing the regulator to the door and the bolts securing the lifting plate to the window channel **(see illustrations)**.
4 Raise the window glass and retain it with adhesive tape. Release the regulator from the door and remove it through the aperture **(see illustration)**.

5 With the window fully lowered unclip the inner and outer mouldings from the window aperture **(see illustration)**.
6 Remove the bolt and screw and pull out the front window channel abutting the corner window **(see illustration)**.
7 Withdraw the corner window and seal.
8 Lift the window glass from the door.

Refitting

9 Refitting is a reversal of removal. If the glass is being renewed, make sure that the lift channel is located in the same position as in the old glass. Ensure that the inner cable is adequately lubricated with grease and if necessary adjust the position of the regulator so that the window moves smoothly.

15.6 Bolt securing the front window channel

16 Tailgate and support struts (Hatchback and Coupe) - removal, refitting & adjustment

Removal

Tailgate

1 Disconnect the battery negative terminal. Open up the tailgate.
2 Remove the inner trim panel by extracting the retaining clips first; use a wide blade screwdriver inserted beneath each retaining clip position in turn **(see illustration)**.
3 Disconnect the wiring connectors situated behind the trim panel and disconnect the washer hose. Also disconnect the wiring connectors from the heated rear screen terminals and free the wiring grommets from the tailgate.

16.2 Removing the tailgate inner trim panel and clips

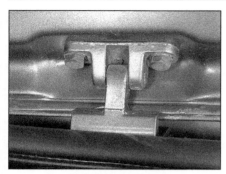

16.5 Tailgate hinge

16.6 Prise out the spring clips before removing the support struts from their balljoint mountings

17.1 Using an Allen key to unscrew the tailgate lock retaining screws

4 Tie a piece of string to each end of the wiring then, noting the correct routing of the wiring harness, release the harness rubber grommets from the tailgate and withdraw the wiring. When the end of the wiring appears, untie the string and leave it in position in the tailgate; it can then be used on refitting to draw the wiring into position. Similarly remove the washer tubing.

5 Using a marker pen, draw around the outline of each hinge marking its correct position on the tailgate **(see illustration)**.

6 Have an assistant support the tailgate, then using a small flat-bladed screwdriver raise the spring clips and pull the support struts off their balljoint mountings on the tailgate **(see illustration)**. Slacken and remove the bolts securing the hinges to the tailgate and remove the tailgate from the vehicle. Where necessary, recover the gaskets fitted between the hinge and tailgate.

7 Inspect the hinges for signs of wear or damage and renew if necessary. The hinges are secured to the vehicle by bolts which can be accessed once the headlining has been freed from the trim strip and peeled back. On refitting ensure that the hinge gasket is in good condition and secure the hinge in position.

Support strut

8 Support the tailgate in the open position, using a stout piece of wood, or with the help of an assistant.

9 Using a small flat-bladed screwdriver raise the spring clip, and pull the support strut off

its balljoint mounting on the tailgate. Note on Coupe models the upper mounting is of pin type and the strut is removed by sliding **off** the pin; recover the washers and spacers noting their positions. Raise the second retaining clip then detach the strut from the balljoint on the body and remove it from the vehicle.

Refitting

Tailgate

10 Refitting is the reverse of removal, aligning the hinges with the marks made before removal.

11 On completion, close the tailgate and check its alignment with the surrounding panels. If necessary slight adjustment can be made by slackening the retaining bolts and repositioning the tailgate on its hinges. If necessary, adjust the tailgate rubber buffers by screwing them in or out.

Support struts

12 Refitting is a reverse of the removal procedure, ensuring that the strut is securely retained by its retaining clips.

17 Tailgate lock components - removal and refitting

Removal

1 Open the tailgate and using an Allen key

unscrew the two lock retaining screws **(see illustration)**. Withdraw the lock and disconnect the wiring and link rod.

2 To remove the lock cylinder first remove the trim from the inside of the tailgate, then working through the aperture extract the circlip from the inner end of the lock cylinder. Insert the key then push out the cylinder from inside and remove from the tailgate.

3 The lock cylinder housing can be removed with the inner trim removed, by removing the handle strip then disconnecting the control rod and pressing out the locking lugs **(see illustrations)**. The housing can then be removed from the tailgate.

4 The lock striker can be removed by unscrewing it **(see illustration)**.

Refitting

5 Refitting is a reversal of removal, but before fully tightening the striker, close and open the tailgate two or three times to centralise it. Tighten the lock retaining screws to the specified torque.

18 Boot lid (Saloon models) - removal, refitting and adjustment

Removal

1 Open the boot lid and mark the position of the hinges with a pencil or marker pen.

2 With the help of an assistant unscrew the

17.3a Removing the screws securing the tailgate handle strip

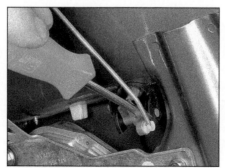

17.3b Disconnecting the control rod from the tailgate lock cylinder

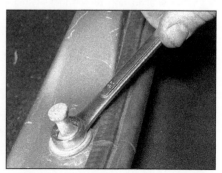

17.4 Removing the tailgate lock striker

bolts and withdraw the boot lid. Recover the spacer where fitted.

3 The boot lock and striker are each secured by two cross-head screws, but when removing the lock it will be necessary to unhook the connecting rod.

Refitting

4 Refitting is a reversal of removal, but make sure that the boot lid is central within the aperture and adjust its position on the hinge bolts. If necessary, adjust the bootlid rubber buffers by screwing them in or out. To adjust the boot lock striker, loosen the mounting screws then tighten them just sufficiently to hold the striker in position. Close and re-open the boot lid and fully tighten the screws. Adjust the stop rubbers if necessary.

19 Boot lid lock components (Saloon models) - removal and refitting

Removal

Boot lid lock

1 Open up the boot, then undo the lock retaining screws. Remove the lock, and detach it from the link rod as it is withdrawn. Recover the plastic cap.

Boot lid lock cylinder

2 Where necessary remove the trim/cover from the inside of the boot for access to the rear of the lock.
3 Unclip the link rod from the lock cylinder.
4 Undo the two retaining screws and remove the lock cylinder assembly from the boot lid. Recover the lock cylinder sealing ring.
5 It is not possible to separate the cylinder from the assembly.
6 Inspect the sealing ring for signs of wear or damage and renew if necessary.

Refitting

Boot lid lock

7 Attach the link rod, then seat the lock and plastic cap in the boot lid and securely tighten its retaining bolts.

Boot lid lock cylinder

8 Fit the sealing ring to the lock cylinder assembly. Insert the assembly into the boot lid and refit the retaining screws tightening them securely.
9 Clip the link rod on the lock cylinder and where necessary refit the trim/cover.

20.6 Exterior mirror control locknut and control knob on the inside of the door

20 Exterior mirror and associated components - removal and refitting

Removal

Non-remote control type

1 Prise the plastic cover from inside the door.
2 Unscrew the cross-head screws and remove the clips.
3 Withdraw the outer cover and mirror.

Remote control type

4 Pull off the adjusting knob and bellows from the inside door pull.
5 Remove the door trim panel (Section 13).
6 Unscrew the locknut and remove the adjusting knob from the bracket **(see illustration)**. If necessary also remove the screws and withdraw the bracket from the door.
7 Prise off the triangular plastic cover then unscrew the cross-head screws and remove the clips **(see illustration)**.
8 Withdraw the mirror together with the adjusting knob and gasket.

Refitting

9 Refitting is a reversal of removal, but fit a new gasket if necessary.

21 Windscreen, tailgate and fixed windows - general information

Removal and refitting of the windscreen and fixed glass windows is best left to a VW garage or windscreen specialist who will have the necessary equipment and expertise to complete the work properly.

22 Sunroof - general information and component renewal

1 The sunroof can be taken out completely as follows. Turn the rotary knob anti-clockwise half a turn to release the tension.
2 Press the two release buttons on the knob

20.7 Removing the triangular plastic cover to reveal the mirror mounting screws

housing, then lift the rear of the sunroof and move it rearwards from the front hinges. Stow the sunroof safely in the luggage compartment.
3 Due to the complexity of the sunroof mechanism, considerable expertise is needed to repair, replace or adjust the sunroof components successfully. Removal of the roof first requires the headlining to be removed, which is a complex and tedious operation, and is not a task to be undertaken lightly. Therefore, any problems with the sunroof should be referred to a VW dealer.

23 Body exterior fittings - removal and refitting

Removal

Wheel arch liners and body under-panels

1 The various plastic covers fitted to the underside of the vehicle are secured in position by screws, nuts or retaining clips and removal will be fairly obvious on inspection. Work methodically around the panel removing its retaining screws and releasing its retaining clips until the panel is free and can be removed from the underside of the vehicle. Most clips used on the vehicle, except for the fasteners which are used to secure the wheelarch liners in position, are simply prised out of position. The wheelarch liner clips are released by pressing out their centre pins and then removing the outer section of the clip; new clips will be required on refitting if the centre pins are not recovered.

Body trim strips and badges

2 The various body trim strips and badges are held in position with special adhesive tape or pop rivets. Removal of trim attached with tape requires the trim/badge to be heated, to soften the adhesive, and then cut away from the surface. Due to the high risk of damage to the vehicle's paintwork during this operation, it is recommended that this task should be entrusted to a VW dealer. Removal of trim secured with pop rivets requires the heads of the rivets to be removed using a drill of suitable diameter.

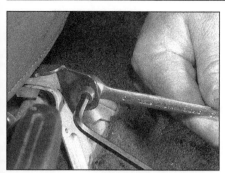

24.1a Remove the screw from the front of the seat . . .

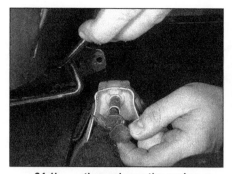

24.1b . . . then release the spring tensioned pin

24.2a Remove the screw . . .

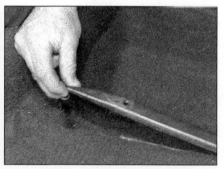

24.2b . . . and withdraw the inner runner cover

24.8 Squab securing screws (split rear seat)

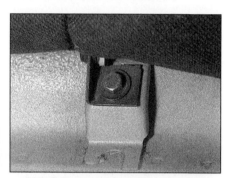

24.9 Split rear seat central mounting bracket bolt

Refitting

3 On refitting wheel arch liners and under-panels, renew any retaining clips that may have been broken on removal, and ensure that the panel is securely retained by all the relevant clips and screws. On refitting the body trim strips and badges, clean the body surface before pressing the tape-secured type, and use new pop rivets when securing the other type.

24 Seats - removal and refitting

Removal

Front seat

1 Using an Allen key and spanner, remove the screw from the front of the seat, then release the spring tensioned pin and withdraw the seat from the mounting bracket **(see illustrations)**.
2 Remove the screw and withdraw the inner runner cover **(see illustrations)**.
3 Slide the seat rearwards from the runners and remove from the car. Where necessary disconnect the wiring for the seat heating.

Rear bench seat

4 Remove the covers and mounting screws from the front of the cushion.
5 Lift the rear of the cushion to disengage the hooks then withdraw the cushion.
6 Working in the luggage compartment prise

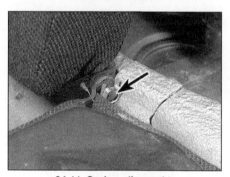

24.11 Spring clip on the centre pivot bracket

the backrest upper hooks from the panel, then withdraw the backrest from the car.

Split rear seat

7 To remove the seat squab, pull the rear of the seats upwards using the plastic pull handles provided.
8 Tilt the seats right forward, which will allow access to the retaining screws. Remove the screws and lift out the seat squabs **(see illustration)**.
9 The seat backrests may be removed by first removing the central mounting bracket bolt **(see illustration)**.
10 Operate the seat back release mechanism and tilt the backrest forward.
11 Remove the spring clip from the centre pivot bracket **(see illustration)**.
12 Now undo the two screws securing each backrest to the luggage compartment floor **(see illustration)**.

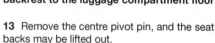

24.12 Screws securing the split rear seat backrest to the luggage compartment floor

13 Remove the centre pivot pin, and the seat backs may be lifted out.

Refitting

14 Refitting is a reversal of removal.

25 Seat belts - removal and refitting

Removal

Front seat belt

1 Push the front seat right forward.
2 Pull back the plastic cover from the lower outer seat belt mounting **(see illustration)**.
3 Count the number of coils in the spring as a guide for refitting.

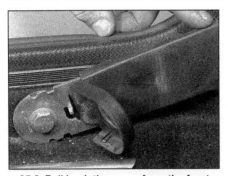

25.2 Pull back the cover from the front seat belt lower mounting

25.4 Unhooking the spring from the front seat belt lower mounting

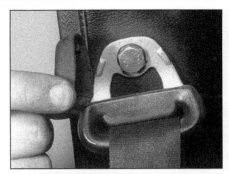

25.7 Removing the plastic cover from the front seat belt upper mounting

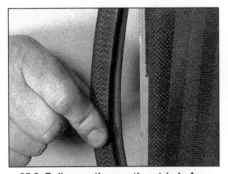

25.8 Pull away the weatherstrip before removing the rear trim panel

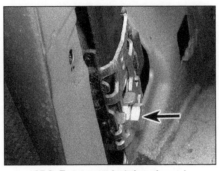

25.9 Front seat belt inertia reel mounting bolt

25.12 Rear seat belt outer mounting

4 Unhook the spring and gently allow the tension to be released by allowing the spring to unwind **(see illustration)**. The spring is normally tensioned by one complete turn.

5 Remove the spring from the retaining bolt head.

6 Unscrew the bolt securing the belt to the inner sill panel.

7 Prise off the plastic cover from the upper mounting and unscrew the retaining bolt **(see illustration)**.

8 Pull away the weatherstrip locally, then remove the trim panel from the side of the rear seat for access to the inertia reel **(see illustration)**. To save time, just the front of the trim needs to be detached in order to reach the inertia reel.

9 Unscrew the retaining bolt holding the inertia reel in place and remove the seat belt from the car **(see illustration)**.

10 The front seat belt central stalk is removed by unscrewing the mounting bolt.

Rear seat belt

11 The rear seat belts are removed in much the same way as the front belts.

12 The outer mountings are held by one bolt **(see illustration)**.

13 The inner mounting is undone after lifting the seat squabs **(see illustration)**.

14 The inertia reel mechanism is held in place in the double skin of the luggage compartment, and the upper mounting bolt is accessed by removing the plastic cover **(see illustrations)**.

Refitting

15 Refitting is a reversal of removal but tighten the mounting bolts to the specified torque.

26 Interior trim and glovebox - removal and refitting

Interior trim panels

1 The interior trim panels are secured using either screws or various types of trim fasteners, usually studs or clips.

2 Check that there are no other panels overlapping the one to be removed; usually there is a sequence that has to be followed that will become obvious on close inspection.

3 Remove all obvious fasteners, such as screws. If the panel will not come free, it is held by hidden clips or fasteners. These are usually situated around the edge of the panel and can be prised up to release them; note,

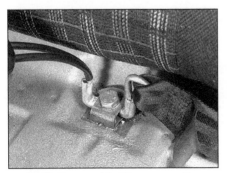

25.13 Rear seat belt inner mounting

25.14a Remove the cap for access to the rear seat belt inertia reel mounting bolt

25.14b Rear seat belt upper mounting

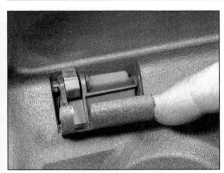

26.11 Glovebox hinge pins

27.2 Unclipping the rubber boot
from the centre console

27.3 Centre console front mounting screw

however that they can break quite easily so replacements should be available. The best way of releasing such clips without the correct type of tool, is to use a large flat-bladed screwdriver. Note in many cases that the adjacent sealing strip must be prised back to release a panel.

4 When removing a panel, **never** use excessive force or the panel may be damaged; always check carefully that all fasteners have been removed or released before attempting to withdraw a panel.

5 Refitting is the reverse of the removal procedure; secure the fasteners by pressing them firmly into place and ensure that all disturbed components are correctly secured to prevent rattles.

Carpets

6 The passenger compartment floor carpet is in one piece and is secured at its edges by screws or clips, usually the same fasteners used to secure the various adjoining trim panels.

7 Carpet removal and refitting is reasonably straightforward but very time-consuming because all adjoining trim panels must be removed first, as must components such as the seats, the centre console and seat belt lower anchorages.

Headlining

8 The headlining is clipped to the roof and can be withdrawn only once all fittings such as the grab handles, sun visors, sunroof (if fitted), windscreen and rear quarterwindows and related trim panels have been removed

and the door, tailgate and sunroof aperture sealing strips have been prised clear.

9 Note that headlining removal requires considerable skill and experience if it is to be carried out without damage and is therefore best entrusted to an expert.

Glovebox

10 The glovebox forms part of the facia panel and it is only possible to remove the lid.

11 Open up the glovebox lid and release the check stop, then remove the hinge pins and remove the lid from the facia **(see illustration)**.

12 Refitting is the reverse of removal.

27 Centre console - removal and refitting

Removal

1 A centre console is fitted to some models. First disconnect the battery negative lead.

2 Unclip and remove the rubber boot from the centre console **(see illustration)**. If necessary remove the gear lever knob.

3 Remove the screws attaching the front of the console to the facia panel **(see illustration)**.

4 Pull the console to the rear so that the guides are unclipped from the pins on the floor.

5 Withdraw the console from the passenger side and recover the seal. If the gear lever knob was not removed, feed the rubber boot through the gear lever hole **(see illustration)**.

6 If necessary remove the retaining plate and the special nut from the facia.

Refitting

7 Refitting is a reversal of removal, but make sure that the seal is correctly located between the console and the facia panel.

28 Facia panel assembly - removal and refitting

Removal

1 Disconnect the battery negative terminal.

2 Where fitted, remove the centre console as described in Section 27.

3 Unscrew the mounting screws and remove the passenger side shelf/trim panel from beneath the facia panel. Also disconnect the diagnostic socket wiring plugs. Note that a pin on the front of the shelf locates in a rubber grommet **(see illustrations)**.

4 Remove the steering wheel, combination switches, and steering lock with reference to Chapter 10, Section 16. It is not necessary to remove the steering column completely.

5 Remove the instrument panel as described in Chapter 12.

6 Remove the radio as described in Chapter 12.

7 Using a screwdriver, carefully prise away the trim plate covering the heater controls.

8 Unscrew the retaining screws and pull the heater control assembly together with cables from the facia panel.

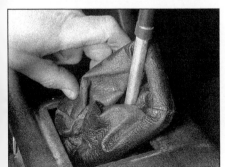

27.5 Feeding the gear lever rubber boot
through the centre console

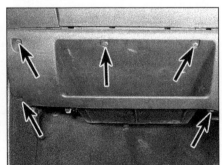

28.3a Passenger side shelf/trim panel
mounting screws

28.3b Removing the passenger side
shelf/trim panel

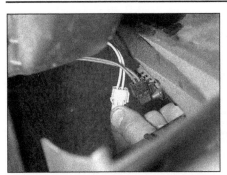

28.3c Disconnecting the diagnostic socket wiring plugs

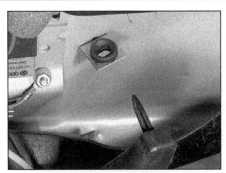

28.3d Shelf/trim panel front pin and rubber grommet

28.13 Facia panel mounting screw next to the steering column

9 Disconnect the wiring from the switches and the cigarette lighter, noting the location of each wire **(see Haynes Hint)**.

Label each wiring connector as it is disconnected from its relevant component. The labels will prove useful on refitting, when routing the wiring and feeding the wiring through the facia apertures.

10 Disconnect the loudspeaker wiring from the left-hand side of the facia.

11 Unscrew the facia panel lower mounting screws.
12 With the glovebox open, unscrew the mounting screw from inside the glovebox compartment.
13 Unscrew the mounting screw located next to the steering column **(see illustration)**.
14 Working inside the engine compartment, unscrew the two mounting nuts on the bulkhead.
15 With the help of an assistant, carefully ease the facia panel away from the bulkhead into the passenger compartment. As it is withdrawn, release the wiring harness from its retaining clips on the rear of the facia, whilst

noting its correct routing **(see Haynes Hint)**. Feed the heater control panel through the hole in the facia, and disconnect the air ducts as necessary.

Refitting

16 Refitting is a reversal of removal. When locating the facia on the bulkhead, insert the central pin in the special guide and the mounting studs in the holes. Make sure that all of the air ducts are correctly reconnected. On completion, reconnect the battery and check that all the electrical components and switches function correctly.

Chapter 12
Body electrical system

Contents

Degrees of difficulty

Easy, suitable for novice with little experience	**Fairly easy,** suitable for beginner with some experience	**Fairly difficult,** suitable for competent DIY mechanic	**Difficult,** suitable for experienced DIY mechanic	**Very difficult,** suitable for expert DIY or professional

Specifications

System type . . . . 12-volt negative earth

Fuses . . . . See Wiring diagrams at end of Chapter

Bulb ratings — **Watts**

Headlight	60/55
Indicator	21
Stop light	21
Tail light	5
Side light	4
Number plate light	5

1 General information and precautions

Warning: Before carrying out any work on the electrical system, read through the precautions in "Safety first!" and in Chapter 5.

1 The electrical system is of 12 volt negative earth type. Power for the lights and all electrical accessories is supplied by a lead/acid type battery which is charged by the alternator.

2 This Chapter covers repair and service procedures for the various electrical components not associated with the engine. Information on the battery, alternator and starter motor can be found in Chapter 5.

3 It should be noted that prior to working on any component in the electrical system, the ignition and all accessories should be switched off. On circuits which are live with the ignition off, the battery negative terminal should first be disconnected to prevent the possibility of electrical short circuits and/or fires.

2 Electrical fault-finding - general information

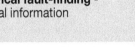

Note: *Refer to the precautions given in 'Safety first!' and in Section 1 of this Chapter before starting work. The following tests relate to testing of the main electrical circuits, and should not be used to test delicate electronic circuits (such as anti-lock braking systems), particularly where an electronic control module is used.*

General

1 A typical electrical circuit consists of an electrical component, any switches, relays, motors, fuses, fusible links or circuit breakers related to that component, and the wiring and connectors which link the component to both the battery and the chassis. To help pinpoint a problem in an electrical circuit, wiring diagrams are included at the end of this Manual.

2 Before attempting to diagnose an electrical fault, first study the appropriate wiring diagram to obtain a complete understanding of the components included in the particular circuit concerned. The possible sources of a fault can be narrowed down by noting if other components related to the circuit are operating properly. If several components or circuits fail at one time, the problem is likely to be related to a shared fuse or earth connection.

3 Electrical problems usually stem from simple causes, such as loose or corroded connections, a faulty earth connection, a blown fuse, a melted fusible link, or a faulty relay (refer to Section 3 for details of testing relays). Visually inspect the condition of all fuses, wires and connections in a problem circuit before testing the components. Use the wiring diagrams to determine which terminal connections will need to be checked in order to pinpoint the trouble spot.

4 The basic tools required for electrical fault-finding include a circuit tester or voltmeter (a 12-volt bulb with a set of test leads can also be used for certain tests); a self-powered test light (sometimes known as a continuity tester); an ohmmeter (to measure resistance); a battery and set of test leads; and a jumper wire, preferably with a circuit breaker or fuse incorporated, which can be used to bypass suspect wires or electrical components. Before attempting to locate a problem with test instruments, use the wiring diagram to determine where to make the connections.

5 To find the source of an intermittent wiring fault (usually due to a poor or dirty connection, or damaged wiring insulation), a 'wiggle' test can be performed on the wiring. This involves wiggling the wiring by hand to see if the fault occurs as the wiring is moved. It should be possible to narrow down the source of the fault to a particular section of wiring. This method of testing can be used in conjunction with any of the tests described in the following sub-Sections.

6 Apart from problems due to poor connections, two basic types of fault can occur in an electrical circuit - open circuit, or short circuit.

7 Open circuit faults are caused by a break somewhere in the circuit, which prevents current from flowing. An open circuit fault will prevent a component from working, but will not cause the relevant circuit fuse to blow.

8 Short circuit faults are caused by a "short" somewhere in the circuit, which allows the current flowing in the circuit to "escape" along an alternative route, usually to earth. Short circuit faults are normally caused by a breakdown in wiring insulation, which allows a feed wire to touch either another wire, or an earthed component such as the bodyshell. A short circuit fault will normally cause the relevant circuit fuse to blow.

Finding an open circuit

9 To check for an open circuit, connect one lead of a circuit tester or voltmeter to either the negative battery terminal or a known good earth.

10 Connect the other lead to a connector in the circuit being tested, preferably nearest to the battery or fuse.

11 Switch on the circuit, bearing in mind that some circuits are live only when the ignition switch is moved to a particular position.

12 If voltage is present (indicated either by the tester bulb lighting or a voltmeter reading, as applicable), this means that the section of the circuit between the relevant connector and the battery is problem-free.

13 Continue to check the remainder of the circuit in the same fashion.

14 When a point is reached at which no voltage is present, the problem must lie between that point and the previous test point with voltage. Most problems can be traced to a broken, corroded or loose connection.

Finding a short circuit

15 To check for a short circuit, first disconnect the load(s) from the circuit (loads are the components which draw current from a circuit, such as bulbs, motors, heating elements, etc).

16 Remove the relevant fuse from the circuit, and connect a circuit tester or voltmeter to the fuse connections.

17 Switch on the circuit, bearing in mind that some circuits are live only when the ignition switch is moved to a particular position.

18 If voltage is present (indicated either by the tester bulb lighting or a voltmeter reading, as applicable), this means that there is a short circuit.

19 If no voltage is present, but the fuse still blows with the load(s) connected, this indicates an internal fault in the load(s).

Finding an earth fault

20 The battery negative terminal is connected to "earth" - the metal of the engine/transmission and the car body - and most systems are wired so that they only receive a positive feed, the current returning through the metal of the car body. This means that the component mounting and the body form part of that circuit. Loose or corroded mountings can therefore cause a range of electrical faults, ranging from total failure of a circuit, to a puzzling partial fault. In particular, lights may shine dimly (especially when another circuit sharing the same earth point is in operation), motors (eg. wiper motors or the radiator cooling fan motor) may run slowly, and the operation of one circuit may have an apparently unrelated effect on another. Note that on many vehicles, earth straps are used between certain components, such as the engine/transmission and the body, usually where there is no metal-to-metal contact between components due to flexible rubber mountings, etc.

21 To check whether a component is properly earthed, disconnect the battery and connect one lead of an ohmmeter to a known good earth point. Connect the other lead to the wire or earth connection being tested. The resistance reading should be zero; if not, check the connection as follows.

22 If an earth connection is thought to be faulty, dismantle the connection and clean back to bare metal both the bodyshell and the wire terminal or the component earth connection mating surface. Be careful to remove all traces of dirt and corrosion, then use a knife to trim away any paint, so that a clean metal-to-metal joint is made. On reassembly, tighten the joint fasteners securely; if a wire terminal is being refitted, use serrated washers between the terminal

and the bodyshell to ensure a clean and secure connection. When the connection is remade, prevent the onset of corrosion in the future by applying a coat of petroleum jelly or silicone-based grease or by spraying on (at regular intervals) a proprietary ignition sealer or a water dispersant lubricant.

3 Fuses and relays - general information

Main fuses

1 The fuses are located beneath the bonnet on the left-hand side of the plenum chamber/bulkhead. Access is gained by squeezing the sides of the plastic lid at the top and bottom (see illustration). Take care not to damage the seal.

2 The fuse circuits are given in the wiring diagrams at the end of this Chapter.

3 Blown fuses are easily recognised by the metal strip being burnt apart in the centre. Make sure that new fuses are firmly held between the terminals.

4 To remove a fuse, first switch off the circuit concerned (or the ignition), then pull the fuse out of its terminals. The metal strip within the fuse should be visible; if the fuse is blown it will be broken or melted.

5 Always renew a fuse with one of an identical rating; never use a fuse with a different rating from the original or substitute anything else. Never renew a fuse more than once without tracing the source of the trouble. The fuse rating is stamped on top of the fuse; note that the fuses are also colour-coded for easy recognition.

6 If a new fuse blows immediately, find the cause before renewing it again; a short to earth as a result of faulty insulation is most likely. Where a fuse protects more than one circuit, try to isolate the defect by switching on each circuit in turn (if possible) until the fuse blows again. Always carry a supply of spare fuses of each relevant rating on the vehicle, a spare of each rating should be clipped into the base of the fusebox.

3.1 Removing the plastic lid from the fuse box

3.7a Relays located beneath the left-hand side of the facia panel

Relays

7 The main relays are near the fusebox in the left-hand side of the plenum chamber/ bulkhead. Other relays are beneath the left-hand side of the facia panel and behind the ECU on the bulkhead (see illustrations).

8 If a circuit or system controlled by a relay develops a fault and the relay is suspect, operate the system; if the relay is functioning it should be possible to hear it click as it is energised. If this is the case the fault lies with the components or wiring of the system. If the relay is not being energised then either the relay is not receiving a main supply or a switching voltage or the relay itself is faulty. Testing is by the substitution of a known good unit but be careful; while some relays are identical in appearance and in operation, others look similar but perform different functions.

9 To renew a relay first ensure that the

3.7b Relay located behind the ECU on the bulkhead

ignition switch is off. The relay can then simply be pulled out from the socket and the new relay pressed in.

4 Switches and cigarette lighter - removal and refitting

Note: *Make sure the ignition and all accessories are switched off before removing any switch. Where switches are live with the ignition switched off, disconnect the battery negative lead before commencing work.*

Ignition switch/steering lock

1 Refer to Chapter 10.

Steering column combination switches

2 Remove the steering wheel as described in Chapter 10.

3 Undo the retaining screws and remove the steering column upper and lower shrouds.
4 Slacken and remove the three retaining screws then disconnect the wiring connectors and remove both switch assemblies from the steering column (see illustrations).
5 Separate the direction indicator switch from the windscreen wiper switch if necessary (see illustration).
6 Refitting is a reversal of removal; refer to Chapter 10 when refitting the steering wheel.

Facia-mounted switches

7 Most facia-mounted switches may be removed by careful levering out with a flat-bladed screwdriver. Place a piece of card on the facia to prevent damage. Some may be removed by reaching up behind the facia and pressing them out. Where applicable, remove the adjacent blanking cover or the radio in order to push out the switch from behind (see illustrations).

4.4a Steering column combination switch retaining screws

4.4b Remove the combination switch from the steering column . . .

4.4c . . . and disconnect the wiring connectors

4.5 Separating the direction indicator switch from the windscreen wiper switch

4.7a Using a screwdriver to prise out the lighting switch

4.7b Prise out the blanking cover . . .

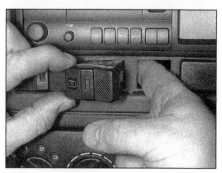

4.7c . . . and push out the adjacent switch

4.8 With the switch removed from the facia, the wiring plug can be disconnected

4.10 Prising off the heater control panel cover

4.11a Removing the ashtray insert mounting screws

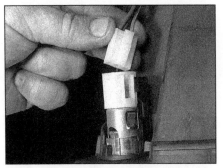

4.11b Disconnecting the wiring plug from the rear of the cigarette lighter

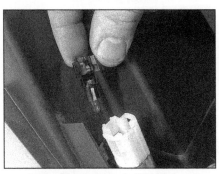

4.12a Slide out the bulbholder . . .

4.12b . . . lever the tab . . .

4.12c . . . withdraw the body . . .

4.12d . . . and remove the plastic surround

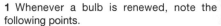

5 Bulbs (exterior lights) - renewal

General

1 Whenever a bulb is renewed, note the following points.

a) *Make sure that the relevant circuit is switched off before starting work.*
b) *Remember that if the light has just been in use the bulb may be extremely hot.*
c) *Always check the bulb contacts and holder, ensuring that there is clean metal-to-metal contact. Clean off any corrosion or dirt before fitting a new bulb.*
d) *Wherever bayonet-type bulbs are fitted ensure the live contacts bear firmly against the bulb contact.*
e) *Always ensure the new bulb is the correct rating and is completely clean before fitting.*

Headlight

2 To remove a headlamp bulb first open the bonnet. On G40 models it is necessary to remove the turbocharger inlet in order to gain access to the rear of the headlight. Move the hinged cover to the rear and pull it out upwards, then unscrew the crosshead screw and disconnect the inlet from the turbocharger.
3 Disconnect the wiring from the rear of the headlamp bulb **(see illustration)**.
4 Remove the rubber dust cap .
5 Unhook and release the ends of the retaining clip and remove the bulb from the

8 With the switch removed disconnect the wiring plug from the terminals and remove from the car. Prevent the wiring slipping back into the facia using adhesive tape **(see illustration)**.
9 Refitting is a reversal of removal. Press the switch firmly into the facia until the plastic tabs hold it in position.

Cigarette lighter

10 The cigarette lighter is located on the ashtray insert in the centre of the facia. To remove the lighter first prise off the heater control panel cover using a screwdriver **(see illustration)**, and remove the centre console (where fitted) with reference to Chapter 11.
11 Remove the ashtray, then unscrew the mounting screws and withdraw the ashtray insert from the facia. At the same time disconnect the wiring plug from the rear of the lighter **(see illustrations)**.

12 Slide the bulbholder from the lighter body, then lever out the tab in order to remove the body. Remove the plastic surround from the ashtray insert **(see illustrations)**.
13 Refitting is a reversal of removal.

Handbrake warning light switch

14 Refer to Chapter 9.

Stop light switch

15 Refer to Chapter 9.

Courtesy light switches

16 Open up the door and unscrew the cross-head screw from the switch.
17 Withdraw the switch and disconnect the wiring. Tie a loose knot in the wire to prevent it dropping into the door pillar.
18 Check the switch seal for condition and renew it if necessary.
19 Refitting is a reversal of removal.

5.3 Disconnecting the wiring plug from the rear of the headlamp bulb

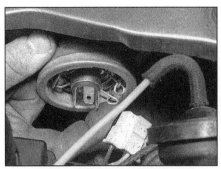

5.5a Release the clips . . .

5.5b . . . and remove the bulb from the rear of the headlight unit

5.10 Removing the front sidelight bulbholder

5.14a Disconnect the wiring . . .

5.14b . . . then remove the bulbholder . . .

5.14c . . . and remove the front direction indicator bulb

5.16 Push the front indicator side repeater to the rear to remove it

14 Reach down behind the front direction indicator light, alternatively remove the indicator light first as described later. Disconnect the wiring, then turn the bulbholder anticlockwise and withdraw it from the light body. Depress and twist the bulb to remove it **(see illustrations)**.
15 Refitting is a reversal of the removal procedure.

Front direction indicator side repeater

16 Push/slide the repeater body to the rear, then withdraw the light from the wing **(see illustration)**.
17 Pull the bulbholder from the body. The bulb is of the capless (push-fit) type and can be removed by simply pulling it out of the bulbholder **(see illustrations)**.
18 To refit the light, first check the seal and renew it if necessary. Insert the bulbholder in its guides then locate the light on the wing

rear of the light unit. Withdraw the bulb **(see illustrations)**.
6 When handling the new bulb, use a tissue or clean cloth to avoid touching the glass with the fingers; moisture and grease from the skin can cause blackening and rapid failure of this type of bulb. If the glass is accidentally touched, wipe it clean using methylated spirit.
7 Install the new bulb, ensuring that its locating tabs are correctly located in the light cutouts, and secure it in position with the retaining clip
8 Refit the rubber dust cap and reconnect the wiring. On G40 models refit the turbocharger inlet.

Front sidelight

9 Carry out the procedure in paragraph 2.
10 Turn the bulbholder anti-clockwise and remove it from the reflector **(see illustration)**.
11 Depress and twist the bulb to remove it. If

necessary the bulbholder may be removed by disconnecting the wiring.
12 Refitting is a reversal of removal.

Front direction indicator

13 Carry out the procedure given in paragraph 2.

5.17a Pull the bulbholder from the body . . .

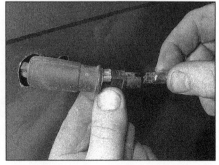

5.17b . . . then remove the bulb

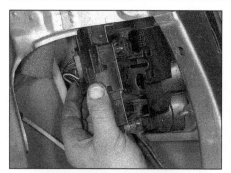

5.24a Squeeze together the plastic tabs . . .

5.24b . . . and remove the rear light cluster bulbholder

5.25 Removing a bulb from the rear light cluster bulbholder

5.27a Remove the screws . . .

5.27b . . . and remove the rear number plate light lens

5.28 Rear number plate light bulb removal

with the front tag in the small hole. Press in the light until the rear clip engages.

Front foglight

19 Apply the handbrake then jack up the front of the car and support on axle stands (see "*Jacking and vehicle support*").
20 Reach up behind the front bumper and disconnect the wiring from the connector plug on the rear cap.
21 Turn the cap anticlockwise and withdraw it from the foglamp. Disconnect the wire connector attached to the bulb.
22 Release the clips and withdraw the bulb using a tissue or clean cloth to avoid touching the glass with the fingers; moisture and grease from the skin can cause blackening and rapid failure of this type of bulb. If the glass is accidentally touched, wipe it clean using methylated spirit.
23 Install the new bulb, ensuring that it is correctly located. The remaining procedure is a reversal of removal.

Rear light cluster

24 From inside the vehicle luggage compartment, squeeze together the plastic tabs and remove the bulbholder from the rear of the light unit **(see illustrations)**.
25 Depress and twist the relevant bulb to remove it from the bulbholder **(see illustration)**. The stop/tail light bulb has offset locating pins to prevent it being installed incorrectly.
26 Refitting is the reverse of the removal sequence ensuring that the bulbholder is securely clipped into position.

Rear number plate light

27 Slacken and remove the retaining screws and withdraw the relevant lens from the tailgate/boot lid **(see illustrations)**. Recover the lens seal and examine it for signs of damage or deterioration, renewing it if necessary.
28 The bulb is of the capless (push-fit) type and can be removed by simply pulling it out of the bulbholder **(see illustration)**.
29 Press the new bulb into position and refit the seal and lens. Do not overtighten the lens retaining screws. Make sure that the lugs on the lens engage correctly with the holes in the bulbholder otherwise the rear number plate light will not be fully illuminated.

6 Bulbs (interior lights) - renewal

General

1 Refer to Section 5, paragraph 1.

Front courtesy light and rear luggage compartment light

2 Using a small flat-bladed screwdriver carefully prise the light unit out of position **(see illustration)**.
3 Release the festoon type bulb from the light unit contacts **(see illustration)**.
4 Install the new bulb, ensuring it is securely held in position by the contacts, and clip the light unit back into position.

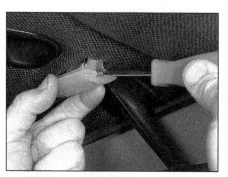

6.2 Use a screwdriver to carefully prise out the front courtesy light

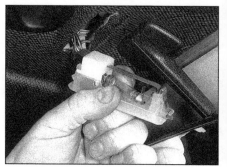

6.3 Remove the festoon type bulb from the contacts

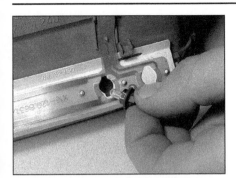

6.6 Removing a bulbholder from the rear of the instrument panel

Instrument panel illumination/warning lights

5 Remove the instrument panel (Section 8).
6 Twist the relevant bulbholder anti-clockwise and withdraw it from the rear of the panel **(see illustration)**.
7 All bulbs are integral with their holders. Be very careful to ensure that the new bulbs are of the correct rating, the same as those removed; this is especially important in the case of the ignition/battery charging warning light. Renewal of the light-emitting diodes should be left to a VW dealer.
8 Refit the bulbholder to the rear of the instrument panel then refit the instrument panel as described in Section 8.

Cigarette lighter/ashtray illumination bulb

9 Remove the ashtray insert from the facia as described in Section 4.
10 Pull the bulbholder from the rear of the cigarette lighter and separate the bulb.
11 Refitting is the reverse of removal.

Heater control panel illumination bulb

12 Withdraw the heater control panel as described in Section 9 of Chapter 3 so that access to the rear of the panel can be gained. Note there is no need to remove the panel completely; the control cables can be left attached.
13 Disconnect the wiring connector then unclip the bulbholder assembly from the rear of the control panel.

14 Unclip the surround from around the bulb then carefully pull the bulb out of its holder.
15 Refitting is the reverse of removal.

Switch illumination bulbs

16 All of the switches are fitted with illuminating bulbs; some are also fitted with a bulb to show when the circuit concerned is operating. These bulbs are an integral part of the switch assembly and cannot be obtained separately. Bulb replacement will therefore require the renewal of the complete switch assembly.

7 Exterior light units - removal and refitting

Note: *Make sure the ignition and all accessories are switched off before commencing work.*

Headlight

1 Using a suitable screwdriver, carefully release the radiator grille upper and lower retaining lugs then move the grille forwards and away
2 Remove the headlight and sidelight bulbs as described in Section 5, then remove the front direction indicator light as described later.
3 Remove the headlight mounting screws (cross-head) and ease the unit away from the crossmember panel **(see illustrations)**.
4 Refitting is a reversal of removal.

Front direction indicator light

5 Remove the front direction indicator light bulb as described in Section 5.
6 Slide the light unit directly forwards from its mounting on the side of the headlight unit **(see illustration)**.
7 Refitting is a reversal of removal but make sure that the light unit is correctly located in the slots on the side of the headlight unit.

Front direction indicator side repeater

8 Push/slide the repeater body to the rear, and withdraw the light from the wing.
9 Pull the bulbholder from the guides. Tie a piece of string to the wiring to prevent it falling back into the wing.
10 Refitting is a reversal of removal.

Front foglight

11 Remove the foglight bulb as described in Section 5.
12 Unscrew the mounting bolts and remove the foglight from the front bumper.
13 Refitting is a reversal of removal.

Rear light cluster

14 Remove the rear light bulbholder as described in Section 5.
15 Unscrew the mounting nuts and withdraw the light cluster from the rear of the car **(see illustrations)**.
16 Refitting is a reversal of removal.

Number plate light

17 Remove the bulb as described in Section 5.

7.3a The two inner headlight mounting screws

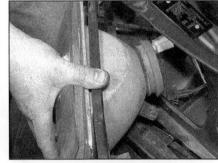

7.3b Withdrawing the headlight from the crossmember panel

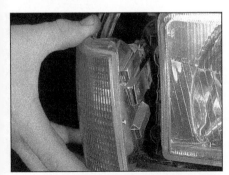

7.6 Slide the front direction indicator light from the headlight unit

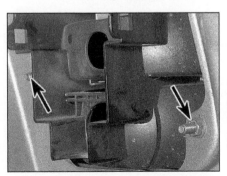

7.15a Two of the three rear light cluster mounting nuts

7.15b Removing the rear light cluster

8.3a Removing the instrument panel with the special tools

8.4 Disconnecting the wiring plug from the rear of the instrument panel

18 Withdraw the light unit and disconnect it from the wiring connector.
19 Refitting is a reversal of removal.

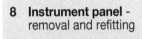

8 Instrument panel - removal and refitting

Note: *Two special U-shaped tools are required in order to remove the instrument panel. The tools are also used to remove the radio and should be available at car accessory shops.*

Removal

1 Make sure the ignition and all accessories are switched off.
2 Remove the steering wheel as described in Chapter 10.
3 Insert the two special tools fully into the holes located on the right- and left-hand edges of the instrument panel. This will release the side clips **(see illustrations)**.
4 Pull the instrument panel from the facia. As it is being removed it will be disconnected from the speedometer cable, and finally disconnect the wiring multi-plug **(see illustration)**.

Refitting

5 Refitting is a reversal of removal. The special tools should be removed before refitting the instrument panel as the side clips will engage automatically **(see illustration)**.

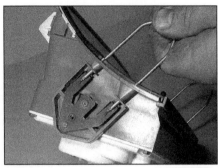

8.3b The special tools are used to hold in the side clips

8.5 Refitting the instrument panel

9 Horn - removal and refitting

Removal

1 The horn is located behind the radiator grille.
2 To remove the horn, first disconnect the battery negative lead.
3 Remove the radiator grille (see Chapter 11).
4 Unscrew the mounting bolt, disconnect the wires, and withdraw the horn.
5 If the horn emits an unsatisfactory sound it may be possible to adjust it by removing the sealant from the adjusting screw and turning it one way or the other.

Refitting

6 Refitting is a reversal of removal.

11.3a Lift the hinged cover . . .

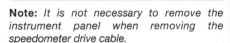

10 Speedometer drive cable - removal and refitting

Note: *It is not necessary to remove the instrument panel when removing the speedometer drive cable.*

Removal

1 Open the bonnet and then reach down behind the engine and unscrew the speedometer cable nut from the gearbox. Recover the washer.
2 Where necessary for improved access, remove the air cleaner and ducting as described in Chapter 3.
3 In the plenum chamber at the rear of the engine compartment, unscrew the plastic nut on the bulkhead then withdraw the speedometer cable and rubber grommet through the secondary panel and remove it from the engine compartment. Release the cable from the clips and cable-ties as necessary.

Refitting

4 Refitting is a reversal of removal.

11 Wiper arm - removal and refitting

Removal

1 Operate the wiper motor then switch it off so that the wiper arm returns to the at-rest position.
2 Stick a piece of masking tape along the edge of the wiper blade to use as an alignment aid on refitting.
3 Lift the hinged cover then slacken and remove the spindle nut and washer **(see illustrations)**. Lift the blade **off** the glass and pull the wiper arm off its spindle. If necessary use a flat-bladed screwdriver to lever the arm off the spindle.

Refitting

4 Ensure that the wiper arm and spindle splines are clean and dry then refit the arm to

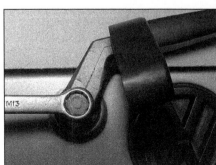

11.3b . . . and unscrew the tailgate wiper arm spindle nut

12.2a Pull off the weatherstrip . . .

12.2b . . . and remove the plastic cover from over the windscreen wiper motor

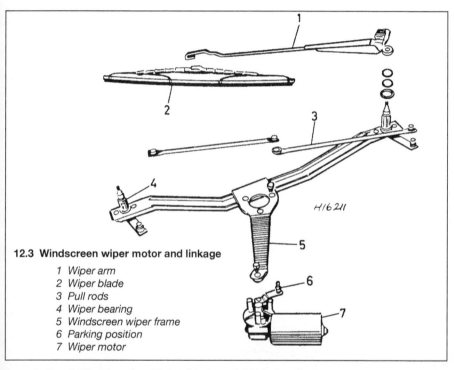

12.3 Windscreen wiper motor and linkage

1 Wiper arm
2 Wiper blade
3 Pull rods
4 Wiper bearing
5 Windscreen wiper frame
6 Parking position
7 Wiper motor

the spindle, aligning the wiper blade with the tape fitted on removal. Refit and tighten the spindle nut then close the hinged cover.

12 Windscreen wiper motor and linkage - removal and refitting

Note: *Make sure the ignition and all accessories are switched off before commencing work.*

Removal

1 Remove the wiper arms as described in the previous Section.
2 Pull the weatherstrip from the front of the plenum chamber and remove the plastic cover **(see illustrations)**.

3 Mark the wiper motor crank and spindle in relation to each other, then unscrew the nut and remove the crank from the motor spindle **(see illustration)**.
4 Disconnect the wiring multi-plug.
5 Unscrew the bolts and withdraw the wiper motor from the frame.
6 To remove the linkage, unscrew the bearing nuts and remove the spacers.
7 Unscrew the frame mounting bolt, then withdraw the assembly from the bulkhead.

Refitting

8 Refitting is a reversal of removal, but when fitting the crank to the spindle (motor in parked position) make sure that the marks are aligned.

13 Tailgate wiper motor - removal and refitting

Note: *Make sure the ignition and all accessories are switched off before commencing work.*

Removal

1 Open the tailgate and carefully prise off the inner trim panel.
2 Remove the wiper arm as described in Section 11, then unscrew the spindle outer nut and remove the spacers **(see illustrations)**.

13.2a Unscrew the tailgate wiper motor outer nut . . .

13.2b . . . and remove the spacer

13.3a Disconnect the wiring plug . . .

13.3b . . . unscrew the mounting bracket bolts . . .

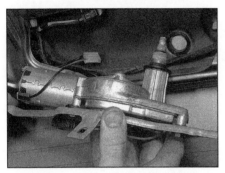

13.3c . . . and withdraw the motor assembly from the tailgate

13.4 Tailgate wiper motor mounting bolts on the bracket

3 Disconnect the wiring plug, then unscrew the mounting bracket bolts and withdraw the motor assembly **(see illustrations)**. Note the location of any spacers and recover the rubber grommet from the tailgate.
4 If necessary, unscrew the bolts and remove the wiper motor from the mounting bracket **(see illustration)**. Inspect the rubbers for signs of damage or deterioration and renew if necessary.

Refitting

5 Refitting is a reversal of removal.

14 Windscreen/tailgate washer system components - removal and refitting

Washer system reservoir

1 Remove the battery as described in Chapter 5. **Note:** *Make sure you know the anti-theft code for the radio so that you can re-activate it on refitting.*
2 Disconnect the wiring connector and the hose(s) from the washer pump.
3 Slacken and remove the mounting nuts and lift the reservoir upwards and out of position. On models equipped with headlight washers it will be necessary to disconnect the wiring connector and washer hose from the headlight pump as the reservoir is removed. Wash off any spilt fluid with cold water.
4 Refitting is the reverse of removal ensuring that the washer hose(s) are securely connected.

Washer pump

5 Empty the contents of the reservoir or be prepared for fluid spillage as the pump is removed.
6 Remove the battery as described in Chapter 5. **Note:** *Make sure you know the anti-theft code for the radio so that you can re-activate it on refitting.*
7 Disconnect the wiring connector and washer hose(s) from the pump.
8 Carefully ease the pump out from the reservoir and recover its sealing grommet. Wash off any spilt fluid with cold water.
9 Refitting is the reverse of removal, using a new sealing grommet if the original one shows signs of damage or deterioration. Refill the reservoir and check the pump grommet for leaks.

Windscreen washer jets

10 With the bonnet open first remove the plastic cover from the plenum chamber. Reach under the grille at the bottom of the windscreen and disconnect the washer hose from the base of the jet. Where necessary, also disconnect the wiring connector from the jet. Carefully ease the jet out from the grille, taking great care not to damage the paintwork.
11 On refitting, securely connect the jet to the hose and clip it into position in the grille; where necessary also reconnect the wiring connector. Check the operation of the jet. If necessary adjust the nozzle using a pin, aiming the spray to a point slightly above the centre of the swept area. Finally refit the plastic cover to the plenum chamber.

Tailgate washer jet

12 The washer jet is located in the top of the tailgate. Carefully prise the jet from the tailgate taking care not to damage the paintwork.
13 Disconnect the washer tube and remove the jet.
14 On refitting ensure that the jet is clipped securely in position. Check the operation of the jet. If necessary adjust the nozzle using a pin, aiming the spray to a point slightly above the centre of the swept area.

15 Headlight washer system components - removal and refitting

Washer system reservoir

1 Refer to Section 14. Two pumps are fitted to the reservoir, the larger one being the headlight washer pump.

Washer pump

2 Remove the washer reservoir as described in paragraph 1.
3 Carefully ease the pump out from the reservoir and recover its sealing grommet. Wash off any spilt fluid with cold water.
4 Refitting is the reverse of removal, using a new sealing grommet if the original one shows signs of damage or deterioration. Refill the reservoir and check the pump grommet for leaks.

Washer jets

5 If necessary for improved access to the jet retaining nut, remove the front bumper as described in Chapter 11.
6 Disconnect the washer tubing then unscrew the mounting nut and remove the jet from the bumper.
7 Refitting is the reverse of removal making sure that the washer jets are correctly aimed at the headlight.

16 Radio/cassette player - removal and refitting

Note: *The following removal and refitting procedure is for the range of radio/cassette units which VW fit as standard equipment. Removal and refitting procedures of non-standard radio/cassettes will differ slightly.*

Removal

Early (pre 1994) models

1 The radio/cassette players fitted prior to 1994 have DIN standard fixings. Two special tools, obtainable from most car accessory shops, are required for removal. Alternatively suitable tools can be fabricated from 3 mm diameter wire, such as welding rod.

16.3a Fitting the special radio removal tools

16.3b Disconnecting the wiring plug from the radio

16.3c Disconnecting the aerial from the radio

2 Disconnect the battery negative lead. **Note:** *Make sure you know the anti-theft code for the radio/cassette so that you can re-activate it on refitting.*
3 Insert the tools into the two holes on each side of the unit and push them until they snap into place. The radio/cassette player can then be slid out of the facia and the wiring connectors and aerial disconnected **(see illustrations)**.

Later (1994 onwards) models

4 The radio/cassette players fitted from 1994 onwards have special fixings and two special VW radio removal tools (No. 3316) are required for removal.
5 Slide tools into the slots on each side of the unit until they snap into place. Slide the radio squarely out of position, disconnecting the wiring connector and aerial as they become accessible. To release the removal tools, push the locating lugs on the side of the unit inwards.

Refitting

6 Reconnect the wiring connector and aerial lead then push the unit into the facia until the retaining lugs snap into place.

17 Loudspeakers - removal and refitting

Removal

1 The loudspeakers are located at each end of the facia panel. Using a screwdriver carefully prise the grille from the top of the facia panel **(see illustration)**.
2 Use a screwdriver to depress the tabs, then withdraw the loudspeaker from the facia and disconnect the wiring **(see illustrations)**.

Refitting

3 Refitting is a reversal of removal.

18 Radio aerial - removal and refitting

Removal

1 The aerial is mounted at the rear of the left-hand side front wing. First jack up the front of the car and support on axle stands (see *"Jacking and vehicle support"*). Remove the left-hand front wheel.
2 Remove the radio as described in Section 16. Also remove the lower shelf from the left-hand side of the facia.

3 Unscrew the screws and remove the wheelarch liner from inside the wheelarch.
4 Note the routing of the aerial then withdraw it from the passenger compartment into the wheelarch.
5 Unscrew the top nut and remove the aerial from under the wing.

Refitting

6 Refitting is a reversal of removal.

19 Heated front seat components - general information

Heater mats

On models equipped with heated front seats, a heater pad is fitted to both the seat back and seat cushion. Renewal of either heater mat involves peeling back the upholstery, removing the old mat, sticking the new mat in position and then refitting the upholstery. Note that upholstery removal and refitting requires considerable skill and experience if it is to be carried out successfully and is therefore best entrusted to your VW dealer. In practice, it will be very difficult for the home mechanic to carry out the job without ruining the upholstery.

Heated seat switches

Refer to Section 4.

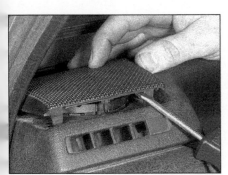

17.1 Use a screwdriver to carefully prise the loudspeaker grille from the facia panel

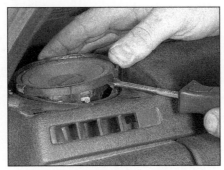

17.2a Depress the tabs to release the loudspeaker from the facia

17.2b Disconnecting the loudspeaker wiring

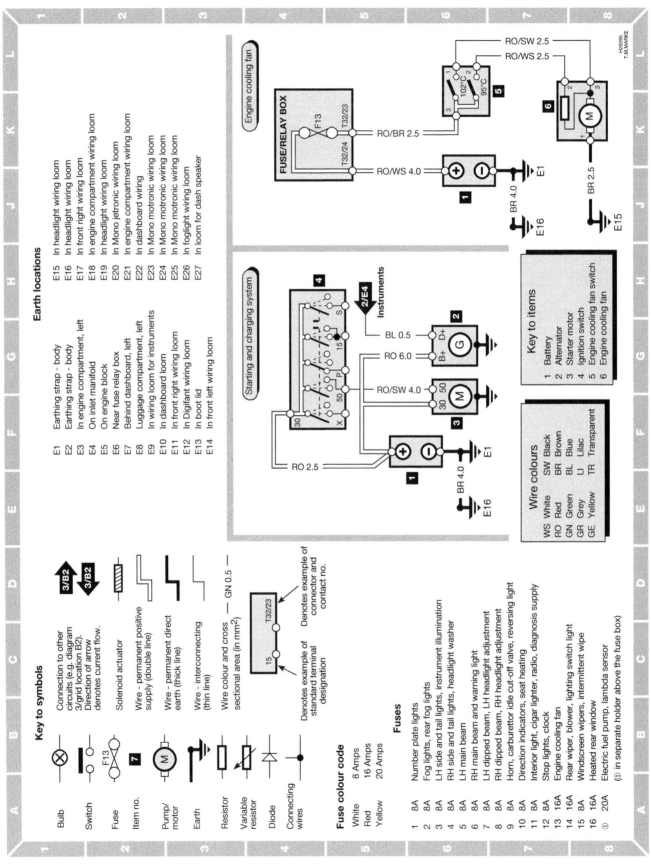

Diagram 1 : Information for wiring diagrams, starting, charging and engine cooling fan

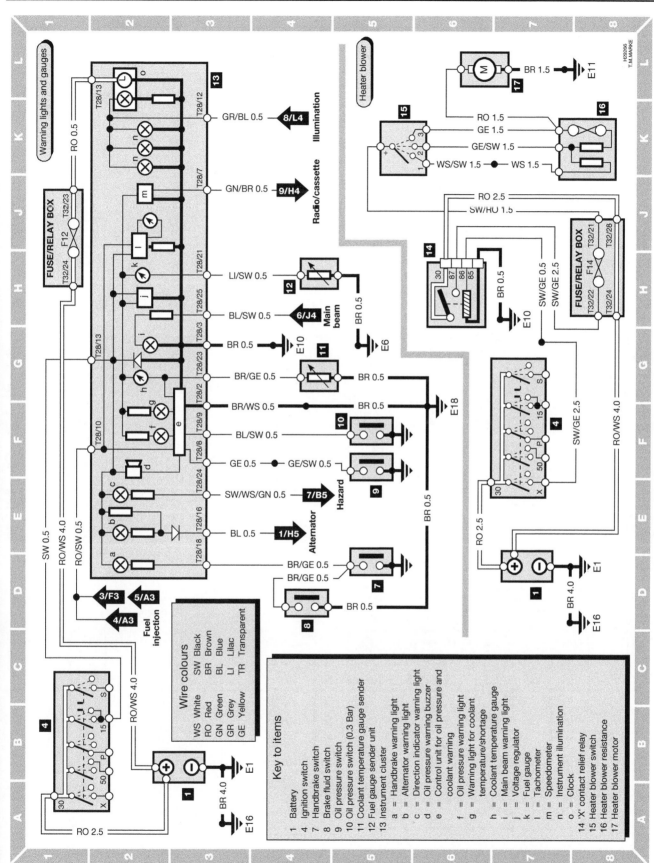

Diagram 2 : Warning lights, gauges and heater blower

Wire colours

WS	White	SW	Black
RO	Red	BR	Brown
GN	Green	BL	Blue
GR	Grey	LI	Lilac
GE	Yellow	TR	Transparent

Key to items

1 Battery
4 Ignition switch
7 Handbrake switch
8 Brake fluid switch
9 Oil pressure switch
10 Oil pressure switch (0.3 Bar)
11 Coolant temperature gauge sender
12 Fuel gauge sender unit
13 Instrument cluster

a = Handbrake warning light
b = Alternator warning light
c = Direction indicator warning light
d = Oil pressure warning buzzer
e = Control unit for oil pressure and coolant warning
f = Oil pressure warning light
g = Warning light for coolant temperature/shortage
h = Coolant temperature gauge
j = Voltage regulator
k = Fuel gauge
l = Tachometer
m = Speedometer
n = Instrument illumination
o = Clock
14 'X' contact relief relay
15 Heater blower switch
16 Heater blower resistance
17 Heater blower motor

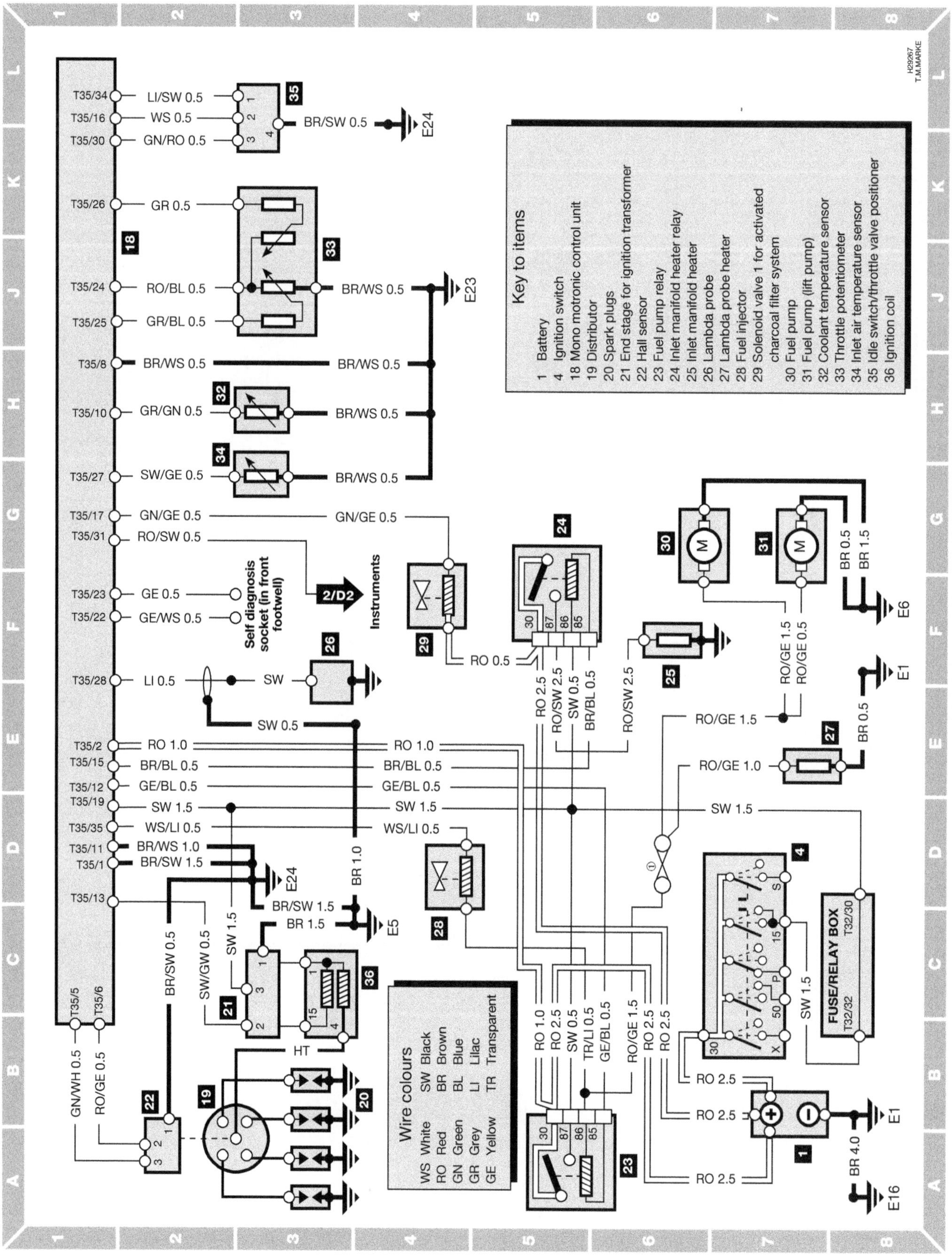

Key to items

1 Battery
4 Ignition switch
18 Mono motronic control unit
19 Distributor
20 Spark plugs
21 End stage for ignition transformer
22 Hall sensor
23 Fuel pump relay
24 Inlet manifold heater relay
25 Inlet manifold heater
26 Lambda probe
27 Lambda probe heater
28 Fuel injector
29 Solenoid valve 1 for activated charcoal filter system
30 Fuel pump
31 Fuel pump (lift pump)
32 Coolant temperature sensor
33 Throttle potentiometer
34 Inlet air temperature sensor
35 Idle switch/throttle valve positioner
36 Ignition coil

Wire colours

WS	White	SW	Black
RO	Red	BR	Brown
GN	Green	BL	Blue
GR	Grey	LI	Lilac
GE	Yellow	TR	Transparent

Diagram 3 : Single-point fuel injection

Self diagnosis socket (in front footwell)

2/D2 Instruments

FUSE/RELAY BOX T32/30 T32/32

H29267
T.M.MARKE

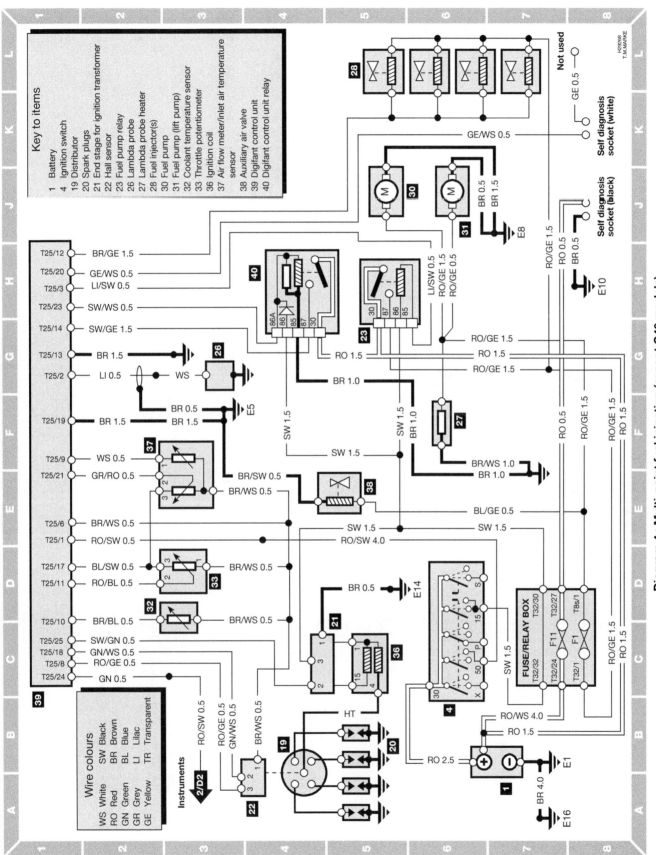

Key to items

1 Battery
4 Ignition switch
19 Distributor
20 Spark plugs
21 End stage for ignition transformer
22 Hall sensor
23 Fuel pump relay
26 Lambda probe
27 Lambda probe heater
28 Fuel injector(s)
30 Fuel pump
31 Fuel pump (lift pump)
32 Coolant temperature sensor
33 Throttle potentiometer
36 Ignition coil
37 Air flow meter/inlet air temperature sensor
38 Auxiliary air valve
39 Digifant control unit
40 Digifant control unit relay

Wire colours

WS	White
RO	Red
GN	Green
GR	Grey
GE	Yellow
SW	Black
BR	Brown
BL	Blue
LI	Lilac
TR	Transparent

Diagram 4 : Multi-point fuel injection (except G40 models)

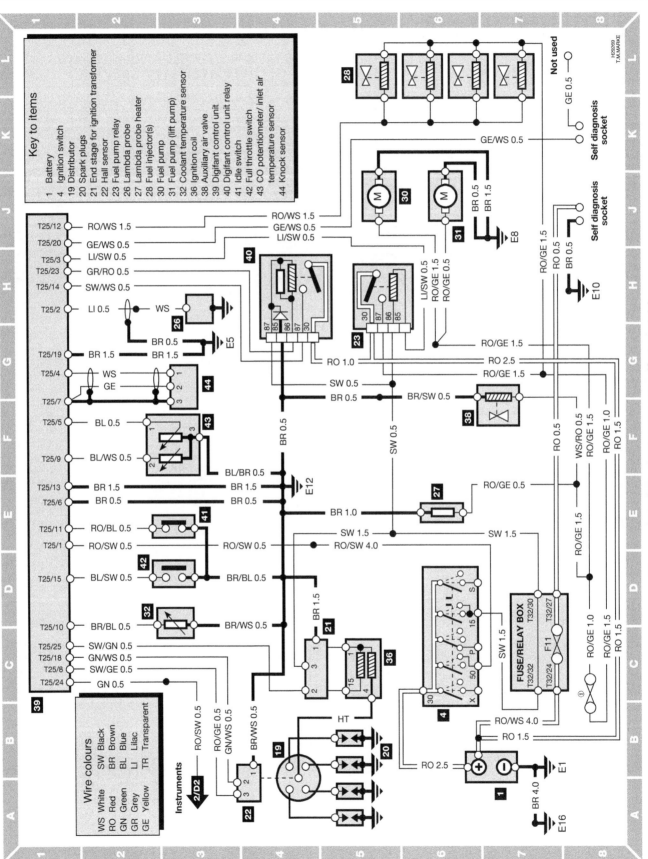

Key to items

1 Battery
4 Ignition switch
19 Distributor
20 Spark plugs
21 End stage for ignition transformer
22 Hall sensor
23 Fuel pump relay
26 Lambda probe
27 Lambda probe heater
28 Fuel injector(s)
30 Fuel pump
31 Fuel pump (lift pump)
32 Coolant temperature sensor
36 Ignition coil
38 Auxiliary air valve
39 Digifant control unit
40 Digifant control unit relay
41 Idle switch
42 Full throttle switch
43 CO potentiometer/ inlet air temperature sensor
44 Knock sensor

Wire colours

WS White   SW Black
RO Red   BR Brown
GN Green   BL Blue
GR Grey   LI Lilac
GE Yellow   TR Transparent

Diagram 5 : Multi-point fuel injection (G40 models)

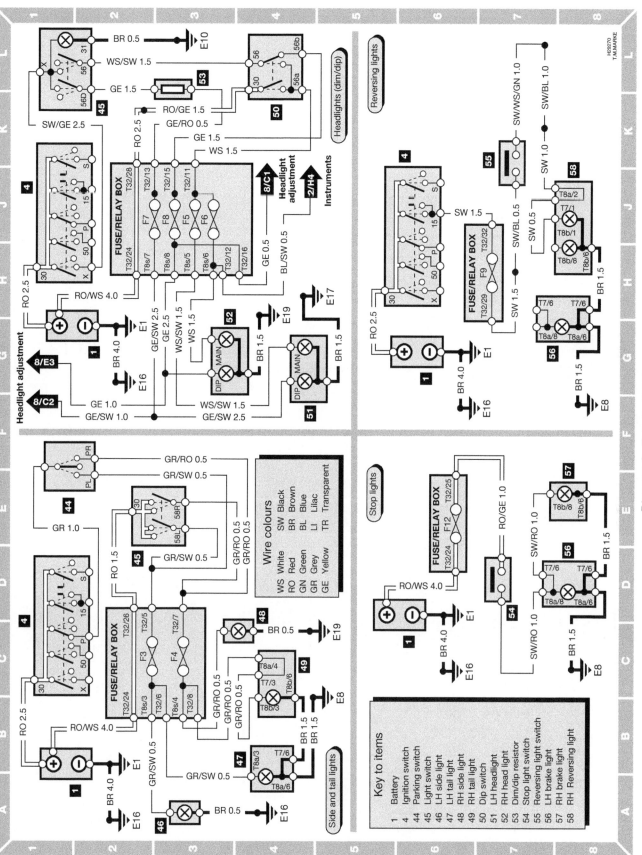

Diagram 6 : Exterior lighting

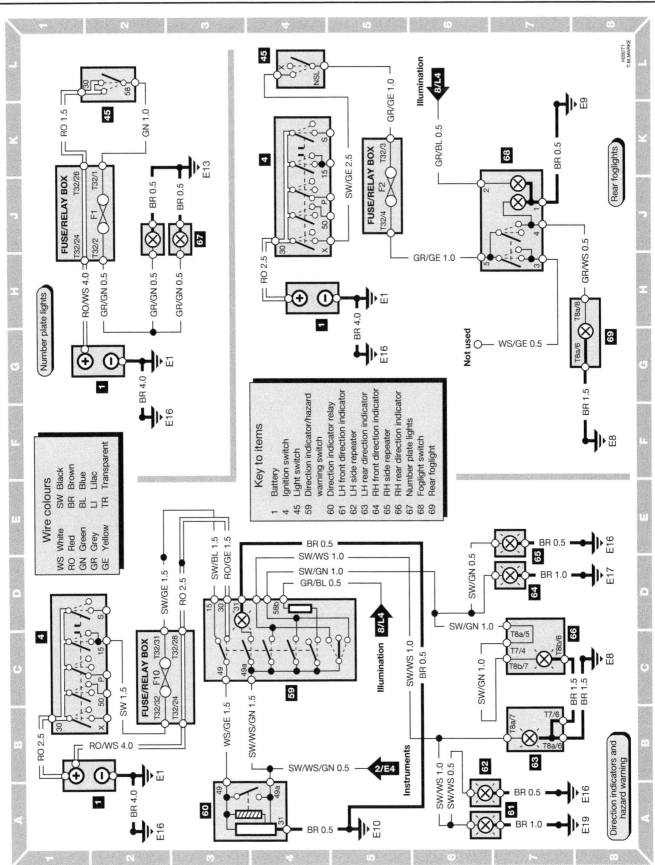

Diagram 7 : Exterior lighting continued

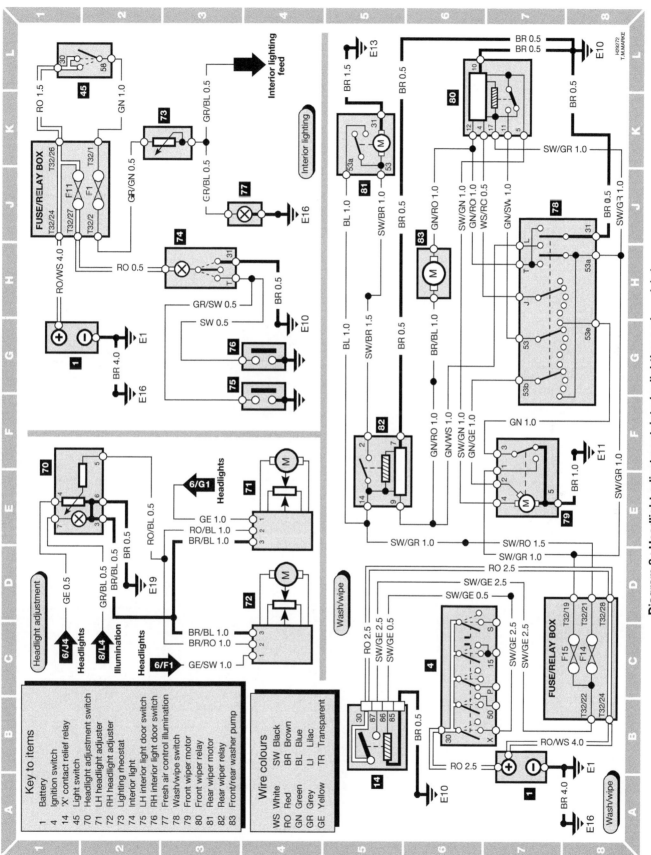

Diagram 8 : Headlight adjustment, interior lighting and wash/wipe

Key to items

1. Battery
4. Ignition switch
14. 'X' contact relief relay
45. Light switch
70. Headlight adjustment switch
71. LH headlight adjuster
72. RH headlight adjuster
73. Lighting rheostat
74. Interior light
75. LH interior light door switch
76. RH interior light door switch
77. Fresh air control illumination
78. Wash/wipe switch
79. Front wiper relay
80. Front wiper motor
81. Rear wiper relay
82. Rear wiper motor
83. Front/rear washer pump

Wire colours

WS	White	SW	Black
RO	Red	BR	Brown
GN	Green	BL	Blue
GR	Grey	LI	Lilac
GE	Yellow	TR	Transparent

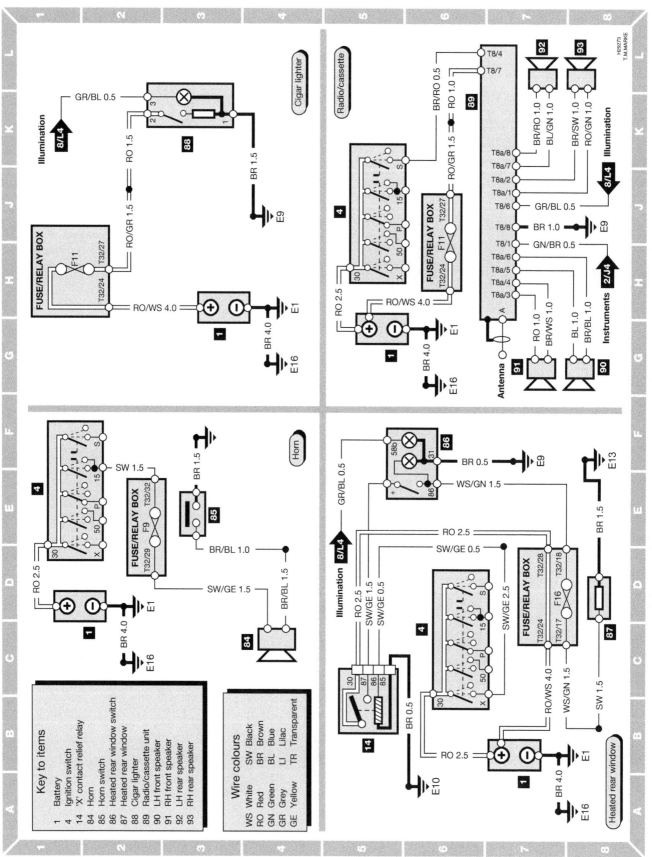

Diagram 9 : Horn, heated rear window, cigar lighter and radio/cassette

Key to items

1 Battery
4 Ignition switch
14 'X' contact relief relay
84 Horn
85 Horn switch
86 Heated rear window switch
87 Heated rear window
88 Cigar lighter
89 Radio/cassette unit
90 LH front speaker
91 RH front speaker
92 LH rear speaker
93 RH rear speaker

Wire colours

WS White   SW Black
RO Red   BR Brown
GN Green   BL Blue
GR Grey   LI Lilac
GE Yellow   TR Transparent

H29273
T.M.MARKE

Reference REF•1

Dimensions and weights

Note: *All figures are approximate, and may vary according to model. Refer to manufacturer's data for exact figures.*

Dimensions

Overall length:
    Hatchback models . . . . 3765 mm
    Coupé models . . . . 3725 mm
Overall width - including mirrors (all models) . . . . 1765 mm
Overall height (unladen) . . . . 1350 mm
Ground clearance at gross vehicle weight:
    Hatchback models . . . . 117 mm
    Coupé models . . . . 95 mm
Turning circle . . . . 10 m

Weights

Kerb weight . . . . 765 to 830 kg*
Maximum gross vehicle weight** . . . . 1230 to 1250 kg*
Maximum roof rack load (all models) . . . . 50 kg
Maximum towing weight**
    Braked trailer . . . . 650 kg*
    Unbraked trailer . . . . 410 kg*
Maximum trailer nose weight . . . . 50 kg
Minimum trailer nose weight . . . . 4% of actual trailer weight (up to 25 kg)
*Depending on model and specification.
**Refer to VW dealer for exact recommendations.

Conversion factors

Length (distance)

Inches (in)	x 25.4	=	Millimetres (mm)	x 0.0394 =	Inches (in)
Feet (ft)	x 0.305	=	Metres (m)	x 3.281 =	Feet (ft)
Miles	x 1.609	=	Kilometres (km)	x 0.621 =	Miles

Volume (capacity)

Cubic inches (cu in; in^3)	x 16.387	=	Cubic centimetres (cc; cm^3)	x 0.061 =	Cubic inches (cu in; in^3)
Imperial pints (Imp pt)	x 0.568	=	Litres (l)	x 1.76 =	Imperial pints (Imp pt)
Imperial quarts (Imp qt)	x 1.137	=	Litres (l)	x 0.88 =	Imperial quarts (Imp qt)
Imperial quarts (Imp qt)	x 1.201	=	US quarts (US qt)	x 0.833 =	Imperial quarts (Imp qt)
US quarts (US qt)	x 0.946	=	Litres (l)	x 1.057 =	US quarts (US qt)
Imperial gallons (Imp gal)	x 4.546	=	Litres (l)	x 0.22 =	Imperial gallons (Imp gal)
Imperial gallons (Imp gal)	x 1.201	=	US gallons (US gal)	x 0.833 =	Imperial gallons (Imp gal)
US gallons (US gal)	x 3.785	=	Litres (l)	x 0.264 =	US gallons (US gal)

Mass (weight)

Ounces (oz)	x 28.35	=	Grams (g)	x 0.035 =	Ounces (oz)
Pounds (lb)	x 0.454	=	Kilograms (kg)	x 2.205 =	Pounds (lb)

Force

Ounces-force (ozf; oz)	x 0.278	=	Newtons (N)	x 3.6 =	Ounces-force (ozf; oz)
Pounds-force (lbf; lb)	x 4.448	=	Newtons (N)	x 0.225 =	Pounds-force (lbf; lb)
Newtons (N)	x 0.1	=	Kilograms-force (kgf; kg)	x 9.81 =	Newtons (N)

Pressure

Pounds-force per square inch (psi; lbf/in^2; lb/in^2)	x 0.070	=	Kilograms-force per square centimetre (kgf/cm^2; kg/cm^2)	x 14.223 =	Pounds-force per square inch (psi; lbf/in^2; lb/in^2)
Pounds-force per square inch (psi; lbf/in^2; lb/in^2)	x 0.068	=	Atmospheres (atm)	x 14.696 =	Pounds-force per square inch (psi; lbf/in^2; lb/in^2)
Pounds-force per square inch (psi; lbf/in^2; lb/in^2)	x 0.069	=	Bars	x 14.5 =	Pounds-force per square inch (psi; lbf/in^2; lb/in^2)
Pounds-force per square inch (psi; lbf/in^2; lb/in^2)	x 6.895	=	Kilopascals (kPa)	x 0.145 =	Pounds-force per square inch (psi; lbf/in^2; lb/in^2)
Kilopascals (kPa)	x 0.01	=	Kilograms-force per square centimetre (kgf/cm^2; kg/cm^2)	x 98.1 =	Kilopascals (kPa)
Millibar (mbar)	x 100	=	Pascals (Pa)	x 0.01 =	Millibar (mbar)
Millibar (mbar)	x 0.0145	=	Pounds-force per square inch (psi; lbf/in^2; lb/in^2)	x 68.947 =	Millibar (mbar)
Millibar (mbar)	x 0.75	=	Millimetres of mercury (mmHg)	x 1.333 =	Millibar (mbar)
Millibar (mbar)	x 0.401	=	Inches of water (inH$_2$O)	x 2.491 =	Millibar (mbar)
Millimetres of mercury (mmHg)	x 0.535	=	Inches of water (inH$_2$O)	x 1.868 =	Millimetres of mercury (mmHg)
Inches of water (inH$_2$O)	x 0.036	=	Pounds-force per square inch (psi; lbf/in^2; lb/in^2)	x 27.68 =	Inches of water (inH$_2$O)

Torque (moment of force)

Pounds-force inches (lbf in; lb in)	x 1.152	=	Kilograms-force centimetre (kgf cm; kg cm)	x 0.868 =	Pounds-force inches (lbf in; lb in)
Pounds-force inches (lbf in; lb in)	x 0.113	=	Newton metres (Nm)	x 8.85 =	Pounds-force inches (lbf in; lb in)
Pounds-force inches (lbf in; lb in)	x 0.083	=	Pounds-force feet (lbf ft; lb ft)	x 12 =	Pounds-force inches (lbf in; lb in)
Pounds-force feet (lbf ft; lb ft)	x 0.138	=	Kilograms-force metres (kgf m; kg m)	x 7.233 =	Pounds-force feet (lbf ft; lb ft)
Pounds-force feet (lbf ft; lb ft)	x 1.356	=	Newton metres (Nm)	x 0.738 =	Pounds-force feet (lbf ft; lb ft)
Newton metres (Nm)	x 0.102	=	Kilograms-force metres (kgf m; kg m)	x 9.804 =	Newton metres (Nm)

Power

Horsepower (hp)	x 745.7	=	Watts (W)	x 0.0013 =	Horsepower (hp)

Velocity (speed)

Miles per hour (miles/hr; mph)	x 1.609	=	Kilometres per hour (km/hr; kph)	x 0.621 =	Miles per hour (miles/hr; mph)

Fuel consumption*

Miles per gallon (mpg)	x 0.354	=	Kilometres per litre (km/l)	x 2.825 =	Miles per gallon (mpg)

Temperature

Degrees Fahrenheit = (°C x 1.8) + 32   Degrees Celsius (Degrees Centigrade; °C) = (°F - 32) x 0.56

It is common practice to convert from miles per gallon (mpg) to litres/100 kilometres (l/100km), where mpg x l/100 km = 282

Buying spare parts

Spare parts are available from many sources, including maker's appointed garages, accessory shops, and motor factors. To be sure of obtaining the correct parts, it will sometimes be necessary to quote the vehicle identification number. If possible, it can also be useful to take the old parts along for positive identification. Items such as starter motors and alternators may be available under a service exchange scheme - any parts returned should always be clean.

Our advice regarding spare part sources is as follows.

Officially-appointed garages

This is the best source of parts which are peculiar to your car, and which are not otherwise generally available (eg badges, interior trim, certain body panels, etc). It is also the only place at which you should buy parts if the vehicle is still under warranty.

Accessory shops

These are very good places to buy materials and components needed for the maintenance of your car (oil, air and fuel filters, spark plugs, light bulbs, drivebelts, oils and greases, brake pads, touch-up paint, etc). Components of this nature sold by a reputable shop are of the same standard as those used by the car manufacturer.

Besides components, these shops also sell tools and general accessories, usually have convenient opening hours, charge lower prices, and can often be found not far from home. Some accessory shops have parts counters where the components needed for almost any repair job can be purchased or ordered.

Motor factors

Good factors will stock all the more important components which wear out comparatively quickly, and can sometimes supply individual components needed for the overhaul of a larger assembly (eg brake seals and hydraulic parts, bearing shells, pistons, valves, alternator brushes). They may also handle work such as cylinder block reboring, crankshaft regrinding and balancing, etc.

Tyre and exhaust specialists

These outlets may be independent, or members of a local or national chain. They frequently offer competitive prices when compared with a main dealer or local garage, but it will pay to obtain several quotes before making a decision. When researching prices, also ask what "extras" may be added - for instance, fitting a new valve and balancing the wheel are both commonly charged on top of the price of a new tyre.

Other sources

Beware of parts or materials obtained from market stalls, car boot sales or similar outlets. Such items are not invariably sub-standard, but there is little chance of compensation if they do prove unsatisfactory. In the case of safety-critical components such as brake pads, there is the risk not only of financial loss but also of an accident causing injury or death.

Second-hand components or assemblies obtained from a car breaker can be a good buy in some circumstances, but this sort of purchase is best made by the experienced DIY mechanic.

Vehicle identification

Modifications are a continuing and unpublicised process in vehicle manufacture, quite apart from major model changes. Spare parts manuals and lists are compiled upon a numerical basis, the individual vehicle identification numbers being essential to correct identification of the component concerned.

When ordering spare parts, always give as much information as possible. Quote the car model, year of manufacture, body and engine numbers as appropriate.

The Vehicle Identification Number (VIN) plate is situated on the front engine bay panel, to the right of the bonnet lock. The chassis number is stamped below the lip of the engine bay bulkhead. **(see illustration).**

The engine number is stamped on the cylinder block, below the ignition distributor flange **(see illustration)**. In addition, a bar code label attached to the timing belt cover contains engine code information.

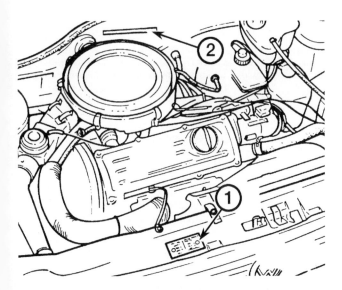

VIN plate (1) and chassis number (2) locations

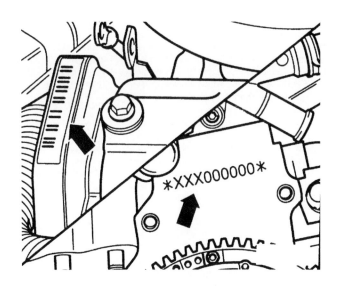

Engine number and engine code locations (arrowed)

Whenever servicing, repair or overhaul work is carried out on the car or its components, observe the following procedures and instructions. This will assist in carrying out the operation efficiently and to a professional standard of workmanship.

Joint mating faces and gaskets

When separating components at their mating faces, never insert screwdrivers or similar implements into the joint between the faces in order to prise them apart. This can cause severe damage which results in oil leaks, coolant leaks, etc upon reassembly. Separation is usually achieved by tapping along the joint with a soft-faced hammer in order to break the seal. However, note that this method may not be suitable where dowels are used for component location.

Where a gasket is used between the mating faces of two components, a new one must be fitted on reassembly; fit it dry unless otherwise stated in the repair procedure. Make sure that the mating faces are clean and dry, with all traces of old gasket removed. When cleaning a joint face, use a tool which is unlikely to score or damage the face, and remove any burrs or nicks with an oilstone or fine file.

Make sure that tapped holes are cleaned with a pipe cleaner, and keep them free of jointing compound, if this is being used, unless specifically instructed otherwise.

Ensure that all orifices, channels or pipes are clear, and blow through them, preferably using compressed air.

Oil seals

Oil seals can be removed by levering them out with a wide flat-bladed screwdriver or similar implement. Alternatively, a number of self-tapping screws may be screwed into the seal, and these used as a purchase for pliers or some similar device in order to pull the seal free.

Whenever an oil seal is removed from its working location, either individually or as part of an assembly, it should be renewed.

The very fine sealing lip of the seal is easily damaged, and will not seal if the surface it contacts is not completely clean and free from scratches, nicks or grooves. If the original sealing surface of the component cannot be restored, and the manufacturer has not made provision for slight relocation of the seal relative to the sealing surface, the component should be renewed.

Protect the lips of the seal from any surface which may damage them in the course of fitting. Use tape or a conical sleeve where possible. Lubricate the seal lips with oil before fitting and, on dual-lipped seals, fill the space between the lips with grease.

Unless otherwise stated, oil seals must be fitted with their sealing lips toward the lubricant to be sealed.

Use a tubular drift or block of wood of the appropriate size to install the seal and, if the seal housing is shouldered, drive the seal down to the shoulder. If the seal housing is unshouldered, the seal should be fitted with its face flush with the housing top face (unless otherwise instructed).

Screw threads and fastenings

Seized nuts, bolts and screws are quite a common occurrence where corrosion has set in, and the use of penetrating oil or releasing fluid will often overcome this problem if the offending item is soaked for a while before attempting to release it. The use of an impact driver may also provide a means of releasing such stubborn fastening devices, when used in conjunction with the appropriate screwdriver bit or socket. If none of these methods works, it may be necessary to resort to the careful application of heat, or the use of a hacksaw or nut splitter device.

Studs are usually removed by locking two nuts together on the threaded part, and then using a spanner on the lower nut to unscrew the stud. Studs or bolts which have broken off below the surface of the component in which they are mounted can sometimes be removed using a stud extractor. Always ensure that a blind tapped hole is completely free from oil, grease, water or other fluid before installing the bolt or stud. Failure to do this could cause the housing to crack due to the hydraulic action of the bolt or stud as it is screwed in.

When tightening a castellated nut to accept a split pin, tighten the nut to the specified torque, where applicable, and then tighten further to the next split pin hole. Never slacken the nut to align the split pin hole, unless stated in the repair procedure.

When checking or retightening a nut or bolt to a specified torque setting, slacken the nut or bolt by a quarter of a turn, and then retighten to the specified setting. However, this should not be attempted where angular tightening has been used.

For some screw fastenings, notably cylinder head bolts or nuts, torque wrench settings are no longer specified for the latter stages of tightening, "angle-tightening" being called up instead. Typically, a fairly low torque wrench setting will be applied to the bolts/nuts in the correct sequence, followed by one or more stages of tightening through specified angles.

Locknuts, locktabs and washers

Any fastening which will rotate against a component or housing during tightening should always have a washer between it and the relevant component or housing.

Spring or split washers should always be renewed when they are used to lock a critical component such as a big-end bearing retaining bolt or nut. Locktabs which are folded over to retain a nut or bolt should always be renewed.

Self-locking nuts can be re-used in non-critical areas, providing resistance can be felt when the locking portion passes over the bolt or stud thread. However, it should be noted that self-locking stiffnuts tend to lose their effectiveness after long periods of use, and should then be renewed as a matter of course.

Split pins must always be replaced with new ones of the correct size for the hole.

When thread-locking compound is found on the threads of a fastener which is to be re-used, it should be cleaned off with a wire brush and solvent, and fresh compound applied on reassembly.

Special tools

Some repair procedures in this manual entail the use of special tools such as a press, two or three-legged pullers, spring compressors, etc. Wherever possible, suitable readily-available alternatives to the manufacturer's special tools are described, and are shown in use. In some instances, where no alternative is possible, it has been necessary to resort to the use of a manufacturer's tool, and this has been done for reasons of safety as well as the efficient completion of the repair operation. Unless you are highly-skilled and have a thorough understanding of the procedures described, never attempt to bypass the use of any special tool when the procedure described specifies its use. Not only is there a very great risk of personal injury, but expensive damage could be caused to the components involved.

Environmental considerations

When disposing of used engine oil, brake fluid, antifreeze, etc, give due consideration to any detrimental environmental effects. Do not, for instance, pour any of the above liquids down drains into the general sewage system, or onto the ground to soak away. Many local council refuse tips provide a facility for waste oil disposal, as do some garages. If none of these facilities are available, consult your local Environmental Health Department, or the National Rivers Authority, for further advice.

With the universal tightening-up of legislation regarding the emission of environmentally-harmful substances from motor vehicles, most vehicles have tamperproof devices fitted to the main adjustment points of the fuel system. These devices are primarily designed to prevent unqualified persons from adjusting the fuel/air mixture, with the chance of a consequent increase in toxic emissions. If such devices are found during servicing or overhaul, they should, wherever possible, be renewed or refitted in accordance with the manufacturer's requirements or current legislation.

OIL CARE
FOLLOW THE CODE

OIL BANK LINE
0800 66 33 66
www.oilbankline.org.uk

Note: It is antisocial and illegal to dump oil down the drain. To find the location of your local oil recycling bank, call this number free.

The jack supplied with the vehicle tool kit should only be used for changing the roadwheels - see *"Wheel changing"* at the front of this book. When carrying out any other kind of work, raise the vehicle using a hydraulic (or "trolley") jack, and always supplement the jack with axle stands positioned under the vehicle jacking points.

When using a hydraulic jack or axle stands, always position the jack head or axle stand head under one of the relevant jacking points, indicated by indentations at the lower edges of the bodywork **(see illustrations)**.

To raise the front of the vehicle, position the jack with an interposed block of wood underneath. **Do not** jack the vehicle under the sill, sump, or any of the steering or suspension components. With the vehicle raised, an axle stand should be positioned beneath the vehicle jack location point on the sill. Position a block of wood with a groove cut in it on the jack head to prevent the vehicle weight resting on the sill edge; align the sill edge with the groove in the wood so that the vehicle weight is spread evenly over the surface of the block

To raise the rear of the vehicle, position the jack with an interposed block of wood underneath. **Do not** attempt to raise the vehicle with the jack positioned underneath the floor pan or axle. With the vehicle raised, an axle stand should be positioned beneath the vehicle jacking location point on the sill. Position a grooved block of wood on the jack as described in the previous paragraph.

Never work under, around, or near a raised vehicle, unless it is adequately supported on stands.

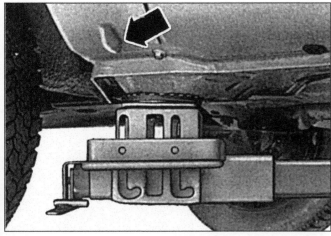

Workshop hoist/trolley jacking point for the front of the vehicle

Workshop hoist/trolley jacking point for the rear of the vehicle

Radio/cassette unit anti-theft system - precaution

The radio/cassette unit may be equipped with a built-in security code, to deter thieves. If the power source to the unit is cut, the anti-theft system will activate. Even if the power source is immediately reconnected, the radio/cassette unit will not function until the correct

security code has been entered. Therefore, if you do not know the correct security code for the radio/cassette unit **do not** disconnect either of the battery terminals, or remove the radio/cassette unit from the vehicle.

To enter the security code, follow the instructions in the radio/cassette handbook.

If an incorrect code is entered, the unit will become locked, and cannot be operated.

If this happens, or if the security code is lost or forgotten, seek the advice of your dealer.

Introduction

A selection of good tools is a fundamental requirement for anyone contemplating the maintenance and repair of a motor vehicle. For the owner who does not possess any, their purchase will prove a considerable expense, offsetting some of the savings made by doing-it-yourself. However, provided that the tools purchased meet the relevant national safety standards and are of good quality, they will last for many years and prove an extremely worthwhile investment.

To help the average owner to decide which tools are needed to carry out the various tasks detailed in this manual, we have compiled three lists of tools under the following headings: *Maintenance and minor repair*, *Repair and overhaul*, and *Special*. Newcomers to practical mechanics should start off with the *Maintenance and minor repair* tool kit, and confine themselves to the simpler jobs around the vehicle. Then, as confidence and experience grow, more difficult tasks can be undertaken, with extra tools being purchased as, and when, they are needed. In this way, a *Maintenance and minor repair* tool kit can be built up into a *Repair and overhaul* tool kit over a considerable period of time, without any major cash outlays. The experienced do-it-yourselfer will have a tool kit good enough for most repair and overhaul procedures, and will add tools from the *Special* category when it is felt that the expense is justified by the amount of use to which these tools will be put.

Maintenance and minor repair tool kit

The tools given in this list should be considered as a minimum requirement if routine maintenance, servicing and minor repair operations are to be undertaken. We recommend the purchase of combination spanners (ring one end, open-ended the other); although more expensive than open-ended ones, they do give the advantages of both types of spanner.

☐ *Combination spanners:*
Metric - 8 to 19 mm inclusive
☐ *Adjustable spanner - 35 mm jaw (approx.)*
☐ *Spark plug spanner (with rubber insert) - petrol models*
☐ *Spark plug gap adjustment tool - petrol models*
☐ *Set of feeler gauges*
☐ *Brake bleed nipple spanner*
☐ *Screwdrivers:*
Flat blade - 100 mm long x 6 mm dia
Cross blade - 100 mm long x 6 mm dia
Torx - various sizes (not all vehicles)
☐ *Combination pliers*
☐ *Hacksaw (junior)*
☐ *Tyre pump*
☐ *Tyre pressure gauge*
☐ *Oil can*
☐ *Oil filter removal tool*
☐ *Fine emery cloth*
☐ *Wire brush (small)*
☐ *Funnel (medium size)*
☐ *Sump drain plug key (not all vehicles)*

Repair and overhaul tool kit

These tools are virtually essential for anyone undertaking any major repairs to a motor vehicle, and are additional to those given in the *Maintenance and minor repair* list. Included in this list is a comprehensive set of sockets. Although these are expensive, they will be found invaluable as they are so versatile - particularly if various drives are included in the set. We recommend the half-inch square-drive type, as this can be used with most proprietary torque wrenches.

The tools in this list will sometimes need to be supplemented by tools from the *Special* list:
☐ *Sockets (or box spanners) to cover range in previous list (including Torx sockets)*
☐ *Reversible ratchet drive (for use with sockets)*
☐ *Extension piece, 250 mm (for use with sockets)*
☐ *Universal joint (for use with sockets)*
☐ *Flexible handle or sliding T "breaker bar" (for use with sockets)*
☐ *Torque wrench (for use with sockets)*
☐ *Self-locking grips*
☐ *Ball pein hammer*
☐ *Soft-faced mallet (plastic or rubber)*
☐ *Screwdrivers:*
Flat blade - long & sturdy, short (chubby), and narrow (electrician's) types
Cross blade – long & sturdy, and short (chubby) types
☐ *Pliers:*
Long-nosed
Side cutters (electrician's)
Circlip (internal and external)
☐ *Cold chisel - 25 mm*
☐ *Scriber*
☐ *Scraper*
☐ *Centre-punch*
☐ *Pin punch*
☐ *Hacksaw*
☐ *Brake hose clamp*
☐ *Brake/clutch bleeding kit*
☐ *Selection of twist drills*
☐ *Steel rule/straight-edge*
☐ *Allen keys (inc. splined/Torx type)*
☐ *Selection of files*
☐ *Wire brush*
☐ *Axle stands*
☐ *Jack (strong trolley or hydraulic type)*
☐ *Light with extension lead*
☐ *Universal electrical multi-meter*

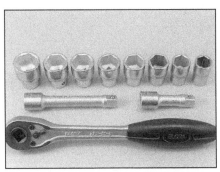

Sockets and reversible ratchet drive

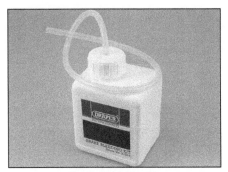

Brake bleeding kit

Torx key, socket and bit

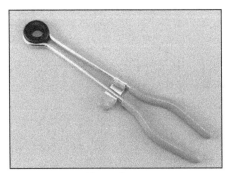

Hose clamp

Angular-tightening gauge

Special tools

The tools in this list are those which are not used regularly, are expensive to buy, or which need to be used in accordance with their manufacturers' instructions. Unless relatively difficult mechanical jobs are undertaken frequently, it will not be economic to buy many of these tools. Where this is the case, you could consider clubbing together with friends (or joining a motorists' club) to make a joint purchase, or borrowing the tools against a deposit from a local garage or tool hire specialist. It is worth noting that many of the larger DIY superstores now carry a large range of special tools for hire at modest rates.

The following list contains only those tools and instruments freely available to the public, and not those special tools produced by the vehicle manufacturer specifically for its dealer network. You will find occasional references to these manufacturers' special tools in the text of this manual. Generally, an alternative method of doing the job without the vehicle manufacturers' special tool is given. However, sometimes there is no alternative to using them. Where this is the case and the relevant tool cannot be bought or borrowed, you will have to entrust the work to a dealer.

☐ Angular-tightening gauge
☐ Valve spring compressor
☐ Valve grinding tool
☐ Piston ring compressor
☐ Piston ring removal/installation tool
☐ Cylinder bore hone
☐ Balljoint separator
☐ Coil spring compressors (where applicable)
☐ Two/three-legged hub and bearing puller
☐ Impact screwdriver
☐ Micrometer and/or vernier calipers
☐ Dial gauge
☐ Stroboscopic timing light
☐ Dwell angle meter/tachometer
☐ Fault code reader
☐ Cylinder compression gauge
☐ Hand-operated vacuum pump and gauge
☐ Clutch plate alignment set
☐ Brake shoe steady spring cup removal tool
☐ Bush and bearing removal/installation set
☐ Stud extractors
☐ Tap and die set
☐ Lifting tackle
☐ Trolley jack

Buying tools

Reputable motor accessory shops and superstores often offer excellent quality tools at discount prices, so it pays to shop around.

Remember, you don't have to buy the most expensive items on the shelf, but it is always advisable to steer clear of the very cheap tools. Beware of 'bargains' offered on market stalls or at car boot sales. There are plenty of good tools around at reasonable prices, but always aim to purchase items which meet the relevant national safety standards. If in doubt, ask the proprietor or manager of the shop for advice before making a purchase.

Care and maintenance of tools

Having purchased a reasonable tool kit, it is necessary to keep the tools in a clean and serviceable condition. After use, always wipe off any dirt, grease and metal particles using a clean, dry cloth, before putting the tools away. Never leave them lying around after they have been used. A simple tool rack on the garage or workshop wall for items such as screwdrivers and pliers is a good idea. Store all normal spanners and sockets in a metal box. Any measuring instruments, gauges, meters, etc, must be carefully stored where they cannot be damaged or become rusty.

Take a little care when tools are used. Hammer heads inevitably become marked, and screwdrivers lose the keen edge on their blades from time to time. A little timely attention with emery cloth or a file will soon restore items like this to a good finish.

Working facilities

Not to be forgotten when discussing tools is the workshop itself. If anything more than routine maintenance is to be carried out, a suitable working area becomes essential.

It is appreciated that many an owner-mechanic is forced by circumstances to remove an engine or similar item without the benefit of a garage or workshop. Having done this, any repairs should always be done under the cover of a roof.

Wherever possible, any dismantling should be done on a clean, flat workbench or table at a suitable working height.

Any workbench needs a vice; one with a jaw opening of 100 mm is suitable for most jobs. As mentioned previously, some clean dry storage space is also required for tools, as well as for any lubricants, cleaning fluids, touch-up paints etc, which become necessary.

Another item which may be required, and which has a much more general usage, is an electric drill with a chuck capacity of at least 8 mm. This, together with a good range of twist drills, is virtually essential for fitting accessories.

Last, but not least, always keep a supply of old newspapers and clean, lint-free rags available, and try to keep any working area as clean as possible.

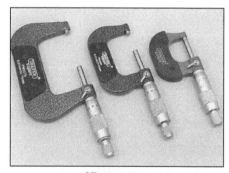
Micrometers

Dial test indicator ("dial gauge")

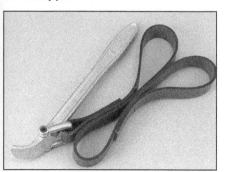
Strap wrench

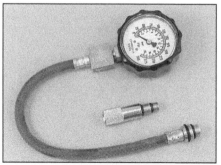
Compression tester

Fault code reader

This is a guide to getting your vehicle through the MOT test. Obviously it will not be possible to examine the vehicle to the same standard as the professional MOT tester. However, working through the following checks will enable you to identify any problem areas before submitting the vehicle for the test.

Where a testable component is in borderline condition, the tester has discretion in deciding whether to pass or fail it. The basis of such discretion is whether the tester would be happy for a close relative or friend to use the vehicle with the component in that condition. If the vehicle presented is clean and evidently well cared for, the tester may be more inclined to pass a borderline component than if the vehicle is scruffy and apparently neglected.

It has only been possible to summarise the test requirements here, based on the regulations in force at the time of printing. Test standards are becoming increasingly stringent, although there are some exemptions for older vehicles.

An assistant will be needed to help carry out some of these checks.

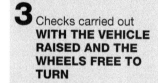

The checks have been sub-divided into four categories, as follows:

1 Checks carried out **FROM THE DRIVER'S SEAT**

2 Checks carried out **WITH THE VEHICLE ON THE GROUND**

3 Checks carried out **WITH THE VEHICLE RAISED AND THE WHEELS FREE TO TURN**

4 Checks carried out on **YOUR VEHICLE'S EXHAUST EMISSION SYSTEM**

---

1 Checks carried out **FROM THE DRIVER'S SEAT**

Handbrake

☐ Test the operation of the handbrake. Excessive travel (too many clicks) indicates incorrect brake or cable adjustment.
☐ Check that the handbrake cannot be released by tapping the lever sideways. Check the security of the lever mountings.

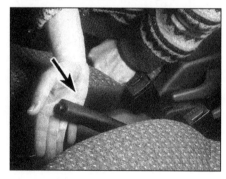

Footbrake

☐ Depress the brake pedal and check that it does not creep down to the floor, indicating a master cylinder fault. Release the pedal, wait a few seconds, then depress it again. If the pedal travels nearly to the floor before firm resistance is felt, brake adjustment or repair is necessary. If the pedal feels spongy, there is air in the hydraulic system which must be removed by bleeding.

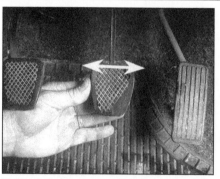

☐ Check that the brake pedal is secure and in good condition. Check also for signs of fluid leaks on the pedal, floor or carpets, which would indicate failed seals in the brake master cylinder.
☐ Check the servo unit (when applicable) by operating the brake pedal several times, then keeping the pedal depressed and starting the engine. As the engine starts, the pedal will move down slightly. If not, the vacuum hose or the servo itself may be faulty.

Steering wheel and column

☐ Examine the steering wheel for fractures or looseness of the hub, spokes or rim.
☐ Move the steering wheel from side to side and then up and down. Check that the steering wheel is not loose on the column, indicating wear or a loose retaining nut. Continue moving the steering wheel as before, but also turn it slightly from left to right.
☐ Check that the steering wheel is not loose on the column, and that there is no abnormal

movement of the steering wheel, indicating wear in the column support bearings or couplings.

Windscreen, mirrors and sunvisor

☐ The windscreen must be free of cracks or other significant damage within the driver's field of view. (Small stone chips are acceptable.) Rear view mirrors must be secure, intact, and capable of being adjusted.

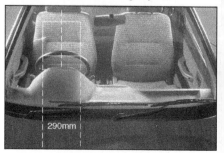

☐ The driver's sunvisor must be capable of being stored in the "up" position.

Seat belts and seats

Note: *The following checks are applicable to all seat belts, front and rear.*

☐ Examine the webbing of all the belts (including rear belts if fitted) for cuts, serious fraying or deterioration. Fasten and unfasten each belt to check the buckles. If applicable, check the retracting mechanism. Check the security of all seat belt mountings accessible from inside the vehicle.

☐ Seat belts with pre-tensioners, once activated, have a "flag" or similar showing on the seat belt stalk. This, in itself, is not a reason for test failure.

☐ The front seats themselves must be securely attached and the backrests must lock in the upright position.

Doors

☐ Both front doors must be able to be opened and closed from outside and inside, and must latch securely when closed.

2 Checks carried out WITH THE VEHICLE ON THE GROUND

Vehicle identification

☐ Number plates must be in good condition, secure and legible, with letters and numbers correctly spaced – spacing at (A) should be at least twice that at (B).

☐ The VIN plate and/or homologation plate must be legible.

Electrical equipment

☐ Switch on the ignition and check the operation of the horn.

☐ Check the windscreen washers and wipers, examining the wiper blades; renew damaged or perished blades. Also check the operation of the stop-lights.

☐ Check the operation of the sidelights and number plate lights. The lenses and reflectors must be secure, clean and undamaged.

☐ Check the operation and alignment of the headlights. The headlight reflectors must not be tarnished and the lenses must be undamaged.

☐ Switch on the ignition and check the operation of the direction indicators (including the instrument panel tell-tale) and the hazard warning lights. Operation of the sidelights and stop-lights must not affect the indicators - if it does, the cause is usually a bad earth at the rear light cluster.

☐ Check the operation of the rear foglight(s), including the warning light on the instrument panel or in the switch.

☐ The ABS warning light must illuminate in accordance with the manufacturers' design. For most vehicles, the ABS warning light should illuminate when the ignition is switched on, and (if the system is operating properly) extinguish after a few seconds. Refer to the owner's handbook.

Footbrake

☐ Examine the master cylinder, brake pipes and servo unit for leaks, loose mountings, corrosion or other damage.

☐ The fluid reservoir must be secure and the fluid level must be between the upper (**A**) and lower (**B**) markings.

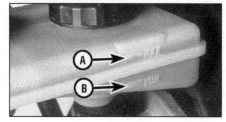

☐ Inspect both front brake flexible hoses for cracks or deterioration of the rubber. Turn the steering from lock to lock, and ensure that the hoses do not contact the wheel, tyre, or any part of the steering or suspension mechanism. With the brake pedal firmly depressed, check the hoses for bulges or leaks under pressure.

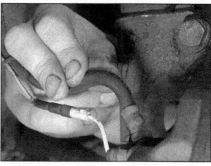

Steering and suspension

☐ Have your assistant turn the steering wheel from side to side slightly, up to the point where the steering gear just begins to transmit this movement to the roadwheels. Check for excessive free play between the steering wheel and the steering gear, indicating wear or insecurity of the steering column joints, the column-to-steering gear coupling, or the steering gear itself.

☐ Have your assistant turn the steering wheel more vigorously in each direction, so that the roadwheels just begin to turn. As this is done, examine all the steering joints, linkages, fittings and attachments. Renew any component that shows signs of wear or damage. On vehicles with power steering, check the security and condition of the steering pump, drivebelt and hoses.

☐ Check that the vehicle is standing level, and at approximately the correct ride height.

Shock absorbers

☐ Depress each corner of the vehicle in turn, then release it. The vehicle should rise and then settle in its normal position. If the vehicle continues to rise and fall, the shock absorber is defective. A shock absorber which has seized will also cause the vehicle to fail.

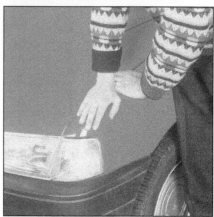

Exhaust system

☐ Start the engine. With your assistant holding a rag over the tailpipe, check the entire system for leaks. Repair or renew leaking sections.

3 Checks carried out **WITH THE VEHICLE RAISED AND THE WHEELS FREE TO TURN**

Jack up the front and rear of the vehicle, and securely support it on axle stands. Position the stands clear of the suspension assemblies. Ensure that the wheels are clear of the ground and that the steering can be turned from lock to lock.

Steering mechanism

☐ Have your assistant turn the steering from lock to lock. Check that the steering turns smoothly, and that no part of the steering mechanism, including a wheel or tyre, fouls any brake hose or pipe or any part of the body structure.

☐ Examine the steering rack rubber gaiters for damage or insecurity of the retaining clips. If power steering is fitted, check for signs of damage or leakage of the fluid hoses, pipes or connections. Also check for excessive stiffness or binding of the steering, a missing split pin or locking device, or severe corrosion of the body structure within 30 cm of any steering component attachment point.

Front and rear suspension and wheel bearings

☐ Starting at the front right-hand side, grasp the roadwheel at the 3 o'clock and 9 o'clock positions and rock gently but firmly. Check for free play or insecurity at the wheel bearings, suspension balljoints, or suspension mountings, pivots and attachments.

☐ Now grasp the wheel at the 12 o'clock and 6 o'clock positions and repeat the previous inspection. Spin the wheel, and check for roughness or tightness of the front wheel bearing.

☐ If excess free play is suspected at a component pivot point, this can be confirmed by using a large screwdriver or similar tool and levering between the mounting and the component attachment. This will confirm whether the wear is in the pivot bush, its retaining bolt, or in the mounting itself (the bolt holes can often become elongated).

☐ Carry out all the above checks at the other front wheel, and then at both rear wheels.

Springs and shock absorbers

☐ Examine the suspension struts (when applicable) for serious fluid leakage, corrosion, or damage to the casing. Also check the security of the mounting points.

☐ If coil springs are fitted, check that the spring ends locate in their seats, and that the spring is not corroded, cracked or broken.

☐ If leaf springs are fitted, check that all leaves are intact, that the axle is securely attached to each spring, and that there is no deterioration of the spring eye mountings, bushes, and shackles.

☐ The same general checks apply to vehicles fitted with other suspension types, such as torsion bars, hydraulic displacer units, etc. Ensure that all mountings and attachments are secure, that there are no signs of excessive wear, corrosion or damage, and (on hydraulic types) that there are no fluid leaks or damaged pipes.

☐ Inspect the shock absorbers for signs of serious fluid leakage. Check for wear of the mounting bushes or attachments, or damage to the body of the unit.

Driveshafts (fwd vehicles only)

☐ Rotate each front wheel in turn and inspect the constant velocity joint gaiters for splits or damage. Also check that each driveshaft is straight and undamaged.

Braking system

☐ If possible without dismantling, check brake pad wear and disc condition. Ensure that the friction lining material has not worn excessively, (A) and that the discs are not fractured, pitted, scored or badly worn (B).

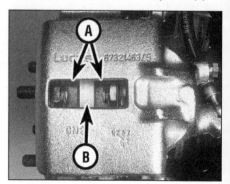

☐ Examine all the rigid brake pipes underneath the vehicle, and the flexible hose(s) at the rear. Look for corrosion, chafing or insecurity of the pipes, and for signs of bulging under pressure, chafing, splits or deterioration of the flexible hoses.

☐ Look for signs of fluid leaks at the brake calipers or on the brake backplates. Repair or renew leaking components.

☐ Slowly spin each wheel, while your assistant depresses and releases the footbrake. Ensure that each brake is operating and does not bind when the pedal is released.

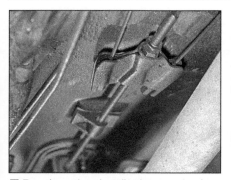

☐ Examine the handbrake mechanism, checking for frayed or broken cables, excessive corrosion, or wear or insecurity of the linkage. Check that the mechanism works on each relevant wheel, and releases fully, without binding.

☐ It is not possible to test brake efficiency without special equipment, but a road test can be carried out later to check that the vehicle pulls up in a straight line.

Fuel and exhaust systems

☐ Inspect the fuel tank (including the filler cap), fuel pipes, hoses and unions. All components must be secure and free from leaks.

☐ Examine the exhaust system over its entire length, checking for any damaged, broken or missing mountings, security of the retaining clamps and rust or corrosion.

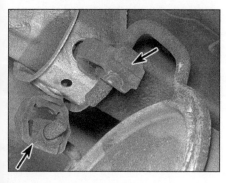

Wheels and tyres

☐ Examine the sidewalls and tread area of each tyre in turn. Check for cuts, tears, lumps, bulges, separation of the tread, and exposure of the ply or cord due to wear or damage. Check that the tyre bead is correctly seated on the wheel rim, that the valve is sound and properly seated, and that the wheel is not distorted or damaged.

☐ Check that the tyres are of the correct size for the vehicle, that they are of the same size and type on each axle, and that the pressures are correct.

☐ Check the tyre tread depth. The legal minimum at the time of writing is 1.6 mm over at least three-quarters of the tread width. Abnormal tread wear may indicate incorrect front wheel alignment.

Body corrosion

☐ Check the condition of the entire vehicle structure for signs of corrosion in load-bearing areas. (These include chassis box sections, side sills, cross-members, pillars, and all suspension, steering, braking system and seat belt mountings and anchorages.) Any corrosion which has seriously reduced the thickness of a load-bearing area is likely to cause the vehicle to fail. In this case professional repairs are likely to be needed.

☐ Damage or corrosion which causes sharp or otherwise dangerous edges to be exposed will also cause the vehicle to fail.

4 Checks carried out on
**YOUR VEHICLE'S EXHAUST
EMISSION SYSTEM**

Petrol models

☐ Have the engine at normal operating temperature, and make sure that it is in good tune (ignition system in good order, air filter element clean, etc).

☐ Before any measurements are carried out, raise the engine speed to around 2500 rpm, and hold it at this speed for 20 seconds. Allow the engine speed to return to idle, and watch for smoke emissions from the exhaust tailpipe. If the idle speed is obviously much too high, or if dense blue or clearly-visible black smoke comes from the tailpipe for more than 5 seconds, the vehicle will fail. As a rule of thumb, blue smoke signifies oil being burnt (engine wear) while black smoke signifies unburnt fuel (dirty air cleaner element, or other carburettor or fuel system fault).

☐ An exhaust gas analyser capable of measuring carbon monoxide (CO) and hydrocarbons (HC) is now needed. If such an instrument cannot be hired or borrowed, a local garage may agree to perform the check for a small fee.

CO emissions (mixture)

☐ At the time of writing, for vehicles first used between 1st August 1975 and 31st July 1986 (P to C registration), the CO level must not exceed 4.5% by volume. For vehicles first used between 1st August 1986 and 31st July 1992 (D to J registration), the CO level must not exceed 3.5% by volume. Vehicles first

used after 1st August 1992 (K registration) must conform to the manufacturer's specification. The MOT tester has access to a DOT database or emissions handbook, which lists the CO and HC limits for each make and model of vehicle. The CO level is measured with the engine at idle speed, and at "fast idle". The following limits are given as a general guide:

At idle speed -
CO level no more than 0.5%
At "fast idle" (2500 to 3000 rpm) -
CO level no more than 0.3%
(Minimum oil temperature 60°C)

☐ If the CO level cannot be reduced far enough to pass the test (and the fuel and ignition systems are otherwise in good condition) then the carburettor is badly worn, or there is some problem in the fuel injection system or catalytic converter (as applicable).

HC emissions

☐ With the CO within limits, HC emissions for vehicles first used between 1st August 1975 and 31st July 1992 (P to J registration) must not exceed 1200 ppm. Vehicles first used after 1st August 1992 (K registration) must conform to the manufacturer's specification. The MOT tester has access to a DOT database or emissions handbook, which lists the CO and HC limits for each make and model of vehicle. The HC level is measured with the engine at "fast idle". The following is given as a general guide:

At "fast idle" (2500 to 3000 rpm) -
HC level no more than 200 ppm
(Minimum oil temperature 60°C)

☐ Excessive HC emissions are caused by incomplete combustion, the causes of which can include oil being burnt, mechanical wear and ignition/fuel system malfunction.

Diesel models

☐ The only emission test applicable to Diesel engines is the measuring of exhaust smoke density. The test involves accelerating the engine several times to its maximum unloaded speed.

Note: *It is of the utmost importance that the engine timing belt is in good condition before the test is carried out.*

☐ The limits for Diesel engine exhaust smoke, introduced in September 1995 are:
Vehicles first used before 1st August 1979:
Exempt from metered smoke testing, but must not emit "dense blue or clearly visible black smoke for a period of more than 5 seconds at idle" or "dense blue or clearly visible black smoke during acceleration which would obscure the view of other road users".
Non-turbocharged vehicles first used after 1st August 1979: 2.5m-1
Turbocharged vehicles first used after 1st August 1979: 3.0m-1

☐ Excessive smoke can be caused by a dirty air cleaner element. Otherwise, professional advice may be needed to find the cause.

Engine 1

☐ Engine fails to rotate when attempting to start
☐ Engine rotates, but will not start
☐ Engine difficult to start when cold
☐ Engine difficult to start when hot
☐ Starter motor noisy or excessively-rough in engagement
☐ Engine starts, but stops immediately
☐ Engine idles erratically
☐ Engine misfires at idle speed
☐ Engine misfires throughout the driving speed range
☐ Engine hesitates on acceleration
☐ Engine stalls
☐ Engine lacks power
☐ Engine backfires
☐ Oil pressure warning light illuminated with engine running
☐ Engine runs-on after switching off
☐ Engine noises

Cooling system 2

☐ Overheating
☐ Overcooling
☐ External coolant leakage
☐ Internal coolant leakage
☐ Corrosion

Fuel and exhaust systems 3

☐ Excessive fuel consumption
☐ Fuel leakage and/or fuel odour
☐ Excessive noise or fumes from exhaust system

Clutch 4

☐ Pedal travels to floor - no pressure or very little resistance
☐ Clutch fails to disengage (unable to select gears)
☐ Clutch slips (engine speed increases, with no increase in vehicle speed)
☐ Judder as clutch is engaged
☐ Noise when depressing or releasing clutch pedal

Manual transmission 5

☐ Noisy in neutral with engine running
☐ Noisy in one particular gear
☐ Difficulty engaging gears
☐ Jumps out of gear
☐ Vibration
☐ Lubricant leaks

Driveshafts 6

☐ Clicking or knocking noise on turns (at slow speed on full-lock)
☐ Vibration when accelerating or decelerating

Braking system 7

☐ Vehicle pulls to one side under braking
☐ Noise (grinding or high-pitched squeal) when brakes applied
☐ Excessive brake pedal travel
☐ Brake pedal feels spongy when depressed
☐ Excessive brake pedal effort required to stop vehicle
☐ Judder felt through brake pedal or steering wheel when braking
☐ Brakes binding
☐ Rear wheels locking under normal braking

Suspension and steering systems 8

☐ Vehicle pulls to one side
☐ Wheel wobble and vibration
☐ Excessive pitching and/or rolling around corners, or during braking
☐ Wandering or general instability
☐ Excessively-stiff steering
☐ Excessive play in steering
☐ Lack of power assistance
☐ Tyre wear excessive

Electrical system 9

☐ Battery will not hold a charge for more than a few days
☐ Ignition/no-charge warning light remains illuminated with engine running
☐ Ignition/no-charge warning light fails to come on
☐ Lights inoperative
☐ Instrument readings inaccurate or erratic
☐ Horn inoperative, or unsatisfactory in operation
☐ Windscreen/tailgate wipers inoperative, or unsatisfactory in operation
☐ Windscreen/tailgate washers inoperative, or unsatisfactory in operation
☐ Electric windows inoperative, or unsatisfactory in operation

Introduction

The vehicle owner who does his or her own maintenance according to the recommended service schedules should not have to use this section of the manual very often. Modern component reliability is such that, provided those items subject to wear or deterioration are inspected or renewed at the specified intervals, sudden failure is comparatively rare. Faults do not usually just happen as a result of sudden failure, but develop over a period of time. Major mechanical failures in particular are usually preceded by characteristic symptoms over hundreds or even thousands of miles. Those components which do occasionally fail without warning are often small and easily carried in the vehicle.

With any fault-finding, the first step is to decide where to begin investigations. Sometimes this is obvious, but on other occasions, a little detective work will be necessary. The owner who makes half a dozen haphazard adjustments or replacements may be successful in curing a fault (or its symptoms), but will be none the wiser if the fault recurs, and ultimately may have spent more time and money than was necessary. A calm and logical approach will be found to be more satisfactory in the long run. Always take into account any warning signs or abnormalities that may have been noticed in the period preceding the fault - power loss, high or low gauge readings, unusual smells, etc - and remember that failure of components such as fuses or spark plugs may only be pointers to some underlying fault.

The pages which follow provide an easy-reference guide to the more common problems which may occur during the operation of the vehicle. These problems and their possible causes are grouped under headings denoting various components or systems, such as Engine, Cooling system, etc. The Chapter and/or Section which deals with the problem is also shown in brackets. Whatever the fault, certain basic principles apply. These are as follows:

Verify the fault. This is simply a matter of being sure that you know what the symptoms are before starting work. This is particularly important if you are investigating a fault for someone else, who may not have described it very accurately.

Don't overlook the obvious. For example, if the vehicle won't start, is there petrol in the tank? (Don't take anyone else's word on this particular point, and don't trust the fuel gauge either!) If an electrical fault is indicated, look for loose or broken wires before using the test gear.

Cure the disease, not the symptom. Substituting a flat battery with a fully-charged one will get you off the hard shoulder, but if the underlying cause is not attended to, the new battery will go the same way. Similarly, changing oil-fouled spark plugs for a new set will get you moving again, but the reason for the fouling (if it wasn't simply an incorrect grade of plug) will have to be established and corrected.

Don't take anything for granted. Particularly, don't forget that a "new" component may itself be defective (especially if it's been rattling around in the boot for months), and don't leave components out of a fault diagnosis sequence just because they are new or recently-fitted. When you do finally diagnose a difficult fault, you'll probably realise that all the evidence was there from the start.

1 Engine

Engine fails to rotate when attempting to start

☐ Battery terminal connections loose or corroded ("*Weekly checks*").
☐ Battery discharged or faulty (Chapter 5A).
☐ Broken, loose or disconnected wiring in the starting circuit (Chapter 5A).
☐ Defective starter solenoid or switch (Chapter 5A).
☐ Defective starter motor (Chapter 5A).
☐ Starter pinion or flywheel ring gear teeth loose or broken (Chapters 2A, 2B and 5A).
☐ Engine earth strap broken or disconnected (Chapter 5A).

Engine rotates, but will not start

☐ Fuel tank empty!
☐ Battery discharged (engine rotates slowly) (Chapter 5A).
☐ Battery terminal connections loose or corroded ("*Weekly checks*").
☐ Ignition components damp or damaged (Chapters 1 and 5B).
☐ Broken, loose or disconnected wiring in the ignition circuit (Chapters 1 and 5B).
☐ Worn, faulty or incorrectly-gapped spark plugs (Chapter 1).
☐ Fuel injection system fault (Chapter 4A or 4B).
☐ Major mechanical failure (eg timing belt) (Chapter 2A or 2B).

Engine difficult to start when cold

☐ Battery discharged (Chapter 5A).
☐ Battery terminal connections loose or corroded ("*Weekly checks*").
☐ Worn, faulty or incorrectly-gapped spark plugs (Chapter 1).
☐ Fuel injection system fault (Chapter 4A or 4B).
☐ Other ignition system fault (Chapters 1 and 5B).
☐ Low cylinder compressions (Chapter 2A).

Engine difficult to start when hot

☐ Air filter element dirty or clogged (Chapter 1).
☐ Fuel injection system fault (Chapter 4A or 4B).
☐ Low cylinder compressions (Chapter 2A).

Starter motor noisy or excessively-rough in engagement

☐ Starter pinion or flywheel ring gear teeth loose or broken (Chapters 2A, 2B and 5A).
☐ Starter motor mounting bolts loose or missing (Chapter 5A).
☐ Starter motor internal components worn or damaged (Chapter 5A).

Engine starts, but stops immediately

☐ Loose or faulty electrical connections in the ignition circuit (Chapters 1 and 5B).
☐ Vacuum leak at the throttle body or inlet manifold (Chapter 4A or 4B).
☐ Blocked injector/fuel injection system fault (Chapter 4A or 4B).

Engine idles erratically

☐ Air filter element clogged (Chapter 1).
☐ Vacuum leak at the throttle body, inlet manifold or associated hoses (Chapter 4A or 4B).
☐ Worn, faulty or incorrectly-gapped spark plugs (Chapter 1).
☐ Uneven or low cylinder compressions (Chapter 2A).
☐ Camshaft lobes worn (Chapter 2B).
☐ Timing belt incorrectly tensioned (Chapter 2A).
☐ Blocked injector/fuel injection system fault (Chapter 4A or 4B).

Engine misfires at idle speed

☐ Worn, faulty or incorrectly-gapped spark plugs (Chapter 1).
☐ Faulty spark plug HT leads - (Chapter 1).
☐ Vacuum leak at the throttle body, inlet manifold or associated hoses (Chapter 4A or 4B).
☐ Blocked injector/fuel injection system fault - (Chapter 4A or 4B).
☐ Distributor cap cracked or tracking internally (Chapter 1).
☐ Uneven or low cylinder compressions (Chapter 2A).
☐ Disconnected, leaking, or perished crankcase ventilation hoses (Chapter 4C).

Engine misfires throughout the driving speed range

☐ Fuel filter choked (Chapter 1).
☐ Fuel pump faulty, or delivery pressure low (Chapter 4A or 4B).
☐ Fuel tank vent blocked, or fuel pipes restricted (Chapter 4A or 4B).
☐ Vacuum leak at the throttle body, inlet manifold or associated hoses (Chapter 4A or 4B).
☐ Worn, faulty or incorrectly gapped spark plugs (Chapter 1).
☐ Faulty spark plug HT leads (Chapter 1).
☐ Distributor cap cracked or tracking internally (Chapter 1).
☐ Faulty ignition coil (Chapter 5B).
☐ Uneven or low cylinder compressions (Chapter 2A).
☐ Blocked injector/fuel injection system fault (Chapter 4A or 4B).

Engine hesitates on acceleration

☐ Worn, faulty or incorrectly-gapped spark plugs (Chapter 1).
☐ Vacuum leak at the throttle body, inlet manifold or associated hoses (Chapter 4A or 4B).
☐ Blocked injector/fuel injection system fault (Chapter 4A or 4B).

Engine stalls

☐ Vacuum leak at the throttle body, inlet manifold or associated hoses (Chapter 4A or 4B).
☐ Fuel filter choked (Chapter 1).
☐ Fuel pump faulty, or delivery pressure low (Chapter 4A or 4B).
☐ Fuel tank vent blocked, or fuel pipes restricted (Chapter 4A or 4B).
☐ Blocked injector/fuel injection system fault (Chapter 4A or 4B).

1 Engine (continued)

Engine lacks power

- ☐ Timing belt incorrectly fitted or tensioned (Chapter 2A or 2B).
- ☐ Fuel filter choked (Chapter 1).
- ☐ Fuel pump faulty, or delivery pressure low (Chapter 4A or 4B).
- ☐ Uneven or low cylinder compressions (Chapter 2A or 2B).
- ☐ Worn, faulty or incorrectly-gapped spark plugs (Chapter 1).
- ☐ Vacuum leak at the throttle body, inlet manifold or associated hoses (Chapter 4A or 4B).
- ☐ Blocked injector/fuel injection system fault (Chapter 4A or 4B).
- ☐ Brakes binding (Chapters 1 and 9).
- ☐ Clutch slipping (Chapter 6).

Engine backfires

- ☐ Timing belt incorrectly fitted or tensioned (Chapter 2A or 2B).
- ☐ Vacuum leak at the throttle body, inlet manifold or associated hoses (Chapter 4A or 4B).
- ☐ Blocked injector/fuel injection system fault (Chapter 4A or 4B).

Oil pressure warning light illuminated with engine running

- ☐ Low oil level, or incorrect oil grade ("Weekly checks").
- ☐ Faulty oil pressure sensor (Chapter 5A).
- ☐ Worn engine bearings and/or oil pump (Chapter 2C).
- ☐ High engine operating temperature (Chapter 3).
- ☐ Oil pressure relief valve defective (Chapter 2A or 2B).
- ☐ Oil pick-up strainer clogged (Chapter 2A or 2B).

Engine runs-on after switching off

- ☐ Excessive carbon build-up in engine (Chapter 2C).
- ☐ High engine operating temperature (Chapter 3).
- ☐ Fuel injection system fault (Chapter 4A or 4B).

Engine noises

Pre-ignition (pinking) or knocking during acceleration or under load

- ☐ Ignition timing incorrect/ignition system fault (Chapters 1 and 5B).
- ☐ Incorrect grade of spark plug (Chapter 1).
- ☐ Incorrect grade of fuel (Chapter 1).
- ☐ Vacuum leak at the throttle body, inlet manifold or associated hoses (Chapter 4A or 4B).
- ☐ Excessive carbon build-up in engine (Chapter 2C).
- ☐ Blocked injector/fuel injection system fault (Chapter 4A or 4B).

Whistling or wheezing noises

- ☐ Leaking inlet manifold or throttle body gasket (Chapter 4A or 4B).
- ☐ Leaking exhaust manifold gasket or pipe-to-manifold joint (Chapter 4A, 4B or 4C).
- ☐ Leaking vacuum hose (Chapters 4A, 4B, 4C, 5B and 9).
- ☐ Blowing cylinder head gasket (Chapter 2A or 2B).

Tapping or rattling noises

- ☐ Worn valve gear or camshaft (Chapter 2A or 2B).
- ☐ Ancillary component fault (water pump, alternator, etc) (Chapters 3, 5A, etc).

Knocking or thumping noises

- ☐ Worn big-end bearings (regular heavy knocking, perhaps less under load) (Chapter 2B).
- ☐ Worn main bearings (rumbling and knocking, perhaps worsening under load) (Chapter 2B).
- ☐ Piston slap (most noticeable when cold) (Chapter 2B).
- ☐ Ancillary component fault (water pump, alternator, etc) (Chapters 3, 5A, etc).

2 Cooling system

Overheating

- ☐ Insufficient coolant in system ("Weekly checks").
- ☐ Thermostat faulty (Chapter 3).
- ☐ Radiator core blocked, or grille restricted (Chapter 3).
- ☐ Electric cooling fan or thermoswitch faulty (Chapter 3).
- ☐ Pressure cap faulty (Chapter 3).
- ☐ Ignition timing incorrect/ignition system fault (Chapters 1 and 5B).
- ☐ Inaccurate temperature gauge sender unit (Chapter 3).
- ☐ Airlock in cooling system (Chapter 1).

Overcooling

- ☐ Thermostat faulty (Chapter 3).
- ☐ Inaccurate temperature gauge sender unit (Chapter 3).

External coolant leakage

- ☐ Deteriorated or damaged hoses or hose clips (Chapter 1).
- ☐ Radiator core or heater matrix leaking (Chapter 3).
- ☐ Pressure cap faulty (Chapter 3).
- ☐ Water pump seal leaking (Chapter 3).
- ☐ Boiling due to overheating (Chapter 3).
- ☐ Core plug leaking (Chapter 2B).

Internal coolant leakage

- ☐ Leaking cylinder head gasket (Chapter 2A or 2B).
- ☐ Cracked cylinder head or cylinder bore (Chapter 2A or 2B).

Corrosion

- ☐ Infrequent draining and flushing (Chapter 1).
- ☐ Incorrect coolant mixture or inappropriate coolant type (Chapter 1).

3 Fuel and exhaust systems

Excessive fuel consumption

☐ Air filter element dirty or clogged (Chapter 1).
☐ Fuel injection system fault (Chapter 4A or 4B).
☐ Ignition timing incorrect/ignition system fault (Chapters 1 and 5B).
☐ Tyres under-inflated ("*Weekly checks*").

Fuel leakage and/or fuel odour

☐ Damaged or corroded fuel tank, pipes or connections (Chapter 4A or 4B).

Excessive noise or fumes from exhaust system

☐ Leaking exhaust system or manifold joints (Chapters 1 and 4A or 4B).
☐ Leaking, corroded or damaged silencers or pipe (Chapters 1 and 4A or 4B).
☐ Broken mountings causing body or suspension contact (Chapter 1).

4 Clutch

Pedal travels to floor - no pressure or very little resistance

☐ Broken clutch cable - cable-operated clutch (Chapter 6).
☐ Incorrect clutch cable adjustment/automatic adjuster faulty - cable-operated clutch (Chapter 6).
☐ Broken clutch release bearing or fork (Chapter 6).
☐ Broken diaphragm spring in clutch pressure plate (Chapter 6).

Clutch fails to disengage (unable to select gears)

☐ Incorrect clutch cable adjustment/automatic adjuster faulty (Chapter 6).
☐ Incorrect clutch cable adjustment/automatic adjuster faulty (Chapter 6).
☐ Clutch disc sticking on gearbox input shaft splines (Chapter 6).
☐ Clutch disc sticking to flywheel or pressure plate (Chapter 6).
☐ Faulty pressure plate assembly (Chapter 6).
☐ Clutch release mechanism worn or poorly assembled (Chapter 6).

Clutch slips (engine speed increases, with no increase in vehicle speed)

☐ Incorrect clutch cable adjustment/automatic adjuster faulty - cable-operated clutch (Chapter 6).
☐ Clutch disc linings excessively worn (Chapter 6).
☐ Clutch disc linings contaminated with oil or grease (Chapter 6).
☐ Faulty pressure plate or weak diaphragm spring (Chapter 6).

Judder as clutch is engaged

☐ Clutch disc linings contaminated with oil or grease (Chapter 6).
☐ Clutch disc linings excessively worn (Chapter 6).
☐ Clutch cable sticking or frayed (Chapter 6).
☐ Faulty or distorted pressure plate or diaphragm spring (Chapter 6).
☐ Worn or loose engine or gearbox mountings (Chapter 2A or 2B).
☐ Clutch disc hub or gearbox input shaft splines worn (Chapter 6).

Noise when depressing or releasing clutch pedal

☐ Worn clutch release bearing (Chapter 6).
☐ Worn or dry clutch pedal bushes (Chapter 6).
☐ Faulty pressure plate assembly (Chapter 6).
☐ Pressure plate diaphragm spring broken (Chapter 6).
☐ Broken clutch disc cushioning springs (Chapter 6).

5 Manual transmission

Noisy in neutral with engine running

☐ Input shaft bearings worn (noise apparent with clutch pedal released, but not when depressed) (Chapter 7A).*
☐ Clutch release bearing worn (noise apparent with clutch pedal depressed, possibly less when released) (Chapter 6).

Noisy in one particular gear

☐ Worn, damaged or chipped gear teeth (Chapter 7).*

Difficulty engaging gears

☐ Clutch fault (Chapter 6).
☐ Worn or damaged gearchange linkage/cable (Chapter 7).
☐ Incorrectly-adjusted gearchange linkage/cable (Chapter 7).
☐ Worn synchroniser units (Chapter 7).*

Jumps out of gear

☐ Worn or damaged gearchange linkage/cable (Chapter 7).
☐ Incorrectly-adjusted gearchange linkage/cable (Chapter 7).
☐ Worn synchroniser units (Chapter 7).*
☐ Worn selector forks (Chapter 7).*

Vibration

☐ Lack of oil (Chapter 1).
☐ Worn bearings (Chapter 7).*

Lubricant leaks

☐ Leaking differential output oil seal (Chapter 7).
☐ Leaking housing joint (Chapter 7).*
☐ Leaking input shaft oil seal (Chapter 7).*

Although the corrective action necessary to remedy the symptoms described is beyond the scope of the home mechanic, the above information should be helpful in isolating the cause of the condition, so that the owner can communicate clearly with a professional mechanic.

6 Driveshafts

Clicking or knocking noise on turns (at slow speed on full-lock)

☐ Lack of constant velocity joint lubricant, possibly due to damaged gaiter (Chapter 8).
☐ Worn outer constant velocity joint (Chapter 8).

Vibration when accelerating or decelerating

☐ Worn inner constant velocity joint (Chapter 8).
☐ Bent or distorted driveshaft (Chapter 8).

7 Braking system

Note: Before assuming that a brake problem exists, make sure that the tyres are in good condition and correctly inflated, that the front wheel alignment is correct, and that the vehicle is not loaded with weight in an unequal manner. Apart from checking the condition of all pipe and hose connections, any faults occurring on the anti-lock braking system should be referred to a VW dealer for diagnosis.

Vehicle pulls to one side under braking

☐ Worn, defective, damaged or contaminated brake pads/shoes on one side (Chapters 1 and 9).
☐ Seized or partially-seized front brake caliper/wheel cylinder piston (Chapters 1 and 9).
☐ A mixture of brake pad/shoe lining materials fitted between sides (Chapters 1 and 9).
☐ Brake caliper or backplate mounting bolts loose (Chapter 9).
☐ Worn or damaged steering or suspension components (Chapters 1 and 10).

Noise (grinding or high-pitched squeal) when brakes applied

☐ Brake pad or shoe friction lining material worn down to metal backing (Chapters 1 and 9).
☐ Excessive corrosion of brake disc or drum. (May be apparent after the vehicle has been standing for some time (Chapters 1 and 9).
☐ Foreign object (stone chipping, etc) trapped between brake disc and shield (Chapters 1 and 9).

Excessive brake pedal travel

☐ Inoperative rear brake self-adjust mechanism - drum brakes (Chapters 1 and 9).
☐ Faulty master cylinder (Chapter 9).
☐ Air in hydraulic system (Chapters 1 and 9).
☐ Faulty vacuum servo unit (Chapter 9).

Brake pedal feels spongy when depressed

☐ Air in hydraulic system (Chapters 1 and 9).
☐ Deteriorated flexible rubber brake hoses (Chapters 1 and 9).
☐ Master cylinder mounting nuts loose (Chapter 9).
☐ Faulty master cylinder (Chapter 9).

Excessive brake pedal effort required to stop vehicle

☐ Faulty vacuum servo unit (Chapter 9).
☐ Disconnected, damaged or insecure brake servo vacuum hose (Chapter 9).
☐ Primary or secondary hydraulic circuit failure (Chapter 9).
☐ Seized brake caliper or wheel cylinder piston(s) (Chapter 9).
☐ Brake pads or brake shoes incorrectly fitted (Chapters 1 and 9).
☐ Incorrect grade of brake pads or brake shoes fitted (Chapters 1 and 9).
☐ Brake pads or brake shoe linings contaminated (Chapters 1 and 9).

Judder felt through brake pedal or steering wheel when braking

☐ Excessive run-out or distortion of discs/drums (Chapters 1 and 9).
☐ Brake pad or brake shoe linings worn (Chapters 1 and 9).
☐ Brake caliper or brake backplate mounting bolts loose (Chapter 9).
☐ Wear in suspension or steering components or mountings (Chapters 1 and 10).

Brakes binding

☐ Seized brake caliper or wheel cylinder piston(s) (Chapter 9).
☐ Incorrectly-adjusted handbrake mechanism (Chapter 9).
☐ Faulty master cylinder (Chapter 9).

Rear wheels locking under normal braking

☐ Rear brake shoe linings contaminated (Chapters 1 and 9).
☐ Faulty brake pressure regulator (Chapter 9).

8 Suspension and steering

Note: Before diagnosing suspension or steering faults, be sure that the trouble is not due to incorrect tyre pressures, mixtures of tyre types, or binding brakes.

Vehicle pulls to one side

☐ Defective tyre ("Weekly checks").
☐ Excessive wear in suspension or steering components (Chapters 1 and 10).
☐ Incorrect front wheel alignment (Chapter 10).
☐ Accident damage to steering or suspension components (Chapter 1).

Wheel wobble and vibration

☐ Front roadwheels out of balance (vibration felt mainly through the steering wheel) (Chapters 1 and 10).
☐ Rear roadwheels out of balance (vibration felt throughout the vehicle) (Chapters 1 and 10).
☐ Roadwheels damaged or distorted (Chapters 1 and 10).
☐ Faulty or damaged tyre ("Weekly checks").
☐ Worn steering or suspension joints, bushes or components (Chapters 1 and 10).
☐ Wheel bolts loose (Chapters 1 and 10).

8 Suspension and steering (continued)

Excessive pitching and/or rolling around corners, or during braking

- ☐ Defective shock absorbers (Chapters 1 and 10).
- ☐ Broken or weak spring and/or suspension component (Chapters 1 and 10).
- ☐ Worn or damaged anti-roll bar or mountings (Chapter 10).

Wandering or general instability

- ☐ Incorrect front wheel alignment (Chapter 10).
- ☐ Worn steering or suspension joints, bushes or components (Chapters 1 and 10).
- ☐ Roadwheels out of balance (Chapters 1 and 10).
- ☐ Faulty or damaged tyre ("*Weekly checks*").
- ☐ Wheel bolts loose (Chapters 1 and 10).
- ☐ Defective shock absorbers (Chapters 1 and 10).

Excessively-stiff steering

- ☐ Lack of steering gear lubricant (Chapter 10).
- ☐ Seized track rod end balljoint or suspension balljoint (Chapters 1 and 10).
- ☐ Broken or incorrectly-adjusted auxiliary drivebelt - power steering (Chapter 1).
- ☐ Incorrect front wheel alignment (Chapter 10).
- ☐ Steering rack or column bent or damaged (Chapter 10).

Excessive play in steering

- ☐ Worn steering column intermediate shaft universal joint (Chapter 10).
- ☐ Worn steering track rod end balljoints (Chapters 1 and 10).
- ☐ Worn rack-and-pinion steering gear (Chapter 10).
- ☐ Worn steering or suspension joints, bushes or components (Chapters 1 and 10).

Lack of power assistance

- ☐ Broken or incorrectly-adjusted auxiliary drivebelt (Chapter 1).
- ☐ Incorrect power steering fluid level ("*Weekly checks*").
- ☐ Restriction in power steering fluid hoses (Chapter 1).
- ☐ Faulty power steering pump (Chapter 10).
- ☐ Faulty rack-and-pinion steering gear (Chapter 10).

Tyre wear excessive

Tyres worn on inside or outside edges

- ☐ Tyres under-inflated (wear on both edges) ("*Weekly checks*").
- ☐ Incorrect camber or castor angles (wear on one edge only) (Chapter 10).
- ☐ Worn steering or suspension joints, bushes or components (Chapters 1 and 10).
- ☐ Excessively-hard cornering.
- ☐ Accident damage.

Tyre treads exhibit feathered edges

- ☐ Incorrect toe setting (Chapter 10).

Tyres worn in centre of tread

- ☐ Tyres over-inflated ("*Weekly checks*").

Tyres worn on inside and outside edges

- ☐ Tyres under-inflated ("*Weekly checks*").

Tyres worn unevenly

- ☐ Tyres/wheels out of balance (Chapter 1).
- ☐ Excessive wheel or tyre run-out (Chapter 1).
- ☐ Worn shock absorbers (Chapters 1 and 10).
- ☐ Faulty tyre ("*Weekly checks*").

9 Electrical system

Note: *For problems associated with the starting system, refer to the faults listed under "Engine" earlier in this Section.*

Battery will not hold a charge for more than a few days

- ☐ Battery defective internally (Chapter 5A).
- ☐ Battery terminal connections loose or corroded ("*Weekly checks*").
- ☐ Auxiliary drivebelt worn or incorrectly adjusted (Chapter 1).
- ☐ Alternator not charging at correct output (Chapter 5A).
- ☐ Alternator or voltage regulator faulty (Chapter 5A).
- ☐ Short-circuit causing continual battery drain (Chapters 5A and 12).

Ignition/no-charge warning light remains illuminated with engine running

- ☐ Auxiliary drivebelt broken, worn, or incorrectly adjusted (Chapter 1).
- ☐ Alternator brushes worn, sticking, or dirty (Chapter 5A).
- ☐ Alternator brush springs weak or broken (Chapter 5A).
- ☐ Internal fault in alternator or voltage regulator (Chapter 5A).
- ☐ Broken, disconnected, or loose wiring in charging circuit (Chapter 5A).

Ignition/no-charge warning light fails to come on

- ☐ Warning light bulb blown (Chapter 12).
- ☐ Broken, disconnected, or loose wiring in warning light circuit (Chapter 12).
- ☐ Alternator faulty (Chapter 5A).

Lights inoperative

- ☐ Bulb blown (Chapter 12).
- ☐ Corrosion of bulb or bulbholder contacts (Chapter 12).
- ☐ Blown fuse (Chapter 12).
- ☐ Faulty relay (Chapter 12).
- ☐ Broken, loose, or disconnected wiring (Chapter 12).
- ☐ Faulty switch (Chapter 12).

Instrument readings inaccurate or erratic

Instrument readings increase with engine speed

- ☐ Faulty voltage regulator (Chapter 12).

Fuel or temperature gauges give no reading

- ☐ Faulty gauge sender unit (Chapters 3 and 4A or 4B).
- ☐ Wiring open-circuit (Chapter 12).
- ☐ Faulty gauge (Chapter 12).

Fuel or temperature gauges give continuous maximum reading

- ☐ Faulty gauge sender unit (Chapters 3 and 4A or 4B).
- ☐ Wiring short-circuit (Chapter 12).
- ☐ Faulty gauge (Chapter 12).

9 Electrical system (continued)

Horn inoperative, or unsatisfactory in operation

Horn operates all the time

☐ Horn push either earthed or stuck down (Chapter 12).
☐ Horn cable-to-horn push earthed (Chapter 12).

Horn fails to operate

☐ Blown fuse (Chapter 12).
☐ Cable or cable connections loose, broken or disconnected (Chapter 12).
☐ Faulty horn (Chapter 12).

Horn emits intermittent or unsatisfactory sound

☐ Cable connections loose (Chapter 12).
☐ Horn mountings loose (Chapter 12).
☐ Faulty horn (Chapter 12).

Windscreen/tailgate wipers inoperative, or unsatisfactory in operation

Wipers fail to operate, or operate very slowly

☐ Wiper blades stuck to screen, or linkage seized or binding (Chapters 1 and 12).
☐ Blown fuse (Chapter 12).
☐ Cable or cable connections loose, broken or disconnected (Chapter 12).
☐ Faulty relay (Chapter 12).
☐ Faulty wiper motor (Chapter 12).

Wiper blades sweep over too large or too small an area of the glass

☐ Wiper arms incorrectly positioned on spindles (Chapter 1).
☐ Excessive wear of wiper linkage (Chapter 12).
☐ Wiper motor or linkage mountings loose or insecure (Chapter 12).

Wiper blades fail to clean the glass effectively

☐ Wiper blade rubbers worn or perished ("Weekly checks").
☐ Wiper arm tension springs broken, or arm pivots seized (Chapter 12).
☐ Insufficient windscreen washer additive to adequately remove road film ("Weekly checks").

Windscreen/tailgate washers inoperative, or unsatisfactory in operation

One or more washer jets inoperative

☐ Blocked washer jet (Chapter 1).
☐ Disconnected, kinked or restricted fluid hose (Chapter 12).
☐ Insufficient fluid in washer reservoir ("Weekly checks").

Washer pump fails to operate

☐ Broken or disconnected wiring or connections (Chapter 12).
☐ Blown fuse (Chapter 12).
☐ Faulty washer switch (Chapter 12).
☐ Faulty washer pump (Chapter 12).

Washer pump runs for some time before fluid is emitted from jets

☐ Faulty one-way valve in fluid supply hose (Chapter 12).

Electric windows inoperative, or unsatisfactory in operation

Window glass will only move in one direction

☐ Faulty switch (Chapter 12).

Window glass slow to move

☐ Regulator seized or damaged, or in need of lubrication (Chapter 11).
☐ Door internal components or trim fouling regulator (Chapter 11).
☐ Faulty motor (Chapter 11).

Window glass fails to move

☐ Blown fuse (Chapter 12).
☐ Faulty relay (Chapter 12).
☐ Broken or disconnected wiring or connections (Chapter 12).
☐ Faulty motor (Chapter 11).

A

ABS (Anti-lock brake system) A system, usually electronically controlled, that senses incipient wheel lockup during braking and relieves hydraulic pressure at wheels that are about to skid.

Air bag An inflatable bag hidden in the steering wheel (driver's side) or the dash or glovebox (passenger side). In a head-on collision, the bags inflate, preventing the driver and front passenger from being thrown forward into the steering wheel or windscreen.

Air cleaner A metal or plastic housing, containing a filter element, which removes dust and dirt from the air being drawn into the engine.

Air filter element The actual filter in an air cleaner system, usually manufactured from pleated paper and requiring renewal at regular intervals.

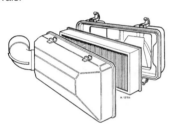

Air filter

Allen key A hexagonal wrench which fits into a recessed hexagonal hole.

Alligator clip A long-nosed spring-loaded metal clip with meshing teeth. Used to make temporary electrical connections.

Alternator A component in the electrical system which converts mechanical energy from a drivebelt into electrical energy to charge the battery and to operate the starting system, ignition system and electrical accessories.

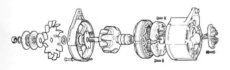

Alternator (exploded view)

Ampere (amp) A unit of measurement for the flow of electric current. One amp is the amount of current produced by one volt acting through a resistance of one ohm.

Anaerobic sealer A substance used to prevent bolts and screws from loosening. Anaerobic means that it does not require oxygen for activation. The Loctite brand is widely used.

Antifreeze A substance (usually ethylene glycol) mixed with water, and added to a vehicle's cooling system, to prevent freezing of the coolant in winter. Antifreeze also contains chemicals to inhibit corrosion and the formation of rust and other deposits that would tend to clog the radiator and coolant passages and reduce cooling efficiency.

Anti-seize compound A coating that reduces the risk of seizing on fasteners that are subjected to high temperatures, such as exhaust manifold bolts and nuts.

Anti-seize compound

Asbestos A natural fibrous mineral with great heat resistance, commonly used in the composition of brake friction materials. Asbestos is a health hazard and the dust created by brake systems should never be inhaled or ingested.

Axle A shaft on which a wheel revolves, or which revolves with a wheel. Also, a solid beam that connects the two wheels at one end of the vehicle. An axle which also transmits power to the wheels is known as a live axle.

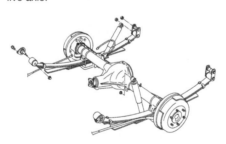

Axle assembly

Axleshaft A single rotating shaft, on either side of the differential, which delivers power from the final drive assembly to the drive wheels. Also called a driveshaft or a halfshaft.

B

Ball bearing An anti-friction bearing consisting of a hardened inner and outer race with hardened steel balls between two races.

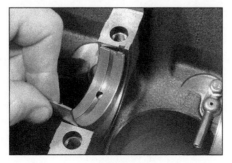

Bearing

Bearing The curved surface on a shaft or in a bore, or the part assembled into either, that permits relative motion between them with minimum wear and friction.

Big-end bearing The bearing in the end of the connecting rod that's attached to the crankshaft.

Bleed nipple A valve on a brake wheel cylinder, caliper or other hydraulic component that is opened to purge the hydraulic system of air. Also called a bleed screw.

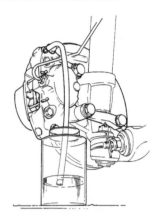

Brake bleeding

Brake bleeding Procedure for removing air from lines of a hydraulic brake system.

Brake disc The component of a disc brake that rotates with the wheels.

Brake drum The component of a drum brake that rotates with the wheels.

Brake linings The friction material which contacts the brake disc or drum to retard the vehicle's speed. The linings are bonded or riveted to the brake pads or shoes.

Brake pads The replaceable friction pads that pinch the brake disc when the brakes are applied. Brake pads consist of a friction material bonded or riveted to a rigid backing plate.

Brake shoe The crescent-shaped carrier to which the brake linings are mounted and which forces the lining against the rotating drum during braking.

Braking systems For more information on braking systems, consult the *Haynes Automotive Brake Manual*.

Breaker bar A long socket wrench handle providing greater leverage.

Bulkhead The insulated partition between the engine and the passenger compartment.

C

Caliper The non-rotating part of a disc-brake assembly that straddles the disc and carries the brake pads. The caliper also contains the hydraulic components that cause the pads to pinch the disc when the brakes are applied. A caliper is also a measuring tool that can be set to measure inside or outside dimensions of an object.

Camshaft A rotating shaft on which a series of cam lobes operate the valve mechanisms. The camshaft may be driven by gears, by sprockets and chain or by sprockets and a belt.

Canister A container in an evaporative emission control system; contains activated charcoal granules to trap vapours from the fuel system.

Canister

Carburettor A device which mixes fuel with air in the proper proportions to provide a desired power output from a spark ignition internal combustion engine.

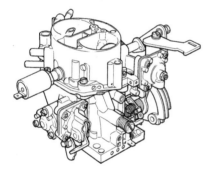

Carburettor

Castellated Resembling the parapets along the top of a castle wall. For example, a castellated balljoint stud nut.

Castellated nut

Castor In wheel alignment, the backward or forward tilt of the steering axis. Castor is positive when the steering axis is inclined rearward at the top.

Catalytic converter A silencer-like device in the exhaust system which converts certain pollutants in the exhaust gases into less harmful substances.

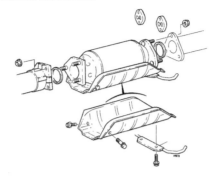

Catalytic converter

Circlip A ring-shaped clip used to prevent endwise movement of cylindrical parts and shafts. An internal circlip is installed in a groove in a housing; an external circlip fits into a groove on the outside of a cylindrical piece such as a shaft.

Clearance The amount of space between two parts. For example, between a piston and a cylinder, between a bearing and a journal, etc.

Coil spring A spiral of elastic steel found in various sizes throughout a vehicle, for example as a springing medium in the suspension and in the valve train.

Compression Reduction in volume, and increase in pressure and temperature, of a gas, caused by squeezing it into a smaller space.

Compression ratio The relationship between cylinder volume when the piston is at top dead centre and cylinder volume when the piston is at bottom dead centre.

Constant velocity (CV) joint A type of universal joint that cancels out vibrations caused by driving power being transmitted through an angle.

Core plug A disc or cup-shaped metal device inserted in a hole in a casting through which core was removed when the casting was formed. Also known as a freeze plug or expansion plug.

Crankcase The lower part of the engine block in which the crankshaft rotates.

Crankshaft The main rotating member, or shaft, running the length of the crankcase, with offset "throws" to which the connecting rods are attached.

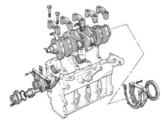

Crankshaft assembly

Crocodile clip See Alligator clip

D

Diagnostic code Code numbers obtained by accessing the diagnostic mode of an engine management computer. This code can be used to determine the area in the system where a malfunction may be located.

Disc brake A brake design incorporating a rotating disc onto which brake pads are squeezed. The resulting friction converts the energy of a moving vehicle into heat.

Double-overhead cam (DOHC) An engine that uses two overhead camshafts, usually one for the intake valves and one for the exhaust valves.

Drivebelt(s) The belt(s) used to drive accessories such as the alternator, water pump, power steering pump, air conditioning compressor, etc. off the crankshaft pulley.

Accessory drivebelts

Driveshaft Any shaft used to transmit motion. Commonly used when referring to the axleshafts on a front wheel drive vehicle.

Driveshaft

Drum brake A type of brake using a drum-shaped metal cylinder attached to the inner surface of the wheel. When the brake pedal is pressed, curved brake shoes with friction linings press against the inside of the drum to slow or stop the vehicle.

Drum brake assembly

E

EGR valve A valve used to introduce exhaust gases into the intake air stream.

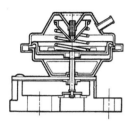

EGR valve

Electronic control unit (ECU) A computer which controls (for instance) ignition and fuel injection systems, or an anti-lock braking system. For more information refer to the *Haynes Automotive Electrical and Electronic Systems Manual.*

Electronic Fuel Injection (EFI) A computer controlled fuel system that distributes fuel through an injector located in each intake port of the engine.

Emergency brake A braking system, independent of the main hydraulic system, that can be used to slow or stop the vehicle if the primary brakes fail, or to hold the vehicle stationary even though the brake pedal isn't depressed. It usually consists of a hand lever that actuates either front or rear brakes mechanically through a series of cables and linkages. Also known as a handbrake or parking brake.

Endfloat The amount of lengthwise movement between two parts. As applied to a crankshaft, the distance that the crankshaft can move forward and back in the cylinder block.

Engine management system (EMS) A computer controlled system which manages the fuel injection and the ignition systems in an integrated fashion.

Exhaust manifold A part with several passages through which exhaust gases leave the engine combustion chambers and enter the exhaust pipe.

Exhaust manifold

F

Fan clutch A viscous (fluid) drive coupling device which permits variable engine fan speeds in relation to engine speeds.

Feeler blade A thin strip or blade of hardened steel, ground to an exact thickness, used to check or measure clearances between parts.

Feeler blade

Firing order The order in which the engine cylinders fire, or deliver their power strokes, beginning with the number one cylinder.

Flywheel A heavy spinning wheel in which energy is absorbed and stored by means of momentum. On cars, the flywheel is attached to the crankshaft to smooth out firing impulses.

Free play The amount of travel before any action takes place. The "looseness" in a linkage, or an assembly of parts, between the initial application of force and actual movement. For example, the distance the brake pedal moves before the pistons in the master cylinder are actuated.

Fuse An electrical device which protects a circuit against accidental overload. The typical fuse contains a soft piece of metal which is calibrated to melt at a predetermined current flow (expressed as amps) and break the circuit.

Fusible link A circuit protection device consisting of a conductor surrounded by heat-resistant insulation. The conductor is smaller than the wire it protects, so it acts as the weakest link in the circuit. Unlike a blown fuse, a failed fusible link must frequently be cut from the wire for replacement.

G

Gap The distance the spark must travel in jumping from the centre electrode to the side

Adjusting spark plug gap

electrode in a spark plug. Also refers to the spacing between the points in a contact breaker assembly in a conventional points-type ignition, or to the distance between the reluctor or rotor and the pickup coil in an electronic ignition.

Gasket Any thin, soft material - usually cork, cardboard, asbestos or soft metal - installed between two metal surfaces to ensure a good seal. For instance, the cylinder head gasket seals the joint between the block and the cylinder head.

Gasket

Gauge An instrument panel display used to monitor engine conditions. A gauge with a movable pointer on a dial or a fixed scale is an analogue gauge. A gauge with a numerical readout is called a digital gauge.

H

Halfshaft A rotating shaft that transmits power from the final drive unit to a drive wheel, usually when referring to a live rear axle.

Harmonic balancer A device designed to reduce torsion or twisting vibration in the crankshaft. May be incorporated in the crankshaft pulley. Also known as a vibration damper.

Hone An abrasive tool for correcting small irregularities or differences in diameter in an engine cylinder, brake cylinder, etc.

Hydraulic tappet A tappet that utilises hydraulic pressure from the engine's lubrication system to maintain zero clearance (constant contact with both camshaft and valve stem). Automatically adjusts to variation in valve stem length. Hydraulic tappets also reduce valve noise.

I

Ignition timing The moment at which the spark plug fires, usually expressed in the number of crankshaft degrees before the piston reaches the top of its stroke.

Inlet manifold A tube or housing with passages through which flows the air-fuel mixture (carburettor vehicles and vehicles with throttle body injection) or air only (port fuel-injected vehicles) to the port openings in the cylinder head.

J

Jump start Starting the engine of a vehicle with a discharged or weak battery by attaching jump leads from the weak battery to a charged or helper battery.

L

Load Sensing Proportioning Valve (LSPV) A brake hydraulic system control valve that works like a proportioning valve, but also takes into consideration the amount of weight carried by the rear axle.

Locknut A nut used to lock an adjustment nut, or other threaded component, in place. For example, a locknut is employed to keep the adjusting nut on the rocker arm in position.

Lockwasher A form of washer designed to prevent an attaching nut from working loose.

M

MacPherson strut A type of front suspension system devised by Earle MacPherson at Ford of England. In its original form, a simple lateral link with the anti-roll bar creates the lower control arm. A long strut - an integral coil spring and shock absorber - is mounted between the body and the steering knuckle. Many modern so-called MacPherson strut systems use a conventional lower A-arm and don't rely on the anti-roll bar for location.

Multimeter An electrical test instrument with the capability to measure voltage, current and resistance.

N

NOx Oxides of Nitrogen. A common toxic pollutant emitted by petrol and diesel engines at higher temperatures.

O

Ohm The unit of electrical resistance. One volt applied to a resistance of one ohm will produce a current of one amp.

Ohmmeter An instrument for measuring electrical resistance.

O-ring A type of sealing ring made of a special rubber-like material; in use, the O-ring is compressed into a groove to provide the sealing action.

O-ring

Overhead cam (ohc) engine An engine with the camshaft(s) located on top of the cylinder head(s).

Overhead valve (ohv) engine An engine with the valves located in the cylinder head, but with the camshaft located in the engine block.

Oxygen sensor A device installed in the engine exhaust manifold, which senses the oxygen content in the exhaust and converts this information into an electric current. Also called a Lambda sensor.

P

Phillips screw A type of screw head having a cross instead of a slot for a corresponding type of screwdriver.

Plastigage A thin strip of plastic thread, available in different sizes, used for measuring clearances. For example, a strip of Plastigage is laid across a bearing journal. The parts are assembled and dismantled; the width of the crushed strip indicates the clearance between journal and bearing.

Plastigage

Propeller shaft The long hollow tube with universal joints at both ends that carries power from the transmission to the differential on front-engined rear wheel drive vehicles.

Proportioning valve A hydraulic control valve which limits the amount of pressure to the rear brakes during panic stops to prevent wheel lock-up.

R

Rack-and-pinion steering A steering system with a pinion gear on the end of the steering shaft that mates with a rack (think of a geared wheel opened up and laid flat). When the steering wheel is turned, the pinion turns, moving the rack to the left or right. This movement is transmitted through the track rods to the steering arms at the wheels.

Radiator A liquid-to-air heat transfer device designed to reduce the temperature of the coolant in an internal combustion engine cooling system.

Refrigerant Any substance used as a heat transfer agent in an air-conditioning system. R-12 has been the principle refrigerant for many years; recently, however, manufacturers have begun using R-134a, a non-CFC substance that is considered less harmful to the ozone in the upper atmosphere.

Rocker arm A lever arm that rocks on a shaft or pivots on a stud. In an overhead valve engine, the rocker arm converts the upward movement of the pushrod into a downward movement to open a valve.

Rotor In a distributor, the rotating device inside the cap that connects the centre electrode and the outer terminals as it turns, distributing the high voltage from the coil secondary winding to the proper spark plug. Also, that part of an alternator which rotates inside the stator. Also, the rotating assembly of a turbocharger, including the compressor wheel, shaft and turbine wheel.

Runout The amount of wobble (in-and-out movement) of a gear or wheel as it's rotated. The amount a shaft rotates "out-of-true." The out-of-round condition of a rotating part.

S

Sealant A liquid or paste used to prevent leakage at a joint. Sometimes used in conjunction with a gasket.

Sealed beam lamp An older headlight design which integrates the reflector, lens and filaments into a hermetically-sealed one-piece unit. When a filament burns out or the lens cracks, the entire unit is simply replaced.

Serpentine drivebelt A single, long, wide accessory drivebelt that's used on some newer vehicles to drive all the accessories, instead of a series of smaller, shorter belts. Serpentine drivebelts are usually tensioned by an automatic tensioner.

Serpentine drivebelt

Shim Thin spacer, commonly used to adjust the clearance or relative positions between two parts. For example, shims inserted into or under bucket tappets control valve clearances. Clearance is adjusted by changing the thickness of the shim.

Slide hammer A special puller that screws into or hooks onto a component such as a shaft or bearing; a heavy sliding handle on the shaft bottoms against the end of the shaft to knock the component free.

Sprocket A tooth or projection on the periphery of a wheel, shaped to engage with a chain or drivebelt. Commonly used to refer to the sprocket wheel itself.

Starter inhibitor switch On vehicles with an

automatic transmission, a switch that prevents starting if the vehicle is not in Neutral or Park.

Strut See MacPherson strut.

T

Tappet A cylindrical component which transmits motion from the cam to the valve stem, either directly or via a pushrod and rocker arm. Also called a cam follower.

Thermostat A heat-controlled valve that regulates the flow of coolant between the cylinder block and the radiator, so maintaining optimum engine operating temperature. A thermostat is also used in some air cleaners in which the temperature is regulated.

Thrust bearing The bearing in the clutch assembly that is moved in to the release levers by clutch pedal action to disengage the clutch. Also referred to as a release bearing.

Timing belt A toothed belt which drives the camshaft. Serious engine damage may result if it breaks in service.

Timing chain A chain which drives the camshaft.

Toe-in The amount the front wheels are closer together at the front than at the rear. On rear wheel drive vehicles, a slight amount of toe-in is usually specified to keep the front wheels running parallel on the road by offsetting other forces that tend to spread the wheels apart.

Toe-out The amount the front wheels are closer together at the rear than at the front. On front wheel drive vehicles, a slight amount of toe-out is usually specified.

Tools For full information on choosing and using tools, refer to the *Haynes Automotive Tools Manual*.

Tracer A stripe of a second colour applied to a wire insulator to distinguish that wire from another one with the same colour insulator.

Tune-up A process of accurate and careful adjustments and parts replacement to obtain the best possible engine performance.

Turbocharger A centrifugal device, driven by exhaust gases, that pressurises the intake air. Normally used to increase the power output from a given engine displacement, but can also be used primarily to reduce exhaust emissions (as on VW's "Umwelt" Diesel engine).

U

Universal joint or U-joint A double-pivoted connection for transmitting power from a driving to a driven shaft through an angle. A U-joint consists of two Y-shaped yokes and a cross-shaped member called the spider.

V

Valve A device through which the flow of liquid, gas, vacuum, or loose material in bulk may be started, stopped, or regulated by a movable part that opens, shuts, or partially obstructs one or more ports or passageways. A valve is also the movable part of such a device.

Valve clearance The clearance between the valve tip (the end of the valve stem) and the rocker arm or tappet. The valve clearance is measured when the valve is closed.

Vernier caliper A precision measuring instrument that measures inside and outside dimensions. Not quite as accurate as a micrometer, but more convenient.

Viscosity The thickness of a liquid or its resistance to flow.

Volt A unit for expressing electrical "pressure" in a circuit. One volt that will produce a current of one ampere through a resistance of one ohm.

W

Welding Various processes used to join metal items by heating the areas to be joined to a molten state and fusing them together. For more information refer to the *Haynes Automotive Welding Manual*.

Wiring diagram A drawing portraying the components and wires in a vehicle's electrical system, using standardised symbols. For more information refer to the *Haynes Automotive Electrical and Electronic Systems Manual*.

Preserving Our Motoring Heritage

< The Model J Duesenberg Derham Tourster. Only eight of these magnificent cars were ever built – this is the only example to be found outside the United States of America

Almost every car you've ever loved, loathed or desired is gathered under one roof at the Haynes Motor Museum. Over 300 immaculately presented cars and motorbikes represent every aspect of our motoring heritage, from elegant reminders of bygone days, such as the superb Model J Duesenberg to curiosities like the bug-eyed BMW Isetta. There are also many old friends and flames. Perhaps you remember the 1959 Ford Popular that you did your courting in? The magnificent 'Red Collection' is a spectacle of classic sports cars including AC, Alfa Romeo, Austin Healey, Ferrari, Lamborghini, Maserati, MG, Riley, Porsche and Triumph.

A Perfect Day Out

Each and every vehicle at the Haynes Motor Museum has played its part in the history and culture of Motoring. Today, they make a wonderful spectacle and a great day out for all the family. Bring the kids, bring Mum and Dad, but above all bring your camera to capture those golden memories for ever. You will also find an impressive array of motoring memorabilia, a comfortable 70 seat video cinema and one of the most extensive transport book shops in Britain. The Pit Stop Cafe serves everything from a cup of tea to wholesome, home-made meals or, if you prefer, you can enjoy the large picnic area nestled in the beautiful rural surroundings of Somerset.

> John Haynes O.B.E., Founder and Chairman of the museum at the wheel of a Haynes Light 12.

< Graham Hill's Lola Cosworth Formula 1 car next to a 1934 Riley Sports.

The Museum is situated on the A359 Yeovil to Frome road at Sparkford, just off the A303 in Somerset. It is about 40 miles south of Bristol, and 25 minutes drive from the M5 intersection at Taunton.
Open 9.30am - 5.30pm (10.00am - 4.00pm Winter) 7 days a week, *except Christmas Day, Boxing Day and New Years Day*
Special rates available for schools, coach parties and outings Charitable Trust No. 292048